Digital Media and Reporting C

Digital Media and Reporting Conflict explores the impact of new forms of online reporting on the British Broadcasting Corporation's (BBC) coverage of war and terrorism. It is based on unique access to the BBC from 2007 to 2011 and reflects the views of more than 100 BBC staff at all levels of the Corporation. It argues that the BBC's practices and values are fundamentally shifting in response to the challenges of immediate digital publication. The contributions of the 'former audience', a more personal style and the presentation of news as process complement and test the BBC's impartial and 'objective' approach to covering war and terrorism. The book demonstrates that the future of journalism will be dependent on the 'uneasy truce' which is brokered between traditional media organisations and the 'collective intelligence' of a networked society.

Daniel Bennett is an independent scholar and author of the blogs Mediating Conflict and Reporting War (The Frontline Club).

Routledge Research in Journalism

Digital Media and Reporting Conflict

Blogging and the BBC's Coverage
of War and Terrorism

Daniel Bennett

Routledge
Taylor & Francis Group
NEW YORK AND LONDON

First published 2013
by Routledge
711 Third Avenue, New York, NY 10017

Simultaneously published in the UK
by Routledge
2 Park Square, Milton Park, Abingdon, Oxfordshire OX14 4RN

First issued in paperback 2016

Routledge is an imprint of the Taylor and Francis Group, an informa business

Library of Congress Cataloging in Publication Data

Bennett, Daniel.
  Digital media and reporting conflict : blogging and the BBC's coverage
of war and terrorism / by Daniel Bennett.
    pages cm. — (Routledge research in journalism)
  Includes bibliographical references and index.
  1. War—Press coverage—Great Britain—History—21st century.
2. Terrorism—Press coverage—Great Britain—History—21st century.
3. Online journalism—Great Britain—History—21st century.
4. Journalism—Objectivity—Great Britain. 5. Blogs—Political aspects—
Great Britain. 6. Blogs—Social aspects—Great Britain. 7. British
Broadcasting Corporation. I. Title.
  PN4784.W37B45 2013
  070.4'3330941—dc23
  2012046677

ISBN 13: 978-1-138-24326-2 (pbk)
ISBN 13: 978-0-415-81921-3 (hbk)

Typeset in Sabon
by Apex CoVantage, LLC

For Kip and Jane
In loving memory of Don and Iris

Contents

Tables

Acknowledgements

It is perhaps fitting that a book chronicling the emergence of a more collaborative form of journalism was the result of a truly collaborative project.

I would like to thank the Arts and Humanities Research Council for funding the project and all of the BBC participants who gave up their time to contribute to the book. I would particularly like to mention Peter Burdin, David Hayward and Jonathan Baker for their support at the BBC.

I am very grateful to my PhD supervisor at the War Studies Department, Dr Peter Busch. The project was his idea and his vision for the book provided me with an excellent framework. He was always generous with his time and it has been a pleasure to work with him. The critique supplied by my PhD examiners, Professor Stuart Allan and Professor Howard Tumber, improved the theoretical grounding of the book's final text.

I have benefited from the oversight of an excellent editor in Felisa Salvago-Keyes at Routledge. I would also like to thank Dominique Jackson for her editorial advice on an initial full draft and Malcolm Balen for reading the book on behalf of the BBC. Martin Belam, Alexandra Eriksson, Stuart Hughes, Chris Vallance and Marie Kinsey kindly read drafts of chapters and provided me with insightful feedback and criticism.

I am grateful to Graham Holliday for offering me the opportunity to blog for the Frontline Club and during the project I have been influenced, encouraged and challenged by bloggers and Twitter users from all over the world. They are too numerous to mention here, but together they formed a 'virtual office' of ideas and information.

Finally, there were a number of people who have shared the journey while I have been writing this book. Their love and support made it possible, and I owe them a great debt of gratitude. I am particularly thankful to my family: Kip, Jane and Owen Bennett and my housemates: Nic Mogford, Dave Jones, and Tom Hill.

I would also like to mention a few of the people whose friendship has been invaluable to me: Carl and Alice Brown, Tom and Marian Carson, Megan Collett, Laura Davies, Jamie Dunn, Alexandra Eriksson, Marco Evans, Alexander Hargreaves, Sarah Hewerdine, Alexandra Johnson, Esther Lloyd, Joe and Sarah-Jane Marshall, Ellie and Luke McLaughlin, Judy Mead, Jeni Mitchell, Kieran Mitton, Maria O'Reilly, Fiona Paterson, Adam and Hannah Stacey, Judith Townend, Lineu and Susan Vargas and Stu and Sian White.

Introduction
The Impact of Blogging on the BBC's Coverage of War and Terrorism

In September 2002, a 29-year-old architect living in Baghdad started a weblog, or blog, to keep in touch with a friend living in Jordan.[1] Writing under the pseudonym 'Salam Pax', the blogger's accounts of everyday life became increasingly popular with the blogging community in the run-up to the US-led invasion of Iraq in March 2003. Salam's blog posts were not only informative but also witty and insightful, attracting attention from all over the world.[2] Speculation over his identity mounted. Some commentators claimed he was a Central Intelligence Agency (CIA) agent; others that he was acting on behalf of Iraqi officials. The BBC's first online article about Salam Pax on 25 March 2003 was cautious, and the BBC asked a technology expert to establish whether he was actually posting from Baghdad.[3] During the invasion Salam was unable to access the Internet and he did not post again until 7 May, when he began to retrospectively update the blog from his notebook diary.[4] Soon afterwards, *The Guardian* established the blogger's identity when Salam revealed that his friend, 'G.',[5] had been doing some translation work for the newspaper.

By September, John Naughton of *The Observer* noted that Salam Pax had 'gone mainstream'—a reference to Salam's appearances in *The Guardian* and on the BBC.[6] The newspaper gave Salam a fortnightly column, BBC Radio 4's flagship news programme *Today*, interviewed him and Guardian Films helped him produce a series of short documentaries for BBC's *Newsnight*. Salam had made a transition: he was no longer simply a 'new media' blogger writing about his life in Baghdad; he had also become a key journalistic source, war correspondent, author and filmmaker. His 'alternative' perspective which initially challenged traditional media coverage of the Iraq war was at least partially incorporated into the established media.[7]

Salam Pax's blog presented BBC journalists with new challenges based on old editorial concerns, but it also provided a way of accessing a compelling voice which might never have been heard without the communication possibilities afforded by the World Wide Web. It is an example of how the context of conflict has proved to be a catalyst for new blogs and the use of blogs by journalists. Blogs offered a straightforward publishing outlet for people who wanted to express their views on events which fundamentally affected their lives. In turn, journalists began to realise the potential of blogs and other digital media to complement their coverage of war and terror.

Taking the BBC as a case study, this book explores how media coverage of war and terrorism has been influenced by the emergence of blogs as a tool which made the Web both 'writable' and 'conversational' for millions of individuals.[8] It documents the BBC's approach to the emergence of 'mass self-communication'[9] and the Corporation's response to a fundamental shift in the relationship between the journalist and the audience[10]—part of a broader process of convergence between producers and consumers.[11] It considers how BBC journalists have altered their approaches to sources of information and the impact that access to a network of digital sources has had on their working practices. It explores the influence of the blogging format as a method of online publication including the adoption of BBC diaries, the establishment of reporters' blogs as part of the BBC blog network and the emergence of 'live blogging' as a means to collaboratively communicate ongoing breaking news stories.

It also analyses the extent to which interactive methods of digital communication have led to a dialogue between BBC journalists and their audience through comments and programme blogs. It thus assesses the BBC's engagement with an emerging 'networked public sphere'[12] through 'conversations'[13] with bloggers and commenters and the development of online communities. In the midst of a revolution in information technology[14] and the continued evolution of the digital media environment, the book is a timely empirical investigation into the impact of new communication technologies on the BBC's journalistic practices, editorial procedures, guidelines and values. A printed format inevitably has weaknesses as a method of documenting the 'runaway world'[15] of digital media, but it also provides a more permanent record of a period of transition in a renascent media landscape.

STUDYING BLOGS AT THE BBC

The BBC's global reach and privileged place in Britain's cultural life mean it has often been the subject of academic study.[16] It is the world's largest broadcasting Corporation employing more than 20,000 people.[17] The Corporation is an ideal unit for investigation as it launched one of the first comprehensive news websites,[18] but there were also concerns over how blogs and blogging might affect the BBC's journalism. Initial understandings of blogs as a vehicle for partial, first-person argumentative comment and opinion appeared to clash with the BBC's brand of journalism; BBC journalists were attempting to report the news 'objectively', impartially and accurately with expertise and authority. For many journalists and editors at the organisation, it seemed that blogs were an interesting media development but that they were not reliable as sources of information and that they could not be written by BBC journalists without compromising the BBC's values. If blogs were written within the BBC's editorial guidelines, there were doubts that the resulting content would be sufficiently engaging. Other BBC journalists shared the concerns of commentators like John Markoff, the *New York Times*' senior Silicon Valley Correspondent, who felt that blogs were merely the latest in a number of short-lived Internet trends.[19] Studying the BBC's response to these issues provides a valuable insight into the challenge of blogs to existing media organisations, changes to journalistic working practices, the evolution of editorial values and the impact that blogs have had on traditional media content.

The BBC's participation in this project as one of its sponsors has facilitated excellent opportunities to access journalists and regularly observe their working practices. The book is based on more than 60 individual interviews with a range of BBC staff members at all levels of the Corporation between 2007 and 2011. Additional evidence was accessed through focus groups, informal conversations, email correspondence, open source material and BBC talks, seminars and events. The book reflects the views of more than 100 BBC staff, past and present, and includes evidence based on previously unpublished editorial documents and internal blog posts. It represents the first comprehensive investigation of the BBC's engagement with digital sources of information and builds on the work of Alfred Hermida in understanding the adoption of blogs for news at the Corporation.[20]

THE RISE OF REPORTING WAR AND TERRORISM USING BLOGS AND ITS PLACE IN ACADEMIC LITERATURE

Although the book does consider the BBC's general approach to blogs for news, it concentrates on one particular aspect of journalism—the reporting of war and terrorism. Media coverage of conflict has already been explored in a number of studies. Academics have usually been highly sceptical of the ability of journalists to represent war and terror accurately. Criticisms include plain bias, 'dehistoricised and dehistoricising reporting',[21] sensationalism, formulaic coverage, the use of existing historical and cultural frames which distort the reality of current events, portrayal of wars as simplistic struggles between the forces of good and evil,[22] providing terrorists with an outlet for their propaganda[23] and the manipulation of photographs and video footage. More recent academic studies have considered changes to war reporting including a shift towards 24/7 live coverage on TV[24] or the rise of Internet reporting.[25]

This book, however, specifically adds to an emerging literature which considers the impact of digital sources of information on the process of reporting war and terror[26] in a world where anybody can potentially act as a journalist.[27] In *Reporting War*, Barbie Zelizer and Stuart Allan suggest that the use of blogs accelerated in response to US involvement in major military operations in the 'war on terror'.[28] Since the war in Iraq, blogs have become an important feature of media coverage of conflict. They provide journalists with important alternative sources of information when first-hand reporting is too dangerous or in contexts when militaries and governments are managing information and access to conflict areas. In the context of terror attacks, blogs have also been used to access eyewitness accounts. Blogging by journalists for media organisations to cover stories about war and terror has also become commonplace. These trends raise significant questions about the journalist's approach to communicating conflict and the nature of future media coverage of war and terrorism. Shorter academic articles, however, have tended to focus on the nature of war blogs[29] rather than the practices which journalists have established for incorporating them into their journalism or, for example, the journalist's experience of live blogging a terror attack. War and terror also provides a valuable context in which to assess the limitations of the influence of blogging on journalism as reporting conflict raises significant editorial and ethical questions for journalists.[30]

CHAPTER OUTLINE

Before considering how blogs have become a feature of the BBC's journalism, the first part of the book, contained in Chapter 1, outlines the nature of blogs covering war and terrorism at the beginning of the 21st century. It documents how blogs have merged with other online genres and the way in which the blogging format has been adopted by governments, militaries, organisations and companies. It not only highlights areas where blogs have challenged traditional media narratives of conflict but also identifies categories of blogs which have been useful for journalists as sources of information. Based on David Altheide's idea of 'progressive theoretical sampling',[31] these categories are not, therefore, statistically representative of all blogs covering war and terror but are instead conceptually relevant, documenting the range of blogs a journalist covering defence and security might use as part of their journalism. The chapter employs a reflexive mixed method approach to identify these categories including a consideration of existing literature, the testimony of BBC journalists and participation in the blogosphere by the researcher.[32]

The second part of the book focuses on how blogs have been used as sources of information by BBC journalists. Chapter 2 places blogs in the context of the BBC's approach to journalism and its organisational culture by looking at existing editorial guidance and internal documents. It also surveys academic literature which analyses journalists' approach to their sources and identifies a process by which BBC journalists overcame misconceptions about blogs and began to incorporate them into their journalism. Blogs were a source of tip-offs for news stories, and they provided journalists with a new network of online sources to supplement existing contact books. BBC journalists began to use these blog posts to represent atmosphere, mood, comment and reaction. The incorporation of blogs into BBC content helped journalists satisfy a dynamic within the organisation for 'new voices', although paradoxically some bloggers developed a closer relationship with the BBC acting as regular contributors, media pundits or freelance journalists. Harnessing the blogosphere was led by specialists at the BBC, who either worked on the User Generated Content (UGC) hub— the BBC's department for collecting material submitted or created by the audience—or journalists who had developed a particular interest in blogs and online communities. Chapter 2 concludes by highlighting several circumstances when blogs became prominent in the BBC's coverage of war and terrorism. Chapters 3 and 4 consider journalists' attitudes to blogs and their understanding of the nature of blogs. Their testimony is used as a basis to explore why journalists use blogs to cover conflict and the limitations of blogs when compared with other sources of information. Based on a broad range of interviews, several focus groups, a number of internal documents and observations at the BBC, these chapters build on Chapter 2 to establish which journalists use blogs and the role of digital sources of information in the BBC's coverage of war and terrorism.

The third part of the book documents another significant response to the emergence of blogging—the adoption of the blogging format by the BBC as a key component of their online news offering. Chapter 5 traces the establishment of the BBC blog network which was the result of a number of experimental ventures and more than a year of debate at the Corporation. It documents discussions within the Corporation over how the BBC's values could be reconciled with a culture of blogging. It demonstrates that weaknesses were initially addressed by placing blogs under long-established editorial principles but that tensions still remain as online news continues to test the BBC's traditional values. Reporters' blogs and their Twitter feeds exposed a fine line between professional judgement and personal opinion, leading to a reaffirmation of the BBC's commitment to impartiality. Although the BBC did not abandon objectivity in favour of subjectivity, reporters' diaries, reporters' blogs and correspondent pages offered news accounts which were more personal in style. The chapter also explains why the BBC's defence and security correspondents have been reluctant to write their own blogs, highlighting that in the BBC context, blogging in the field of war and terrorism has been limited.

In a media environment facilitating unprecedented possibilities for interactivity between the audience and a news organisation, the BBC also started blogs which attempted to cultivate this relationship. Editors' blog posts were used as a tool of accountability.[33] It was a response to the ease with which the audience could communicate criticism online and the challenge from some bloggers who demanded greater transparency in the news process. The BBC also used blogs in support of radio and television programmes in an attempt to facilitate a dialogue between journalists and the audience. Chapter 6 compares the experience of the BBC's *World Have*

Your Say programme—a radio phone-in show[34]—with BBC Television's *Newsnight* programme, which analyses the day's news events. The chapter is based on interviews, observations and an analysis of the content of their programme blogs.

The fourth part of the book focuses on the influence of blogs on the content of the BBC's journalism. Chapters 7 and 8 provide two detailed cases studies of the BBC's coverage of war and terrorism. The former uses a mixture of methods to detail how the BBC covered the Mumbai terror attacks in November 2008 using live updates, a format which draws on 'live blogging'. BBC journalists were observed covering the event on 27 November to understand the news process. A content analysis was undertaken of 49 hours of online coverage to assess which sources journalists used in the live updates and the extent to which blogs were included. Finally, BBC journalists were interviewed to explore their editorial thinking in greater detail and to present them with the results of the content analysis. The chapter demonstrates how the live blogging format has been adopted as a response to the challenge of blogs, enabling journalists to publish material from a variety of sources at speed. It also analyses the impact that live blogging has had on the way journalists operate and their understanding of reporting accurately online in a breaking news environment.

Chapter 8 takes a broader approach and considers how the BBC incorporated blogs into their radio, TV and online coverage of the war in Gaza in 2009. Using the categories identified in Chapter 1, it documents how a selection of blogs covered the conflict and compares their approach to war reporting with the BBC's output during one week of the war. The chapter explores the limits of convergence by tracing fundamental differences between the BBC's reporting on the Gaza conflict and the coverage available on blogs. It suggests that the BBC retains a dominant role in the news network and that the incorporation of blogs is dependent on bloggers providing content which complements the BBC's news agenda.[35] It demonstrates that in the context of a conflict which was particularly sensitive, the BBC's journalism appeared cautious, preventing journalists from making more use of blogs.

The conclusion considers how blogging has influenced the BBC's key editorial practices and values in the context of its coverage of war and terror. It argues that the BBC's response to the challenges and opportunities of blogging can be likened to Janus, the Roman god of gatekeepers and doors, who looks both forwards into the future and backwards into the past.

In adapting to the new media landscape, the BBC has perhaps inevitably drawn on its experience of the past, and there are significant limits on the extent to which the culture of blogging has influenced the BBC's long-standing editorial approach to its journalism. News agendas and sources of information in the BBC's main radio and TV news bulletins and the BBC's broad aim of reporting accurately, impartially and objectively with expertise and authority remain relatively unchanged. The BBC has consistently maintained that their journalists' use of blogs is consistent with the Corporation's existing journalistic values and editorial procedures. Journalists usually say that the incorporation of blogs into their journalism does not deviate from their practices with any other source, while a BBC blog post has been described by the Director-General as 'a fact-checked' piece of 'broadcast journalism'.[36]

Paradoxically, the emphasis on the principles of the past is evidence that the BBC's journalism has been influenced by blogging, and the Corporation has reevaluated aspects of its understanding of impartiality, accountability and accuracy. Initiatives such as the Editors' blog are part of a shift towards greater openness about decision making and the limitations of the news process. The adoption of the personal tone and the organisation of content around individual journalists have become regular features of the BBC's online offering. The personalities of news correspondents are promoted online to complement more detached and distanced reportage in support of the BBC brand. Blogs and their digital offspring such as Twitter accounts and 'correspondent pages' are vehicles for the authoritative, expert voices of the BBC's correspondents, occasionally blurring the line between professional judgement and personal opinion. The BBC's off-air producers, researchers and editors are also more visible than they would have been in the past through their personal engagement in the online environment.

The working practices of journalists are also changing as they evolve strategies to access, verify and report information from multiple sources. The book points to a future model of journalism which is more collaborative. Digital connectivity in a 'networked society'[37] provides journalists with 'a map' of the social world which is less dependent on bureaucratic structures;[38] blogs helped facilitate the inclusion of authentic voices from conflict zones and witnesses to terror attacks in the BBC's coverage. The opportunities and challenges of finding and incorporating audience material led to fundamental organisational changes including the development of the UGC hub, the appointment of a Social Media Editor and the establishment of a social media training course. The emergence of the live blog format is identified as a key development enabling BBC journalists to present a 'multi-perspectival',[39] 'live' and instantly collaborative flow of news information about a conflict or terror attack which includes contributions from digitally connected members of the audience.

Attempting to graft the face of the future onto the BBC's existing values, however, has not always been successful. Although programmes such as *World Have Your Say* have managed to move to a more interactive news model, a shift towards news as conversation between the journalist and the audience has proved fundamentally problematic for the BBC. More generally, tensions remain between the foundations of the BBC's editorial approach and a new face of journalism, which is consciously subjective, transparent, publishes as it verifies and seeks to harness the 'collective intelligence'[40] of the audience. Developing trust in the BBC's journalism is now dependent on a balancing act between remaining impartial on matters of public controversy and a new limited transparency which reveals more about the personalities of individual journalists and the news process. The nature of accuracy has been reevaluated in light of immediate digital publication enabling the BBC to engage with material which its staff are still working to verify. The future of the BBC's journalism will depend on how it continues to negotiate an 'uneasy truce' between the challenges posed by the news-making practices of a digitally networked society and its existing editorial practices and values.[41]

WHAT IS A BLOG?

Before focussing specifically on blogs concerning war and terrorism in the first chapter, it is worth pausing to consider what a blog has been and what it is becoming. The term *weblog* was coined in 1997,[42] but it was not until the development of user-friendly software after 1999 that weblogs began to become more widespread. A weblog or 'blog' became a simple Web-based publishing tool which could be set up within minutes. Anyone with access to a computer and the Internet could publish information very easily. The number of blogs grew rapidly from several thousand by the end of 2000 to an estimated 4.12 million by October 2003.[43] By January 2009, Technorati. com claimed it had followed more than 133 million blogs since 2002.[44]

When somebody publishes information on a blog he or she produces a date-stamped 'blog post' or 'post'. A blog usually displays the most recent post at the top of the page, and previous posts are archived in folders on the blog. The very first blogs consisted of links to interesting websites—it was a way of 'logging' webpages and new developments online—and some blogs still have 'blogrolls' which provide a list of links to other blogs and websites. A reader may also be directed to other locations on the World Wide Web through a hyperlink in the text of a post. Blogs might also include audio, photos, graphics or video. They usually have a space for visitors to the site to comment on the posts. A blog is said to be written by a 'blogger'. Bloggers were initially stereotyped as 'computer geeks' because many early blogs were written on computer technology subjects and required a certain level of programming knowledge to start and maintain.[45] Today bloggers come from a variety of backgrounds, places and countries; it is difficult to generalise about bloggers apart from their ability to use blogging software and their desire to publish information.[46]

Early content analyses of blogs by both Susan Herring et al. and Zizi Papacharissi distinguished between personal blogs and 'filter' blogs.[47] Personal blogs were usually written by one author and took the form of an online diary where a blogger chronicles his or her everyday life. Filter blogs tended to focus on a certain topic, 'filtering' out other information, although it would perhaps be more useful to describe them as 'specialist' or 'niche' blogs. They were normally more outward looking, offering opinion, comment and analysis on external events rather than focussing on the day-to-day life of the author. These blogs were more likely to be authored by more than one blogger.

Enthusiasts for blogging particularly emphasised the advantages of the interactivity offered by blogs as a publishing tool over more static websites. As blogging software allowed users to comment and link to other websites, blogs facilitated asynchronous and sometimes near instantaneous communication between bloggers around the world. This not only enabled like-minded bloggers to develop supportive communities but also facilitated opportunities for disagreements which ranged from the civil to the vitriolic. A 'buzz' was said to occur in the blogosphere when a topic or issue attracted the attention of a large group of bloggers and numerous blog posts were written on the subject in a short time.[48] Blogs were part of a self-correcting network with peer-review mechanisms. The ideas presented in one blog post could be developed or refuted in the form of a comment on the blog, and factually inaccurate posts might be called to account.

A network of blogs is known as a 'blogosphere'. According to Mark Tremayne, the total blogopshere is 'a classic social network'; he emphasises three features.[49] First, the form of communication is textual, recorded and archived. Second, the network is held together by the process of linking to other bloggers. Third, he notes that this linking process favours the established blogs, or those which are most popular, because new bloggers tend to start by linking to these blogs. Juan Merelo and Beatriz Prieto define the blogosphere as 'readers/writers, which establish long-running relationships; these communities include weblog owners/writers or editors, people that post comments to weblog stories, and *silent* but persistent readers, both of whom might [or might not] have their own weblog'.[50] Researchers have studied smaller blogospheres such as the Persian blogosphere[51] or the Australian political blogosphere[52] which form part of an overall blogosphere.

THE CHALLENGE OF BLOGS TO THE TRADITIONAL MEDIA

A number of bloggers began fact checking, critiquing and publicly pointing out the deficiencies of traditional media coverage. They claimed blogs were quicker at breaking news or offered greater depth of coverage by mobilising a section of the blogosphere to investigate a story. They highlighted perceived bias in reporting and were critical of a lack of transparency about how news was produced and the way journalists sourced stories. They also did not necessarily follow the traditional media's existing conventions, publishing news stories that had been ignored or tackling issues which had not been deemed newsworthy.

Many media organisations became defensive when 'amateurs' began probing their own practices and procedures.[53] Journalists responded by emphasising the value of established newsgathering procedures; the editorial process as a safeguard of accuracy and objectivity; and bloggers' failure to separate fact from opinion. In the US, several high-profile incidents stoked the debate between 'amateur' 'bloggers' and 'professional' journalists: The Drudge Report's publication of the Monica Lewinsky scandal in 1997,[54] bloggers' role in bringing national attention to allegedly racist remarks made by Senator Trent Lott in 2002,[55] and their involvement in the exposure of faked documents used by CBS News in 2004.[56]

Initially 'the discourse of weblogs as journalism' was organised 'around the idea of challenging mainstream journalism',[57] but some successful multiauthor blogs, such as the Daily Kos and the Huffington Post, grew into substantial websites with full time editorial staff. Although the Huffington Post still produced blog posts, it began describing itself as 'The Internet Newspaper', demonstrating that conceptually, blogs and media websites are not necessarily discrete entities. Blogs also developed alongside a number of other emerging Internet genres including social networks such as Facebook; Internet forums; microblogging services like Twitter; audio and video blogs; social bookmarking and recommendation sites; and geolocation services like Foursquare. By 2011, the overlap between these genres was significant. They will continue to evolve as part of a nascent online medium, and it is possible that a first era of blogging is coming to an end.[58] A number of features of the blogging genre, however, continue to have a fundamental impact on the nature of news and information online including a more personal or subjective voice; the presentation of the most recent information at the top of a webpage to create streams of information; and the use of the hyperlink and comments to create participative, networked online communities. The first chapter of the book traces the evolution of blogs in the area of war and terrorism in order to provide an understanding of the nature of blogs which are available to a BBC journalist covering defence and security.

Part I

1   The 'War and Terror' Blogosphere

On 22 October 2008, the BBC's Technology Correspondent wrote a blog post titled 'Is blogging dead?' The irony was not lost on Rory Cellan-Jones:

> According to an article in *Wired* Magazine, Twitter, Flickr and Facebook make blogs look 'so 2004'. Oh dear. My response was to go straight home—and write a blog post.[1]

In the *Wired* article cited by Cellan-Jones, commentator Paul Boutin urged readers not to start a blog. For Boutin, blogs were not what they used to be. 'The blogosphere', he argued, was 'once a freshwater oasis of folksy self-expression and clever thought'.[2] By 2008, it had 'been flooded by a tsunami of paid bilge. Cut-rate journalists and underground marketing campaigns now drown out the authentic voices of amateur wordsmiths'.[3]

In addition to the entry of the official, the corporate and the professional, Boutin argued that blogs were too text-heavy compared to the new social networks on offer. The development and spread of faster broadband Internet connections made photo and video sharing on sites such as Flickr and YouTube more accessible. Meanwhile, microblogging in the form of the 'status update' on social networks like Facebook and dedicated sites such as Twitter attracted burnt out bloggers. But other commentators suggested that the convergence of blogging with these new forms of Internet communication and those which already existed would help reignite blogging. By 2011, blog functionality had developed to such an extent that it was possible to build a substantial, multiple-page website using blogging software, blurring the boundaries between what had previously been identifiable as distinct Internet genres. Blogging might have been entering a new era, but it was only 'dead' in the sense that it had become ubiquitous as a variety of individuals, organisations, companies and governments adopted the format or emerging variations.

Blogs in the field of war and terrorism did not remain untouched by these general trends. This chapter chronicles some of the key stages in the development of blogs in this area and identifies several categories of blogs and bloggers that might be of particular interest to journalists. Indeed, the aim is not to identify categories based on statistical sampling but to consider the question from the perspective of working journalists by outlining which sources of information are available to them and the opportunities and challenges these blogs present to their journalism. This approach draws on David Altheide's notion of 'progressive theoretical sampling',[4] whereby a researcher is able to select categories which are more theoretically or conceptually relevant by gaining a deep understanding of the topic. In order to achieve this, a mixture of methods was employed including a consideration of the academic literature, the incorporation of trends identified from interviews with BBC journalists and the immersion of the researcher in the blogosphere.

So-called citizen journalists have written about their experiences of war and terrorism using blogs since the attacks on the World Trade Center in 2001.[5] As blogs evolved and merged with other genres, eyewitnesses to major news events could publish material using a variety of multimedia tools. Interested individuals also collated news articles, blog posts, Twitter updates and imagery using their own 'live blogs'. The experience of those involved in conflict could be amplified by diasporic bloggers—such as Lebanese living abroad during the Second Lebanon War—or by a network of bloggers like the military blogging community in the US. Independent journalists, nongovernmental organisations (NGOs) and activists began using blogs as a means of communicating stories outside traditional media spaces highlighting the plight of victims of conflict. Militaries adopted blogs as a tool to explain their operations and the experiences of their servicemen and -women, while specialist defence and security reporters, analysts and academics updated blogs which covered issues surrounding war and terrorism in detail.

This chapter demonstrates that these blogs and bloggers provide opportunities for journalists to access eyewitness accounts to conflict, background information, military news, and specialist and expert comment. But they also present challenges to traditional journalism: a number of blogs are deliberately written in order to present an alternative picture to existing media narratives; specialist blogs can highlight deficiencies in journalists' content; other blogs can be co-opted as tools for public relations or propaganda campaigns; and networks of bloggers can actively pressurise journalists who are deemed to be inaccurate or biased.

This chapter provides a backdrop to the book outlining which blogs are available to BBC journalists, how blogs concerning war and terrorism have evolved in the 21st century and why blogs represent a challenge to traditional news narratives of war.

BLOGS FROM WAR ZONES AND WITNESSING TERROR

The mobile phone and the Internet have formed the vanguard of a revolution in communications technology by which the ability to publish information has been distributed to a much wider group of people.[6] Anybody with access to these technologies can participate in instant global publication via the World Wide Web. In practice, most people publish information over the Web to a relatively small audience and a few websites dominate Internet traffic, but the potential to reach larger audiences is often only one hyperlink away. Individuals caught up in conflict or terror attacks often seek to communicate their shock, anxiety, grief, suffering and pain. Blogs have been used by eyewitnesses to major news events to document their experiences sometimes catapulting their blogs to a larger audience. Throughout the first decade of the 21st century these accounts have provided an alternative to news and information available in media organisations. They have also been incorporated by the traditional media into their coverage.

During the Kosovo war, the word *blog* was yet to receive mainstream recognition,[7] but then the development of easy-to-use blogging software, such as Blogger and LiveJournal, was in its infancy in mid-1999.[8] The people communicating on the Web about the war in Kosovo were not using blogs but were instead updating their own webpages, writing emails or using message boards and chatrooms. Relief organisations were also updating websites with news from the bombing zones. International journalists had been ordered to leave Serbia in March 1999,[9] and many journalists were forced to rely on emails being sent to them from the ground. A Serbian monk, Father Hieromonk Sava, provided firsthand accounts suggesting that NATO's bombing campaign was not as precise as it was claiming. The emails of a 16-year-old Albanian Muslim girl in Kosovo were read out on CBS News. Nenad Ćosić, a graphic designer in Belgrade, published time-stamped email updates of NATO airstrikes in a style which might now be referred to as a 'live blog'.[10] These personal accounts offered a different perspective from the 'narrow prism of views' and the 'ubiquitous aerial photos' available on network news.[11]

By 2001, 'weblogging' was beginning to emerge. The use of blogs by individuals to document their reaction to the events of September 11 pointed towards a future in which they would play a more significant role in the reporting of news events.[12] James Marino, for example, had been updating a blog-style celebrity news and gossip website in New York on the day that al-Qaida operatives flew two planes into the towers of the World Trade Center.[13] Marino had a view of the towers from his office window and as he watched the events of that morning unfold, he continued to update his website. He offered short updates which provided a mixture of factual information and emotional response to what he was seeing. Marino demonstrated that eyewitnesses to the news did not have to be mediated by traditional media organisations in order for their accounts to be accessed.

As the use of blogs became more widespread the potential for a blogger to be documenting a newsworthy event increased. During the Iraq war, a number of Iraqis began blogging about their experiences of life in a conflict zone. Bloggers such as Salam Pax, Riverbend and Healing Iraq attracted significant audiences as media attention focused on the country. Their accounts provided access to voices offering a more nuanced view of the conflicting hopes and aspirations of many Iraqis. They drew readers into a world unfettered by editorial restrictions, traditional media frames, news values and agendas.[14]

By the middle of the decade, blogs written by eyewitnesses to news events had caused a number of journalists to reconsider their scepticism of the value of blogging. Bloggers provided accounts of the tsunami in Southeast Asia in 2004, the London bombings in July 2005, the Second Lebanon War in 2006 and the ongoing conflicts in Iraq and Afghanistan. Commentators regularly referred to this phenomenon as one aspect of 'citizen journalism', and bloggers were problematically labelled 'citizen journalists'.[15] Bloggers often did not see themselves as journalists, and their blog posts were not of broader media significance until a news event occurred in their vicinity. Many bloggers were only acting as journalists or reporters for short periods of time or at a particular stage in the journalistic process. They committed 'random acts of journalism' which, in some cases unwittingly, led to much wider fame.[16] Nevertheless, their inclusion in media reports meant online news was becoming 'a collaborative endeavour, engendering a heightened sense of locality'.[17]

As the number of bloggers grew, other bloggers began collating, curating, aggregating and organising their posts. Often these were small topic focused blogs. Jeffrey Schuster, for example, started Iraqi Bloggers Central to help him track the Iraqi blogosphere,[18] but more substantial projects also emerged. In 2005, Harvard fellows Ethan Zuckerman and Rebecca MacKinnon founded a blog called Global Voices to collect blog posts from bloggers all over the world on one site. Their starting point was a belief in freedom of expression and an awareness that the traditional media did not always reflect various strands of thought. Relying on volunteers, Global Voices aimed to 'redress some of the inequities in media attention by leveraging the power of citizens' media'.[19] The project is maintained by a community of more than 300 bloggers and translators.

EYEWITNESSES IN THE EVOLVING DIGITAL MEDIA LANDSCAPE

Towards the end of the decade blogging was diversifying and eyewitness material could be found on a variety of Internet platforms. Images and videos which were initially uploaded on websites such as Flickr, Vimeo and YouTube were embedded into blog posts and other websites. The widespread incorporation of a camera, which takes both still and moving images into mobile phone technology, has meant that people are potentially continuously in a position to capture images of a breaking news event and upload them within minutes to the Web. In the aftermath of the attacks on Mumbai in November 2008, Vinukumar Ranganathan uploaded photos of damaged and bloodstained streets to Flickr which were more widely distributed by bloggers and news organisations.

YouTube played a significant role in the Iran election crisis in 2009 providing access to imagery which otherwise would have been unavailable. The disturbing raw footage of Neda Agha-Soltan, a female demonstrator who was killed in a government crackdown on protesters and who was filmed as she died on a street in Tehran, became synonymous with the cause of the reformist movement. After the Moscow metro system was attacked by two female suicide bombers in March 2010, a video was uploaded on YouTube by photographer Alexey Baranov which showed people evacuating Park Kultury metro station where one of the bombs exploded. The viewer could see dead passengers strewn across the platform and inside a train. The video appeared on a number of Russian LiveJournal blogs and was used by France24's website.[20] During the uprisings in the Middle East and North Africa in 2011, videos shot by activists, uploaded onto YouTube and incorporated into traditional media news coverage documented the often bloody struggle for political change. The pictures of Tunisians toppling President Zine El Abidine Ben Ali helped inspire Egyptians to occupy Tahrir Square to remove Hosni Mubarak from power, while activists successfully bypassed attempts by the governments in Libya and Syria to suppress media coverage of these countries' civil wars.

Microblogging, particularly on Twitter, but also via the status update feature of Facebook, is another method for eyewitnesses to news events to quickly relay information. Twitter limits users to only 140 characters encouraging brevity and immediacy. The service rapidly became a hub for breaking news and acted as an unofficial and customisable wire service. After a series of bomb blasts in Bangalore killed two people in July 2008, technology entrepreneur Mukund Mohan demonstrated how Twitter could be used to provide real time updates in the context of a terror attack. Mohan travelled to the scene where one of the bombs had exploded and acted as a reporter speaking to eyewitnesses and the police.[21] At first, he used his mobile phone to update his Twitter account, but a slow Internet connection speed made it difficult to keep up with all the information he was receiving.[22] He decided to collect several mobile phone numbers of contacts at the blast sites before returning to a nearby office to continue to update his Twitter feed on his PC. It was probably the first example of Twitter being used as a reporting tool by a 'citizen journalist' to cover a terror attack.

Twitter updates can be incorporated into blogs or websites, but particularly in the context of an ongoing breaking-news situation the use of Twitter has become more prominent than longer-form blogs. In November 2008, one of the BBC journalists covering the Mumbai attacks noted that rather than updating their blogs many Indians were using Twitter instead.[23] While microblogging might be quicker for instant breaking news, longer form blogs are still used by individuals to write about their experiences of conflict and terrorism. In addition, 'live blogs' are started by individuals as a way of collating material in an ongoing crisis.

A blog, therefore, is one of a number of online genres which an eyewitness might use to communicate a news event concerning war and terrorism.

Blogging enabled a larger group of 'citizens' to upload news information to the Web and many bloggers have contributed—whether consciously or otherwise—to the process of journalism. Bloggers' access to a conflict zone or their presence at the scene of a terror attack allied to the possibilities of low-cost and increasingly mobile digital publication meant they could be better positioned to perform the role of the newsgatherer than are many journalists. This challenge to the role of the journalist was met by the widespread incorporation of blogs and other material produced by the 'former audience' into traditional journalism.

NGOs, ACTIVISTS AND INDEPENDENT JOURNALISTS

Bloggers such as James Marino and Salam Pax started blogging because a monumental event had interrupted their everyday lives and they felt compelled to share their stories. But other bloggers were impinging even more directly on the role of traditional media journalists by travelling to conflict zones. They were motivated by a desire to bring attention to untold stories or illuminate the plight of the suffering. A few were independent adventurers, several were freelance journalists and a growing number were employees or volunteers for charities, nongovernmental organisations or civil society groups with the specific aim of influencing the political agenda.

In 2003, Christopher Allbritton, a former AP and *New York Daily News* journalist, raised more than US$10,000 from blog readers to fund an independent reporting project to Iraq.[24] In return, donors would have access to exclusive content. Hoping to build a spirit of trust and engagement, Allbritton was open about his opposition to the war in Iraq and responded to readers' questions and criticisms. Blog readers were also invited to suggest stories and offer feedback acting in the stead of an assignments editor. Although he was a trained journalist, Allbritton eschewed traditional forms of journalism: 'It's not Associated Press inverted pyramid-style writing, but I didn't think people wanted that on a site such as this. My reporting combines the personal, the micro and the macro'.[25] Allbritton struggled to make donations alone pay for this independent form of journalism. He only stayed in Iraq for 20 days in 2003 and during a second trip to Iraq in 2004 admitted he would have to accept freelance work to cover his costs.[26]

He also disputed his status as a 'blogger'. On a blog post responding to New York University journalism professor Jay Rosen, who had cited Allbritton as an example of a blogger performing original reporting, Allbritton asked to be omitted from 'the lists showing bloggers doing journalism':

> I am not a 'blogger.' I am a journalist who chose to blog to make a career move. I am still a journalist, proudly embedded in the so-called mainstream media, which generates about 99.9999% of the original reporting today.[27]

Other journalists followed in Allbritton's footsteps. Michael Yon, a former Green Beret with US Army Special Forces, has become renowned for his embedded dispatches from Iraq and Afghanistan. Although his blog moved to a more standard website in 2005 he followed Allbritton's model by soliciting donations from readers and built a more 'intimate and trusting' relationship with his readers than traditional journalists.[28] Despite his preference for embedded journalism, Yon managed to retain his often outspoken independent voice. As a former member of the Special Forces, Yon was generally sympathetic to the military and in particular serving soldiers, but he was not afraid to offer his opinion on the progress of the wars in Iraq and Afghanistan and the conduct of senior politicians and military figures.[29]

Independent journalists were not the only actors looking to escape the constraints of traditional journalism—so too were charities and nongovernmental organisations. Civil society groups have also used blogging in post-conflict situations in an attempt to promote lasting peace.[30] According to Sarah Wilson, a Christian Aid media officer, 'aid agencies tend to want to give . . . a much more detailed account . . . than usually the conventions of journalism allow'.[31] Dissatisfied with the limited space available in conventional print and broadcast media, organisations such as Oxfam and Médecins Sans Frontières employ their own journalists and produce their own journalism. In addition to working with media organisations and providing content for them, NGOs have also begun to use blogging as a tool for communicating their work. Oxfam started a news blog on its main website in 2008 and launched a dedicated website for blogs by Oxfam workers including several from conflict zones.[32] Similarly, Médecins Sans Frontières collate blog posts written by their employees.[33]

Independent journalists, NGO workers and activists began writing blogs to escape the conventions of the traditional media. They found that they could tell the stories of people on the ground outside the news agendas, editorial guidelines and story structures imposed by media organisations.[34] These bloggers play a role in amplifying the voices of those in conflict zones who might not be easily accessible to news organisations. The ability to publish at low cost meant they could continue to provide information about an ongoing conflict long after the traditional media news agenda had moved elsewhere. These blogs can represent a challenge to the more sporadic coverage of conflict offered by the traditional media where stories must compete for editorial space with a range of other news items. But these bloggers' coverage of a conflict zone also offers opportunities for traditional journalists and media organisations. Independent journalists often sell their content to traditional media organisations on a freelance basis to fund their projects, while collaborations between NGOs and traditional media journalists are often mutually beneficial. The NGO gains more publicity while the journalist gains access to local sources, knowledge and expertise. The decline of permanent foreign bureaux[35] means that media organisations might rely increasingly on the contributions of NGOs and independent journalists in the future.

FRONT-LINE MILITARY BLOGGING

In addition to eyewitnesses, independent journalists, NGO workers and activists, soldiers were also offering their perspective of war and terror using the blogging genre. Indeed, the US' 'global war on terror' was the catalyst for the emergence of the military blog. The war in Iraq divided political opinion, and military bloggers began discussing both the merits of the invasion of the country and the portrayal of the conflict by the traditional media.[36] As the war stagnated bloggers both questioned and defended the 'war on terrorism'. Many of these bloggers were based in the US, but the construction of significant military bases in Iraq and Afghanistan enabled soldiers to communicate with friends and families via the Web. Some started blogs which attracted much larger audiences than merely a few interested relatives and friends. Although these front-line blogs were rare, several attracted media attention, and a number were collated into a book by former US Army Major Matthew Burden.[37]

These blogs were compelling because they offered a different picture of war to that being presented in the traditional media. One of the first military bloggers to gain notoriety was US Army Specialist Colby Buzzell. His blog, My War, captured the raw experience of his life in Iraq as a US soldier. In June 2004, he had decided to set up an anonymous blog with the aim of keeping it 'under the radar for as long as possible'.[38] He was not very successful. Buzzell wrote a vivid account of a firefight in Iraq in which he recorded that US troops had been low on ammunition and water. This information formed part of an article in *The News Tribune* by journalist Mike Gilbert which ultimately alerted Buzzell's commanders to his blog. Although his blog was not shut down immediately, it was not long before he was ordered to stop writing.

When Buzzell's blog made headlines in 2004, a US Army spokesperson stated that blogs would be tolerated as long as they did not 'violate operational or informational security'.[39] In practice, blogs which became controversial for a variety of political reasons tended to be closed by their authors under pressure from military superiors. Buzzell discovered that his right to freedom of expression under the First Amendment, which he quoted on his blog, would be firmly challenged by the power of military command and control.

Buzzell was not the only soldier who explored the limitations of democratic freedoms through a blog. Capt. Matt Gallagher, who wrote Kaboom: A Soldier's War Journal from Iraq during 2007 and 2008, stopped blogging after he had vented his frustration at the US Army's internal politics on a blog post.[40] Similarly, a British military blog, written by a Royal Air Force (RAF) technician, ended after he wrote a blog post which had offered Condoleezza Rice 'some pointers' following her visit to Kandahar airbase. The blogger concluded his post by suggesting that the then US secretary of state would be better advised not to visit again.[41] A Ministry of Defence (MoD) press officer said the blogger, known only as 'Sensei Katana', had taken his blog down of his own accord after realising that 'posting some of the information was not a particularly sensible thing to do'.[42] While the MoD claimed Sensei Katana was 'not forced' to delete the blog, it was clear that his commanders had become aware of his online activity, and it was unlikely that his sarcastic advice to such a senior figure in the NATO alliance was welcomed.

Bloggers such as Buzzell, Gallagher and Sensei Katana entered the online world in the hope that it was a place where they could 'speak the truth', and they took advantage of a window of opportunity whereby their blogs were unknown by their professional superiors or the wider world. But open and honest accounts revealing some of the inner workings of military life inevitably attracted attention and military blogs written from the front lines were featured in traditional media articles. As military commands became increasingly aware of blogs, the freedom to publish unadulterated accounts was reined in both formally, through military directives, and informally, through self-censorship.

The US military led the way on blogging policy and was exceptional in having to do so—in Iraq and Afghanistan it had more potential front-line bloggers than any military in the world. In April 2007, the US military revised Army Regulation 530–1 on Operations Security (OPSEC) to specifically cover blogs. Military bloggers were subsequently required to consult their 'immediate supervisor and their OPSEC Officer for an OPSEC review prior to publishing'.[43] (In August 2007, the British MoD published a similar set of regulations.[44]) Although straightforward in theory, in practice the US military lurched between actively encouraging their servicemen and -women to tell their stories on blogs and outright censorship. It reflected the conflicting views towards the use of digital media by serving soldiers across services and ranks, the adoption of policies which could be widely interpreted and the fraught process of institutional learning and change in a rapidly evolving environment.

The revisions to AR530–1 and existing guidance under 'Multi-National Corps—Iraq' from 2005[45] discouraged some milbloggers from continuing their blogs and others from starting them.[46] The US Marines banned its members from using social networks on military computers in August 2009 on the grounds that the sites were 'a proven haven for malicious actors and content and particularly high risk due to information exposure'.[47] At the same time, engagement with digital media was receiving backing from the highest echelons of military command including Lt. Gen. Caldwell, Adm. Mike Mullen and Gen. Petraeus. By February 2010, the Department of Defense's first official policy on social media was branded as switching the default position to 'open' and suggested that military computers could be used to update personal blogs and microblogs. But it also allowed for temporary bans on access to blogging and microblogging sites.[48]

As militaries became much more aware of blogging and introduced additional guidance to servicemen and -women, military bloggers necessarily began to avoid the raw accounts which had seen others censored. In December 2009, a number of military bloggers held a silent protest in support of blogger C. J. Grisham, who had been disciplined by his chain of command for a blog post concerning his dissatisfaction with the conduct of a school Parent Teacher Association meeting.[49] Although this was not a post from the front line, it led to more general consideration about the state of milblogs. Blackfive.net raised concerns about the decline in 'combat blogs' from Afghanistan compared to Iraq and the 'level of self-censorship that is creeping in'.[50] Another blogger suggested that 'many field grade officers and senior NCOs' [noncommissioned officers] not only failed to support blogging but were issuing verbal and written reprimands against 'active duty milbloggers and milspouses'.[51] A number of serving US soldiers continue to blog about life on the front line, but they are aware that their blogs are almost certainly being read by the military hierarchy. They are more circumspect than their predecessors, and blogs written by soldiers serving in other militaries remain exceptionally rare. Within the British context, there have been very few examples of blogs written from the front line which have not been completely officially sanctioned by the MoD as part of a public relations project.

A number of soldiers started blogs because they were dissatisfied with media coverage of conflict. They hoped to offer a more personal, raw account of the experience of war. As Bart Cammaerts and Nico Carpentier note, Buzzell's blog challenged the military's and media's 'ideological model of war' by highlighting the irrationality and indiscriminateness of conflict.[52] Soldiers' blogs from the front line potentially offered a fascinating insight into the life of the combat soldier and, at times, blogs such as those written by Buzzell and Gallagher provided journalists' with the possibility of including alternative angles on conflict. Both the challenge and opportunity for journalists has been limited, however, by the increased awareness and control of blogs by military organisations. In the cases of Buzzell and Gallagher, it was evident that more widespread media attention and the military's internal politics ultimately led to the demise of their blogs. Whereas previously military authorities were only vaguely aware of the blogosphere, now it is taken far more seriously. As a consequence, the level of self-censorship by military bloggers appears to have increased. The window of opportunity for journalists to incorporate these blogs into their journalism, therefore, appears to be small and if a journalist takes advantage of the blog as a source, it may inadvertently lead to the window being permanently closed.

DIASPORIC BLOGGERS AND WAR REPORTING: THE SECOND LEBANON WAR

Influential bloggers are not isolated on the World Wide Web: they read other blog posts, link to one another and comment on other blogs. Individual blogs are usually part of connected blogging networks which often coalesce around certain topics or interests forming regional, language or subject-oriented blogospheres. In the context of war and terrorism, blogs written from the front lines of conflict situations are supported or challenged by wider blogging communities.

During the Second Lebanon War in 2006, bloggers in Lebanon were supported by a blogging diaspora. Sune Haugbolle notes that a coherent blogosphere discussing Lebanese issues first emerged in response to the assassination of Rafiq Al-Hariri in February 2005 and the conflict between Israel and Hezbollah.[53] Several blogs, such as Siege Notes and Kerblog, were being updated from Lebanon during the war in 2006.[54] But a number of the key blogs identified by Haugbolle in the Lebanese blogosphere at this time were based abroad. Across the Bay, From Beirut to Beltway and the Angry Arab News Service were written from the US. The author of Beirut Spring had also left Lebanon, and several blogs about the conflict were being updated from Jordan and Syria.[55] A transnational media community was commenting on the war.[56]

These diasporic bloggers were at once both connected and disconnected from the conflict zone. As they were former residents or had relatives in the affected country, they had links, contacts and experience upon which to base blog posts. But they were not subject to the difficulties and constraints faced by individuals living in the war zone. Ethan Zuckerman has described these and similar individuals as 'bridgebloggers'.[57] Knowledge of their own culture and their adopted culture allows these bloggers to act as a 'bridge' between the two cultures mediating the concerns of people at home to a new audience abroad. During the Lebanon war, bloggers on the ground and in the diaspora cooperated in an attempt to disseminate their own version of the conflict.

Diasporic bloggers helped amplify the message of those blogging from Lebanon by distributing news and adding their own commentary. The email updates of Hanady Salman, the editor of Beirut-based newspaper As-Safir, were collated by a friend on the Beirut Journal blog.[58] Similarly, freelance writer Rasha Salti's Siege Notes were also distributed by bloggers.[59] Widespread coverage on Lebanese blogs brought the accounts to the attention of the traditional media which subsequently used them in their coverage. Although these accounts were incorporated into the journalism of traditional media organisations, they also sat alongside traditional media as alternative sources of news about the progress of the war. A number of bloggers featured photographs which had been passed to them by Hanady Salman; gruesome images of the dead and wounded which the editor of As-Safir knew would not be shown by the Western media.[60] The testimony of Lebanese on the ground did not always sit comfortably with the perceived bias and actual limitations of media reports which people in the Lebanese diaspora were consuming. As'ad AbuKhalil felt the US media was biased in favour of Israel and used his blog to sarcastically criticise editorials in the *New York Times*.[61]

Haugbolle regarded these blogs as an 'indispensable addition to the daily dose of BBC and Lebanese media',[62] while Fadda-Conrey described them as 'necessary information lifelines for the diasporic Lebanese'.[63] She believed their 'first-person perspective' served 'to humanise the Arab voice . . . creating an archive of much-needed alternative stories'.[64] Although several blogs were incorporated in traditional media coverage for these very reasons, diasporic bloggers also challenged journalists approach to the publication of sensitive imagery by publishing disturbing images and bloggers openly attacked narratives of the conflict portrayed in the traditional media. For journalists, these bloggers may provide access to sources and information from conflict zones which can be incorporated into their journalism, but bloggers can also act as pressure groups, rounding on journalists and media organisations that are deemed to be misrepresenting a conflict.

NETWORKED BLOGGERS AND WAR REPORTING: THE US MILITARY BLOGGING COMMUNITY

In the US, the role of scrutinising and criticising the media's coverage of conflict has been adopted by a military blogging community which has emerged as a media actor in the area of war and terrorism. As previously noted, a number of military bloggers began blogging because they were dissatisfied with traditional media reports from the wars in Afghanistan and particularly Iraq.[65] The blogs were written by a variety of people including servicemen or –women who began blogging on deployment and continued to do so after they returned home; veterans of the wars in Afghanistan, Iraq and previous US military engagements; military spouses; and other interested parties.

Although they usually had a common interest in defending the reputation of the US Armed Forces, the military blogging community grew to incorporate a variety of political views. Military bloggers not only supported and encouraged one another but also engaged in lively debate. They linked to one another, quoted one another and used contacts with serving members of the US Forces to put forward concerns on their behalf. Several websites such as The Sandbox for Slate and MilitaryBlogging.com aggregate blog posts from around the military blogosphere. Links and contacts between bloggers are cemented at an annual military blogging conference which has convened every year since 2006.

Individually, they probably would have made little impact, and like bloggers in other fields they were usually dismissed by traditional media journalists as a noisy irrelevance. But when they mobilised as a community they became a pressure group as *The Telegraph* discovered in October 2008 when military bloggers were alerted to a report on the newspaper's website by journalist Nick Meo.

Meo had been embedded with National Guardsmen in Afghanistan when the armoured vehicle he was travelling in from Kandahar to a base in

Helmand was hit by an improvised explosive device (IED). Guardsman Corporal Scott Dimond died in the attack. Meo described his experience in an online article for *The Telegraph* which included a piece of video he had shot in the aftermath. A US public affairs officer for ARSIC-South, First Lt. Amy Bonanno, was unhappy with several features of Meo's article. She listed fourteen complaints including Meo's comparison of the US National Guard with the British Territorial Army, his criticism of a guardsman's Mohican hair cut, allegedly initially refusing to tell a US investigating officer whether he had taken video footage of the attack, inconsistencies in the article over whether US soldiers had night-vision equipment, dramatising the article by allegedly falsely claiming that in the aftermath of the attack the US military listed Meo as 'Killed in Action', and his alleged refusal of an offer to attend the ramp ceremony for Cpl Dimond.[66]

Amy Bonanno was planning to issue an official rebuttal but also decided to contact Troy Steward of Bouhammer.com and Matthew Burden at Blackfive.net, two influential military blogs. Both bloggers ran posts highlighting Bonanno's criticisms. Meo and *The Telegraph* were the subject of several highly critical follow-up posts on other blogs and Meo personally received a number of abusive emails which he described as 'extremely vicious personal attacks'.[67] Meo responded in a second online article for *The Telegraph*. He did not retract any part of the story, nor did he directly address any of Bonanno's criticisms. The article only sparked further posts by military bloggers. Meo found it 'puzzling that the bloggers are making all kinds of wild claims. Exactly why the bloggers have attacked the story with such venom has also been rather difficult to understand'.[68] Meo said he had not been invited to the ramp ceremony, had not received an official complaint from the US military and felt Bonanno's claims would not have been sustained by any official procedure. Bonanno said she would have taken more formal action had military bloggers already not done 'more than the military would have been able to accomplish'.[69]

The incident between Meo, Bonanno and the military bloggers highlighted the consequences of a journalist's audience being immediately global and not merely national. Perhaps more important, it had shown that military blogs were new players in the online media landscape. Although in this instance their influence had been consciously mobilised by the US military's public affairs department, military bloggers had demonstrated that they were able to apply pressure to a journalist and a media organisation by attempting to discredit a news article online. Embedded journalists, such as Meo, were already under constraints and pressures from the military machine, but they now also potentially faced flak from a well-connected network of military bloggers. Reporting a story which was critical of US soldiers had become an even more fraught enterprise.

Casting military bloggers merely in opposition to the traditional media, however, would be inaccurate. Journalists can take advantage of these networks to facilitate their journalism. As Lebanese bloggers contributed to media reports during the war in Lebanon in 2006, so too have military blog-gers become integrated into traditional media coverage. Some bloggers, such as Troy Steward, the author of Bouhammer.com, are regularly interviewed by the traditional media including the BBC.

THE ENTRY OF 'ELITE' SOURCES INTO THE BLOGOSPHERE: OFFICIAL MILITARY BLOGS

Earlier in the chapter, it was noted that blogs written by US soldiers had raised awareness within the military command of the online world. In addi-tion to closing down blogs which were deemed to be 'off message' or a threat to operational security, militaries also sought to communicate their own narratives of conflict using blogs. The entry into the blogosphere of the US military and other 'official', elite, government and corporate actors funda-mentally altered the nature of blogging on war and terrorism. Blogs became a tool of official public relations campaigns, and it is also possible they were being used more covertly in psychological or intelligence operations.[70]

An article on the US Department of Defense website claims that the first official military blog was written by Capt. Steve Alvarez for the *Orlando Sentinel* newspaper as part of his official duties while deployed to Iraq in 2004–2005.[71] Like a number of early blogs it was a personal online column with limited functionality. Alvarez said that he had permission to write the blog from Maj. Gen. Paul Eaton in 2004 and then later Lt. Gen. David Petraeus. Alvarez noted, however, that it caused 'a lot of heartache': he claims that at one point he was told by the Commandant of the Defense Information School that for 'the good of his career' and 'until they could figure out a position on blogs' he should shut it down.[72]

The Department of Defense's New Media Directorate was established in October 2006, but official US military blogs only emerged in significant numbers during 2008 and 2009.[73] One of the first was started by the US Army Accessions Command in partnership with Weber Shandwick PR and Communications Agency. Army Strong Stories aimed to publish interesting posts written by soldiers and to provide an online space where potential recruits could ask questions about life in the US Army.[74] It was followed by the Chief of Information in the Department of the Navy in January 2008, by the US Army Corps of Engineers the following month and by a Department of Defense blog hosted on Blogger in April 2008.[75]

A number of US military public affairs officers also began experimenting with the blog format as a way of providing news and information about individual military units. 10th Mountain Division started a blog in 2008 as a way for 'Task Force [Mountain] leaders to share their thoughts . . . with our troops, friends and supporters back home'.[76] Perhaps surprisingly the unit allowed blog commenters to debate some sensitive topics. One post in April 2009 stated that 'the Army is experiencing an unacceptable level of sexual assaults against female soldiers' and asked for thoughts on how the Army should reverse this trend.[77] By the end of 2009, the US Navy, Air Force and Army as well as the Department of Defense were all updating official blogs. Chief Public Affairs Officer, Maj. Gen. Kevin Bergner, noted that the US Army had witnessed the 'value of blogs': 'they are powerful tools of communication for our soldiers, veterans, family members and others'. He said 'many great stories' had been told through the blogosphere and that the Army was 'excited to join that community'.[78]

Other militaries were also experimenting with blogging. The UK MoD's Defence News Daily section of the website, which started in July 2006, was renamed the Defence News blog. Although it collated and linked to other defence news stories it remained closed to comments until May 2010 when it was re-launched on a more interactive format. The blog's aim, however, remained within the bounds of a traditional approach to public relations: 'The purpose of this blog is to summarise significant stories about defence and the Armed Forces, respond to press reports, highlight coverage of defence issues elsewhere on the internet, and advertise forthcoming events'.[79]

Front-line blogging by members of the British forces occurred almost exclusively in an official capacity. Whereas their US counterparts often started blogs independently, which were subsequently vetted by superiors, British service member blogs were usually either initiated or quickly co-opted into an official blog offering. Initially these were sporadic projects such as the blogs written by the Commanding Officers of HMS *Somerset* and HMS *Nottingham* or a video diary by SAC Paul Goodfellow of the RAF. In August 2010, a blog written by RAF airman Alex Ford was the first to be given a MoD 'Sponsored blogger' badge, indicating that he would blog within MoD guidelines in return for receiving online advertising from MoD referrals.[80]

Two years previously, Maj. Paul Smyth, a Territorial Army soldier who runs his own PR firm, started the Basra Blog. It provided news and information about the British deployment in Southern Iraq. The MoD already had a blog of that name, hosted on their website which was only updated every few weeks. Smyth said he 'deliberately launched a competitive blog' to highlight the potential of blogging and other online tools to the MoD and provide 'a strategic viewpoint' of the campaign.[81] Hosted on a standard blogger template, Basra Blog lasted a year, closing several months after British troops had officially withdrawn from Iraq in April 2009.

In January 2009, a similar venture, Helmand Blog, was started by Maj. Smyth for the UK's Afghanistan operations prior to his own deployment on Operation Herrick 11. This project also incorporated Twitter, Facebook, YouTube and Flickr accounts. Smyth said he built on the lessons from Iraq to develop a social networking tool which he could use when he arrived in Afghanistan. By October 2009, he claimed the blog had developed an 'established audience' including a 'following of international journalists', and he regarded it as 'valuable platform for delivering media operations' from

Afghanistan.[82] An offshoot of Helmand Blog, called Front Line Bloggers—Afghanistan, collated blog posts written by servicemen and -women serving in Afghanistan.[83] Although Smyth claimed these projects offered a 'different flavour'[84] of what was happening in Afghanistan, the fact that any soldier who contributed was aware that it was an MoD project meant posts never wavered from the 'official line'. Posts were vetted by Smyth and the theatre media operations team for operational security violations.

Smyth's approach was evident in a more centrally operated blogging venture—UK Forces Afghanistan. Launched on 1 July 2010, the project established separate blogs for each of the three services. The MoD officially described it as the 'first-ever mass blogging initiative' by British forces in Afghanistan.[85] These blogs aimed to inform the public about the work of the men and women 'at the forefront' of the mission in Afghanistan. The project was operated by the Joint Media Operations Centre in Camp Bastion.

Official blogs by the US and British Armed Forces were established in the context of ongoing, existing operations in Iraq and Afghanistan. But blogs were also used in other circumstances. During the Russo-Georgia war in 2008, a number of Georgian government and news websites were forced to close down after distributed denial of service (DDoS) attacks.[86] On 11 August 2008, the Ministry of Foreign Affairs announced that Georgian websites had been disrupted by 'a cyber warfare campaign'.[87] The Georgian government was forced to seek alternative hosting options. The President's website was subsequently hosted by Tulip Systems, an US company based in Atlanta,[88] while the Ministry of Foreign Affairs started updating a Google blog.[89] By using Google's Blogger servers the Ministry of Foreign Affairs was much less vulnerable to DDoS attack, enabling it to continue to distribute the Georgian perspective of the ongoing conflict. At the height of the crisis, from 9 August to the end of the month, the Ministry wrote 124 blog posts.

Conflict also spurred the establishment of the Israel Defense Forces (IDF) spokesperson blog at the end of 2008 as the IDF prepared to invade the Gaza strip as part of Operation Cast Lead. Initially, digital media did not figure prominently in Israel's public relations plan, and it was hastily conceived merely days before the start of the operation.[90] The IDF set up a YouTube channel,[91] a Twitter feed and the IDF spokesperson blog, which began publishing information hours before the first aerial bombardments of the Gaza strip began on 27 December 2008. The three channels were closely interlinked but were not interactive. 'New' media formats were co-opted as vehicles for 'old' media messaging. Although the digital media element of the IDF's campaign was criticised,[92] both British and US commanders believed they could learn from the IDF's engagement in the 'new media battlespace'.[93]

The official military entry into digital media was not straightforward for large, hierarchical and bureaucratic organisations used to the 'one to many' delivery of information. Militaries faced technical difficulties and skill shortages as they attempted to mediate messages themselves rather than through traditional media channels and cultural challenges in adapting to a participative media culture.[94] By 2011, military organisations such as the International Security Assistance Force (ISAF) in Afghanistan and the Kenyan Army were also countering the respective Twitter accounts of insurgent actors—the Taliban (@alemerahweb) and the Somali-based insurgent group Al-Shabaab (@HSMPress). The emergence of these insurgent microblogging campaigns posed new problems for militaries because their 'official' military Twitter accounts were initially designed to inform and influence domestic and international allied audiences, not to engage in a war of words with an online 'enemy'. Nevertheless, this development helped consolidate the establishment of several militaries as a permanent online media presence allowing the public to access information which was usually reserved for journalists. By utilising blogs, militaries were attempting to mediate messages to the public without the interference of the traditional media, and they could use blogs as a method of accessing audiences online. Militaries have become substantial media producers in an attempt to influence the online environment.

The extent to which these blogs offer an opportunity for traditional media journalists to access information and incorporate them into their journalism appears to be limited. While the Jack Speak blog claims to offer an 'unlimited view' of the Royal Navy; for example, there are many operational security, political and linguistic constraints placed on official military blogs. Some journalists at the BBC are concerned that they would not find newsworthy information on such tightly controlled platforms or at least nothing more than they already receive through existing communications from the military. Commenting on the UK MoD's mass blogging announcement in July 2010, the BBC's World Affairs Producer, Stuart Hughes, said it was an 'interesting, if pointless initiative': 'I don't think I'll be holding my breath for an explosive indiscreet leak on the MoD's blogs that's going to make the lead on the Ten [O'Clock News]'.[95] Major Paul Smyth acknowledges that to obtain national media coverage, he needs to offer news organisations an "incredible story" regardless of the regularity and speed of his blogging initiatives.[96]

EXPERTS, ANALYSTS AND SPECIALISTS

Academics, interested specialists, independent analysts and critical observers have also started blogs in the field of war and terrorism. Their views had often been sought by traditional media organisations in the past and incorporated into news coverage, but blogs enabled them to easily and regularly publish their thoughts to niche and sometimes larger audiences.

Juan Cole, the Professor of History at Michigan University, began his Informed Comment blog as a hobby in 2002. Using his expertise in the area of Shiite Islam as a basis for commenting on the progress of the US invasion of Iraq, Cole attracted a substantial readership which had grown to

250,000 readers a month by 2004 during the Shiite uprising. The popularity of his blog led to appearances on CNN, National Public Radio (NPR) and before the Senate Foreign Relations Committee. An article for *Foreign Policy* magazine noted that academics such as Cole were using blogging to substantially increase their visibility.[97]

Rather than blogging individually, academics have also started blogging in groups to help manage the burden of regular updates and to provide a broader range of topics. The Arms Control Wonk blog features scholars from various universities where they dissect nuclear proliferation and security,[98] while academics at the War Studies Department at King's College, London collaborate to produce the Kings of War blog which covers contemporary defence and security issues.[99]

In addition to providing a platform for academics to more substantially influence the media landscape, discussions on specialist blogs, such as the Small Wars Journal[100] and Abu Muqawama,[101] helped shape debate over US counterinsurgency strategy in both Iraq and Afghanistan.[102] An essay on counterinsurgency by Australian Army Colonel David Kilcullen titled 'Twenty-Eight Articles: Fundamentals of Company-level Counterinsurgency' appeared on the Small Wars website in April 2006. It was later expanded and appeared as Appendix A in the 2006 edition of US Army Field Manual 3–24: Counterinsurgency.[103]

Blogs were also used as a way of collating news and information about Islamist militarism. The Jihadica blog, founded by William McCants and subsequently run by several researchers at the Norwegian Defence Research Establishment, describes itself as a 'clearinghouse for materials related to militant, transnational Sunni Islamism, commonly known as Jihadism'.[104] The blog offers translations, summaries and commentaries of media releases, discussions on web forums and other papers produced by jihadi groups.

These and similar blogs provide a greater degree of specialisation and report stories which would find no place in a more general news agenda. In the UK, the Defence of the Realm blog[105] written by independent defence analyst Dr Richard North was highly critical both of the Ministry of the Defence and the traditional media's coverage of Britain's military operations in Iraq and Afghanistan. His research and blog posts were particularly influential in exposing the mistakes made by the MoD in its reliance on the use of Snatch Land Rovers in Iraq. Thirty-eight British soldiers died in the vehicles despite foreknowledge that they offered little protection from the IEDs used by insurgents.[106] North was often scathing in his criticism of the coverage of defence issues in the media, claiming few journalists understood the technical details of military vehicles and lambasting the traditional media's fascination with human interest stories rather than providing detailed analysis of strategy and tactics.

Journalists have long used experts, specialists and analysts to lend authority to their news stories and blogs offer a new way for journalists to access their analysis, comment, opinion and reaction to news events. But these bloggers also represent a significant challenge to the traditional journalist, particularly if the latter is not a specialist or has not established a similar level of expertise. Previously experts would usually be mediated by journalists through short quotes in stories or sound bites. Even where they were asked to contribute longer articles in newspapers and magazines, journalists and publishers retained control. While the ability of journalists to access and incorporate the views of these individuals into their journalism is still a key part of their cultural capital, it has been undermined by the expert's entry into widespread publication online. In particular, blogs have enabled an increasing number of these individuals to play a role in the media landscape. Although they still tend to be read by specialist niche audiences, their ability to reach wider audiences has the potential to expose nonspecialist journalists as anything but authoritative and expert. Furthermore, most of these specialist blogs are available for free on the Internet, meaning that individuals who are interested in specific areas or topics can sometimes access more detailed information at no additional cost. The disparity in expertise has been highlighted by a number of specialist blogs which have dissected inaccuracies in media reports. They have been able to devote coverage entirely to their specialist area and incorporate contributions on their blogs from a knowledgeable audience.

THE CHALLENGES AND OPPORTUNITIES OF BLOGS FOR JOURNALISTS REPORTING WAR AND TERROR

This chapter has demonstrated that blogs and related genres of online publication represent both a challenge and an opportunity to traditional journalism.[107] Blogs have presented journalists with raw eyewitness accounts of conflict and terror attacks, access to alternative sources and specialist material, but they have also emerged as significant actors in the media landscape challenging traditional media narratives of conflict and terror. In numerous instances, blogs might overtly or unconsciously criticise traditional media portrayals of conflict while also being incorporated into media coverage.

In the first decade of the 21st century, a variety of individuals, organisations, governments and militaries have entered the blogosphere as actors in a broader media landscape. Where previously traditional news organisations acted almost exclusively as media producers, the Internet space is a competitive environment where any number of players can mediate war and terror to the public.

Front-line soldiers felt their experience of war was not adequately captured in traditional media formats. They wanted to offer a raw, emotional and personal account of the dilemmas, frustrations and fears of combat. Although for the most part, military bloggers have been reined in by military commands, their blogs still challenge aspects of traditional media coverage of warfare. Similarly, diasporic bloggers' exposure to traditional media reports has often acted as a spur to blogging because of their heightened awareness of the disparities between media reports and necessarily emotive first-hand testimony from relatives and friends caught up in a conflict zone.

The emergence of networked communities of bloggers is an important development. A blogger will not usually have much impact individually but by acting in concert with like-minded bloggers or attracting the attention of the traditional media they can quickly bring attention to issues which might otherwise have been ignored. In the field of war and terrorism, the military blogging community in the US has become a significant media actor, supporting US troops and their operations and scrutinising press coverage.

Militaries have also adopted the blogging format. The British, US and Israeli militaries have all begun official blogging projects as a tool in public relations and strategic communication campaigns. These blogs are used to convey the experiences of their soldiers and offer a narrative of conflict online which is unmediated by the traditional media.

Blogs have impinged most directly on the role of the traditional media journalist when they have been used as a primary medium for news reporting by individuals and organisations. Unlike the traditional media, independent journalists, NGOs, charities and activists often continued to cover stories from conflict zones on their blogs regardless of the news agenda and without the constraints of limited editorial space. Sometimes they also used blogs as a means of building a more intimate and trusting relationship with an audience than traditional media journalists of the past, using comments to reply to readers' questions and having a smaller community of readers rather than substantial audiences. Meanwhile experts, specialists and analysts have highlighted the limitations of the journalist as generalist. While specialist journalists are not uncommon, experts, academics and analysts previously constrained by their incorporation into traditional media frames and practices have now begun publishing blogs gaining their own readerships. Some bloggers have deliberately focussed on holding the media to account, highlighting overly simplistic reporting, factual errors or facile analysis.

As a way of meeting the challenge from blogs, the traditional media sought to incorporate accounts from blogs into their journalistic offering.[108] Wilson Lowrey sees such a move as a strategy whereby media organisations can address their vulnerabilities to blogs,[109] although these collaborations have often benefited both parties. For the blogger, the media organisation offers significantly increased exposure; for the media organisation, bloggers provide accounts and opinions which expand the range of news coverage.

Traditional media organisations have formed mutually beneficial alliances with other bloggers to enhance their coverage of conflict. They have entered into collaborative partnerships with NGOs, charities, activists and independent journalists to offer stories from places which are too dangerous to access and have relied on their expertise to help them access sources on the ground. Journalists have also used diasporic bloggers, such as the

Lebanese bloggers during the Second Lebanon War, and networks of blogging communities as a way of accessing a conflict zone through relatives and friends who can speak on behalf of those who are experiencing war.

Front-line military bloggers have been incorporated into traditional media organisations' coverage of war although it is apparent that the same publicity can precipitate the end of a military blog, particularly if the blogger violates operational security or comments on internal military politics. As military commands have become more aware of blogs and brought in guidelines for the use of digital media, military bloggers have noted that they are increasingly self-censoring. It is difficult for journalists to find potentially explosive accounts on military blogs. Official military blogs appear even more limited. Journalists might use these blogs for background information but they should not expect much to be revealed on these outlets which they do not already know. Similarly, blogs often provide journalists with an alternative method of contacting experts, specialists and analysts, many of whom will probably already be existing sources.

Blogs and other digital tools, such as Twitter, YouTube and Flickr, have made the most impact on traditional journalism in times of crisis, specific terrorist incidents, or in the midst of conflict when eyewitnesses have used them to capture, report and reflect on an event or news story. By the end of the decade, eyewitness accounts had become increasingly multimedia with the proliferation of high-speed internet connections and mobile phones equipped with cameras. Although their images could not match professional photography, their access to a momentous story trumped journalists who were scrambling to reach the scene. Blogs, in the form of live blogs, still play an important role in collating, aggregating and sharing information even if initial breaking news often appears to be shared first through a status update on Twitter or on a social networking site.

Journalists and news organisations have been keen to harvest these eyewitness reports or incorporate first-hand experience of conflict written on blogs in their journalism. The volume of material created by the public in the aftermath of events such as the London bombings in 2005, the Iran election crisis in 2009 and the uprisings in the Middle East and North Africa in 2011 has precipitated fundamental changes in the organisation of media newsrooms and the creation of new journalistic posts in the area of curation and community. More generally, by the end of the first decade of the 21st century many journalists were aware that the blogosphere was a place where they could access accounts of conflict. The following chapter explores how BBC journalists began harnessing blogs as a source of information and incorporating them into their coverage of war and terrorism.

Part II

2 Blogs

'Rumour, Prejudice and Gossip' or 'Standard' BBC Source?

Early understandings of blogs within the traditional media suggested they were highly unreliable as sources of information.[1] In an online article for the BBC website in 2003, technology commentator Bill Thompson emphasised that 'often' blogging was 'as far from journalism as it is possible to get': blogs contained 'unsubstantiated rumour, prejudice and gossip masquerading as informed opinion'.[2] The perceived culture of blogging did not seem to fit with the values associated with the BBC's brand of journalism which was built on accurate, impartial, independent and fair reporting.[3] Within the BBC, blogs were the cause of significant confusion for some journalists[4] and incorporating these new sources of online information in BBC journalism appeared to represent a professional minefield.

In the US, bloggers were becoming more prominent. They criticised media organisations for their lack of accuracy, their perceived and actual bias and their lack of openness. A few were making the news by breaking stories. Although the traditional media often subsequently cast blogs in opposition to the established media order, some journalists were realising that blogs offered them alternative sources of information which could become part of their journalism. A blogger was not necessarily a technology geek, political polemicist or introverted personal diarist. He or she might also be an eyewitness to a news event or be in a position to offer an insightful opinion on current affairs. As journalists experimented with accessing blogs as a way of covering news, perceptions about blogging within newsrooms began to change. Jay Rosen argues that it was their usefulness in reporting major news events such as the Indian Ocean tsunami in 2004 and the London bombings in 2005 which underlined their importance to the future of journalism.[5] At the BBC, an understanding of the potential of blogs for news was driven by the curiosity of staff at various levels of the organisation.

This chapter provides an outline of the incorporation of blogs as sources of information in the BBC's journalism. It highlights how initial concerns were gradually overcome as journalists began featuring blogs in news stories. It also traces the evolution of significant uses for blogs in the BBC's coverage of conflict, war and terrorism. In this respect, several areas are identified including accessing eyewitness accounts, providing alternative voices and collating reaction to major news events. It demonstrates that blogs proved particularly useful in accessing news and information when traditional means of news-gathering were not readily available. During the Iraq war, blogs provided first-hand accounts from places that BBC journalists could not easily cover safely. Reporting bans and state media control in the context of protests in Burma and Iran also encouraged BBC journalists to turn to the blogosphere for information. But in order to assess how far the emergence of blogging has broadened BBC journalists' source base and facilitated 'multiperspectival' news,[6] it is worth first considering the nature of the journalist–source relationship. This chapter begins by placing the use of blogs within the context of the literature on the journalist's sources of information and explores the BBC's particular relationship with 'official sources'.

THE JOURNALIST'S SOURCES OF INFORMATION

The relationship between journalists and their sources has formed a central area of research in academic literature which can be organised around two contrasting models. Epitomised by the uncovering of the Watergate scandal by investigative reporters Bob Woodward and Carl Bernstein, the first model pictures an adversarial relationship. Here, the role of the journalist is holding the powerful to account by accessing sources who are willing to reveal the failings of institutional, governmental and corporate power in order to expose them for the benefit of the public. In contrast, an exchange model emphasises the mutual interest of journalists and their sources of information. A study published in 1961 by Walter Gieber and Walter Johnson identified a level of assimilation between the interests of city hall journalists and local officials.[7] Cooperation was based on shared values and an understanding of their respective functions in society. Journalists require news on a regular basis while their sources desire the publication of material in news outlets to communicate information to a broad audience. Although the aims of journalists and their sources may not always overlap completely, it has often since been argued that news is usually a product of this 'transactional' or 'symbiotic' relationship.[8]

Indeed, journalists' dependency on news and information from their sources has led a number of scholars to conclude that the relationship is weighted towards 'official' or powerful sources. A 'manufacturing consent' school, based on Edward S Herman and Noam Chomsky's news propaganda model, emphasises the mass media's 'symbiotic relationship with powerful sources of information by economic necessity and reciprocity of interest'.[9] Herman and Chomsky argue that powerful sources dominate the news by denying and providing access to important information; offering credible and regular information at a lower cost than dissenting, critical sources; using significant information operations; and co-opting experts.[10] Similarly, Pierre Bourdieu maintains that sources of authority and power limit the autonomy of the journalist through the application of 'economic pressure' and 'their monopoly on legitimate information'.[11] Although he acknowledges that journalists could attempt to 'manipulate' these sources to obtain an exclusive, Bourdieu emphasises the 'exceptional symbolic power' given to state authorities to define the news agenda.[12]

Empirical evidence supporting the theory that the media are influenced by powerful elites has been documented in various studies of news organisations. Gaye Tuchman notes during her observation of reporters in New York that 'people with power serve as sources',[13] while Mark Fishman's study of the justice reporter on an American newspaper concludes that the journalist's 'information sources almost exclusively have a formally organised, governmental bureaucratic character'.[14] Although in theory sources could come from anywhere, Herbert Gans maintains that 'in practice, their recruitment and their access to journalists reflect the hierarchies of nation and society'.[15] He argues that 'incentives, power, ability to supply information, and geographic and social proximity [to the journalist]' increased the likelihood that a source would have access to the news.[16] A transnational study by Peter Golding and Philip Elliot demonstrates that 'even in highly equipped and financed news organisations there is an enormous reliance on the news gathering of agencies and on a few prominent institutional sources'.[17] More recent accounts from within the UK media industry also support these findings. In his book *Flat Earth News,* journalist Nick Davies criticises the news media's tendency to swallow and reiterate the official line. He argues that journalists are placed under personal pressure from powerful individuals, governments and companies.[18]

According to Robert W. McChesney, the structure of journalism, rather than 'morally bankrupt' or 'untalented journalists', is responsible for the deep-seated professional bias inherent in the production of news.[19] Academics have focussed on two interrelated areas of structural deficiency to explain what has been regarded as an over-reliance on 'official sources' of information. The first emphasises the problems arising from the news values of journalists and their professional goals; the second concerns the limitations of the process of news production. Where these 'professional demands' combine with 'practical pressures', it has been argued that they 'produce a systematically structured over-accessing to the media' of the powerful and institutionally privileged.[20]

Looking first at news values and professional goals, Stuart Hall and his colleagues maintain that journalists require sources which are efficient and enable them to achieve 'objectivity', 'impartiality' and 'balance'.[21] Reporters consequently invite certain 'accredited' sources to comment on the news in order to ground their journalism in authoritative statements from those holding institutional power, a 'representative' status or expert knowledge. These sources, therefore, act as 'primary definers' of news topics: by framing the problem and setting the limit for all subsequent discussion, they ensure the salience of their 'primary interpretation' of events. For Hall et al, journalists play a 'secondary role' in 'reproducing' issues that have already been defined and thus the media's role is structurally subordinate to these sources.[22] Similarly, in his study of US news during the Vietnam war, Daniel Hallin maintains that, for the most part, the media was 'a follower rather than a leader'.[23] In an effort to achieve 'objectivity', journalists renounced a role as interpreters of reality by presenting '"just the facts"'. As official sources were efficient, powerful and authoritative providers of these 'facts', they were able to fill 'a vacuum of meaning'.[24]

Turning to the news process, studies by Herbert Gans and Mark Fishman identify significant limitations in the range of sources used by journalists which could be attributed to the production of news. Media organisations require reliable information at speed meaning they utilise the wire services or other news media to find news stories and rely on 'official' governmental and organisational sources of information to verify their accuracy.[25] Gans describes the journalist's overriding aim in the selection of sources as efficiency: obtaining the most suitable news from the fewest number of sources as quickly as possible and with the least strain on the media organisation's budget.[26] He identifies six factors which journalists take into account when selecting a source: past suitability, productivity, reliability, trustworthiness, authoritativeness and articulateness.[27] Fishman argues that journalists need sources which enable them to quickly detect potential news stories, providing them with 'a map of relevant knowers for any topic of newsworthy events'.[28] These 'authorised knowers' provide a regular supply of newsworthy information to fill the demand for journalistic output and save the journalist from time-consuming investigative work.[29] Reliable sources are deemed to require less fact-checking: journalists can 'source' a story by attributing information to them without necessarily verifying the accuracy of every detail.[30]

Research which attempts to understand the media–source relationship from the perspective of both news sources and journalists further illuminates the workings of the negotiated and contested construction of news. Leon Sigal concludes from his study of Washington politics and US newspapers that 'news is an outcome of the bargaining interplay of newsmen and their sources'.[31] Sigal highlights how the routines of news production at the *New York Times* and the *Washington Post* reflected the routines of governmental information arguing that news sources controlled media output through calculated information releases. In *Reporting Crime*, Philip Schlesinger and Howard Tumber demonstrate that political actors were 'obliged to be serious about media relations' and that key institutional sources such as the police and the Home Office had developed an array of sophisticated techniques in an attempt to capture and shape the news agenda.[32] They argue that journalist–source relations in the UK in the 1980s and 1990s were 'not simply reducible to an economic exchange of information for publicity'.[33]

The dominance of official sources as a consequence of the exchange model, therefore, can be overstated. Schlesinger and Tumber highlight that journalists' relationships with their sources is 'quite varied'. They can also 'change over time' as a consequence of a more proactive approach to media relations by sources or clashes of interest.[34] The journalist–source relationship has been characterised, therefore, as a 'dance' or 'a tug of war'.[35] In *Negotiating Control,* Richard Ericson and his colleagues argue that the news media in Toronto were not merely passive 'secondary definers', producing news at the whim of institutional sources.[36] Although official sources were often successful in controlling the flow of information, they were concerned that journalists' influence over the representation of an event gave them 'the upper hand'.[37] Journalists could deny access, offer their own interpretation of the news and produce negative coverage. More generally, journalists do resist the powerful[38] and many journalists would still regard exposing institutional or governmental malpractice as a significant professional coup.

'Nonofficial' sources of information are capable of making their voices heard in the news, although studies tend to emphasise that the regularity of their access remains limited when compared with the 'habitual access' afforded to official sources.[39] Harvey Molotch and Marilyn Lester highlight that whereas the US president is able to contact the media regardless of time or issue, nonofficial sources' access to the media 'ebbs and flows' with time and place.[40] In the 1970s, Edie Goldenberg's study of 'resource-poor', largely radical interest groups in Boston demonstrates that these groups could only gain occasional (rather than regular) access to newspapers under favourable conditions.[41] Other studies have argued that in order to obtain media coverage nonofficial sources were dependent on financial resources, expert knowledge and news management techniques including the adoption of specific tactics and strategies.[42]

For Hallin, nonofficial sources only penetrated media coverage of the Vietnam war when the issues they were discussing had been legitimised by official sources. He maintains that the media failed to reflect the antiwar movement in reporting of Vietnam until elements of discontent began to emerge in the political mainstream.[43] Similarly, in W. Lance Bennett's 'indexing hypothesis', nonaccredited or nonofficial voices are only included in news stories when they 'express opinions already emerging in official circles'.[44] Furthermore, when these voices are included, they often appear in the context of stories relating to protests, civil disobedience or illegal acts which undermines their credibility and legitimacy.[45] Critics have also suggested that journalists are lax at cultivating contacts among those who could be deemed to be part of 'a sphere of deviance'—potential sources which society might have rejected as 'unworthy of being heard'.[46] Gans's work, for example, implicitly criticises journalists for not engaging with poorer sections of society,[47] while Fishman observes that a US justice reporter, he was studying had no regular contact with prisoners, jails or deviant subcultures.[48]

THE IMPACT OF THE INTERNET ON THE JOURNALIST'S SOURCES

Since many of these studies were published, the development of straightforward online publication first made possible through blogging has potentially changed aspects of journalists' relationship with official and nonofficial sources. First, digital media offered journalists more points of access to non-official sources from all over the world.[49] Second, nonofficial sources could easily provide journalists with news content online.[50] Third, nonofficial sources could interact with journalists more easily and quickly than they had done in the past.[51] Fourth, official and nonofficial sources were no longer solely dependent on the traditional media for more widespread publication and distribution of their messages.[52]

Viewed in the terms identified by Gans and Fishman, several notable differences between journalism prior to the Web and 21st-century journalism can be identified. Journalists operating in an information age have virtual 'geographic proximity' to thousands of sources online making it far more straightforward to identify and contact individuals for news stories.[53] The Web also provides journalists with a searchable 'map of relevant knowers', voices and experiences constructed from blogs and social networks.[54] This digital map of the social world exists because of the participation of the 'former audience' in the production of their own 'news' online. It means journalists are no longer necessarily so reliant on official sources and bureaucratic locations for the detection of 'newsworthy' events,[55] as they are more easily able to contact and monitor nonofficial sources through their online publication activities.

Blogs were undoubtedly becoming sources of information for journalists in the 2000s. The *New York Times* suggested that 'warblogs', for example, were becoming well-known in 2002 because 'mainstream journalists' were 'mentioning them in their copy or on the Sunday morning talk shows'.[56] Content analyses of traditional media coverage and surveys of journalists provided more detailed evidence of the emergence of the blog as journalistic source. Marcus Messner and Marcia Watson Distaso's content analysis of the *New York Times* and the *Washington Post* between 2000 and 2005 demonstrates that these newspapers legitimised weblogs as credible sources of information. In 2002, blogs were used as news sources in only 15 articles; by 2005, they appeared in 436 articles.[57] From a survey of 72 foreign journalists covering China in 2006, Rebecca MacKinnon concluded that blogs had become 'an essential part of the media diet for most China correspondents'.[58] Journalists were reading blogs and contacting bloggers: 46 journalists replied to a question which asked them how often they had interviewed a blogger for a story in the previous three months. 66% said they had done so on at least one occasion.[59] The adoption of the blog format as a news production tool also increased journalists' awareness of blogs as sources; journalists writing news blogs who replied to Paul Bradshaw's survey in 2008 spoke of a 'broadening of the range of contacts and of the sources of ideas for potential stories'.[60] Nic Newman's 2009 report looking at the impact of social media on traditional journalism for the Reuters Institute for the Study of Journalism suggested that 'influential bloggers', 'community networks' and 'activists' were all becoming alternative sources of news.[61]

Advocates for the transformative power of the Internet and the blogging genre heralded the potential for the democratisation of the news. In 2001,

John Pavlik suggested that the 'new media present the promise of democracy fulfilled'.[62] New sources of news would facilitate a journalism no longer based on 'objectivity' but on 'a complex blend of perspectives on news stories and events'.[63] For Dan Gillmor, the ability of the 'former audience' to publish online would offer 'more voices and more options' creating a 'massive conversation'.[64] Clay Shirky argues that the definition of news had changed. Rather than being an 'institutional prerogative', it had become part of 'a communications ecosystem' which consisted of 'formal organisations', 'informal collectives' and individuals.[65] Traditional media organisations would have to adapt to the new media environment by adopting a participative definition of journalism which engaged in a two-way dialogue rather than a one-way discourse: a shift that ultimately would better serve democracy.[66]

Critics have subsequently identified several limiting factors in a news revolution. Manuell Castells argues that global multimedia corporations have maintained their role as programmers of the decisive network—'the meta-network of communication networks'.[67] Although the rise of 'mass self-communication' created opportunities for social movements and insurgent politics to enter the public sphere, Castells states that they 'must adapt to the language of the media' and to the media's 'formats of interaction'.[68]

Certain dynamics of change in the media—such as the increased speed of the news cycle online—are also having a limiting influence on journalists' ability to search for alternative perspectives on events. The paradox of the end of the 'deadline delirium of twentieth century journalism'[69] was its replacement with 'the tyranny of real time'.[70] Without deadlines, news agencies and news organisations competed online to be first for breaking news, precipitating a culture of reporting events as they happen and the establishment of minute by minute journalism. The speed of the news cycle is one factor that leads Angela Phillips to conclude that rather than democratising the news, 'the overall effect of the Internet on journalism is to provide a diminishing range of the same old sources albeit in newer bottles'.[71]

The nuanced impact of the Web on the inclusion of nonofficial sources in journalism can be lost in generalisations. Neil Thurman's study of the use of User Generated Content initiatives including blogs by UK media organisations demonstrates that the nature of the news story might also be considered as an important factor. He concludes that the 'former audience' was contributing material for 'out of the ordinary' events such as earthquakes and large fires. He was not convinced, however, that these sources could be used to 'adequately report' news concerning 'elite persons' or nations.[72]

THE BBC'S RELATIONSHIP WITH 'OFFICIAL' SOURCES

If a new digital communications environment was to facilitate a transformation in the nature of news sourcing at the BBC, then it would also have to influence the Corporation's particular relationship with official sources.

According to Ian Hargreaves, BBC journalism is magnificent in its range, carefulness and resources, but it does tend towards an establishment view of the world.[73] Georgina Born suggests BBC journalists traditionally rely on official contacts, exclude less powerful sources and are not sufficiently committed to airing alternative viewpoints.[74]

Uniquely, BBC journalism has always been practised against the backdrop of its constitutional relationship with the UK government through the Royal Charter. Subject to parliamentary review every 10 years, the charter identifies the Public Purposes of the BBC. Members of the BBC Trust, who are appointed on the recommendation of the government, are tasked with ensuring that the BBC delivers on the remit set out in the Charter and a more detailed accompanying document known as the Agreement. Licence fee arrangements, which are responsible for funding most of the BBC's operation, must also be negotiated with government. These arrangements mean the government has 'formidable weapons' to pressurise the BBC if it is not satisfied with its performance.[75]

Throughout the history of the Corporation, the BBC's unusual relationship with the government has influenced its journalism. Official historian Asa Briggs suggests the Corporation's broadcasts during the General Strike in 1926 'greatly assisted the government of the day'.[76] Briggs argues that Director-General John Reith did manage to retain 'a precarious measure of independence'[77] but Jean Seaton describes the Corporation's strategy in the 1920s and 1930s as one of self-protection by self-censorship.[78] Seaton points to the development of what she describes as unhealthy links with civil servants and the Foreign Office which made the Corporation vulnerable to indirect pressure through threats against the licence fee.

In the build up to the Second World War, the BBC became involved in Britain's domestic and foreign affairs, helping to found the Ministry of Information in 1939.[79] In more recent times, the relationship between the government and the BBC has been far less intimate. Clashes between the government and the BBC demonstrate how the organisation's unique constitutional position has placed its journalism under pressure to report the government line from official sources at the behest of 'the national interest'. This is particularly relevant in times of war.

During the 1980s, Prime Minister Margaret Thatcher described the political troubles in Northern Ireland as a national war and she felt it was necessary to demand more responsible coverage from the BBC. She was especially concerned about the media providing 'terrorists' with the 'oxygen of publicity'.[80] Failings by the BBC and other media organisations to self-censor culminated on 19 October 1988 when Home Secretary Douglas Hurd announced the Broadcasting Ban, which made it illegal to cover 'the utterances by the representatives or supporters of pro-terrorist organisations in Northern Ireland'.[81] The BBC was reluctant to submit to the government's demands. Journalists managed to circumvent the ban by using actors' voices and by exploiting a loophole which allowed reporters to interview loyalists and republicans in a personal capacity.[82] The ban was revoked in 1994.

BBC management, however, did delay several Panorama documentaries seemingly out of fear of the government's reaction: in 1991, on the involvement of British manufacturing in the building of Saddam Hussein's 'Supergun' and in 1992 on the collapse of the UK economy. The former was stopped by Director-General John Birt on the grounds that it was not in the national interest when British troops were preparing to fight the Gulf War.[83] Concessions such as these did not appear to avert direct pressure from the government nor did the end of 28 years of Conservative government in 1997. Two years later, Tony Blair's decision to support NATO action in the Balkans led to government criticism of John Simpson's reporting from Sarajevo.[84] This incident, however, proved to be nothing more than a skirmish compared to the battle which broke out over the preparation of the intelligence dossier on Iraq in 2003.

THE HUTTON REPORT

Few could have predicted the consequences of the 6.07am live two-way between the BBC's defence reporter, Andrew Gilligan and the presenter of the Today programme, John Humphrys on the 29 May 2003. Although Gilligan was aware he was breaking a significant story, his allegations on Radio 4 that the government had 'sexed up' the intelligence dossier to gain support for military action against Saddam Hussein's Iraq proved to be the opening shot in a bruising encounter between the BBC and the government. One of the central features of the intelligence dossier was the government's claim that Iraq could prepare weapons of mass destruction within 45 minutes. Based on the testimony of an anonymous source, Gilligan said the government 'probably knew that that forty-five minute figure was wrong, even before it decided to put it in' and had deliberately altered 'a bland production' to make it sound 'more exciting'.[85] Alastair Campbell, Tony Blair's director of communications and strategy was furious at the implication that the prime minister had deliberately lied in leading the country to war and demanded an apology.[86] In July, Dr David Kelly, a government scientist and weapons expert, was revealed as the source of the story. He became the subject of intense media interest, and three days after a gruelling appearance in front of the Foreign Affairs Select Committee he was found dead near his home in Oxfordshire, having committed suicide.

The subsequent publication of Lord Hutton's inquiry into the death of David Kelly triggered 'the biggest crisis in BBC journalism's 80-year history'.[87] Exonerating the government and the intelligence services of any wrongdoing, Hutton's report castigated the BBC's journalism for the publication of 'unfounded allegations'.[88] Critics of the report argue that Hutton's judgement was a whitewash and that his limited remit, defined by Downing Street, meant he failed to address some of the wider issues surrounding the intelligence case which supported the decision to go to war.[89] Some were dismayed that the government seemed to have exercised considerable power over the BBC and Chairman Gavyn Davies reflected on 'threats, veiled and not so veiled, from 'government sources' to take revenge on the BBC by reducing its funding, removing its director-general and changing its charter'.[90] But it was also clear that the BBC had made some serious mistakes. The acting Director-General, Mark Byford, ordered an internal review into the state of the BBC's journalism chaired by Ron Neil, former Director of BBC News and Current Affairs.[91]

Building on existing editorial guidelines and what was described as the 'formidable professionalism' which already underwrote the organisation's practices, the Neil Report reiterated the values of 'BBC Journalism'. As a starting point, the report considered 'some of the guiding principles which should always be at the heart of BBC journalism'.[92] It described the 'DNA of the BBC' as 'accurate, robust, independent, and impartial journalism'. The report identified 'five basic editorial values, on which there could be no compromise'—'a code of conduct for every person who practises journalism in the BBC at whatever level'.[93] The first of these values was truth and accuracy: establishing the 'truth of what has happened as best we can' through well-sourced information, sound evidence, fact checking, precision in the use of language, provision of context and avoiding unfounded speculation. Throughout, the report emphasised the organisation's commitment to impartiality, urging the BBC to stand against the pressure to produce partisan and opinionated journalism.

EARLY USES OF BLOGS AS SOURCES OF INFORMATION AND SALAM PAX, THE BAGHDAD BLOGGER

These editorial axioms, early conceptions about the nature of blogosphere, the journalist's tendency to rely on 'official sources' of information and potential pressure from the government all suggested that blogs would not make suitable sources for the BBC. Many media commentators had already expressed major doubts about the suitability, reliability and authenticity of blogs. BBC technology commentator Bill Thompson argued that the unedited nature of blogs meant it was 'generally impossible to rely on anything one finds in a blog without verifying it somewhere else—often the much-maligned mainstream media'.[94] In March 2003, Mike Smartt, editor of the BBC News website between 1997 and 2004, believed 'dissemination of information is great, but how much of it is trustworthy? They [blogs] are an interesting phenomenon, but I don't think they will be as talked about in a year's time'.[95]

A few BBC journalists, however, had long since begun to use blogs to inform their journalism. As early as 1999, an online article about computer viruses by Internet Correspondent Chris Nuttall included information from the 'contributors to a discussion on the Slashdot Weblog'[96] and by July 2003,

Mark Ward, BBC Online Technology Correspondent, had noted that 'blogs are starting to become an unofficial source of eye-witness news'.[97] At the end of 2004, an article on the BBC website reflected on how blogs had become an important facet of the discourse surrounding the US election and also highlighted the uptake of blogs in China and Iran. It suggested that journalists 'increasingly use blogs as a barometer for how much coverage a topic deserves'.[98] Blogs and bloggers also featured in the BBC's radio output. The World Service radio programme *Go Digital* made a number of programmes in 2003 featuring blogs, including a show on the 'power of blogs' and one on bloggers from Iraq and Iran.[99]

The potential for bloggers to play an important collaborative role in the production of journalism was epitomised by Salam Pax, an Iraqi blogger writing from Baghdad in 2002, whose incorporation into both *The Guardian* and the BBC's media coverage was documented in the introduction. Using Salam Pax as a source of information did not fit with guidance the BBC had established for gathering material.[100] First, a BBC reporter had not witnessed the events which Salam was describing nor could a reporter be sent to verify the information Salam was posting on his blog given the impending military conflict in Iraq. Second, the BBC Producer Guidelines stated that journalists 'should be reluctant to rely on a single source'.[101] Furthermore, if the BBC does rely on a single source, it should preferably be 'a named on the record source', of 'proven credibility and reliability, as well as in a position to have sufficient knowledge of the events featured in the story'.

Salam Pax was a pseudonym and the BBC decided to cautiously report the information on Salam's blog as his own personal opinion rather than using the blog as the factual basis for a news story. After *The Guardian* had established Salam Pax's identity and reliability in May 2003, however, the BBC was far happier to incorporate him more extensively into their news coverage. An interview with Anita Rice for the BBC website in 2004 reveals how far Salam had climbed the BBC's hierarchy of sources on Iraq. His belief that the only way forward in Iraq was through free and fair elections was treated as newsworthy enough for an article on the website.[102] It was similar to the way in which 'elite' sources create news simply by giving their opinion on a relevant topic. The story of Salam Pax provided BBC journalists with an excellent example of how a blogger could be comprehensively utilised in the BBC's coverage.

BLOGGERS VERSUS JOURNALISTS

The incorporation of bloggers into BBC journalism was not always so straightforward. The traditional media, both explicitly and implicitly, often characterised bloggers as being in opposition to journalists. A number of bloggers did revel in this role, but the norms and practices of traditional journalism also had the potential to alienate bloggers. The reporting of the deployment of white phosphorus by the US Army in Iraq reveals how differing approaches could cause friction between the BBC and bloggers.

On 15 November 2005, the BBC's *Ten O'Clock News* led with a story about the use of white phosphorus in Iraq by then Defence Correspondent Paul Wood. The Pentagon had previously acknowledged that white phosphorus was being used legally in Iraq as a method of illuminating the landscape to assist operations, but defence officials had consistently denied that it was being fired as an incendiary weapon to 'flush out' enemy positions. A week prior to the BBC's report, a documentary had been shown on RAI, the Italian state broadcast channel. Titled 'Fallujah: A hidden massacre', it claimed that US forces had killed Iraqi citizens using white phosphorus. The BBC refused to run a story on the grounds that the evidence in the documentary was too flimsy.[103]

Paul Wood, however, described how the situation changed when the March–April 2005 issue of the US Army journal *Field Artillery* 'surfaced on the internet'.[104] In the article, US Army officers described using white phosphorus as a 'potent psychological weapon against the insurgents in trench lines and spider holes'.[105] This was clear evidence that white phosphorus was not merely being used to illuminate the landscape. Wood's description of the article appearing on the Internet failed to mention the contribution of Mark Kraft, who was writing a blog on LiveJournal. Kraft had found the Field Artillery article and submitted a piece to a website called Scoop on 11 November. He also passed the information to Gabriele Zamparini, author of The Cat's Dream blog.[106] Zamparini subsequently discovered a declassified US military document explicitly referring to white phosphorus as a chemical weapon which he published on his blog.[107]

In Paul Wood's package for the BBC *Ten O'Clock News*, Lt. Col. Barry Venable, a US military spokesman, admitted that contrary to previous denials, US forces had made use of white phosphorus as an incendiary weapon during the Battle of Fallujah in November 2004. But neither Kraft nor Zamparini's role in bringing the story to light were mentioned. Zamparini was frustrated that the traditional media had not credited his role in the story, a point which might have been made even more strongly by Kraft. This expectation was driven by the culture of acknowledging sources in the blogosphere often through the use of hyperlinks. Traditional media journalists often reuse material from other sources without crediting them and in the broadcast medium there is simply not enough space to mention every source. In this instance, Wood argues that the information was posted and reposted on the Web, making it difficult to trace the original source. He said he was more concerned to spend time authenticating the *Field Artillery* journal article.[108] In a separate online article, Paul Reynolds did note that bloggers had 'ferreted out' the *Field Artillery* article, but neither Kraft nor his blog were specifically mentioned.[109]

ADVOCATES FOR BLOGS AS SOURCES AT THE BBC

More frequent contact between bloggers and BBC journalists and the contribution of blogs to high profile stories such as the Iraq war helped raise awareness of blogs at various levels of the Corporation. Richard Sambrook, then Director of Global News, started an internal blog in June 2005. He was keen to explore blogging as an Internet phenomenon. In one of his first posts, he referenced Salam Pax's blog, noted that 'there are blogs aggregating information about hard to reach territories—like North Korea' and encouraged colleagues to inform him of 'any really valuable blogs'.[110]

The editors of the BBC website were also keen to explore the editorial value of blogs. Not long after he had blogged the US election for the BBC at the end of 2004, journalist Kevin Anderson[111] was asked by World Editor of News Interactive, Steve Herrmann, to write an internal report on blogs for Pete Clifton, the Editor of the BBC News website, and Nic Newman, Head of Product Development and Technology for News Interactive.

Kevin Anderson said his report, titled 'BBC blogs: News as conversation',[112] was an attempt to understand blogging as an 'editorial proposition'—how the BBC's involvement might be different from what it did already and the extent to which it should be dedicating resources to blogging.[113] Anderson concluded that the BBC should be 'embracing blogging', claiming it would 'sharpen' the BBC's journalism, 'introduce' journalists to new sources' and 'widen' the BBC's 'agenda'.[114] As well as writing their own blogs, the BBC should be comprehensively integrating the content of blogs into its journalism; he argued that bloggers should be interviewed to provide quotes and audio clips for stories. He also suggested the BBC use a 'blog-tracker' to monitor blogging on particular stories and to keep abreast of the blogosphere.[115]

Anderson's advocacy of using blogs to inform the BBC's news journalism was not confined to internal reports. He and other colleagues who felt there was value for journalists in blogs were keen to show how they could be used to provide perspectives on news events. On 7 June 2005, Anderson and Martin Asser tracked the Iraqi media and blogs for news and comment for the One Day in Iraq project.[116] Several extracts from blogs appeared on the website including one written by a 16-year-old girl in Mosul, a piece by 'A Family in Baghdad' and an extract from a US military blogger. Some of these bloggers were interviewed for Radio 5 Live.[117]

Anderson was also involved in the beginnings of a Radio 5 Live programme called *Pods and Blogs*. In June 2005, Anderson, Howard Benson, Rhod Sharp and Chris Vallance started the one-hour segment for BBC Radio 5 Live's *Up All Night* programme. It aimed to provide an alternative angle on the world by viewing it through the eyes of bloggers and podcasters. The programme was broadcast between 0h200 and 03h00, was available as a podcast and had an accompanying programme blog. In the second post for the blog, Anderson wrote a piece about the potential of blogs as sources of information:

> There are thousands if not millions of weblogs out there that are not much more than online journals full of the small details of everyday life. But as we're trying to show on the programme, there are also soldiers capturing both the tedium and terror of war. There are activists in Iran and China who find that weblogs are one of the few means of free expression that they have.[118]

Developing one of these themes, Anderson wrote an article for the BBC website in December 2005, chronicling the rise of military blogging by US servicemen.[119] He wanted to highlight military blogs as additional sources of information which were offering an alternative perspective on the war in Iraq. Anderson said he was not merely informing the audience: he was also trying to convince his colleagues of the editorial value of blogs.[120]

Similarly, after the white phosphorus story in November 2005, BBC News Online World Affairs Correspondent Paul Reynolds wrote an analysis piece which suggested that bloggers' 'influence must not be under-estimated these days'.[121] A few months later, he described the blogosphere as 'a source of criticism that must be listened to and as a source of information that can be used'.[122]

'FROM SEESAW TO WAGON WHEEL': USING BLOGS TO OFFER ALTERNATIVE VIEWS

Increasingly blogs were being used as a way of accessing alternative angles on the news and they were thus assisting BBC journalists in their efforts to fulfil the Corporation's commitment to impartiality. One of the recommendations of the Neil Report charged the BBC with 'reflecting all significant strands of opinion, by exploring the range and conflict of views'.[123] In 2007, an impartiality report for the BBC Trust, subtitled 'from seesaw to wagon wheel', argued that the Corporation's approach to impartiality was necessarily shifting from juxtaposing two opposing viewpoints to including a broader representation of views.[124] Although not specifically mentioned in the report, the incorporation of bloggers into the BBC's journalism can be seen as one aspect of the Corporation's multifaceted conception of impartiality. BBC News online began publishing articles which provided a round-up of views from the blogosphere on an ongoing story or news event, while BBC radio and TV also used bloggers to access alternative angles on the news.

Following the 'One Day in Iraq' project, BBC News online started collating extracts from Iraqi blogs. In December 2006, four contributions from bloggers writing from Baghdad were published at a time when Iraq was experiencing its worst levels of violence since 2004.[125] Similar reviews of the Iraqi blogosphere were published on 12 January 2007 after the execution of Saddam Hussein and in May of the same year.[126] Unlike the piece in January, the May article was not published in reaction to any significant news event and appears to have been commissioned on the basis that blogs offered an insight into Iraq, 'far away from that offered by the mainstream media'.[127] In January 2008, the BBC was continuing to cover the violence in Kenya after disputed election results. On 4th January an article was written which provided 'a snapshot of some of the bloggers [sic] contributions'.[128] It included extracts from blogs written by Kenyans both within the country and from the diasporic community. A year later, bloggers were incorporated into the BBC's online coverage of the conflict in Gaza.

BBC Monitoring also regularly produces reports summarising content on blogs from various parts of the world which can be used by BBC journalists. In 2008, Vivienne Sands, then Head of the Emerging Media Team at BBC Monitoring, said they were looking at blogs 'quite extensively'.[129] Monitors were 'dipping into blogs based around news events', producing weekly round-ups of blogs from individual countries and also following up particular queries from the BBC.[130] Teams of country and regional specialists used their own methods of searching for blogs but they often accessed Web portals where blogs posts were collated. BBC journalists can make requests to BBC Monitoring for blogs on a certain subject, and BBC Monitoring produces media features which appear directly on the BBC website.

Although their natural outlet was on the BBC website, blogs and bloggers have also featured in the BBC's radio and television output. In March 2008, the Editor of *The World Tonight* programme on Radio 4, Alistair Burnett, described how the editorial team was looking for a new angle on the conflict between Israelis and Palestinians in the Gaza Strip. Violence had escalated in the region with rocket attacks from Gaza at Israel and ground operations by Israel Defense Forces. Burnett noted,

> We often discuss . . . how we can shed new light on what can sound a very repetitive story given that politicians and officials on both sides are so entrenched in their positions.[131]

The team made a conscious decision to search for alternative views and found a blog called Life Must Go on in Sderot-Gaza.[132] They managed to contact the authors of the blog, who were campaigning for peace in the region through their joint authorship of the blog from either side of Gaza's border with Israel. The World Tonight team interviewed the bloggers about their perception of the mood in and around Gaza and the difficulties of finding peace.[133]

In 2010, the BBC joined forces with Global Voices as part of a special 'SuperPower' season on the impact of the Internet.[134] The Global Voices website collates the views of bloggers and citizen journalists from around the world.[135] They were incorporated into a number of features as part of the SuperPower series. The BBC updated a Blogworld blog for the duration which included bloggers from Iraq and Afghanistan.[136] Some of the bloggers were also featured on a TV segment on World TV.[137]

CIRCUMVENTING GOVERNMENT AND MILITARY CONTROL OF INFORMATION

Blogs were often used at the BBC as a means to complement traditional journalism by providing alternative angles on the news, but their importance to BBC journalists increased in circumstances where access to the BBC's usual sources of information proved inadequate or was hindered in some way. During periods of conflict, blogs could be used to penetrate military information management and helped capture the impact of warfare on civilians on the ground.

Senior Broadcast Journalist Chris Vallance said he used blogs to cover the progress of the war in Iraq for BBC radio because he felt a significant perspective on the conflict—namely, the views of Iraqi citizens—was not being heard by the outside world.[138] This was for two reasons. First, the US and British military information strategy revolved around tightly controlled embeds, and second, the war in Iraq proved to be a very dangerous conflict for journalists, many of whom could not leave the fortified Green Zone. Through blogs, Chris Vallance managed to obtain an insight into life on the ground in Iraq and his contact with bloggers made him aware of the Sunni Awakening Movement, a development which helped to quell violence in the country. He described the use of blogs to cover conflict in this manner as 'a real revolution'.[139]

Blogs also came to prominence when state media control was prohibiting an opposition movement from using traditional press and broadcast outlets to voice their discontent. The pro-democracy demonstrations in Burma in 2007 provide an example of how bloggers could attempt to circumvent government control of information. In August, the Burmese people had begun protesting against an increase in the price of fuel and foodstuffs in the country. When monks decided to back the protest withdrawing their religious services from military families, the military regime began a severe crackdown in an attempt to end the uprising. Foreign journalists were unable to enter Burma, and traditional media organisations such as the BBC and CNN were forced to report from neighbouring Thailand.[140] The dangers of reporting from the country were made plain when a Japanese photographer was shot dead in Rangoon. But blogs and other Internet communication tools, such as the social networking site Facebook, enabled supporters of the uprising to provide news and information from inside Burma and mobilise awareness outside the country. Comparing the protests with those of 1988, a BBC online news article claimed that 'thanks in part to bloggers, this time the outside world is acutely aware of what is happening on the streets of

Rangoon, Mandalay and Pakokku and is hungry for more information'.[141] The article highlighted the way London-based blogger Ko Htike had set up his blog as 'a virtual news agency' providing reports, pictures and video from a network of contacts inside Burma.

The BBC's experience of covering Burma using alternative sources was called on again during the Iran election crisis in June 2009. Following Mahmoud Ahmadinejad's reelection as president, thousands of Iranians protested on the streets of Tehran in support of his defeated rivals. Forming the Green Movement, they disputed the validity of the election results and demanded a re-run. There was a widespread media crackdown by Ahmadinejad's regime which included a number of measures against the BBC. The BBC's Iran Correspondent, Jon Leyne, was expelled,[142] BBC reporters in Iran were told they were not permitted to cover antigovernment demonstrations[143] and there were accusations that the Iranian government was electronically jamming the satellite broadcasting BBC Persian TV.[144] The Iranian regime also controlled state media broadcasts so the opposition movement turned to digital media, particularly YouTube and Twitter. The BBC and other media organisations came to rely on Twitter for links to bloggers, pictures on Flickr and video on YouTube to furnish the details of the story. Trushar Barot, who was working on the UGC hub during the postelection protests, believes the BBC's experience of covering Iran 'changed the mindset amongst the more traditional reporters within foreign newsgathering'.[145]

A BLOGGER BECOMES A NEWS STORY

As the number of blogs multiplied during the first decade of the 21st century it was increasingly likely that a blogger might become the news story. In the context of the war in Afghanistan, blogs were used by the BBC to provide background information on individuals who had lost their lives during the conflict. Territorial Army rifleman Andrew Fentiman was killed on patrol in Afghanistan on 15 November 2009. A number of media organisations quoted extracts from a blog post he had written on the Planet Lotus website. The post revealed that merely days before he was killed he had said he was 'still waiting on these new body armour and helmets that were promised to us'.[146] His words sparked further coverage of whether the government and the Ministry of Defence were adequately equipping troops fighting in Afghanistan.

The BBC also made use of blogs to cover the death of Dr Karen Woo, a medic who was killed in Afghanistan in August 2010. She was part of a group of 10 aid workers who died during an attack in Badakhshan province. Woo's death was confirmed on the Bridge Afghanistan blog[147] which had been set up by a group of people raising money for Afghanistan. Journalists working on the BBC website's UK desk also discovered Woo had written her own personal blog.[148] The BBC said the blog 'offered a human insight into the aid mission to the war-torn country' and devoted a separate online article to Woo's blog posts.[149] They described aspects of her daily work in Afghanistan, her interactions with Afghans and her motivations, doubts and fears.[150]

EYEWITNESS ACCOUNTS AND INSTITUTIONAL CHANGE: THE UGC HUB

While individual journalists and programmes were incorporating blogs into their journalism, blogs were also having a more fundamental impact on the organisation and structure of the BBC's newsroom as part of the emerging phenomenon of 'citizen journalism'.[151]

By the middle of the decade, the 'former audience'[152] was 'an active, important participant in the creation and dissemination of news information'.[153] The BBC's UGC hub was set up in 2005 as an experiment to see whether more audience contributions could be included in the BBC's journalism.[154] Vicky Taylor, the Editor of Interactivity, was the driving force behind the project. She wanted to test the value of the increasing number of text messages, emails and pictures which were being sent to the BBC. Reflecting on the establishment of the hub five years later, Assistant Editor of Social Media Development Matthew Eltringham said the project was 'met with some scepticism from senior quarters in BBC News and very nearly didn't happen'.[155]

Taylor and Eltringham describe the London bombings in July 2005 as a 'turning point'.[156] On 7 July, the four journalists working on the User Generated Content hub were inundated with media content from eyewitnesses on the ground.[157] Video clips and stills taken on mobile phone cameras from inside the underground trains, where three bombs had been detonated, ran on rolling BBC news coverage. The BBC *Ten O'Clock News* used two sequences of film shot on a mobile phone and the main image on the BBC News website was taken by a passer-by.[158] The iconic image of the wreckage of the number 30 bus on which the fourth suicide bomber had struck near Tavistock Square was sent to the BBC website within 45 minutes of the attack. The Director of Global News, Richard Sambrook, described the BBC's reporting of the attacks as 'a genuine collaboration'.[159] Although they were not directly sourced by the hub, blogs also featured in BBC content in the days that followed the bombing. BBC journalist Alan Connor chronicled the reaction to the London bombings on blogs,[160] while Rachel North, who survived one of the blasts, wrote a blog for the BBC website.[161]

Since 2005, the UGC hub has become an increasingly important player in identifying bloggers who might provide eyewitness accounts in major breaking news situations. During events such as the Mumbai bombings in 2008, the Iran election crisis in 2009, or the Arab Spring in 2011 the hub is tasked with finding eyewitnesses and verifying audience material published online or emailed directly to the BBC.[162] As part of the reorganisation of BBC News during 2007 and 2008, the UGC hub was moved from the seventh floor of Television Centre to a central role in the BBC's new multimedia newsroom. It was a signal of the growing importance of UGC contributions to the BBC's journalism. By 2010, the hub consisted of 23 journalists with up to 8 working on the hub on a daily basis.[163] Although UGC journalists have long searched for Web content, a social media role was formalised in April 2009, meaning at least one journalist was specifically searching for digital media content—including blogs—on any given day. Several months later, the BBC announced the appointment of its first Social Media Editor, Alex Gubbay,[164] whose role was to manage the hub and 'coordinate high-quality UGC newsgathering and effective comment and debate' across all BBC News platforms.[165] Commenting on the appointment, then Head of the BBC Newsroom Mary Hockaday said that 'new social media platforms allow audiences to get, share and comment on the news'—'the way audiences consume and interact with news is changing'.[166] Gubbay was given the task of building an 'open relationship' with the BBC's interactive viewers, listeners and readers not only as a means of sourcing news and comment but also to distribute the BBC's journalism to online audiences.

JOINING THE CONVERSATION: BBC PROGRAMME BLOGS

In addition to the UGC hub, the BBC also began its own blogging projects in order to harness bloggers as sources. Kevin Anderson's internal report into blogging in 2005 suggested that merely using blogs as traditional sources failed to tap into the latent potential of the blogosphere. Successful blogs were involved in a 'conversation' with other blogs made possible by 'a web of links'.[167] Rather than searching for blogs as and when a journalist required information, Anderson advocated placing the BBC at the heart of existing conversations within the blogosphere. If the BBC embraced blogging and 'linked to bloggers who have information of value to our audience we [the BBC] will bring new voices into our journalism'.

One strategy to achieve this aim—the development of the BBC's own blogs to add the voices of their journalists to the blogosphere—is documented in Chapter 5. Another avenue the BBC explored was the use of programme blogs as a tool to cultivate a more interactive relationship with radio and TV audiences. These blogs would provide a space where the BBC could discuss the content of programmes with the audience and offer them the opportunity to engage with the BBC's journalism. Anderson was convinced that bloggers would want to contribute to BBC blogs because so many of them already linked to BBC content: '[t]here is a conversation going on in blogs around our content. The only thing missing is us as active participants'.[168]

Some of the expertise and experience developed by Pods and Blogs in this area was transferred to Radio 4 at the end of 2007, when *iPM* started as an offshoot of the *PM* programme. *PM*, an hour-long radio programme at 17h00, was first broadcast in 1970 aiming to sum up the day's news and current affairs. *iPM* had a similar remit but with an emphasis on looking at events using the reporting resources available on the World Wide Web. This meant establishing a programme blog where listeners could submit their story ideas and a promise to 'source what we do through the best blogs, passionate 'ear catching' online debate as well as comments and recommendations of others'.[169] In the past, the *iPM* team have published blog posts featuring an early running order of each day's programme which listeners were invited to comment on or change altogether by suggesting different story ideas. In March 2010, the *iPM* blog merged with the *PM* blog,[170] but the programme still aimed to give the audience a greater stake in the news process by using audience suggestions as a starting point for the programme. In January 2011, *iPM* was continuing to collate a 'Your News' bulletin based on single sentences submitted by listeners offering their personal news of the week.[171]

A similar idea is being pursued by the *World Have Your Say* programme for the World Service.[172] The show began in October 2005 and aims to provide a space for a 'global conversation'.[173] The programme regularly asks for the opinions of bloggers and at one stage kept a list of the bloggers who had featured on the show.[174] The audience is invited to interact with the programme by supplying ideas on a programme blog, and presenter Ros Atkins also sends an email to 1,500 subscribers in 45 countries outlining story ideas which the team is discussing.[175] In Atkins's view the advantage of interacting with the audience in this way is that it provides an opportunity for listeners to come to the journalists with ideas and contributions. He says it makes producing the programme more straightforward:

> People are actually coming to you and saying: 'I'm interested in this, this is my phone number, this is my experience and I'd like to take part'. And this is revelatory really . . . it can help you, as programme makers, to reach people who you may never otherwise have reached.[176]

NEW SKILLS FOR 'NEW' MEDIA: BBC KNOWLEDGE SHARING AND TRAINING

Specific training initiatives did not drive the establishment of programme blogs or the incorporation of blogs into the BBC's journalism. There were, however, more informal ways that BBC journalists shared their experiences and sought to learn how to take advantage of blogs.[177] The College of Journalism and World Service Training set up several blogging masterclasses where BBC journalists discussed and debated blogging. Robin Hamman, Senior Broadcast Journalist and acting head of the BBC's blog trial, spoke at several of these masterclasses. He regularly delivered talks, seminars and workshops to BBC journalists which demonstrated how they could use blogging and other social media tools to augment their journalism. Other bloggers, journalists and media academics, such as Dan Gillmor and Jeff Jarvis, were also invited to the BBC to share their experience and knowledge of blogging.[178]

By 2009, the BBC was beginning to recognise that there was a skills shortage in Web-based information retrieval and the exploitation of Internet sources by their journalists. Claire Wardle, who had just completed a multifaceted study into the BBC's UGC hub, was asked to design a social media training course for the BBC's College of Journalism on behalf of the newsgathering department. The one day course aimed to teach journalists how to use the power of the Web to improve their journalism by finding case studies for stories, accessing alternative angles on the news and tapping into the potential of online communities.

The course introduced journalists to a number of tools, including RSS feeds,[179] Delicious, Flickr, Twitter and YouTube. But the course was structured around questions that journalists have always asked such as 'How to find stories? How to find sources? How to find images?'.[180] According to Wardle this was deliberately emphasised to convince potential sceptics that while 'the tools' may 'have changed', the journalistic 'questions still remain the same'.[181] The first course was held in November 2009, and a year later more than 1,500 BBC staff had completed the course.[182] Attendees came from all levels of the BBC from local radio journalists through to senior BBC managers. In December 2010, Wardle noted that changing journalists' working practices was not straightforward and that a new phase of training had begun which embedded trainers alongside journalists.[183]

CHANGING ATTITUDES TO BLOGS AS SOURCES AND THE EMERGENCE OF PRIMARY USES FOR BLOGS

The tendency of journalists to use 'official sources' of information, the context of the BBC's approach to journalism and early understandings of the nature of blogging suggested that blogs would not make suitable sources for BBC journalists. This chapter has documented a process by which these concerns and limitations were overcome by BBC journalists. First, bloggers were making their own case to be taken more seriously by the traditional media, whether that was Salam Pax providing insights into life in Iraq or the investigative work undertaken by Mark Kraft and Gabriele Zamparini in relation to the US Army's use of white phosphorus. Second, a number of BBC journalists were leading by example demonstrating that blogs could be used to inform the Corporation's journalism. Third, there was an acceptance of the potential of blogs at a variety of levels of the organisation evident in Nic Newman and Pete Clifton's commissioning of Anderson's report for the BBC into blogging and the interest shown in the blogging phenomenon by the Director of Global News, Richard Sambrook. Fourth, the BBC adapted its organisational structure to help journalists around the Corporation take advantage of blogs and other user-generated content. The UGC hub, which began as a small experiment in 2005, was placed at the heart of the newsroom by 2008, enabling UGC hub journalists to more effectively distribute

digital material that had been sent to the BBC and search for content created on blogs and websites. New editorial roles were also created including
a Social Media Editor post which became active in January 2010. Fifth, the
BBC started their own blogs as a way to engage in online conversations and
encourage bloggers to contribute to BBC journalism. Finally, the BBC has
encouraged knowledge sharing: initially through seminars and workshops,
and then, since 2009, through a specific social media training course which
helps journalists learn how to exploit online sources.

This chapter has shown that blogs have come to prominence in BBC content in several specific circumstances in the context of the BBC's coverage of
conflict, war and terrorism. On some occasions a blogger has become the
story and the BBC has used an individual's blog to provide additional material and background information. Blogs have been used to access eyewitness
accounts in the aftermath of terror attacks and they provide an opportunity to present alternative voices on conflict. Blogs have proved particularly
important in contexts where traditional methods of newsgathering have
been hindered such as state control of media outlets or where the danger of
reporting from war zones has prohibited access. BBC News online regularly
represents bloggers' voices on webpages dedicated to their views, but bloggers have also featured in the BBC's radio and TV coverage.

The BBC was keen to ensure that the incorporation of blogs could be
reconciled with the BBC's brand of journalism by reaffirming its commitment to professional standards. It is notable that new sources were utilised
with reference to traditional editorial policies and practices. Trushar Barot
highlights that during the Iran election crisis several Twitter accounts were
tested for accuracy by their adherence to wire copy over a time. Similarly,
although Claire Wardle's social media training introduces journalists to a
variety of new Internet tools, the course was couched in the structure of traditional journalistic aims of obtaining stories, interviewees and case studies.

At the same time, the BBC was reconceptualising elements of its approach
to journalism. Blogs were one feature of an emerging media landscape which
enables a wider range of views to be aired. This has undoubtedly influenced the BBC's understanding of impartiality as being broader than a 'traditional', 'rather safe middle of the road', 'model' that 'neutrally' balanced
two perspectives.[184] Building on the conclusions of a BBC Trust report of
2007,[185] Peter Horrocks, then Head of the Multimedia Newsroom, argued
that the BBC needed to 'embrace an idea of "radical impartiality" that is
of a much broader range of views than before'.[186] The bloggers' round ups
published on the BBC website during the Iraq war can be viewed as a practical outworking of this philosophy.

This chapter has described a process of institutional change and provided
an overview of the uses of blogs by BBC journalists in the first decade of
the 21st century. The following chapter explores the latter in more detail by
documenting BBC journalists' understanding of how and why they use blogs
as part of their journalism.

3 Reporting Conflict from News Needles in Digital Haystacks

As their understanding and experience of the blogosphere grew, BBC journalists realised that blogs and bloggers did not always clash with the Corporation's values. Even when bloggers did not share the BBC's commitment to impartiality, accuracy and fairness, it was clear that blogs could still be incorporated into the BBC's journalism. As importantly, blogs proved their usefulness in major news stories, and they became more regularly used by BBC journalists as sources of information. In the past, using blogs might have been deemed unusual, but by 2008 one BBC journalist claimed that across the Corporation, 'there's an understanding and an awareness that blogs are a place a journalist can turn to'.[1]

This chapter explores how and why BBC journalists use blogs as sources of information when they are covering conflict, war and terrorism. It considers how journalists read blogs and search for them. In light of the BBC's editorial guidelines, it also seeks to understand journalists' approach to verifying material found on blogs and builds on the previous chapter by chronicling their experiences of incorporating blogs into their journalism. Finally, the chapter considers how a number of BBC journalists have used blogs as part of an online beat which informs their journalism.

One of the aims of the chapter is to more fully establish which journalists use blogs at the BBC and why they use them. The chapter is based on interviews and focus groups with a variety of BBC journalists who fall loosely into the following groups: First, the BBC's defence, security and foreign correspondents who are all experienced journalists and have been reporting for the Corporation for a number of years. Interviews were also conducted with their producers and researchers. These journalists work in the World Affairs Unit at the BBC and are primarily responsible for providing radio and TV reports although they also contribute to online output. Second was a group of journalists working for the BBC's World Service radio news programmes. The third group included journalists writing the main news stories for the BBC website and colleagues who author additional online content. Fourth were journalists who work regularly with blogs out of personal interest or as part of their role on the BBC's User Generated Content (UGC) hub.

These groups were selected because they covered a broad range of journalists across the BBC's TV, radio and online output. They include journalists who perform different roles in the production of news content and reflect a variety of experience in terms of working for the BBC, using blogs and reporting war and terror. Through semistructured interviews and focus groups, several key themes were explored with journalists including their understanding of blogging, their methods for locating blogs, their use of blogs, the value they feel blogs bring to their journalism, and their approach to verifying information on blogs. Conducted between 2007 and 2011, these interviews and focus groups were supplemented by time spent observing journalists at work, material from internal and external BBC documents and other BBC events where blogging was discussed.

Before considering the role of blogs in the news process of BBC journalists, this chapter begins by offering some background on BBC journalists' attitudes to blogs and bloggers. Although the wide range of views expressed might not illuminate the nature of blogging, journalists' perceptions do help reveal why they may or may not use blogs as part of their journalism.

BBC JOURNALISTS ON THE NATURE OF BLOGS AND BLOGGING

In the introduction to his internal paper on blogging for the BBC in 2005, BBC journalist Kevin Anderson provided a 'broad definition' of a weblog by media consultant Amy Gahran. She described blogs as 'a kind of website'— 'an easy and versatile way to publish all kinds of content'.[2] She refused to generalise, emphasising that blogs varied in content, function, style, tone, quality and credibility. Using the definition as a starting point, Anderson attempted to address 'the level of confusion' which existed within the Corporation. BBC journalists are now usually much more aware of blogging, but there remains no consensus within the BBC of what a blog is or who bloggers are. This reflects the growing number of uses for blogs over the last decade, the evolving nature of the online medium and journalists' varying experiences of blogs both personally and professionally.

This book has already demonstrated that the definitional boundaries between blogs, forums, social networks and websites are becoming increasingly blurred as online genres merge. This was also evident from discussions with BBC journalists. The popular military website Army Rumour Service (ARRSE) and the Professional Pilots Rumour Network (PPRuNe) were both described as blogs by some BBC journalists, and there were disagreements over whether these sites should be defined as blogs, message boards or forums. BBC journalists also considered whether a blog could be written by both groups and individuals, while one journalist, interviewed in 2008, debated whether the Huffington Post should be described as a 'blog' or an 'online newspaper'.[3]

A number of journalists emphasised the difficulties of defining blogs and the people who write them. BBC journalist Jamillah Knowles has worked on the

BBC's UGC hub and presents Radio 5 Live's *Outriders* programme, formerly *Pods and Blogs*. She described a blog as 'a space for anyone online',[4] highlighting how the genre was adopted by people outside the technology community:[5]

> It used to be for techy people talking about technical stuff online. And then very much a few small voices who wanted to have a go at it following them and then everybody had a go at it. It is really hard to define now.[6]

Chris Vallance played a key role in starting Radio 5 Live's *Pods and Blogs* programme. He said 'it's impossible to generalise' about blogs and bloggers. A blog is 'just a tool', 'a piece of technology' which is widely available. 'It's like a microphone and we sort of talk about it as if it is a way of life. Or as though it defines an individual and it absolutely doesn't'.[7] A blogger is 'just a person like any other'; the 'only thing bloggers have in common is that they know how to use this piece of software and they like writing'. It's 'unwise' to talk about them 'en masse'.

Blogging is rarely described as a form of journalism by BBC journalists. One BBC producer described blogs as 'a stream of consciousness',[8] while a BBC correspondent said they were a 'kind of thinking out loud that wouldn't have necessarily got into a written piece of journalism or a broadcast piece'.[9] Others emphasised personal opinion and comment. One BBC News online journalist described blogs as 'very subjective':

> '[A blog is] one person's view and if that one person is just a member of society, that's all you can take a blog as—the view of one particular member of society.'[10]

A few journalists acknowledged that blogs are spaces where one might find 'journalism'. Chris Vallance noted that some bloggers are 'already media outlets in their own right', while others share the journalist's 'mission to tell the story'.[11] But BBC News online journalist Adam Blenford believed that stories on blogs do not replicate traditional journalism—'bloggers will take up an issue and discuss it in a very free form way'.[12]

FINDING AND FILTERING BLOGS

In order to use blogs as sources of information, journalists need to know how to find useful blogs among the millions that are available on the World Wide Web. Usually BBC journalists say they have identified a handful of blogs that they might read on a regular basis. Often journalists bookmark these blogs in their Web browsers. Security Correspondent Gordon Corera, for example, said he read a blog called Arms Control Wonk every other day.[13] It covers nuclear proliferation, a subject which Corera says he is 'particularly nerdy on'.[14] Similarly, World Service Defence and Security Correspondent

Rob Watson identified the Small Wars Journal, the Long War Journal and the Counterterrorism blog as places that he will regularly visit online.[15]

When journalists are looking for blogs they do not regularly visit, they use a variety of methods to locate them. Most journalists will look for blogs reactively: they will try to find a relevant blog in the wake of a news story for a specific purpose rather than monitoring them on a daily basis. In these instances, journalists often use Google blog search, which scans the World Wide Web specifically for blog posts. Others rely on word of mouth or the expertise of their BBC colleagues in finding blogs for them.[16] A number of comments revealed that in some cases, searching for blogs was often not systematic. One BBC producer described the process as trial and error,[17] while a News online journalist described his engagement with blogs as random: 'if I find something interesting somewhere else, then I Google it and what comes up are blogs'.[18]

Some journalists have attempted to formulate more reliable ways of filtering information on the Web. Gordon Corera has established a series of Google news alerts which inform him when new information is published on a variety of search terms including individuals and organisations. Often, he said, these news alerts will point him in the direction of a blog.[19] In March 2009, Adam Blenford was trying to develop a strategy to work out which sources to access online. He said the problem with using a Technorati or Google blog search in the context of news journalism is that 'you don't always know what you're looking at and then you might also retrieve something random about local cookery'.[20] He was aiming 'to settle on a variety of key sources' which in turn would lead him to other sources of information. He was also hoping to identify blogs which collated news and provided links to stories.

At the time, Blenford used Netvibes, an RSS feed reader, as a way of keeping track of information published on the Web. The RSS software standard strips salient information from Web pages turning them into a data feed. A Web user can subscribe to a feed which will deliver the information to their e-mail inbox or an RSS reader such as Google Reader or Netvibes. Subscribing to RSS feeds for blogs in particular is advantageous because as a BBC producer acknowledges some blogs are 'not very systematic'—'some days they'll publish something on the blog and other days they will have nothing or it won't be anything particularly relevant'.[21] Rather than having to constantly visit websites to see if they have been updated, an RSS feed enables a website to automatically alert a Web user when the site has been updated.

Setting up an RSS reader, however, still requires an initial investment of time and energy, while maintaining one—so that the Web user continues to collect relevant information—is an additional burden. Blogs can often be short-lived and subscribing to a blog might only be valuable for a number of months. Adam Blenford said the problem with his Netvibes page was that RSS feeds would regularly need updating as interesting blogs were closed and new ones were started.[22] Journalists are also looking for prompt access to news information unless they are undertaking background research for a longer-term project. The fact that there can be a delay, sometimes a significant one, between a post being published and it appearing in an RSS reader is a weakness for a working journalist.

Several journalists in this study said they used RSS readers, but they were in the minority. In 2007, one journalist believed that 90% of the people working in his office would not know how to use them,[23] while a BBC correspondent who had heard of RSS feeds said she did not use them because she is part of the 'non-techy generation'.[24] Claire Wardle, who set up the BBC's social media training course, said that by January 2010, only a few of the 150 journalists she had taught had known what RSS was or used it.[25] Just over a year later, she estimated that approximately 2% of the 2,000 journalists trained on the scheme had previously been aware of RSS or had used it in the past.[26] Although the social media training course continues to teach journalists how to use RSS feeds, by 2011 some journalists, such as Adam Blenford, have turned away from RSS readers as they have adopted Twitter to monitor news online.[27]

Journalists who regularly use blogs to inform their journalism tend to tap into the power of online communities to help them find valuable material. Charlie Beckett describes this process as 'networked sourcing': 'instead of occasional forays into the public sphere they [journalists] will be intimately connected to that network on a perpetual basis'.[28] In the past, Chris Vallance has worked with people who had already filtered blog posts for relevant information such as the volunteers behind the Global Voices website. He also picks up interesting new blog posts via a network of online contacts who message him by email, through Gmail instant messaging or through Twitter. Similarly, Jamillah Knowles is engaged with the online world both at and away from work. She cannot quantify how many blogs she uses because she reads so many and bookmarks many more which she does not have time to read. Her access points to blogs are varied including Facebook, Google Reader, Twitter and the 'links that bloggers are putting up'.[29]

'PART OF MY READING': TRENDS, CONTEXT AND BACKGROUND

All the journalists interviewed in this study claimed to read blogs at least occasionally in relation to their work. A number of journalists said blogs provide useful background information, context and an insight into ongoing trends. Defence Correspondent Caroline Wyatt would look for blogs if she wanted additional background information on US military operations.[30] Her colleague Rob Watson said his main use for blogs was providing him with additional context around a news story:

> I'm looking less for stories, but more for context and for mood . . . If there's a detailed entry on a blog relating to a specific conflict, whether it's Afghanistan, Iraq or Pakistan, then I will use that as context.[31]

A number of journalists said blogs were useful for informing and broadening their perspectives. Chris Vallance described blogs as a useful way of ensuring that journalists did not merely consider the 'received opinion' around a news topic.[32] Similarly, a journalist working for the World Service suggested that reading blogs is a valuable way of challenging her own 'quite narrow perceptions'.[33] Middle East Editor Jeremy Bowen reads blogs that 'analyse' the news or offer him 'fresh ways of looking at things'.[34] Gordon Corera said he primarily uses blogs to build up his 'knowledge base'—they inform his view and perspective rather than being directly used on air.[35]

BBC researcher Alison Baily said blogs could be used to identify ongoing trends that the news agencies would not report. In contrast to the testimony of other journalists around the Corporation who tend to need information at speed, she had been tasked with a longer-term investigation into online jihad in 2008:

> News agencies will pick out big news stories but without giving much context. For example, a new speech threatening the West from Osama Bin Laden will be reported on without much background by the news agencies. In the Jihadica blog, well-known academic experts on the global jihad will put the speech in context, give analysis and pick up on other things which the news agencies wouldn't because they don't have the specialist expertise.[36]

For some journalists, background information represents the extent of blogs' utility; one BBC producer described how once she has an idea and is developing a story, 'there wouldn't be any place for a blog really'.[37]

EXPERTS

BBC correspondents, in particular, said the blogs they read are written by people who are knowledgeable in their specialist areas of interest. These experts fulfil at least several of Herbert Gans's criteria for a journalistic source—reliability, authority and credibility.[38] With the advent of easy to use blogging software a number of experts in the field of war and terrorism have started blogs. According to Security Correspondent Gordon Corera, when journalists make use of these blogs it does not necessarily represent a 'radical change'.[39] He noted that 'on the whole it's people, who you'd access or be interested in anyway. It's just a new means of achieving that—getting access to their thoughts and information'.

The blogs that Jeremy Bowen reads on a regular basis are written by experts. Part of his beat as Middle East Editor is Iran and the politics surrounding its nuclear development programme. Bowen reads Gary's Choices, a blog by Gary Sick, to help him keep up to date.[40] Sick served on the National Security Council under three US presidents and became a research scholar at the School of International and Public Affairs at Columbia University. Sick's blog provides links to Web content discussing Iran interspersed with his own personal commentary. Bowen said it enables him to identify trends which will subsequently appear in the output of traditional media organisations. He also uses the blog as a reliable way of making sure his 'memory bank' on Iran is up to date for occasions when he might not have much time to spend researching a story:

> If I have to do suddenly something in a hurry, it's there already. I don't have to make ten phone calls beforehand. I'm up to date with what I need to be.[41]

Bowen uses Daniel Levy's Prospects for Peace in a similar fashion for coverage of Israeli politics.[42] Bowen said he is not 'a big consumer of blogs' and does not always have confidence in the 'provenance' of a lot of Web material. But Bowen reads the blogs of experts because he has confidence in their authorship; he knows Daniel Levy and respects his judgement.

Gordon Corera uses Arms Control Wonk, a blog about nuclear proliferation for a variety of reasons. It provides 'technical answers for everything' and a 'level of detail and analysis that you wouldn't get anywhere else'.[43] Indeed, he claimed the blog points out deficiencies in the content of articles in the *New York Times* and other newspapers. In the aftermath of a mysterious Israeli aerial raid allegedly on a Syrian nuclear plant in September 2007, Corera said he used Arms Control Wonk to find out 'what informed experts were thinking [had] happened'. The blog is primarily written by Dr Jeffrey Lewis, Director of the Nuclear Strategy and Non-proliferation Initiative at the New America Foundation but also includes contributions from, among others, Dr Geoffrey Forden at the Massachusetts Institute of Technology and Joshua Pollack, a consultant to the US government.[44] By 2011, Gordon Corera had noted an increase in the number of quality 'specialist blogs' available online.[45] He said blogs such as Arms Control Wonk and several counterterrorism blogs contained very useful factual information rather than lengthy arguments which descend into 'noise'.

'EARLY WARNING RADAR': TIP-OFFS ON BLOGS AND TWITTER FOR BREAKING NEWS

Journalists have always relied on tip offs from carefully cultivated contacts to provide them with newsworthy information. A source would usually contact a reporter or a news desk directly via letter or telephone or in person. The journalist would use the tip-off to investigate the story. Sometimes the journalist would discover that the information he received would be unfounded rumour; on other occasions the journalist was able to corroborate and publish the story. Message boards, forums and the emerging

blogosphere provided potentially useful new sources of tip-offs for journalists. In an online article for Salon in 2002, Scott Rosenberg highlighted
a trend in US newsrooms whereby 'time-strapped reporters and editors in
downsized, resource-hungry newsrooms are increasingly turning to blogs
for story tips and pointers'. He encouraged 'good journalists' to do likewise,
claiming they 'would be fools *not* to feed off blogs'.[46]

A number of BBC journalists do read blogs to identify possible stories
as Rosenberg suggested. In the past, Defence and Security Producer Stuart
Hughes found that blogs have acted as an 'early warning radar'.[47] He said
links on blogs pointed him in the direction of 'interesting stories' which he
would not have otherwise identified.[48] Senior Broadcast Journalist Chris
Vallance described blogs as a 'starting point for the kind of journalism you
would do ordinarily'.[49] In the context of war and terrorism he said that reading US military blogs had been 'very valuable' enabling him to 'get ideas for
stories' which he would not have been able to access unless he was embedded with the troops. Adam Blenford is not convinced a news story 'exists
on blogs in the same way as it does in newspapers or on news websites'.[50]
Hence, he believes journalists need to be alert to the possibility that news
stories might be hidden away in online conversations:

> You don't immediately identify it as news. But if you read around and
> follow blog posts, you suddenly realise that you've been tracking this
> issue for two or three days and it's a news story.

Increasingly, however, both Adam Blenford and Stuart Hughes are turning to Twitter as their source of tip-offs, and the 'microblogging' service
is replacing longer form blogs in this newsgathering role. Chris Vallance
said the adoption of Twitter by BBC journalists was 'quite widespread' by
2011.[51] Twitter enables journalists to monitor hundreds of sources of information and the 140-character limit on updates enforces brevity and encourages immediacy. Both Blenford and Hughes have observed that Twitter is
becoming quicker than the agency news wires at providing information.[52]
Twitter can also easily be updated using a mobile phone, facilitating the
publication of tweets from the scene of news events.

Compared to other digital tools, Hughes described Twitter as 'the closest
fit to a traditional wire service', allowing journalists to copy-taste rather
than having to sift through long blog posts.[53] He said it is a 'more effective
newsgathering tool' for finding potential news stories than are longer-form
blogs. In June 2010, Hughes said he had found only one or two stories
on blogs which have been 'worth following up' in the last year. Through
Twitter, he believed he had discovered around a dozen stories which he felt
warranted further investigation in just two weeks. Twitter users can also
organise tweets that are relevant to the same event or topic using a hashtag.
Adam Blenford said that following these Twitter hashtags enables him to
access 'new and useful information'.[54] Although tweets with hashtags were

'not solid enough to be immediately included in a story', Blenford said following Twitter updates in this manner 'can give a sense of where a story is going, or what to look out for'. In 2011, Hughes said he was first made aware of the Domodedovo airport bombing in Moscow via Twitter[55] and noted that HootSuite—a Twitter client—had 'replaced' the BBC's internal Electronic News Production System (ENPS)[56] as his 'first port of call for the latest details on unfolding events'.[57] Hughes believed Twitter was having 'a massive effect in the newsroom'.[58]

FACT CHECKING AND VERIFICATION: EDITORIAL GUIDANCE

Having identified relevant blogs and possibly even discovered a potential news story on a blog, journalists are required to check and verify the information provided on a blog before they can use it in a news story. Although the philosophical notion of objectivity is rarely cited as a journalistic aim in the postmodern era, attempting to accurately report the facts remains a key concern of BBC journalists. The principles of accuracy, fairness and truthfulness remain enshrined in the BBC's editorial guidelines, and according to one broadcast journalist those working for the Corporation remain 'obsessed' with getting stories 'right'.[59]

Before turning to BBC journalists' approaches to fact checking and verification it is worth noting the level of editorial guidance which they are offered on blogs. The BBC's 2005 Editorial Guidelines were revised in June 2010. The updated version included content from a separate set of guidelines for Online Services which had been developed in 2005 to address specific editorial issues around online content. The guidelines make it clear that journalists should apply rigorous editorial standards to all forms of information, but 'particular care' is urged when sourcing material from the Internet.[60] The BBC aims to be accurate by gathering material from first-hand sources, cross-checking and validating the authenticity of digital material.[61] The guidelines state that 'normally reliable sources of information' on the Web 'may not always be accurate'.[62] Journalists are urged to ensure that a website is not a hoax, check who is running a site and confirm that material is genuine.[63] The guidelines recommend tactics such as performing a WHOIS search to access the registration details of the website and cross-checking details on the About Us page of a website.[64]

User–generated content should be verified and eyewitness accounts submitted by email should be corroborated by talking to the eyewitness on the phone.[65] The guidelines note that pictures sent to the BBC should be verified by the UGC hub before they are distributed to other journalists. Journalists are advised to check that contributors 'are who they say they are' when using material submitted through social media via Facebook or Twitter accounts. Usually UGC material does not go directly on air, but the guidelines acknowledge that the speed of the news cycle is pressurising editorial procedures—during breaking-news situations there might be a 'very tight turnaround between receiving and viewing material and broadcasting it'.[66]

FACT CHECKING AND VERIFICATION: JOURNALISTS' EXPERIENCE

Knowing the provenance of a source—in this instance, accurately identifying a blogger—is a key part of the verification process. A number of BBC journalists were concerned about what they perceived to be the anonymous nature of the blogosphere even though academic research suggests that a significant number of bloggers do provide their real names or are identifiable. A Berkman Center study of over 4,000 Arabic blogs found that 64% of bloggers use their name when writing, despite limitations on freedom of speech in the Middle East.[67] Although for a BBC journalist, a key question which was not explored in the research would be whether these bloggers were telling the truth about their real name.

Some BBC journalists highlighted strategies relating to the technical features of a blog which they might specifically use to identify a blogger or verify the accuracy of information. Echoing the advice in the guidelines, Adam Blenford said he would look at a blog's About Me page, a section of a blog which usually has some biographical information about the blogger.[68] He would also read the comments and links on the blog in an attempt to make a judgement about the blog's reliability.

Blenford nevertheless believes he relies on his 'instincts to identify the wheat from the chaff', and BBC journalists tend to emphasise treating blogs with the same rigour as they would any other source. Defence Correspondent Caroline Wyatt, for example, described verifying information on blogs as akin to any other form of journalism. She said she uses her 'normal journalistic instinct' and tries to contact the person blogging to find out if the person is genuine.[69] Journalists working on the BBC News website also said contacting the blogger is important: Krassimira Twigg always tries to ring people in order to ascertain if somebody is at the scene of an event rather than rely solely on their blog,[70] while Adam Blenford advocated emailing the blogger and commencing a dialogue.[71] Broadcast Journalist Jamillah Knowles said the only real difficulties she has faced working with bloggers is when they do not put an email or a telephone contact on their blog.[72] She said that although blogs need to be 'checked and rechecked' they are becoming increasingly trustworthy sources. She nevertheless emphasised the importance of verifying eyewitness accounts using 'traditional journalism': 'Nothing serious gets quoted just straight off a blog. So you want to talk to them and you want to find out who is writing'.

Correspondents Gordon Corera and Caroline Wyatt also mentioned cross-checking other sources to ascertain whether information on a blog is accurate. Indeed, in order to use information on blogs, BBC journalists usually highlighted the importance of the ritual of 'triangulation': 'checking with other source material and assessing the credibility of sources'.[73] One journalist working for the BBC News website said that during this process a blog's use as a source might not subsequently appear in a published news story.[74] Factual claims made on a blog could be used in a news story if they were confirmed by 'corroborating evidence—like the wires or another sort of more official source of information'.[75] Subsequently, however, the fact that the story had started with a journalist looking at a blog 'would be expunged from the record because there wouldn't be any need to mention that in a news story'.[76]

Nevertheless, other journalists do use triangulation while recognising a blog as the source of a story in their output. Chris Vallance used this technique to broadcast a piece on Radio 4's *iPM* programme on the Awakening Councils in Iraq in 2007. Vallance made contact with 'Last of Iraqis', the pseudonym of an Iraqi blogger living in Baghdad.[77] Last of Iraqis had travelled to Adhamiya, a suburb of the Iraqi capital, where he had discovered that an Awakening Council had apparently brought 'a semblance of calm' to an area of the city which had previously been exceptionally dangerous.[78] Chris Vallance asked Last of Iraqis to record some audio describing what he had seen. Vallance confirmed Last of Iraqis' testimony by speaking to both Amit Paley, the *Washington Post*'s reporter in Baghdad, and Admiral Gregory J. Smith, the US military's Chief Military Spokesperson. Indeed, the audio was edited so that the assertions of Last of Iraqis about the presence of the Awakening Movement were put to Paley by *iPM* presenter Eddie Mair.[79] The *Washington Post* reporter confirmed the main factual claims of Last of Iraqis' story, and in a subsequent interview Admiral Smith told Eddie Mair that the US military were paying Iraqis, including some insurgents who had previously fought against them, to join Awakening Councils as part of their counterinsurgency operations.

Vallance said he 'could not vouch for everything' Last of Iraqis had said without going to Baghdad himself, which was 'impossible' at the time.[80] He differentiated between using blogs to access somebody's personal opinion to discuss a news issue and using a blog as the basis for the factual elements of news stories. For significant matters of fact, a journalist 'must check claims made on blogs as thoroughly' as anything else. In the case of the Awakening Movement story, Vallance had gathered sufficient evidence to trust the blogger. He had heard from other people that Last of Iraqis 'is who he says he is', and the main factual basis of the news story—that Awakening Councils were springing up in Baghdad suburbs—was confirmed by other sources.

INCORPORATING BLOGS INTO THE BBC'S JOURNALISM

Journalists who have found blogs and verified the information on them can subsequently incorporate blogs into their journalism. But why use a blog when so many other sources are available in an era of information overload? The previous chapter identified several circumstances when blogs came to prominence in BBC coverage. Blogs provided access to people and places that were otherwise difficult to reach. They were also particularly evident during coverage of a major breaking news crisis and as a way of providing comment and reaction on a news story. This section of the chapter explores journalists' experiences of reporting using blogs in these circumstances in more depth and offers an insight into why they decide to include blogs in the BBC's journalism.

Virtual Geographic Proximity: Getting 'Closer' to News Stories

Several journalists mentioned how useful blogs were in accessing stories during the Iraq war. During the Day in Iraq project in 2005, Kevin Anderson said that the BBC managed to contact an army intelligence officer serving in the 'Sunni Triangle' via his blog.[81] Similarly, Chris Vallance said blogs were very useful in obtaining first-person testimony from outside the Green Zone in Baghdad:

> How do you talk to the dentist in Baghdad who has just witnessed a bombing? It's quite hard. But you can do it because he's blogging. He's the local guy and he's able to record something and email it to us. That's the kind of access, that as a producer in London, it would be very very hard for me to have any other way.[82]

Vallance was clear about some of the limitations that information on blogs provided. He emphasised the importance of placing a blog in its context and of informing the audience that the blogger is not necessarily representative of the wider population. But bloggers provide a journalist with an alternative perspective:

> It's not that everything they say is completely unfiltered or the unvarnished truth or is somehow more true than [other] stuff. It's just different . . . a whole new channel of information, personal views and experience.

In addition to the viewpoints of Iraqi bloggers, Vallance also found the military blogs written by personnel serving in the US Armed Forces illuminating. He was struck by the potential for avoiding traditional gatekeepers of news—in this case military press officers—and speaking to serving soldiers directly by contacting them through their blogs. Vallance said blogs have provided a way to hear US military viewpoints and have helped him understand the complexities of their world.

The potential to get 'closer' to otherwise inaccessible 'situations or stories' through blogs also appeals to other BBC journalists:

> There's been some very interesting Iraqi bloggers who have been talking about their day to day experiences and there's been a few other blogs that I've been reading on the situation in China . . . So [I'm] getting close in to new sources of ordinary people who are already recording their experiences.[83]

This trend is perhaps even more pronounced in the context of the use of YouTube videos by BBC journalists covering conflict. BBC UGC hub journalist Alex Murray played an important role in the BBC's coverage of the conflict in Libya during 2011. He was one of the journalists responsible for contacting Libyans on the ground, working out whether videos posted online were genuine and documenting the conflict on the BBC website. Murray was acting as a 'glocalised war reporter': at once benefiting from global access to sources online which afforded him multiple windows on the conflict in Libya, but at the same time facing the challenges of being tethered 'locally' to his desk in London.[84]

In a blog post reflecting on his journalism, Murray acknowledged that he has never got his 'boots dirty' and has 'absolutely no concept of what it's like to be in a war zone', but he felt that in a 'strange way', he was 'closer to seeing what is happening than some correspondents [in the field]'.[85] The YouTube videos uploaded from inside Libya gave him an immersive virtual experience of what was happening. He was watching 'videos of people bleeding to death' on his screen 'from about the same distance as many of them have been filmed'. The BBC's 'forensic' approach to verifying these videos by checking weather patterns, identifying small details on objects and clothing and cross-referencing location using Google's mapping tools meant Murray would often watch each video several times.[86]

Murray said he lost count of the number of casualties he had witnessed on the Internet and that many of the 'injuries were hard to forget'. He experienced the sound of warfare through his headphones at his desk—mortar fire, gunfire and the crack of artillery; occasionally he jumped up from his desk in surprise. He was also able to locate some of the intimate details of the battlefield almost as if he were present:

> I can tell you pretty definitively which corner of Tripoli Street in Misrata was the place in which a tiny group of civilian resistants turned the tide against the full force of Qadhafi's military.[87]

And yet at the same time, he acknowledged that his experience was not the same as that of a war reporter on the scene: '[u]ntil I see that street with my own eyes, I will always feel that there is something missing in my experience and understanding of the events'. First-person accounts mediated through digital media genres nevertheless appear to offer a powerful sense of proximity which journalists and audiences alike find intriguing.[88]

Circumventing Censorship

Accessing personal perspectives on blogs and other digital media platforms becomes even more important to the BBC when the organisation is reporting a news story in the context of a country with state-controlled media or where press freedom is underdeveloped.[89] BBC journalists particularly mentioned the antigovernment protests in Burma in 2007, stories covering

China and the Iran election in June 2009. BBC journalists do not usually rely on blogs to form the factual basis of a news story, but in these circumstances the BBC's commitment to impartiality and balance is fulfilled by reporting from blogs and unofficial media. Often there has been governmental interference in traditional methods of newsgathering leading the BBC to explore alternative options.

Trushar Barot, who was working on the UGC hub during the Iran election crisis, said the BBC used blogs and social networks to identify 'chatter' on the Web, to pick up rumours, to access potential eyewitness accounts and to source details of future demonstrations. These were circulated around the BBC via internal emails so that they could be followed up and verified or to ensure that BBC journalists were aware of potential developments.[90] Barot noted that 'after a week or so, there were certain bloggers and Twitter accounts that we felt had credibility because everything they were saying turned out to be true by wire copy that would come out later on'.[91] After this vetting process, several key Twitter accounts were identified as being reliable sources of information. Unlike longer form blogs, it is apparent that BBC journalists are more closely following the Twitter feeds of 'official' primary sources of information which provide journalists with news updates. For example, one of the Iranian opposition leaders, Mir Hossein Mousavi, regularly updated his own official Facebook and Twitter accounts.

BBC News online journalist Joe Boyle described stories like Iran as 'probably the closest you get to a breaking news situation where blogs are an official kind of source'.[92] Director of Global News Richard Sambrook believed that the experience of Iran demonstrated why news organisations need to harness new technologies, but he couched the process of verifying blogs and Twitter feeds in terms of basic journalistic skills and editorial judgement.[93]

Breaking News and Eyewitness Accounts

The use of Twitter feeds and other online sources to cover the Iran election crisis was prefigured as early as 2001. During the attacks on the World Trade Center on 11 September, smaller websites and blogs became a vital tool for disseminating information as phone networks in New York collapsed.[94] The event highlighted the potential for sourcing stories when alternative communication channels were not available in a crisis situation. Former BBC journalist Kevin Anderson recalled a similar situation when he was covering the Mumbai train bombings in July 2006. Anderson said the BBC had difficulty getting in touch with its own journalists on the ground because landline and mobile phone networks were jammed or overwhelmed. Unable to use more traditional means, Anderson used his knowledge of blogs to access a source. He managed to find a blogger from the Global Voices website who could speak to the BBC via Skype about the relief efforts in Mumbai.[95] Two years later BBC journalists also used blogs and Twitter feeds to help them report the terror attacks in the same city in 2008.

Blogs and Twitter feeds have therefore proved useful when journalists are 'scrambling to reach voices who will tell us anything' and put them on air as quickly as possible.[96] A journalist working on the BBC News website said that in a situation where there is no information on an event, then a 'blog comment' or an 'eyewitness' or 'a subjective perspective on it' is 'more useful just at that point'.[97] Increasingly, Twitter is replacing blogs in this role because of its 'immediacy' and 'speed'.[98] In a 'pressured newsroom environment' there is 'simply not time to scroll through pages and pages of blogs',[99] although Twitter updates will often help journalists find interesting blog posts and video content related to an event.

A blog or Twitter feed can be a way of contacting an eyewitness to a news event on the ground and in the rush to broadcast comprehensive fact checking cannot always be practised. Normally, a BBC journalist requires two sources before any major piece of information is reported, but one World Service journalist said that BBC journalists do sometimes use agency reports as a sole source with attribution. Comparing this practice with blogs, she said, '[W]e're never going to say: "we're reading on blogs about such and such"' but then noted,

> We often put people on air who we just can't verify who they are: anyone who can tell us anything about what they are seeing—a person in the street, a hotel receptionist who was near the blast, anyone. And we do that quite often.[100]

Attributing the information to the source and explaining to the audience that the BBC cannot be certain of the veracity of the account is often used in these circumstances to distance the Corporation from responsibility for the accuracy of the information. But the journalist's testimony demonstrates how regard for the BBC's editorial guidelines cannot always be adhered to as rigorously in breaking-news situations. Another BBC journalist believed that during the BBC's coverage of the London bombings, 'a lot of the rules went out of the window straight away because there was just so much material coming in'.[101]

'New Voices': Comment, Reaction and Opinion

The previous chapter also identified that blogs are often used as a supplements to traditional reporting providing 'colour', reaction, comment and opinion. The BBC has long used a combination of opinion and comment to construct news programmes: Radio 5 Live hosts phone-ins where members of the public are invited to offer their viewpoints on news topics; the BBC website hosted Have Your Say pages where Web users were given the opportunity to discuss a current debate; and the BBC News Channel often has segments where representatives from different sides of an argument offer their views. Bloggers' perspectives on a news story are most usually hosted on an individual webpage on the BBC news website. Olivia Cornes, one of the

BBC website's Middle East specialists, has collated several of the bloggers' round ups identified in the previous chapter on Iran, Iraq and Gaza. She suggested that accessing and representing these voices does help to 'democ-ratise' news,[102] and the BBC's commitment to impartiality is often achieved by representing and contextualising competing opinions.

Although some BBC journalists feel rather overwhelmed by the sheer volume of opinion and comment available on the Web, many welcome blogs because they offer access to 'new voices' on the news which they can incor-porate into their journalism. One World Service journalist talked of the insti-tutional pressure to find 'new locations, new insights, new ways of looking at the world—new, new, new, new'.[103] She felt she was not yet fully tapping into 'the wider blogging world' but saw great potential in 'an almost endless source of new voices' in the blogosphere.

There is, however, a tension at the heart of finding people to comment on news programmes between 'new voices' and contributors with a 'track record':

> As a journalist you are constantly trying to balance getting that new, exciting, eyewitness voice as opposed to getting someone who you know to be accurate, reliable and impartial.

Who is deemed suitable to provide comment and opinion on a news story seems to vary considerably across the BBC. It is dependent on the nature of the news story, the perceived audience, the culture of the news programme and whether the comment is used within news bulletins or news features. Joe Boyle, who works for BBC News online's world desk, highlighted that while he could use opinion and comment from blogs for news features, there is a different 'level' of comment for daily news:

> In a news story . . . you would have to be straight down the line. You could look at institutional level comments. You are looking at govern-ment type agencies or NGOs [nongovernmental organizations] or chari-ties. You are looking for that kind of level of comment.[104]

For defence and security news on the website and for radio and television news, expert comment and opinion is regarded as the norm. BBC produc-ers working in the World Affairs Unit emphasised that asking a US military blogger to provide comment on a news story is 'great' for the World Service's *World Have Your Say* programme but would not be their first instinct for 'straight' defence and security stories:

> If [Defence Correspondent] Caroline Wyatt's been reporting something you couldn't really have a blogger on to back up a point.[105]

Indeed, BBC correspondents tend to use blogs as a way of gauging reaction to major defence or security news stories rather than incorporating them into their reports. Caroline Wyatt said she searched the Web for reaction to the appointment of the new Chief of the General Staff and the First Sea Lord of the Air Force in October 2008.[106] Frank Gardner has looked at Internet forums to monitor reaction to events such as the US election and developments in Afghanistan.[107] He said Web sources add 'colour' and 'enrich' the BBC's journalism, although both Gardner and Wyatt stated they found forums more useful for this purpose than blogs.[108]

DEVELOPING TRUST THROUGH EMBEDDING IN ONLINE COMMUNITIES

Having considered BBC journalists' general approach to blogs and chronicled their experiences of using blogs, the final section of this chapter elaborates on an idea which has been touched on throughout. It demonstrates how BBC journalists are increasingly adopting a more collaborative and participative approach to incorporate blogs into their journalism.

Media academics, such as Jeff Jarvis and Charlie Beckett, argue that an emerging news model can be described as 'networked journalism'.[109] For Jarvis, the term

> takes into account the collaborative nature of journalism now: professionals and amateurs working together to get the real story, linking to each other across brands and old boundaries to share facts, questions, answers, ideas, perspectives.[110]

As part of this process journalists have built relationships with ready-made online communities of interested 'amateurs' in the blogosphere.[111]

In the past, journalists' approach to bloggers was not always beneficial to building useful collaborative partnerships. Some journalists and editors were not particularly effective at openly communicating with their audience by inviting them to contribute to the process of journalism. BBC journalist Jamillah Knowles suggested there used to be an elitism in the journalistic profession towards bloggers, whereby some journalists would 'steal their stuff' but would then claim they were superior to bloggers because they were 'real journalists'.[112] As blogging and other forms of digital publication online have become increasingly commonplace, however, journalists' attitudes have shifted significantly. Increasingly BBC journalists are able to harness the journalistic potential of blogs and other material on the Web as a consequence of their own engagement in online communities.

Chris Vallance and Jamillah Knowles are representative of a number of pioneering BBC journalists who have built relationships with bloggers on a variety of levels for a number of years. They write their own personal blogs, have Twitter accounts, use RSS feeds and interact with other Web users on a regular basis via email and instant messaging. By participating in a genuine and transparent fashion they hope to both contribute and benefit from the distribution of knowledge and information. Their activity is not always directly connected to their journalism and is for social purposes or personal interest. Bloggers can be friends, regular work contacts or occasional acquaintances, and the nature of their relationships with bloggers is fluid rather than discrete. Although no different to friendships and contacts formed with other groups of people, the networked nature of the Web allows journalists to maintain a greater number of loose relationships or 'weak ties' with individuals.[113]

By 2011, it was no longer unusual for BBC journalists to actively participate online in an open manner through forums, Facebook accounts and, particularly, Twitter, which has been adopted by a wide variety of journalists at the organisation. Digital networks provide BBC journalists with an awareness of the issues affecting a wide variety of people both on- and offline. Cultivating trust and working relationships with bloggers by developing an 'online beat'[114] complements existing contacts enabling journalists to tap into the knowledge and expertise of online communities. Journalists' participation as trusted members of these communities encourages bloggers and Twitter users to contribute to their journalistic activities, whether tipping them off about a story, putting them in contact with a source or providing them with an interview.

TRANSPARENT JOURNALISM: ENGAGING WITH BLOGGERS AND ONLINE COMMUNITIES

Chris Vallance argues that journalists 'need to work with bloggers in the same way that we work with [other] sources',[115] and BBC journalists tend to discuss their approach to online communities in terms of traditional journalism. Nevertheless, experience of online culture has illuminated potential pitfalls. Vallance said it is important for media organisations to avoid a 'silo mentality'. In his view, 'the first step in engagement with social media or User Generated Content is being open to ideas, something as simple as saying: "Hey look, I'm the editor of this programme. If you've got a great story, tell me"'.

Approaching people online and learning online social conventions are also skills which need to be acquired in the same way that journalists learn how to approach people in public or on the phone. Matthew Eltringham, Assistant Editor of Social Media Development, gave an example at an internal event on social media of a BBC journalist who attempted to engage with a local New Orleans message board community just prior to Hurricane Gustav's devastation of the Louisiana coastline in 2008.[116] As an outsider to the message board community, the journalist was unlikely to receive a warm response but invited a series of hostile comments by posting a message which suggested the journalist was only interested in speaking to certain types of people to fit the news agenda of the programme.

Eltringham said the incident demonstrated that journalists had to learn how to 'behave', 'operate' and 'engage with the audience and social websites'. He noted that rather than 'completely twisting the agenda', journalists need to engage in conversation, treat people with respect and be aware of the environment in which they operate.

Jamillah Knowles suggested that journalists should be aware of their potential impact in order to work amicably with bloggers. Although blogs are usually published for a global audience, she noted that some bloggers, who write for a small readership of friends and family, might still be surprised by national or international media interest. Knowles said a lot of people ask her, 'How did you find my blog?'.[117] She claimed that approaching people online can seem rather sudden when compared to meeting them in person because a journalist carries equipment which makes him or her look like a journalist.[118] When people can see a journalist coming, they can decide whether to talk to the journalist or not, whereas online, a journalist 'arrives' on a website without prior warning. She believes 'there are ways of approaching people even on message boards':[119]

> The anonymous nature of many message boards can mean that people react quickly and without thinking. A journalist's approach online should be just as respectful and open as talking to someone face to face. You need to be clear, polite and open about your intentions.[120]

In the past, the majority of the journalist's interactions with sources were mostly concealed; now, when there is no way of emailing, directly messaging or phoning a blogger, it is not unusual for journalists to make an appeal for information under public scrutiny. Knowles noted, for example, that 'a lot of people have Twitter plugged into their blog and that might be their main form of communication'.[121] She regularly contacts bloggers through Twitter and is aware of the risk of being turned down when she wants information or, worse, being criticised in public.

In this instance and in similar circumstances, journalists and their news organisation are more exposed as what is published online can be viewed and commented upon by Web users around the world. Matthew Eltringham warned BBC journalists of the potential backlash from an online faux pas:

> Everything you put online has an afterlife and will start circulating and it will have an impact not just on you and your programme but on the whole of the BBC. So you need to think really carefully about how you go about engaging in social media.[122]

ANCHORING A PARTICIPATIVE AND COLLABORATIVE APPROACH TO TRADITIONAL JOURNALISTIC PRACTICES

Previously dismissed as irrelevant to the practice of journalism, blogs, as this chapter has demonstrated, perform a number of roles as a source of information at the BBC. It has identified that different journalists use blogs for varying purposes depending on their journalistic experience and role within the Corporation. For the BBC's correspondents, blogs tend to form part of their background reading. They particularly read blogs by 'experts' and occasionally dip into blogs to search for mood, colour or reaction on a story, while their producers and researchers use blogs to research stories and search for leads.

In the past, longer form blogs have also been used as an 'early warning radar' system but this role in the newsgathering process has been replaced by Twitter. The microblogging service enables journalists, such as World Affairs Producer Stuart Hughes and BBC News online journalist Adam Blenford, to monitor multiple sources of information quickly and efficiently. Twitter thus acts as a real-time global news wire, an 'awareness system' which allows journalists to monitor 'ambient journalism'.[123] It is becoming an indispensable tool for journalists working in breaking news.[124]

Journalists working from London, who are not usually sent abroad to cover foreign news stories, particularly benefit from the way that blogs and other digital media sources allow them to have some access to voices and stories. It offers them 'virtual geographic proximity' to a range of sources providing an insight into potential news issues. They feel they can get 'closer' to a story, and the blogging network provides a way of searching for interviewees on a variety of topics. Blogs also enable BBC journalists to fulfil an institutional expectation of introducing new voices into their journalism—a more multiperspectival approach which is held in tension with the need for sources to adhere to Herbert Gans's criteria of reliability, authority and efficiency.

The BBC's UGC hub journalists play a specific role in accessing sources and case studies through blogs and social networks for other BBC news programmes while the website's regional specialists, such as Olivia Cornes, collate bloggers' views to appear on the BBC website. Usually blogs provide comment, reaction or opinion on a news event offering an alternative perspective to traditional accounts of war and terrorism. Bloggers tend not to be used by journalists to form the factual basis of news stories in daily news. This chapter, however, has demonstrated how blogs and Twitter can be used in this manner whether in the context of Chris Vallance's reporting on Iraq or Trushar Barot's description of a number of Twitter feeds becoming credible sources on the Iran election crisis.

Following the lead of journalists like Chris Vallance, Jamillah Knowles, Trushar Barot, Stuart Hughes and others, BBC journalists are increasingly incorporating blogs and other digital material into their journalism as a consequence of a participative and collaborative approach to online communities. By monitoring RSS feeds, writing their own blogs, updating Twitter accounts and being aware of a variety of social networks they are effectively embedded in online communities. They hope to both contribute to and benefit from this participation through the distribution of knowledge and information. Their status as participants and their subsequent understanding of online culture enables them to harness the journalistic potential of the blogosphere. Their personal interest in social interaction with bloggers is not always directly connected to their journalism, but this helps facilitate the professional development of an 'online beat' which benefits their journalistic output. The networked nature of the Web also provides them with a method of maintaining effective contact with a significant number of 'weak ties'[125] increasing the scope of their 'news net'[126] and the range of sources they incorporate in their journalism. Vallance's reporting of the Awakening Movement in Iraq in 2007 is an example of war reporting which resonates with a 'networked journalism' model.[127] Previously exceptional, incorporating 'amateur' news material available on blogs and other platforms in the context of stories concerning war and terrorism at the BBC has become more commonplace.

As a consequence of online engagement, journalism has also become a more transparent process. Appeals for news information and requests for sources are now sometimes conducted under public scrutiny online. Journalists also need to be aware of the potential consequences of 'virtual doorstepping' and consider how to approach people in the online environment.[128] BBC journalists nevertheless reiterate their adherence to the standards and practices of traditional journalism in their approach to fact checking and verification of blogs as sources.

Apart from mentioning a few technical aspects of blogs, journalists tended to emphasise applying the same editorial standards and processes to blogs as they would to any other source. In this respect, the chapter echoes the findings of a Cardiff University study of the BBC's UGC hub in which the authors concluded that 'the vast majority of the journalists . . . articulated their approach to working with "UGC" using the lens of traditional journalistic techniques and values'.[129] Journalists said they use their professional instincts, emphasise contacting bloggers through email or on the phone and highlight a process of cross-checking with other sources through the ritual of triangulation. If the face of journalism's future points towards a more collaborative and networked approach, then the shift is being articulated as anchored to the existing practices and standards of journalism's past.

BBC journalists are still learning strategies for finding blogs and filtering the vast quantities of information on the Web. Although few journalists were using RSS feeds, Twitter has been widely adopted to assist in this process. The pace at which journalists must learn new Web tools is a problem that the BBC's social media course is attempting to address. It is, however, merely one of a number of limitations preventing BBC journalists from using blogs as sources of information when they report war and terrorism. These are explored in the following chapter.

4   Information Overload, the 24/7 News Cycle and the Turn to Twitter

The previous two chapters have examined how and why BBC journalists use blogs as sources of information particularly exploring the way they have been incorporated into the BBC's journalism to provide access to news stories, report major terror attacks and offer alternative perspectives on the news. Blogs are, however, merely part of a broad range of material available to journalists: this chapter considers their limitations as sources of information.

For some journalists, searching for stories on blogs is viewed as anathema to their independent approach to journalism which involves going to the site of a story and speaking to people face-to-face. Others remain concerned about the difficulties of navigating a potentially anonymous sea of material in search of a trustworthy piece of news information. The focus of this chapter, however, is on the institutional culture of the BBC, the limitations imposed by the nature of the newsgathering process in the 21st century and the practical weaknesses of blogs for a working journalist.

The chapter highlights the challenges facing journalists who are charged with reporting the news in today's pressurised, real-time and multimedia news environment. In a competitive media landscape, the shift towards rolling news on TV and online has led to a breaking-news culture whereby a number of journalists are expected to provide the news almost immediately.[1] The difficulties appear to be particularly acute for online journalists reporting daily news. The chapter also considers the limitations imposed by the proliferation of outlets for which a BBC correspondent is expected to produce content.

In these circumstances, journalists require information which is produced on a regular basis, at speed and which can be trusted to be accurate. Finding the time to access blogs and verify information on them does not always meet journalists' requirements when they are trying to quickly understand and report the factual basis of a news story. Institutional fear of making a mistake also means that potential stories appearing on blogs might be deemed too much of a risk. In this respect, reporting defence and security is regarded as more sensitive than is covering other news topics.[2]

Journalists covering war and terror face a variety of editorial challenges.[3] Immediate reporting of military operations or hostage situations might provide information which could be used by other actors to harm the individuals involved.[4] Journalists are under pressure from powerful governmental or military sources to report conflict in a manner which is in the 'national interest',[5] but they also receive criticism from interest groups and activists.[6] Journalists are required to make difficult judgements as they attempt to communicate the reality of war while considering the potential impact of coverage on victims and the audience.[7] Reporting war and terror thus provides a lens through which the challenges facing journalists are brought most sharply into focus.[8]

Throughout this chapter, blogs are compared to other sources of information available to a BBC journalist including official sources, news agencies and other media organisations. It is based on similar methods used in the previous chapter—primarily interviews with BBC journalists supplemented by focus groups, internal documents and observations at the Corporation.

REPORTING WAR AND TERRORISM: THE BBC'S WORLD AFFAIRS CORRESPONDENTS

BBC correspondents working in defence and security are experienced journalists. Several began their careers in an era when all journalists had was a car and a landline telephone. They had to 'go and find out what was going on'.[9] World Service Defence and Security Correspondent Rob Watson joined the BBC in 1984. He recalled a time when he felt he was 'a real pioneer working in international news . . . you were really mining at a coal face where there weren't very many others going before you'.[10] This spirit of independent journalism remains strong.[11] Despite vast quantities of information available from the comfort of his base in London, Security Correspondent Frank Gardner maintains that 'the journalism is not done here in this building. The journalism is done going out and meeting people'.[12] Middle East Editor Jeremy Bowen has been travelling to the scene of news stories for the BBC for more than two decades. He believes 'the best idea you get of a situation is to go there yourself. It's a real basic rule of journalism—narrow the distance between yourself and the story'.[13]

Blogs might provide a journalist with an insight into a conflict situation, but BBC correspondents would much rather investigate a story first-hand. In the words of Rob Watson, there is 'no substitute for what you see with your own eyes'[14] while Jeremy Bowen said the BBC would not be 'doing news properly' if correspondents did not travel to stories:

> I remember going off for a trip to Cairo and I'd been swatting up on it on the Internet for a week before. We were doing stuff on the Muslim Brotherhood. I learnt more in half a day than [in the time] I spent reading stuff on the Web, just because you get there, you can sniff it, you can feel it, you can get the body language.[15]

Unlike some of their colleagues in other media organisations and within the Corporation, BBC correspondents are also usually able to travel to the scene of stories. In an era when foreign bureaux are being closed and there is speculation that the 'foreign correspondent' may be a dying breed, the BBC remains committed to sending correspondents into the field. In 2009, then Director of Global News Richard Sambrook said the BBC was not immune to the cost pressures which were seriously undermining the old model of international newsgathering but maintained that the BBC's licence fee funding did mean the Corporation was still capable of sending reporters to news stories abroad. Sambrook was an advocate for the value of the material provided through blogs, social media and 'citizen journalism': it is an 'extremely valuable supplement' and provides a story with 'authenticity'.[16] But he argued it was not a substitute for BBC reporting. The Corporation still required 'the expertise of professional seasoned journalists'.[17]

Blogs hardly figure, if at all, in daily working routines when BBC correspondents are out in the field covering a significant story. Correspondents usually have access to first-hand sources and contacts on the ground; there is often no need to turn to blogs. Reflecting on his coverage of Afghanistan between 2006 and 2008, Alastair Leithead noted that he did not 'look at blogs so much':

> We'd use the mobile phone to contact our local people and get information fed that way . . . I had people on the ground who would go out and film for me, do interviews and provide information. We built our own relationships with the police, the Afghan security forces, the Afghan government as well as the local tribal leaders.[18]

In addition to local knowledge, Leithead supplemented his understanding by sharing information with other journalists based in Afghanistan. He said the 'small tight knit group of journalists in Kabul' offered him a sense of what was happening in places where he did not go. In any case, Leithead was unlikely to have recourse to many blogs on Afghanistan given the lack of development in the country.

During Jeremy Bowen's coverage of Israel's incursion into Gaza in January 2009, his 18-hour working day meant that he had very little opportunity to read material from other news sources:

> If I had a chance of reading a Reuters wire story summing up the main statements of the day I'd be doing quite well. When I'm out covering a news story, I read very little about what other journalists write. That's partly deliberate—I tend to think I should do it my way. And I'm not really bothered about what they're doing.[19]

When BBC correspondents talk about their journalism the emphasis is on individual inquiry. It is a different emphasis than in the collaborative and participative model identified in the previous chapter by some journalists at the BBC who regularly use blogs in their journalism. In part, this is because

BBC correspondents are able to report foreign news stories from abroad whereas some of their colleagues are tasked with reporting conflicts around the world from London.

THE DEMANDS OF A 24-HOUR MULTIMEDIA NEWS CYCLE

BBC correspondents are in demand as the most-recognisable faces and voices of the BBC. When they are reporting from London, they are often fully occupied providing content for an array of BBC outlets. The number of BBC news platforms increased significantly towards the end of the 20th century. In 1991, CNN's coverage of the Gulf War heralded the beginning of 24-hour rolling news, and the uptake of the Internet by news organisations signalled an era of multimedia news. BBC Radio 5 Live, which began broadcasting in 1994, was designed to provide rolling news and sport updates. In 1997, two more outlets in the form of BBC News 24 and the BBC News website were launched.

The resulting BBC news machine requires constant feeding with live journalism a priority. By 2004, Georgina Born stated that the 'demand to produce news twenty-four hours a day changed journalism': 'journalists had even less time to research or to refresh ongoing stories'.[20] Brian McNair described a shift in the role of the journalist from describing 'that which has happened' to 'that which is happening'.[21] Echoing these views, Middle East Editor Jeremy Bowen said there is little time to find new sources for stories:

> There are only a certain number of hours in the day. When it's busy I have so much to do anyway in terms of just writing, getting stuff out there and trying to find out what is going on.[22]

The problem of servicing BBC outlets has only been exacerbated in the digital media age. A number of correspondents now update their own blogs in addition to online articles for the website. They are also asked to do bespoke material for the BBC's On Demand services. Talented BBC staff end up re-versioning correspondents' content rather than investigating their own stories. Frank Gardner noted that 'behind the scenes', more is done with the news material he produces—not by him, but by his colleagues.[23]

At the same time, efficiency savings mean correspondents say they have less producer support than they have in the past. One correspondent describes the World Affairs Unit—the London base of the BBC's foreign correspondents—as having 'scarce resources', highlighting that several correspondents share producers and others 'do their own thing'.[24] Editors at the BBC worry about the impact of having to do more journalism with fewer journalists. Kate Robinson used to be the Assignments Editor in charge of Home Newsgathering and was responsible for domestic security stories. She said the BBC had too many outlets and fewer correspondents to cover stories than in the past.[25] Another editor was concerned that assigning correspondents to fill airtime on the News channel distorted the news agenda: 'the 24 hour news cycle is not about journalism anymore'.[26]

In these circumstances, there is increased importance placed on the speed and reliability of journalists' sources of information and Herbert Gans's conclusion that the most important concern for journalists when using sources is efficiency seems particularly relevant.[27] For some journalists, blogs are not sufficiently efficient—trawling through blog posts for information, which subsequently requires verification, is too time-consuming when a report needs to be prepared quickly for several BBC outlets.

NEW INFORMATION AND BLOGS

When correspondents are back in London, they do use blogs to provide them with background knowledge, expert analysis, reaction and personal opinion, but they do not usually regard blogs as sources of reliable new information. Although a number of specialist blogs provide Security Correspondent Gordon Corera with novel and valuable material, he noted that other blogs only offered him 'a lot of comment and argument'. This is 'fine and interesting', but it is not what he is 'really after'—'new information and new facts'.[28] Corera suggested that, for the most part, bloggers do not have the level of contacts, or the resources, to do the sort of significant investigative research undertaken by large media organisations. Similarly, Security Correspondent Frank Gardner said he cannot afford to get 'bogged down' with opinion and must 'stick to facts and real information'.[29] Despite a few examples where blogs have uncovered news stories, such as the use of white phosphorus in Iraq discussed in Chapter 2, BBC correspondents felt that it would be unlikely that new information in their field would be revealed on a blog.

The journalists who help them find stories agreed: Defence and Security Producer Stuart Hughes has rarely picked up a story just on a blog. He said blogs 'haven't thrown up that many original stories . . . they're not so good at breaking news'.[30] The previous chapter highlighted the markedly different experience that Hughes has had using Twitter to access breaking-news stories than longer-form blogs.

Paradoxically, while there are millions of blogs, BBC correspondents working in defence and security stated there was a shortage of blogs which would be relevant to their journalistic practice. In 2007, Gordon Corera said it would be interesting to read the blog of a radical young Muslim in Bradford, but he was 'not sure' if such a blog was available.[31] A year later, Caroline Wyatt noted that although Google offered her a million websites for a search of 'British military blogs', there were very few British soldiers updating on deployments.[32] She would welcome more blogs offering her access to 'direct, personal and unmediated experience' from Afghanistan. Rob Watson said the sources he would like to contact were 'unlikely to have blogs' because they would be constrained by the Official Secrets Act or similar legislation in other countries.[33] 'In the area of security', Frank Gardner identified 'a sliding scale'. There is 'an inverse correlation—between how much people know and how much they will say publicly'.[34] He suggested that 'the people who know nothing spout forever on the websites' but the people who 'really know what is going on say very little'.[35]

Consequently, correspondents felt that 'official blogs' were of limited value. Diplomatic Correspondent Paul Adams said he read the blog posts of David Miliband when he accompanied the foreign secretary on a trip to China in February 2008. Adams briefly mentioned Miliband's blog in a diary he wrote for the BBC website,[36] but he maintained that it did not offer him anything to which he would not already have access:

> Blogs are about personal opinions and, I suppose, to give a little extra insight into your own genuinely held beliefs . . . [But] he [Miliband] can't really add much because he can't really say what he really thinks. He can't. His considered opinions will come out in the form of press releases.[37]

In 2007, Stuart Hughes said the 'former Chief of Defence Staff' was 'not going to write down his intimate thoughts in a blog', but he might talk to the BBC off the record.[38] Chapter 1 highlighted how the UK military has significantly increased its digital media presence since 2008. By 2010, the Ministry of Defence's (MoD's) Afghanistan blog regularly included posts from front line soldiers, but Stuart Hughes said he rarely read posts that have appeared as part of the MoD's blogging projects. He already had access to similar material and maintained that 'the chances of finding out something [that would be newsworthy] from an official MoD blog are pretty slim'.[39]

The idea that a lot of information on blogs is not particularly relevant to the role of a BBC correspondent is summarised by Frank Gardner: 'reading blogs is really entertaining but it's not doing my job of reporting on . . . what has happened, where it has happened, what has been done about it and what is this going to mean'.[40] Gardner welcomed blogging as 'a window onto the public'—'it's really interesting and it gives a lot of colour'. But he saw a fundamental difference between blogging and the values of conventional journalism:

> I don't think that we should fall into the trap of putting too much credibility on citizen journalism because it simply doesn't go through the same editorial filter and standards. I know that's going to sound backward, anachronistic and perhaps a little pompous. But editors are there to make sure that journalism meets certain standards of impartiality, of balance and of truth and accuracy. Blogging doesn't have those standards . . . don't confuse it with properly edited and accountable journalism.

Gardner said 10% of his reporting might be 'what people are saying on blogs' about a news event but maintained that, for him, this aspect of the story is not 'the core issue'.

THE ANONYMITY OF THE WEB

Certain areas of the BBC have held a conservative attitude towards the World Wide Web. One BBC journalist who worked on attachment with the World Service suggested that some of the people he worked alongside did not know how to use the Internet—'the level of technophobia in radio is stunning'.[41] Similarly, one BBC correspondent admitted to being 'bad at new media in some ways' joking that they could 'just about use the Internet'.[42]

For one BBC correspondent the Web was described in terms of an unexplored and daunting world:

> 'I have this image and it's a blanket one and a rather ill-informed one of this ocean of comment out there . . . I've just been nervous at dipping my big toe in this rather unknown quantity'.[43]

Others were concerned about the transient nature of a constantly updated medium 'where a lot of the time people are maliciously changing things'.[44] Defence Correspondent Caroline Wyatt was critical of a lack of scepticism and rigour among some of her younger colleagues:

> I say: 'Can you do some research on X, Y and Z?' Then they'll come and dump a Wikipedia page on the desk and say: 'Oh, here it is.' Now that is not acceptable. Wikipedia is not 100% correct and you can get a primary source. If I want to know how many people died in Afghanistan and Iraq, I'd rather get that from the MoD website. On Wikipedia, you don't know who is adding to it.

Wyatt was concerned that relying on the Web in pressurised news situations was leading to mistakes. Journalists writing an introduction to a news piece working in television and radio would turn to the Web because of time pressures and use information which turned out to be incorrect. This, she said, was not the case in the past:

> Before the Web existed, you would have made a phone call. You can take what is on the Web as a source, but you still need to either make that phone call or go to a primary source to make sure it's right.

'The one thing' which really worried Caroline Wyatt about the Web was 'the anonymity of it'—a view shared by a number of her colleagues.[45] Given the sensitive politicised nature of his beat, Gordon Corera said he must be 'quite certain of the authenticity' of what he was reading, which cannot always be ascertained sufficiently quickly on blogs.[46] Frank Gardner highlighted the difficulties with a hypothetical example:

> You could get a blogger who is not declaring their hand because they are anonymous, but actually they are representing one side or another in a conflict. They may be incredibly eloquent and have a very well-argued point, but they may not be who they are pretending to be.[47]

Similarly, Middle East Editor Jeremy Bowen was 'a bit suspicious' about some things which were on the Internet. He usually only reads blogs to inform his knowledge if he knows the person who is blogging: 'if you don't know the provenance, it could be some bloke in a sitting room with his own opinion'.[48]

The issue of anonymity was undoubtedly made more pertinent by the conflation of web forums and blogs by BBC journalists.[49] Several 'blogs' that were often mentioned by BBC journalists, such as the Army Rumour Service (ARRSE) and the Professional Pilots Rumour Network (PPRuNe), are large anonymous forums in which it is difficult to establish the identity of the author of a comment. For example, Caroline Wyatt directly likened the problems of blogs to the Army Rumour Service website—'it's a bit like ARRSE, you don't always know what you are reading and you don't know who is currently serving in the Armed Forces and who is not'.[50] She advised caution against potential hoaxers.

These attitudes mean BBC correspondents tend to place greater faith in the contacts they have established over years rather than new sources potentially available on blogs. Jeremy Bowen emphasised the sources he had built up travelling as a journalist in the Middle East, while Rob Watson said he liked to 'contact people on the telephone' and 'meet people' so he could 'have confidential conversations about sensitive issues'—even if he uses the Internet 'a lot' and 'can't imagine life as a journalist without it'.[51]

COVERING DAILY NEWS ONLINE FOR THE BBC WEBSITE

BBC correspondents do contribute to coverage on the BBC website, but the main news pages are updated by a different team of journalists. When BBC journalists first experimented with putting news online, it began as an enterprise which was largely separate from the rest of the BBC's output. BBC journalists working for the website could research and write their own stories. In November 2007, the BBC's news operation was fundamentally overhauled: TV and Radio News and News Interactive became integrated into a single multimedia newsroom department. The changes, which would be rolled out over the course of the following year, were a response to financial pressures and what was described as a 'revolution in the way our audience consumes what we create, driven by technology and the growth of On Demand platforms like the web'.[52] The website became a much more central part of the BBC's wider operation, but as a consequence a number of journalists working for the website found they had far fewer opportunities for their own reporting.

The journalists who currently work in daily news for BBC News online are a case in point. Their primary role is to constantly update the website with the latest world news. In an increasingly competitive media market-place, delivering reliable information to the public as quickly as possible has become paramount.[53] Alluding to the emergence of a real-time media environment, one BBC online journalist said writing news for the website forced journalists 'to publish things immediately all the time'.[54] He noted that the news website could be 'a bit of a sausage factory at times'. In the course of a 10-hour shift, he would be expected to 'churn out' four or five international stories; as soon as one is finished, 'you just get plonked with another story and you start the same thing again'. The BBC journalist estimated that he only worked on his own news stories three or four times a year.

BBC News online journalist Adam Blenford often writes the top world news story for the BBC website. He was also concerned that online journalists were not performing as much original journalism as they once did: 'It's the pressure of the news cycle and the shift patterns. Everybody knows it but there's very little we can do about it'.[55] Another News online journalist described the BBC as a 'big beast'. In such a large organisation, he said, 'a lot of people go in essentially as journalists' and then 'become a cog—a kind of production person'.[56] The testimony of this journalist echoed Nick Davies' criticism in *Flat Earth News* that too much journalism in the 21st century is 'churnalism'.[57] A colleague working on the BBC website agreed: 'the BBC's terrible at that and I guess that's what we're there for. I guess we're there to plonk out stuff'.[58]

In this environment, blogs are not regarded by online journalists as particularly useful sources of information. The nature of their role in the BBC machine, in which they have to process stories for the website constantly and at speed, usually precludes them from using blogs as part of their journalism. Chapter 3 highlighted that blogs are useful to add colour or provide eyewitness accounts and their colleagues working for the website regularly collate bloggers' views on certain news events. But in order to regularly update the website with the latest news, they need less time-consuming, more consistent and more reliable sources of information to form the factual basis of daily news stories.

BLOGS COMPARED WITH OTHER SOURCES AVAILABLE TO BBC JOURNALISTS

Many BBC journalists still rely on the Essential News Production System (ENPS), a piece of computer software developed by the Associated Press

(AP) which the BBC first installed in 1996.[59] It manages news information for BBC journalists on their computers and a steady stream of breaking-news flashes appear at the top of the screen with new information. The production system enables journalists to access news from several main sources: stories written by World Service journalists for radio news bulletins and updates from BBC correspondents and a number of international news wires including Reuters, AP and Agence France Press (AFP).

A basis of trust between a media organisation and the news agencies is partly built on a financial relationship. The BBC pays agencies to provide their journalists with news information, and the news agencies' business would suffer if they consistently delivered inaccurate material. Hence, BBC journalists tend to trust news agencies because the latter's 'reputation is at stake'[60] and they have a 'track record' of providing accurate and reliable information.[61] This does not mean that news agencies are regarded as faultless. An output editor for Persian TV said BBC journalists can usually remember occasions when news agency reports have contained substantial errors, meaning they are inclined to 'assess sources carefully'.[62] She said she would note the name of the news agency reporter to help her decide on the reliability of the information. Experience allows BBC journalists to work out which parts of reports to trust.[63]

BBC journalists do not only rely on news agencies. Particularly on sensitive issues, a story will not be run on the BBC website until a BBC correspondent using their own sources has independently confirmed its veracity. According to Joe Boyle a lot of BBC journalists 'like a BBC source' and 'they'll stick with it in foreign places like Afghanistan and Pakistan', waiting for confirmation of a story even if all the wires are already reporting it.[64] When he was covering stories in the US, Adam Blenford said he would look at newspaper articles in publications such as the *Washington Post* and the *New York Times*—'authoritative sources' that perform 'newsgathering' and provide 'expert knowledge'.[65]

The news agencies, BBC correspondents and certain newspapers have significant advantages over blogs in the eyes of BBC journalists working for the website. These sources have built up a 'track record' of producing generally reliable and accurate information. BBC journalists know that these outlets will provide the news and information they need to file a report, whereas a blog might only sporadically cover an event. In particular, the process of verifying material is far quicker with these sources than with blogs especially where a journalist is unsure about the provenance of the source. Online journalists are trying to get a version of the story out as quickly as possible. They do not have time to search for 'blogs and then corroborate who these people are'—bloggers 'could write anything [and] they could make anything up'.[66] Moreover, online journalists often have 'enough information' about the stories the BBC is covering 'not to necessitate looking anywhere else'.[67]

BREAKING NEWS: HOW TWITTER HAS ADDRESSED
THE WEAKNESSES OF BLOGS

BBC News online journalist Adam Blenford said that longer form blogs do not often have 'much of a place in the breaking news cycle' because they 'don't gather the news'.[68] It is only 'very rarely in extreme circumstances that an issue blows up and they set an agenda'.[69] Even if a breaking-news story were to appear on a blog and was picked up BBC journalists, they would be reluctant to use factual information without first checking the facts with other sources. A BBC correspondent would be asked to verify the information, or the wires would be consulted to see if the news agencies were reporting the story. This method would be used to fulfil the BBC's requirement of having 'two sources' before publishing a news story.

There are exceptions to the rule whereby the BBC would report a piece of news from one source. In order to distance the BBC from the veracity of the information journalists would attribute the news to the source, but there are usually different practices for blogs and news agencies.[70] If a blog was reporting that a bomb had gone off in the blogger's neighbourhood, that would be 'a great lead,' according to Joe Boyle, 'but you would never report that as fact. You'd never even report it as attributed to that person either—you'd have to find a second source. And that second source would have to be more official or more "solid"'.[71] Another BBC News online journalist said that even if he found 'a really good piece of information' on a blog, he would struggle to get those above him to take much notice until it had appeared on a wire service:

> The people who are editing the site [say] there's too much work, it's going to take too much time, it's too dodgy, or why is this not on the wires? That is kind of their first reaction to everything: 'Why is this not on the wires? Because it's a good story, why haven't they even filed on it?' That's their first reaction—it very rarely gets past that.[72]

By 2010, it was apparent that Twitter was having a fundamental impact on the way journalists operate and the microblogging site has proved to be a very useful newsgathering tool for breaking news. In 2009, if Adam Blenford arrived on a shift to find a bomb had exploded somewhere in the world he would have begun to formulate an online news story using the news agencies 'because the point of a news wire is that it's quick and authoritative: they usually have reporters at the scene and they usually get eyewitnesses'.[73] A year later, he said that 'very often the wires are not as quick as Twitter'.[74]

Twitter has addressed some of the weaknesses of longer form blogs for breaking news. Microblogging acts more like a wire service, providing journalists with immediate updates from a variety of sources. The relatively rapid uptake of Twitter by news agencies, media organisations, governmental departments, military organisations and other 'official sources', and the potential for anybody to quickly and easily update an account from their mobile phone at the scene of a news event provides journalists with a customisable, multiple-source, networked news wire. The ability of users to pass on information by retweeting it to their own Twitter followers also enables news to be distributed at speed.

Adam Blenford highlighted that the practical outworking of the 'two-source' requirement—whereby BBC journalists have to verify information from two separate sources before publishing information—was changing as a consequence. Previously journalists would have had to 'pick up the phone' or wait for a second wire report to confirm a piece of information before they reported the news. By the end of 2010, journalists were 'instantly searching the web for confirmation of the story' using Google News or Twitter.[75] A story appearing in a wire report through ENPS can be double-checked using Web sources or a tip-off on Twitter could be verified using wire reports. Although not all journalists yet possess the skills to use Twitter in this manner, the role of ENPS—previously BBC journalists' main platform for information if they worked in daily news production—appears to be shifting.[76]

INFORMATION OVERLOAD

In the past, news and information was relatively scarce; today BBC journalists talk of 'massive information overload'.[77] They welcome the 'phenomenal range of material available' which can be used to develop a 'more nuanced and varied picture' of an event,[78] but they struggle to effectively filter the 'fire pressure hose of information coming in'.[79] Middle East Editor Jeremy Bowen described his email inbox alone as a 'nightmare'.[80] He recounted one occasion when over a period of about 10 days, he built up 10,000 emails in his inbox. He had to spend a day at home deleting 7,000 emails from his BBC email account, still leaving him with 3,000 messages to manage.

BBC journalists must prioritise, and blogs do not necessarily rank highly on their reading lists. If Bowen is filming all day, he struggles to keep up with 'very legitimate stuff that's well-worth reading', such as reports from the Carnegie Endowment in Washington and the International Crisis Group. On a busy news day, Frank Gardner said he did not have time to read eight 'really important articles' about the attacks on Mumbai in November 2008. If he was unable to read 'the really important stuff', he 'definitely' did not have time to read additional blog posts.[81] More generally he was concerned that there was 'no time for a mass of opinion'.[82] Gordon Corera agreed that 'time is at a premium'.[83] He regularly visits several blogs, and he uses Google News alerts to help him extract information on a variety of topics which often leads him to blogs. But he is wary of spending too much time reading 'stuff which is junk': 'sifting through information is such a big part of the job—you don't want to increase the amount of sifting through unless it's going to be productive'.[84]

In the previous chapter, it was noted that some journalists at the BBC do make use of RSS and other methods of filtering the Web such as social bookmarking and other social media sites, particularly Twitter, in an attempt to combat information overload.[85] Frank Gardner, who started updating a Twitter account in November 2010, said he was still wary of the volume of material appearing on Twitter, but the ability to 'choose the right people' to follow has 'enhanced' his ability 'to cover moving stories'.[86] It is likely that journalists are using Twitter to access blog posts, but further research would be required to establish the nature of the sources they are following and the links they click on in Twitter updates.

At an internal event in 2008, a BBC executive producer urged the Corporation to improve efforts at curating news and information available online. He bluntly stated that the BBC had been 'appalling' at fulfilling its remit of being a trusted guide to the Web.[87] For many journalists, it has so far proved difficult to find time to curate and produce news content. It is debatable whether BBC journalists would benefit from spending more time individually monitoring blogs in such a multifarious organisation. In the context of the volume of user-generated content being sent to the BBC, Deputy Head of BBC Newsgathering Jonathan Baker acknowledged the difficulties of keeping track of electronic source material and assessing what was valid. But he said the BBC was flexing its organisational muscle to do a significant amount of filtering.[88]

Similarly, rather than personally taking time to locate and track blogs, a BBC journalist can always call on colleagues who take a keen interest in the blogosphere or the expertise of people in other departments such as BBC Monitoring and the User Generated Content (UGC) hub. Silvia Costeloe, who has worked on the UGC hub, believes that focus and dedication is necessary to sift through blogs and other online information. She regards finding sources and angles on stories—'these gems' or the 'needles in the haystack'—as a 'very specific skill' requiring time and patience. She suggests it is not possible to combine this journalistic role with live reporting or producing stories for a number of outlets.[89]

CAUTION AT THE BBC: IS SOURCING NEWS FROM A BLOG WORTH THE RISK?

As a publicly funded organisation, the BBC's journalism is constantly under scrutiny. The BBC Trust produces reports into the standards of BBC journalism; external organisations examine the BBC for perceived bias, and press articles and blogs criticise BBC coverage. Georgina Born argues that 'crisis is a cast of mind that has haunted the Corporation since its inception',[90] and since 2007, the BBC has endured several high-profile controversies.[91] Staff members at all levels of the Corporation are aware of the potential consequences of making a mistake, leading to a cautious approach to journalism that manifests itself when journalists talk about using blogs.

Previous mistakes are not forgotten and become ingrained in the cultural mindset. In the context of sourcing stories online the Union Carbide story is recalled by BBC journalists. In 2004, the BBC was hoaxed by a man from a pressure group pretending to be a spokesperson for the Union Carbide chemical company. In an interview which was broadcast live on News 24 from the BBC's studio in Paris, the hoaxer claimed that the company was prepared to compensate the victims of an industrial accident in the Indian city of Bhopal 20 years earlier. Thousands had died in the incident from leaked toxic gases from a pesticide plant. 'Pandemonium ensued' as other media outlets rang the BBC wanting to talk to the spokesperson as compensation would have run into millions.[92] But the BBC had been conned. The hoax included a fake website, which was used by the BBC to verify the story from a news agency report and to contact the hoaxer. Four years on, the story was brought up by World Service journalists in a focus group as an example of the BBC being hoaxed online before.[93] The incident was also recalled without prompting by Defence Correspondent Caroline Wyatt, who was based in Paris at the time. She described it as 'a failure of research at the most basic level'.[94]

Journalists are fearful that making a mistake in a news story will have significant consequences: an error might result in legal action against the BBC or have personal consequences for the individual journalist's career at the Corporation. The shadow of the Hutton Inquiry may be receding, but it is not forgotten and in a media era of near-instantaneous interactivity audiences are quick to alert the BBC even to the smallest of journalistic errors. In November 2007, Paul Adams revealed new concerns over the safety of the Nimrod aircraft after a log report from a forced landing in Kandahar was leaked to the BBC. During a live two-way on BBC News, he erroneously referred to Ben Knight as the pilot of a Nimrod which had crashed in September 2006, killing all 14 crew members. Knight had died, but was not the pilot. As Adams changed his report for subsequent outlets on Radio 5 Live and Radio 4, he noted that as a BBC journalist it is 'these sort of details that you can't afford to get wrong'.[95]

According to one BBC News online journalist there is an institutional obsession with 'reporting something that is not right'; if he made a fundamental error in a report, he felt it would be 'taken to huge levels at the BBC'—'the whole thing just comes down on you'.[96] Similarly, BBC News online journalist Alexis Akwagyiram said he is 'more cautious' working for the BBC than when he was a newspaper journalist.[97] Using blogs can consequently be viewed as an unnecessary gamble:

> There's a risk factor of reporting things on blogs that generally isn't worth it . . . No matter what you find on blogs, you're going to struggle to convince yourself that it's worth a punt. Then you're going to have an even bigger struggle to convince any of the higher ups that's worth a punt.[98]

Risk is multiplied by the 'politicised, sensitive' nature of war and terrorism stories.[99] One of the 'higher-ups'—Kate Robinson, the Assignments Editor for Home Newsgathering—said she held a position in the BBC hierarchy which meant she would be held responsible for an error in the BBC's news reporting. Terrorism stories are particularly sensitive, and her experience of covering them led her to distrust any source as a starting point for investigation whether they were government sources or extremists. There are significant legal implications of reporting a story inaccurately and she noted that 'it would be a disaster if the BBC collapsed a terrorism trial'.[100] It would also be morally and ethically wrong to put lives at risk in an ongoing terror attack. The upshot of these concerns is that home news reporters under Robinson's management covering terrorism in the UK very rarely used blogs as sources of information. They might occasionally have accessed information on Web forums to pick up a lead, but Robinson said they did 'old-fashioned journalism' by phoning people and talking to them.

BBC journalists often compared reporting war and terrorism to reporting politics. One BBC producer noted that before she began working on defence stories she used to work on politics in the BBC's office at Millbank near the Houses of Parliament. Here she used to look at blogs 'the entire time because all the MPs keep their own blogs'.[101] Similarly, when Adam Blenford covered US politics for BBC News online, there were 'lots of blogs', and he could 'distinctly find BBC friendly balance: two on this side, two on the other side'.[102] World Affairs Correspondent Paul Adams did look at some US blogs for the US election in 2008, but he described that as a 'different experience' from covering war.[103] He is more nervous about 'reading the observations or opinions of someone who may or may not be a journalist' in the area of conflict:

> I think I just have a respect for a trained hack who's been around, who understands warfare which is complicated and difficult and noisy and confusing and so I haven't found myself turning to the blogs.

THE WEAKNESSES OF BLOGS FOR BBC JOURNALISTS AND THE TURN TO TWITTER

This chapter has shown that attitudes to the Web and blogging affect how journalists use blogs; those who spend less time immersed in online culture were more wary of making use of material on blogs. Among correspondents there was a certain level of scepticism of the transient nature of the Web, a perception that a lot of material is posted anonymously and a concern that unscrupulous fact checking on the Web leads to mistakes. This lack of trust in blogs sits uneasily alongside Charlie Beckett's assertion in *SuperMedia* that 'the bloggers online currency is their trustworthiness and the other bloggers are ferocious at maintaining its values. The untrustworthy or irrelevant blogger tends to be ignored'.[104]

Some correspondents at the BBC suggested they might simply have been 'slow to recognise the potential of blogs' and might benefit from some of the techniques developed by some of their more 'Web-savvy' colleagues.[105] Although it should not be overstated, there does appear to be a slightly different emphasis in the way experienced foreign correspondents visualise their journalism in comparison with colleagues who regularly use blogs in their reporting. In the previous chapter, a more collaborative and participative approach was identified, whereas the correspondents in this chapter tended to have a more independent, individual conception of journalism. This might be construed as a cultural generational shift, but it is also structural: a consequence of correspondents being far more often able to travel to stories while their colleagues in London are finding creative ways to report war and security from afar.

This chapter has also demonstrated that there are a number of fundamental problems with using blogs in an age of 24-hour, real-time, multimedia news where the pressure to deliver content at speed to a variety of outlets has never been so great. BBC journalists maintained that blogs do not fulfil some of Herbert Gans's key tests for useful journalistic sources of information. The demand for reliable information at speed means journalists often do not turn to blogs. BBC correspondents in particular emphasised the value of witnessing events and their reliance on trusted sources and contacts. If journalists have to use secondary sources they tend to make use of better-placed BBC journalists, the news agencies or certain established media organisations. Compared to these sources, blogs were deemed to be too time-consuming to access and verify.

Journalists have little time at work to formulate strategies for monitoring blogs and sorting the 'wheat from the chaff'.[106] They complained paradoxically both that there is too much information for them to filter and too few blogs offering them useful material relevant to their journalism. There is 'a hell of a lot of blogs', but finding 'new facts' is described as looking for 'a needle in a haystack'.[107] Their perception of blogs is that too many of them consist of opinion and comment; too few provide new factual information or undertake significant research especially on sensitive topics. Blogs written by official sources of information were also not considered to provide significant new material in the area of war and terrorism. The chapter thus highlighted the difficulties of using blogs as sources of information in the daily news cycle. It was a problem emphasised most by the journalists who are responsible for writing news for the BBC website and was particularly adjudged to be an issue in the context of reporting defence and security stories.

Microblogging in the form of Twitter, however, has addressed a number of weaknesses of longer-form blogs. The format encourages shorter updates which can be distributed at speed through Twitter networks and allow journalists to more easily monitor multiple sources simultaneously. Blogs are not deemed to play a regular role in the breaking-news cycle whereas Twitter has often beaten the traditional media to the news. Previously, the latter phenomenon was regarded as the exception rather than the norm: in 2009 Adam Blenford believed that it was still 'very rare' to see news stories on Twitter before the news agency wires.[108] The following year, the number of Twitter users grew considerably: 44% of all Twitter users by August 2010 had joined in the previous eight months.[109] Perhaps in part because of this uptake, by December 2010, Adam Blenford noted that 'very often Twitter would be quicker than the wires with the news'.[110] Blenford described an emerging shift in the way BBC journalists corroborate information using 'two sources' whereby Twitter can be used to verify news agency reports and vice versa. This approach is undoubtedly made possible because various news agencies, media organisations, journalists, governments and eyewitnesses to news events are all using Twitter to communicate information.

In respect to both blogs and Twitter, tension will always exist between the need to report information at speed and the organisation's reputation for accurate and trustworthy information. The institutional penalties for making a mistake were deemed to be significant. In an effort to maintain the values of the BBC's journalism and more pragmatically to keep their jobs, BBC journalists are cautious when using blogs. Concerns over accurate reporting are amplified in the context of defence and security, where erroneous reporting might cost lives bringing the organisation under legal or moral scrutiny.

The limitations of blogs as sources of information—the need to protect the BBC news brand, the time-consuming difficulties of verifying, monitoring and filtering information on blogs and concerns surrounding their factual accuracy—contribute to the role for blogs in BBC journalism identified in the two previous chapters.

Part III

5 'Outside the BBC Universe?'
Blogging at the BBC

The first two parts of this book have considered the use of blogs as sources of information by the BBC as a response to the challenge of blogging. They explored how blogs and bloggers have been incorporated into the BBC's journalism, and documented the emergence of a more collaborative approach to war and terror reporting.

In *Blogging, Citizenship and the Future of Media*, Mark Tremayne noted that media organisations were also addressing the blogging challenge by hiring their own bloggers and by commissioning their own journalists to write blogs.[1] The blog was being adopted as a tool of the professional journalist; Chapters 5 and 6 explore how and why BBC journalists began writing their own blogs particularly reporters' blogs and programme blogs.

Wilson Lowrey suggests that the production of 'blog-like content' and the 'hiring of high-profile bloggers' may have been calculated—a movement by media organisations to maintain control over blogging rivals.[2] Similarly, Susan Robinson argues that the traditional media began using blogs in 'an attempt to recapture journalism authority'.[3] It seems, however, that the adoption of blogging at news organisations was often driven by curious journalists who wanted to experiment with the format. Several pioneers who advocated the potential of blogs saw through early cultural distinctions between blogging and journalism and the arguments between bloggers and journalists. They regarded the former as a false argument based on a category mistake and the latter as a hindrance to the potential for a productive working partnership. These journalists simply viewed a blog as a useful tool—they were attracted by the possibilities of straightforward online publication as a method of presenting news and information. The blog provided more space, fewer stylistic conventions and the prospect of a more fluid exchange with their audiences through comments.

Journalists adopting the blog format were not always encouraged by their employers, who often did not believe that blogging could be a form of journalism. CNN journalist Kevin Sites, for example, was told to stop writing his personal blog during the Iraq war after it received significant media attention. His employers said covering war was a 'full time job' and Sites should concentrate on filing TV reports.[4]

Nevertheless, by 2004, Robinson notes that the journalism or j-blog frequently 'served as daily news' on the websites of US traditional news organisations.[5] In the UK, blogs had not yet reached the same level of popularity or influence as they had done in the US, fostering a feeling of general indifference towards the use of blogging by the media. Interviews conducted by Neil Thurman in 2004 reveal a sceptical attitude among UK media editors towards claims that blogging represented a revolution in journalism.[6] *The Guardian* newspaper online was a notable exception to the general trend in the UK establishing a blog as early as 2000.[7]

For the BBC, integrating blogging into their journalistic output was a particular challenge. The BBC's reputation is founded on a long-standing institutional commitment to impartiality, fairness and accuracy whereas successful blogs were deemed to rely on partiality and opinion. This chapter documents the BBC's early experiments with blogs and considers how blogging was reconciled with the BBC's values. It also explores why the BBC's Defence and Security correspondents have not embraced the format in the same way as some of their colleagues.

EXPERIMENTS WITH PARTICIPATORY
MEDIA AND PERSONAL BLOGGING

The BBC, like many traditional media organisations, appeared to be slow in formally adopting blogs as a tool for journalism.[8] The Corporation had, however, led a number of online initiatives through the launch of BBC Online in 1997[9] and was experimenting with several participatory media projects in the early 2000s including Digital Storytelling, iCan and h2g2.[10] These projects aimed to help facilitate the participation of the audience in journalism by encouraging them to use media tools to share news and build online communities.

Blogging was another format that offered the potential for greater participation in journalism. Alfred Hermida notes that 'tentative steps into blogging took place within areas of the BBC that enjoyed an unusually high level of independence from BBC news management'.[11] In 2002, a group of production staff at Scotland Interactive started Scotblog. Former Senior Development Producer Martin Belam describes it as 'the first thing on the BBC that *looked* like a blog'.[12] It provided links to 'internet-based items and resources, featuring executive summary and unique perspectives on the web'.[13] It also had an RSS feed.

In 2003, BBC Scotland Interactive joined forces with the Scottish Executive for a project called Island Blogging that provided PCs and an Internet connection to homes in the Scottish Islands. The BBC set up a platform allowing island bloggers to post to the BBC website in an attempt to encourage hyperlocal newsgathering, 'community connection', Web literacy and participation in the BBC's journalism.[14] A report on Island Blogging in

2005 raised a number of issues which would reappear in future discussions within the organisation. Concern was expressed about the moderation of comments, the nature of links to other sites and the content of trackbacks posted on BBC webpages. The report highlighted the need to protect the BBC's brand of journalism from bloggers who could potentially write whatever they liked.[15]

BBC staff members had also begun keeping their own blogs as a way of experimenting with the technology. In 2002, Euan Semple's DigiLab Unit[16] pioneered the adoption of 'workblogging' at the BBC, establishing internal wikis and blogs.[17] By 2005, BBC journalist Kevin Anderson believed there were around 150 internal blogs at the BBC, which staff could use as a way of exchanging information about their work. Outside of the BBC firewall, BBC staff members were participating in the blogosphere as well. At the end of 2002, Martin Belam started his own blog after noticing that a number of his colleagues were writing blogs including Matt Jones, Euan Semple and Tom Dolan.[18]

Personal blogs, both internal and external, raised the profile of the genre within the organisation not least because the information posted on these blogs occasionally had interesting consequences. Richard Sambrook's blog, for example, was quoted by union leaders as evidence of a split in the management's approach to a cost-saving programme.[19] A new set of editorial guidelines for external personal blogs was drawn up by Nick Reynolds, the Senior Advisor in Editorial Policy, in 2005 as the BBC became aware of the potential impact of staff blogging.[20]

Whatever the fallout from either internal or external BBC staff blogs, Kevin Anderson nevertheless believed that they provided an ideal training ground—'a good way to become familiar with the tools and the editorial approach to blogging'.[21] Moreover, Lucy Hooberman, then working in the BBC's New Media and Technology Division, believed that Euan Semple's work had 'revolutionised' the BBC's intranet to such an extent that it was 'a necessary precondition' for the establishment of the BBC blog network in 2006.[22] The cross-divisional nature of the BBC's blogging project was made possible by a more collaborative, internally networked working environment.

BLOGGING THE NEWS: NICK ROBINSON LEADS THE WAY

In 2001, Nick Robinson and the future Editor of BBC News blogs, Giles Wilson, began The Campaign Today in the run-up to the UK General Election.[23] Written for BBC News online, Robinson provided regular updates on what he observed and witnessed as the BBC's Political Correspondent. It was missing some of the characteristic elements of blogs, particularly a visible comments section and links to other sites, but visitors could put comments to Robinson via email. His online diary also had a sense of immediacy and a limited feel of interactivity. It was more than merely an online column and according to Wilson 'pretty much' the BBC's 'first experience with blogging in news'.[24]

The project was deemed to be a success and Nick Robinson's Newslog was launched later in December 2001.[25] Newslog aimed to be 'a unique diary from the heart of the news' specifically mentioning that its inspiration came from the weblog phenomenon.[26] More emphasis was placed on audience participation in Newslog: 'In true weblog style . . . you are free to add your comments, questions and thoughts'.[27] Reflecting on Newslog several years later, Giles Wilson said there was a period when he was trying to work out 'what the beast was and what it was for':[28]

> It took us a while to work it out really. Was it for breaking news? Or was it for analysis? Or was it for diary items? We bowed out of using it for breaking news really because there are other ways you get breaking news.

Robinson and Wilson decided that the blog should be about Robinson's job, 'covering the comings and goings of the Westminster political scene'.[29]

DODGING THE BBC'S RULES: PAUL MASON'S *NEWSNIGHT* BLOG

Early experiments, both within and outside of the BBC's website, demonstrated that working out what a blog was, what it was for and perhaps most importantly whether and how the BBC could and should be using blogs was not straightforward. Although the BBC had been producing content which drew on the blogging phenomenon, the use of blogs in news had been sporadic and uncoordinated. By 2005, several dynamics were pushing forward a move towards a more coherent approach to blogging across the BBC.

In June, Paul Mason started a blog for Newsnight, which covered the G8 Summit, with the approval of his editor, Peter Barron. Mason aimed to write 'personalised analysis, using the same self-control as on Newsnight; my producer or the web editor would run an eye over anything controversial and keep an eye on balance'.[30] The blog ran 'silent' for three days before Barron managed to negotiate the necessary approval for it to be promoted by the Newsnight team.[31] Reflecting on his blogging experience in July 2005, Mason described the blog's birth:

> I decided to do a 'proof of concept' blog and show it to Newsnight's editor. He liked it, our web editor got it signed off and that was it. Apparently the BBC bosses had just had a big away day where they decided to stop being clipboard merchants and prioritise innovation, so no one felt like nixing it. And yet there was nothing that said it should be allowed. As one person put it: 'this is outside the BBC universe'—and I thought: that puts it rather well . . . [32]

The technical limitations of the BBC website meant Newsnight decided to host the blog outside of the bbc.co.uk domain using Typepad's external blogging software. According to Nick Reynolds, Mason's blog caused 'all sorts of ructions'.[33] There were questions over whether the blog could be hosted using Typepad within the terms of the BBC's technology contract with Siemens and Reynolds became involved in an email conversation with Peter Barron about whether the latter had gained permission from Editorial Policy for the project.[34] Nevertheless, Reynolds did not want to stand in the way of what he regarded as 'good journalism'. Mason said he 'did not so much break the BBC rules when setting up the blog but shimmied through them like Tana Umaga'.[35] It was another 'spur for the BBC to get its act together'.[36]

BBC BLOGS AND 'NEWS AS CONVERSATION': KEVIN ANDERSON'S REPORT

As Newsnight was launching its first blog, Kevin Anderson was in the final stages of drafting a report on a role for blogs in the BBC's journalism for the Editor of the BBC News website, Pete Clifton, and the Head of Product Development for Technology for News Interactive, Nic Newman. Nick Robinson's Newslog had been halted when he left the BBC to join Independent Television News (ITN) in October 2002, but BBC editors were keen for Robinson to start a BBC blog on his return in 2005.[37] One of the reasons Robinson had given for returning to the BBC as Political Editor was an opportunity to write a blog.[38] In part, Pete Clifton commissioned Kevin Anderson to write his report on blogging as an important first step in the process.

Anderson was chosen for the task on the strength of his work blogging the US election in 2004 for the BBC website—the first major blogging project in news after Robinson's Newslog. Anderson updated the election blog several times a day in the course of the three-week project and engaged the audience by using their comments as a starting point for his posts.[39] According to Martin Belam, Anderson's 'real on-the-ground understanding of how blogging could play a vital part in his journalism'[40] formed the basis of his conclusions for Newman and Clifton.[41]

Titled BBC Blogs: News as Conversation, Anderson identified several BBC failings including an 'inconsistent use of language' and 'approach to weblogs'.[42] He said the BBC had 'confused audiences', 'alienated bloggers' and 'missed opportunities'. His decision to devote a considerable amount of space to a section titled 'What Is a Blog?' naturally followed from an assertion that 'blogs are the latest internet phenomenon of which much is said and little understood'. Anderson made one of the final versions of this report available to colleagues on 26 July 2005. Three days later, Pete Clifton, published an article on the BBC website titled BLOG BAN. Citing Anderson's work, Clifton admitted the BBC's approach to blogs had been confusing and embarrassing:

> The site has called all manner of things blogs in recent months, even, briefly, this column. None of them have been blogs and our publishing system does not currently have the tools to produce them properly. So we've looked pretty dumb.[43]

He issued a ban on calling anything on bbc.co.uk a blog until the BBC 'could do them technically'. Looking forward, he identified only one priority: turning the Editor's Desktop column into a blog. The BBC's blog trial proved to be considerably more ambitious.

THE ORIGINS OF THE BBC BLOG TRIAL: THE BLOGGING SUMMIT

Blogging was 'emerging from the cracks between the nailed down floorboards of the BBC'.[44] There had been various blogging experiments in news and current affairs, internal blogging was well established and a significant group of staff members were interested in the journalistic potential of blogs. Innovation at the periphery of the BBC was also making its presence felt at the centre.

Julie Adair, the Head of New Media for Scotland Interactive, who had been running Island Blogging, was enthusiastically advocating blogs to Innovation Executive Lucy Hooberman, in New Media and Technology. Hooberman was in contact with Nic Newman and Jem Stone, Executive Producer for Engagement in New Media and Technology, who were also interested in blogging. Having obtained support at board level for a blogging project from the Director of Global News, Richard Sambrook, Hooberman decided to organise a summit for interested parties across the BBC in July 2005. She encouraged participation by informing potential attendees that 'decisions would be made'.[45] The summit was delayed because of the terror attacks on London on 7 July, but eventually convened on 16 September 2005. It was a result of 'a year of debate, some rants, lots of action outside the BBC and a growing movement and demand inside'.[46]

The pan-BBC blog summit was a meeting which brought together between 15 and 20 staff members from a variety of departments and backgrounds within the BBC.[47] Representatives from different departments gave presentations outlining their interest in blogging. Subsequent discussions covered the need for cultural change within the organisation, a technical solution to provide a working blogging platform and the editorial value of blogging.[48] Two projects emerged as front runners. The first was a decision to 'jump in and get involved' by setting up some blogs to test them as an editorial proposition.[49] The second was a way of tracking what was being said in the blogosphere using a system called Crsstal.[50]

Jem Stone produced the third draft of a proposal for a BBC blogging trial on 14 November 2005.[51] He highlighted issues which chimed with Anderson's assessment of the BBC's approach to blogs. Stone criticised the launch of '"blogs" that don't in any way offer standard blog functionality', noting that some BBC teams were launching blogs '"under cover"', others could not develop valid propositions and everybody suffered from a lack of advice about 'best practice, cost implications, [and] guidelines and recommendations about whether a blog was a right approach'.[52]

The BBC blog trial aimed to address these problems by providing a coherent approach to blogging. It would establish between 20 and 40 blogs with dedicated blogs.bbc.co.uk addresses, the installation of blogging software onto the BBC's servers to provide blog functionality,[53] and 'a framework to govern new blog launches, moderation, technology and their features'.[54] The decision to start blogging under trial status meant blogs could be launched more quickly, provided the BBC with more room for mistakes and allowed public value testing to be carried out as the BBC blogged rather than incurring further delays.

A steering group was set up to guide, fund and manage the project even though several of those who attended the summit in September were against the idea. There was a group who argued that 'bloggers are great individualists . . . many prefer to exist outside mainstream frameworks'.[55] At the meeting they had suggested that BBC bloggers might be allowed to set up their own accounts using external software as Paul Mason had done and pursue their own projects, but Jem Stone, among others, was convinced that 'the BBC should provide journalists, broadcast journalists, or talent, or production teams with their own platform to do it'.[56] It was indicative of the clash between the cultural assumptions of blogging and the BBC's bureaucratic organisational practices. But Stone believed the trial had the necessary support:

> By the end of 2005, there was pretty much a consensus around the BBC that this was the right thing to do . . . at a production and at a senior level. We needed to have the right technology and the right platform to do it. We'll experiment with a few high profile blogs and a few of a different nature. And we'll see what we learn.

THE TRIALS OF THE BBC'S BLOG TRIAL

The blog trial, which was initially scheduled for late January, did not launch until March 2006.[57] Lucy Hooberman wrote an article for *Ariel* magazine encouraging BBC teams to submit proposals for new blogs. These were discussed by the steering group in two phases in February and June. By November 2006, there were 43 BBC blogs.[58] The BBC soon began struggling with substantial technical problems. In order to start the project quickly a number of mistakes were made installing the system, and even by the begin-ning of 2007 the software was 'not production ready'.[59] The version of Mov-able Type the BBC was using had also not been particularly well designed for the scale of the BBC's blogging project.[60]

The technical situation became so troublesome by the end of 2006 that the New Media steering group, which approved new blog proposals, was facing a significant dilemma: 'everybody wanted a blog and everybody knew the technology wasn't up to it'.[61] A 'slightly arbitrary ruling' was put in place: 'no more blogs'.[62] Blogs were still launched,[63] but Aaron Scullion, who worked under Giles Wilson for the BBC News blogs team, says the intervention of then Deputy Director General Mark Byford was required for the BBC's regional political editors to be given blogs for the elections in May 2007.[64]

Several months earlier, Jem Stone had apologised to readers of Radio 4's *PM* blog for persistent difficulties but admitted that because blogs were operating under trial status the BBC could 'not allocate the same kind of technical resource to them as we would to a full service; to do so would, in the long run, detract from other important projects'.[65] Although he could not say so at the time, he was mainly referring to the expensive development of iPlayer, the BBC's 'on demand' catch-up service for radio and television.[66]

'OUTSIDE THE BBC UNIVERSE': CAN A BBC JOURNALIST BE A BLOGGER?

Jem Stone was aware that technical difficulties were merely one potential pitfall as the BBC launched the blog trial. The cultural and editorial risk he identified was whether a BBC journalist could be a good blogger.[67] Even by 2005, blogging was regarded as an 'alien activity'; 'a really brave thing for the BBC to be doing'.[68] At a senior level, Richard Sambrook, the Director of Global News, who was acting as a sponsor for the project, noted that man-agers were 'very suspicious about blogging'.[69] They were concerned about 'editorial standards and control' and there were 'all sorts of crazy debates about it'.[70]

Kevin Anderson described the 'response [to blogs] from most in the main-stream media as 'fear and defensiveness'.[71] And his report did not exempt the BBC from these attitudes. Writing for the BBC website in 2003, technology commentator Bill Thompson had concluded that blogging is 'often . . . as far from journalism as it is possible to get'.[72] There were also considerable doubts about whether blogging could or should be incorporated into BBC journalism. Mike Smartt, then editor of the BBC News website, was not con-vinced of the durability of blogging: '[t]hey are an interesting phenomenon, but I don't think they will be as talked about in a year's time'.[73]

Audience expectations of blogs and of the BBC's journalism also posed a potential stumbling block. Research by the BBC in 2006 concluded that 'people's gut understanding of blogs centres on single authorship and complete freedom of expression, often of unorthodox views—which poses problems in the context of BBC blogging'.[74] The research suggested that audiences perceived a clash between the BBC's factual, trustworthy and balanced reportage and the opinionated, personal and unmoderated information offered by blogs. Senior Broadcast Journalist Robin Hamman, who became acting head of the BBC's blog trial,[75] expressed similar concerns. He noted that in 'some respects, our name and our values, as well as audience (and regulators') expectations of us actually make it difficult for us to fully engage'.[76]

BBC journalists who took up the blogging mantle were particularly aware of the problems. Reflecting on his experience of blogging for *Newsnight*, Paul Mason wondered whether the BBC could fully meet the blogging challenge. He believed that journalists should be offering the content which made blogs attractive to audiences rather than producing 'faux blogs', but he recognised that the BBC was 'hidebound by extra rules on impartiality as well as fairness and accuracy'.[77]

Abandoning the BBC's editorial principles was never regarded as an option. It was taken as axiomatic that BBC blogs should be impartial, balanced, fair, accurate and adhere to the BBC's existing editorial standards. The 'idea of blogging' sat 'awkwardly'[78] alongside these values which Defence and Security Producer Stuart Hughes identified as a 'fundamental problem':

> If you take a BBC reporter and you give him a blog, he's going to have to be more careful and apply the same standards that he would do to his work. To me, that in some ways undermines the whole spirit of what blogs are about.[79]

Anderson's report maintained that blogs written by BBC journalists could be a successful part of the BBC's output. 'Writing a weblog,' he stated, 'does not need to conflict with our journalistic values. In fact, it will help us communicate those values to our audience'.[80] He argued that BBC blogs should be written in a conversational tone, ask questions of the audience, link to other websites and reply to comments made by readers. They should be interactive and facilitate a conversation with the audience. Anderson believed that by engaging in the blogosphere, the BBC brand would be more visible around the World Wide Web, enhancing the BBC's trust, reach and credibility.

The BBC's audience research had similarly pointed to a middle ground, indicating that BBC blogs could become part of a 'less maverick and confrontational blog community . . . where expertise and trustworthiness have a role to play'.[81] The report suggested that the BBC will never embody the core values of blogging, but could retain a sense of immediacy, energy, informality and conversational dialogue without compromising the BBC's editorial standards.

Nick Robinson's blog played a significant role in convincing a number of doubters of the ability for BBC journalists to be successful bloggers.

Importantly, Robinson was decisive in describing himself as a 'blogger' in one of his first posts for Newslog after its relaunch in 2005.[82] Robinson's blog is cited by Richard Sambrook as an important step in the evolution of the use of blogging at the BBC: 'he was high profile and he got it right very quickly and early'; 'he was very able to do it, very suited to do it and had the right tone of voice'.[83] Similarly, Aaron Scullion described Robinson's conversational yet neutral approach as 'a template' which 'everybody else has followed'.[84]

Some BBC staff believed the use of blogs by journalists such as Nick Robinson and Business Editor Robert Peston transformed the BBC's working practices. Peston describes his blog as 'an absolute cornerstone' of the way he works—'central to everything' he does at the BBC.[85] Peston, a former print journalist, says his blog was a natural progression from a daily email he would send to BBC staff about stories he was covering that day. He uses it as a personal diary to formulate his thinking around the news, a way of informing BBC news desks about his thoughts on business stories and an outlet to present stories to the audience.[86] He argues that the blog reinforces the BBC's authority allowing him to publish scoops, stories and news lines that would not make the cut for the *Ten O'Clock News*. According to Kevin Marsh, the Executive Editor of the College of Journalism, BBC bloggers such as Robert Peston have transformed the BBC's approach to old ideas of what constituted 'a story', 'a deadline' and sufficient material to publish a piece of information.[87] Although Peston says that he has 'a paternalistic view of journalism' and that his expertise is important, he also believes his journalism has been 'improved enormously' by feedback on his blog.[88]

ADDRESSING WEAKNESSES: MOULDING BLOGS TO FIT THE FACE OF THE BBC'S VALUES

Despite the application of the BBC's editorial standards to blogs, there have been times when engaging in a 'slightly unguarded genre'[89] has impinged on the BBC's journalistic values. In 2007, one of Robert Peston's blog posts was criticised in a BBC Trust report for 'a scathing attack' on the Microsoft Vista operating system.[90] The report said the Business Editor's post appeared to disregard 'the BBC's guidelines which state that blogs are subject to the same level of editorial care as other content'.[91] During the financial crisis in 2007 and 2008, Robert Peston's blog came under even greater scrutiny when his posts were alleged to have had a significant impact on trading on the London Stock Market. In this case, Peston's blog was widely regarded as being exceptionally accurate, and in February 2009 he was praised for his coverage by fellow journalists giving evidence to a Commons Select Committee investigating the influence of the media on the banking crisis.

Critics of the BBC had suggested that mistakes were being made. Writing in *The Observer* in October 2008, Peter Preston claimed that BBC blogs 'don't go through anxious committees of editors, pondering deeply. They are self-publication, performed at the double'.[92] Two months later, Stephen Glover in *The Daily Mail* cited Peston's blog as an example of a wide-ranging breakdown of the 'old distinction between reporters and pundits' on the BBC's blogs:

> My problem is with Mr Peston, and other BBC reporters, increasingly presenting themselves as pundits and opinion formers. This increasingly takes place on the blogs . . . on the BBC's website. The point about these blogs is that they are not simply opinionated. The opinions they offer are often Leftist or *bien pensant*.[93]

Peston's reporting of the financial crisis brought renewed attention to the editorial procedures for blogs at the BBC and the fine line between 'personal opinion' and 'professional judgement'.[94] The BBC's blogs had already been placed under similar editorial standards to other online content prior to the articles written by Preston and Glover, although Robin Lustig, who writes the BBC's World Tonight blog, suggested in 2008 that practices may not initially have been as vigorous for blogs as they were for other forms of content. He said he used to write his blog 'very late at night' when there was no readily available editorial oversight.[95] By the end of the year, Lustig said this was no longer the case.

When weaknesses were found or where they were perceived by critics, the BBC responded by publicly emphasising that their blogs adhered to existing editorial standards and practices. Peter Preston's article prompted a letter to the same newspaper from the Director of BBC News, Helen Boaden, in which she stated that BBC blogs were subject to a system of 'editorial oversight'.[96] Little more than a week later Mark Mardell, then Europe Editor, told a BBC Feedback programme on Radio 4 that there were far more editorial checks with blogs than on live TV or live radio.[97] In December 2008, Giles Wilson also rejected Glover's charge that BBC's blogs were full of opinion. Writing for the Editors' blog, Wilson argued that the BBC's 'expert editors' use blogs to 'tell us what has happened, to explain why it is or isn't important, what it means, and even what might be the effect'.[98]

Behind the scenes, editorial control over blogs was tightened as part of a wider BBC review of editorial compliance triggered by the Ross/Brand affair.[99] In November 2008, Wilson emphasised the strict editorial rigour with which blogs were handled at an internal BBC conference. While 'authenticity' may be a key audience attraction of a BBC blog, it was always subordinate to impartiality. The BBC's blogs were not blogs in 'the sense of somebody just writing what they want to write and publishing it'.[100] The BBC's bloggers were 'expected to engage with controversial subjects in a lively way and have a different tone, but they must never be seduced by the apparent informality of this blog environment to letting their impartiality drop'.[101] Reflecting on this period in 2010, Giles Wilson argued that this did not represent 'a sea-change', but he said processes were codified and the BBC made sure it knew which senior figures were acting as a 'second pair for eyes' for each blogger at the BBC.[102]

Fully embracing an existing culture of blogging would have required a fundamental realignment of the BBC's values. It was notable that the latest set of revisions to the BBC's editorial guidelines published in 2010 inserted a new phrase—'rooted in evidence'—to distinguish between the analysis offered by BBC journalists and opinionated journalism.[103] Although there were 'theoretical risks' with a 'slightly unguarded genre',[104] BBC blogs were moulded to fit the BBC's existing journalistic culture. BBC journalists often repeat the advice of 'not writing anything in a blog that you would not say on air', and a blog team is responsible for checking blog copy. Members of the team can refer to a set of internal 'Blog Guidelines' which implores journalists to ask a series of questions of blog post content before it is published.[105] In May 2009, the Director-General, Mark Thompson, linked the BBC's blogging future with its journalistic past, describing a BBC blog post as a 'piece of, essentially, broadcast journalism'—'fact-checked' by a 'senior editorial manager'.[106]

'HERE COMES EVERYBODY'[107]: COMMENTS ON BBC BLOGS

At the same time, BBC blogs were supposed to offer more than merely another outlet for the BBC's journalists to broadcast the news. A central feature of that offering was the opportunity for a journalist to directly engage with an audience through comments on a blog post. In his 2005 report *BBC Blogs: News as conversation*, Kevin Anderson had urged the BBC to use blogs to engage in an informal online conversation. Aware that moderating comments would be time-consuming, he nevertheless emphasised that bloggers needed to respond to blog comments or the 'conversation' would 'break down'.[108] In a BBC blog post in April 2008, Giles Wilson told readers that 'all our research, as well as our instincts, tell us how important it is that one should be able to add comments to a blog'.[109] He recognised that, for some readers, the ability to comment 'is the defining characteristic of a blog—and when a blog author takes part in the comments you can see the value of it'.

Wilson's post was written in the aftermath of a blogging software upgrade which had fixed the technical problems blighting the BBC's blogs throughout 2007. With no money available to fix the technology, the BBC had struggled on with the same blogging platform throughout most of 2007. A BBC Trust report claimed that the BBC was publishing 1.5 million comments on blogs and message boards every month.[110] The BBC's blogs had been 'strangled' by spam;[111] bloggers and commenters alike found they were plagued by error messages, which meant they could not post to the BBC's blogs. These technical difficulties had two salient consequences. First, it was 'very frustrating' for journalists trying to produce news content using blogs.[112] Second, it had significantly undermined one of the central editorial propositions of blogs—the development of a conversation between the BBC and their audience. As Peter Barron, the editor of Newsnight, pointed out in a piece for the Editors' blog:

> Many of you have been writing in to complain about problems getting through both on the Editors' blog and on the Newsnight blog pages. I sympathise. Often I try to respond to a comment or complaint about the programme and end up gnawing my knuckles in frustration as the response either doesn't appear for many hours or fails to materialise at all. Hardly the best way to have a free flowing dialogue with our viewers.[113]

By November 2007, blogs were receiving as many as 50,000 spam comments a week and the BBC had been forced to abandon Movable Type's comment system and use in-house comment software.[114] The *World Have Your Say* team had already given up on blogging with the BBC's technology. They decided to move their blog to Wordpress and did not return inside the BBC firewall until March 2010.[115] 'In hindsight', Jem Stone admitted that he and his colleagues running the blog trial 'should probably have fixed that [technical] issue at the beginning of 2007 and we didn't start doing it until the end of 2007'.[116]

Blogs were finally moved onto a more stable platform in April 2008, and a new registration system for commenters was introduced. Although the technology did improve the technical aspects of the commenting experience, the editorial difficulties surrounding comments had not been solved. Despite the BBC's enthusiasm for comments in public, comment moderation had become time-consuming and expensive.[117] As part of the upgrade in April 2008, comment moderation for all BBC news blogs was outsourced to an external company called Tempero. Moderators working for the company check comments for compliance with the BBC's House Rules, rejecting comments which contain advertising, spam, racism or break the law. Tempero decides whether to approve comments in the first instance, thus performing the 'lion's share of comment moderation' according to an internal BBC document.[118] BBC producers are still expected to read comments which are approved by Tempero as a way of double-checking that they are suitable to be displayed and that they are not 'off topic'—a process called 'second-line moderation'.[119]

Despite this filtering process, BBC journalists who had written blog posts could not possibly read all the comments published on their blog or reply to them. Aaron Scullion noted that 'a particularly popular, high-profile or inflammatory piece might have 1500 comments'.[120] The level of noise in blog comments is undermining the BBC's desire for 'clear, useful, constructive debates' which provide editorial value both to BBC journalists and their audience.[121] 'Incredibly high value discussions' that were to be found on Robert Peston's blog during its early days were swamped 'as soon as business became an emotive issue that people had a stake in'.[122] BBC blogs were suffering from an intractable problem of scale identified by Clay Shirky in 2002 whereby the dynamics of a small community of readers could not be replicated when applied to a much larger audience.[123]

By 2010, the limitations and difficulties of blog comments for the BBC were being aired in public by some of the BBC's most senior journalists. Nick Robinson acknowledged that while he initially 'liked the interactivity' offered by his blog, he discovered that over time 'a huge percentage of comments' 'are frankly just abusive'.[124] He acknowledged that he did not read the comments on his blog as much as he did previously and was looking for a way to 'cut through' the 'white noise' to reach some meaningful dialogue. Similarly, Cricket Correspondent Jonathan Agnew revealed that he had decided to abandon his BBC blog because it had become 'full of appalling comments'.[125] He returned to writing comment pieces on the BBC website. There was speculation that the BBC was 'falling out of love' with blogging.[126]

Comments on blogs and on the BBC website remained a 'live issue' at the BBC.[127] In 2009, Aaron Scullion stated that the BBC needed to act and could not 'live in denial about the fact that the BBC will have a lot of comments'.[128] He said the Corporation ought to find a way to 'represent', 'slice' and display the best comments to audiences. Comments should also be searchable and visualised in an interesting manner. But progress was slow. There were sensitivities to accusations of censorship in light of the BBC's public funding, and while the BBC recognised that publishing lots of comments did not necessarily improve the organisation's journalism, selecting 'the best' comments would lead to editorial dilemmas. Who would select comments? On what grounds would they be selected? And would there be a backlash against those selections? One solution allowed website users to recommend comments, a system used by *The Daily Mail* website. At a major media conference in 2010, Matthew Eltringham revealed that the BBC was considering this approach as an option, and it was adopted as part of the BBC's overhaul of its blogging platform in March 2011.[129] Within the Corporation's walls, however, BBC staff were concerned that other media organisations were ahead in their use of comments, and Kevin Anderson's vision of 'news as conversation' and interactivity with the audience remained elusive.[130]

REPORTING WAR AND TERRORISM: BBC PRODUCER STUART HUGHES'S PERSONAL BLOG

Alfred Hermida notes that not all of the blogs launched as part of the BBC blog trial were news and journalism blogs.[131] Only about 13 of the 43 blogs were primarily outlets for news and current affairs, and the BBC's use of blogs to cover war and terrorism has been fairly sporadic. Interestingly, the BBC had an example of how a defence blog might work in the form of Stuart

Hughes's chronicle of his time in Iraq, although it was a personal blog which was hosted on Blogger, not on the BBC website.

Then BBC Defence and Security Producer Hughes was part of a team sent to cover the impending US-led invasion of Iraq in February 2003. He started Blog from Northern Iraq as a way of keeping in touch with friends and family back in the UK and did not view it as a form of journalism at first: 'I wasn't looking to become a blogger or keep a blog; I was looking for a way to keep a diary that other people could access'.[132]

Prior to being seriously injured in a landmine explosion in April 2003, Hughes provided a 'behind-the-scenes' insight into the work of the BBC as it covered the northern advance of the invasion of Iraq. He posted photos, audio and links to other websites on his blog. It was 'an addition' to his BBC work: a 'scrapbook for all the stuff that falls on the floor when you're working'.[133] By the end of March, Hughes's blog had featured in a number of press articles including *The Guardian* and the *Washington Post*. Hughes' awareness of a wider audience did change what he wrote, but he said there was no interference from his employers in the early years: 'I self-censored to an extent but I didn't feel the BBC was watching over my shoulder'. He did not believe 'BBC managers really understood what blogs were about':

> By the time they cottoned on to the fact I was expressing my own personal opinions on a blog I'd had my accident—and I think they thought it unwise to add insult to injury by complaining about it! I've never sought permission from my BBC bosses over my blog—nor have they asked for it.[134]

After Hughes had recovered from his landmine accident, he returned to blogging about his life covering the news for the BBC. He chronicled stints in Washington, Iran and Spain, commenting on the aftermath of the Madrid train bombing in March 2004. One post revealed that while working 20-hour days, blogging was a secondary part of Hughes's agenda:

> I had planned to give regular updates on developments here in Madrid . . . but since I arrived just keeping up with the demands of my 'real' job has been tough enough.[135]

In June 2004, Hughes claimed to have broken the news that the handover of Iraqi sovereignty would be brought forward to 30 June.[136] While he was filing material for the BBC's main news outlets, he 'bashed out a couple of lines onto the blog' probably beating other news organisations to the story.[137] Technology website Boing Boing claimed that this was a sign of how news would be broken in the future.[138] Hughes himself was sceptical:

> The interesting thing about the 'scoop' is that some people are seeing it as an example of how blogs can break news first. That's only half true. I

only got the story in the first place because I'm a journalist with a traditional news organisation—albeit one with my own personal blog which
allows me to flash stories as quickly as the big boys.[139]

Hughes was never approached by anybody at the BBC asking him to move
the blog onto the BBC website.[140] He was blogging long before the BBC
began the blog trial and if he had been approached it is not certain he would
have accepted. He enjoyed the freedom of feeling he could write whatever
he wanted and decided to wind up the blog when he realised BBC managers were 'taking more of an interest'.[141] In 2006, Editorial Policy had contacted him with reference to the new editorial guidelines which had been
drawn up regarding personal blogs kept by BBC journalists.[142] He felt that
he might risk disciplinary action for discussing issues in the news on his blog;
Beyond Northern Iraq came to an end after his colleague, Alan Johnston,
was released from captivity in Gaza in 2007.

Hughes's blog was very much an exception, and although he demonstrated how a BBC blog might cover defence and security, BBC journalists
covering these topics have been reluctant to take up the blogging mantle for
the Corporation.

REPORTING WAR AND TERRORISM: BBC REPORTERS' LOGS AND DIARIES

BBC journalists have written reporters' diaries for BBC News online. These
'reporters' logs' appear to have been influenced by the blogging format,
evident in the style of short updates from reporters on a daily basis, the use
of the word *log* and the way they are occasionally referred to inside the Corporation as 'blogs'. One of the earliest and most significant in this subject
area was a group reporters' log covering the invasion of Iraq in March and
April 2003.[143] BBC foreign correspondents who were embedded with British
and US units, were stationed in the region or were based in other parts of the
world contributed to an 'entire patchwork of blogs' in an attempt to provide
a complete picture of the invasion of Iraq.[144]

Alastair Leithead has kept several diaries for the BBC during embeds
with British military units in Afghanistan.[145] Writing long after Pete Clifton,
then Editor of BBC News Interactive, had banned frivolous uses of the word
blog on the BBC website, Leithead nevertheless began an entry in November
2006 from Helmand province with the following words:

> I'm writing this blog outside an Afghan National Police checkpoint,
> bolstered up by British forces for another night.

These reporters' diaries are similar to blogs in the way they tell the personal
story of the journalist on a daily basis as well as relating news to the audi-

ence. However, they lack many other features which often appear on blogs, particularly the opportunity to engage with the audience and Leithead's diary was not an ongoing project, only covering one week in November. Mark Urban has been updating a dedicated War and Peace blog in his role as *Newsnight*'s Diplomatic Editor, but his posts have tended to be similar to the analysis pieces that he was already writing for the BBC website.

(NOT) REPORTING WAR AND TERRORISM: WHY DEFENCE AND SECURITY CORRESPONDENTS HAVE NOT BECOME BBC BLOGGERS

A number of news correspondents have so far not taken up possible opportunities to write a regular, dedicated BBC blog about defence or security issues. In November 2008, Defence Correspondent Caroline Wyatt discussed setting up a blog with Fiona Anderson at the BBC's College of Journalism.[146] Anderson was encouraging women correspondents to blog as she felt 'the predominantly male BBC blogs' did not match her 'experience of the demographic out in the wider blogosphere'.[147] She had previously approached Wyatt when the latter became Defence Correspondent in October 2007. Then, Wyatt said she 'couldn't possibly do a blog' because she had 'nothing to blog about at that stage'.[148] The following year, she felt writing a blog 'would be a really interesting thing to do' and saw the potential to provide a space where she could build 'a sense of personal connection':

> I think you could build up a good rapport with the audience—people in the military, parents, families of people serving. A blog would give them the opportunity to respond to the stories that we're doing.[149]

Despite this vision Wyatt was not persuaded to pursue Anderson's suggestion any further. For Wyatt, a blog should offer something different from television and radio output. It should also be honest. She feels military matters are often 'too sensitive, too raw or too controversial' and reporting them relied on background briefings and off-the-record conversations. In her opinion, a blog would have to be disingenuous if it were not to compromise her contacts:

> I just think that you couldn't probably be honest enough in what you thought . . . because you would probably lose all of your contacts . . . they'd be worried that they talk to you [and] that goes straight on your blog.

Rob Watson, the Defence and Security Correspondent for the World Service, shared Wyatt's concern. He felt he could not have lunch with a military source and then go and blog about it.[150]

The perceived and real reticence of the Ministry of Defence to share information, both for operational and political purposes, as well as policies which prohibit employees from speaking directly to the press 'on-the-record' undoubtedly contribute to the difficulties facing a blogging journalist.[151] Wyatt cites information from military briefings as potentially excellent material for a blog, for example, but notes that they are usually 'on background' and cannot be published:

> So what do you blog about it? Do you say: 'Well, that was a fascinating briefing but I can't tell you about it'. Or do you say: 'I believe . . .', or 'defence sources say . . .'? Then you disguise the source so much you don't know who it came from and then it's not credible.

Frank Gardner, the BBC's Security Correspondent, has also turned down the opportunity to write a blog for the BBC. He identifies a clash between the culture of blogging and the importance of remaining impartial as a BBC journalist:

> It's hard to a do a blog properly without putting your opinions in. And when we start putting our own subjective opinions in then we lay ourselves open to all sorts of accusations of bias.[152]

Gardner's main reason for refusing a blog, however, was time. He says he would only be able to blog on 'quiet days' and 'the time people really want to read blogs is when you are flat out covering Mumbai or Somali pirates'.[153] 'It would be a disaster'; 'it's better just not to start a blog than doing it half-heartedly'. Wyatt notes that it 'takes a lot' to blog properly and was concerned about having to spend half the day defending blog posts in lieu of carrying out other work.[154]

Middle East Editor Jeremy Bowen has wanted to write a blog for the BBC for some time. Initially, he said there were concerns at the BBC about it being 'hijacked by interest groups and people with very strong views'.[155] In 2009, he believed these had largely been resolved but that he and the BBC had 'not got our act together to do it'. Two years later, he said the blog was 'finally sanctioned' but various BBC parties with an interest in the project had been caught up in some 'big news stories'.[156] In the context of a busy start to 2011, during which he had covered major political upheaval across the Middle East and North Africa, Bowen also remained concerned that 'doing it properly' would require devoting time that was not currently available. The project remains 'on the back burner'.

It is worth noting that these defence and security correspondents are positions filled by journalists with years of experience. One correspondent wondered whether the reason why there were not more BBC blogs in this area is because he and his colleagues were 'too old'.[157] They have established working patterns and primarily came into the BBC as broadcasters. They see blogging as a potentially burdensome extension of their existing work for radio, television and the BBC website, and they have developed an understanding of blogs that includes a cultural element. For them, blogging is not merely a publishing tool. It comes with certain expectations in terms of style, tone, content and regularity, to which they do not feel they can currently adhere as BBC journalists covering defence and security. It is possible that a future generation of war and security correspondents might view blogging differently, more in keeping with Business Editor Robert Peston who claims his blog 'gives shape' to his journalism.[158]

REPORTING WAR AND TERRORISM: TWITTER AND MICROBLOGGING

The brevity of Twitter has also encouraged more journalists to become 'bloggers'. The format lowers the amount of content which journalists are expected to produce, and Twitter accounts can be easily updated by text message on a mobile phone. It is increasingly being adopted by BBC journalists to deliver short news updates online. Laura Kuenssberg was the first officially sanctioned BBC correspondent to use Twitter as a reporting tool in her role as Political Correspondent.[159] Official accounts are usually marked by having 'BBC' in the Twitter account title and have the same editorial procedure as 'live broadcasting', whereby tweets are checked by senior editors as they are published.[160] The BBC's editorial guidance for Twitter often reflected previous advice on online publishing such as running tweets past 'a second pair of eyes'[161] and imploring journalists to ask themselves the question, 'Would I be comfortable saying this on Radio 5 Live?'.[162]

One of the first significant uses of Twitter by a foreign correspondent at the BBC was from Thailand by Alastair Leithead in May 2010. Reporting on antigovernment protests in the capital, Bangkok, the Asia Correspondent said he initially started using Twitter as a way of keeping track of what was happening on the ground. By following photographers, fellow journalists and colleagues he 'knew' and 'respected', Leithead had an idea of what was occurring in other parts of the city in real time. 'When something happened or the atmospherics changed in a particular place', Leithead would be alerted via Twitter, and he could travel with his cameraman to capture the story.[163] Leithead also contributed to the flow of information among journalists on the ground by reporting what he was seeing. His Twitter feed subsequently gained a much larger audience after the BBC promoted it on television. In one tweet, Leithead reported that he had just seen a 'black shirt' protester shooting at the Army.[164] Leithead said that particular news line was 'really important' to disseminate as 'there were very few pictures or first hand reports of protesters shooting at the soldiers'.[165]

By the beginning of the uprisings in the Middle East and North Africa in 2011, the practice of providing live streams of information on Twitter about major news stories was becoming widespread. Twitter was facilitating the publication of news material online at speed and journalists from a number of news organisations were tweeting live updates during the Arab Spring.[166] For the BBC, Producer Jonathan Hallam even provided Twitter updates from close to the battle of Sirte during the struggle for the control of Libya. His tweets were incorporated into the BBC's live page coverage of the conflict.[167]

The key role played by digital media and social networking sites in telling the story of the Arab Spring and BBC journalists' personal experience of using the microblogging site increased the Corporation's awareness of the importance of Twitter within the media industry. When BBC correspondent Adam Mynott tweeted about a Tunisian militia searching his hotel in Tunis, the BBC news desk began receiving inquiries from rival news organisations. Perhaps most importantly, critics argued that Middle East Editor Jeremy Bowen had 'lost out' on a scoop to Christiane Amanpour after the ABC correspondent broke news lines on Twitter from an exclusive joint interview with the then embattled leader of Libya, Muammar Gaddafi.[168] While Bowen prepared a package for the BBC's radio and TV news bulletins, the interview became known as 'ABC's scoop' thanks to Amanpour's engagement on Twitter. BBC journalists and editors played down the incident noting that the *6 O'Clock News* has far more viewers—4 to 5 million—than many journalists have followers on Twitter. Bowen nevertheless started a Twitter account soon afterwards, and the incident was mentioned by the Director of Global News, Peter Horrocks, at a BBC Social Media Summit a few months later.

REPORTING WAR AND TERRORISM: PROGRAMME BLOGS AND 'LIVE BLOGGING'

In addition to individual blogs and Twitter accounts, the BBC has experimented with other blogging formats which are more fully explored in Chapters 6 and 7. The *World Have Your Say* blog provides a space for the audience to discuss issues around war and terrorism. Although blogging is not the only factor in their decision to pursue this participative approach to journalism, it does help facilitate wider audience involvement and feedback.

The BBC also started using 'live text commentary', which is akin to 'live blogging', to cover major news and sports events. The format draws on the blogging genre by delivering the news in short, time-stamped updates and by displaying the most recent material at the top of a webpage. Live text commentary is regularly used in situations where there is a continuous stream of new material available; it offers a way for journalists to display significant quantities of information on one page from a variety of sources. The Mumbai attacks in November 2008 represented a major development in the use of the format in the context of reporting an ongoing terror attack. Live text commentary has also been adopted by the BBC to cover Prime Minister's questions in the UK; elections in the US (2008), Israel (2009), Afghanistan (2009) and the UK (2010); the Moscow Airport bombing (2011); and significant political crises such as those in Egypt and Libya (2011).

BBC NEWS BLOGS ARE DEAD, LONG LIVE BLOGGING THE NEWS

By the end of 2010, nearly a decade since Giles Wilson and Nick Robinson first began experimenting with the use of blogs to cover news online, the BBC Blog Network had expanded to 209 blogs. Giles Wilson believes that blogging has established itself as 'a central part of our coverage on any given story'.[169] The BBC's blogs moved to a new format in 2011 which aggregates the content of a BBC correspondent on a single webpage. These 'correspondent pages' also incorporate the Twitter feeds of BBC correspondents.

The BBC has not always been entirely comfortable with the term *blog*, and the move to 'correspondent pages' suggests the term will quietly disappear from the BBC's news offering, but the legacy of blogging remains fundamental. It appears that news and information online will continue to be organised around the personalities of individual journalists, while reporters will also present news 'live' to an online audience in streams of short updates complementing longer-form reporting. The aspiration to encourage the participation of the audience in news, one of the driving forces behind the adoption of the format,[170] also remains an important feature of the BBC's journalism.

The development of blogging at the BBC was a protracted process and several key stages can be identified. In the first stage, innovation was driven from the bottom up and at the periphery of the organisation by individuals with the support of a few key senior editors and managers. Experiments with personal blogging, workblogging, blog-like formats for news output and participatory media projects demonstrated the value of blogging, but the BBC decided it needed a coherent Corporation-wide approach to blogs. The second stage of the process was the development of a pan-BBC blog trial which began to take shape in 2005. There were numerous tensions to resolve in light of the blog trial's cross-departmental nature and differing conceptions of how the BBC could successfully adopt the blogging format. When it was launched in March 2006, the blog trial included a steering group to oversee new blogs and, in BBC News, a blog team to oversee journalists' copy.

A third stage explored the limits of the BBC's blogging project as it encountered technical and editorial challenges. The technical difficulties which culminated in the strangulation of the BBC's blogs by spam in 2007 were solved by technology upgrades in April 2008 and March 2009. Editorially, a BBC blog was never going to be 'something written off the top of a reporter's head',[171] and tensions existed between the BBC's efforts to offer 'authentic' blogs while remaining true to the BBC's commitment to impartiality. It was a balance which was regulated by the application of the BBC's existing editorial standards and practices to the blogging format.

Indeed, where weaknesses have been exposed or perceived by critics, the BBC has responded by reemphasising the Corporation's commitment to editorial rigour on blogs. The BBC's reporters' blogs thus look both ways. On one hand they offer unique news content 'delivering additional context, analysis and insight'[172] and have helped change the BBC's attitudes to stories and their relationship with the audience. At the same time, however, the Director-General described a blog post as a 'fact-checked' piece of 'broadcast journalism' overseen by a 'senior editorial manager'.[173] The BBC's reporters' blogs are regarded as a way of enhancing the authority of their journalists and showcasing their expertise on the Web. The personal voice and informal tone of the BBC's senior blogging journalists are deemed to reinforce the quality and values of the BBC's institutional brand.

This chapter has also demonstrated that the extent to which BBC reporters and correspondents have used the blogging format to cover war and terrorism has been limited compared with other areas of news and sport. There have been a number of online ventures which have drawn on the blogging format in the field of defence and security. In 2003, BBC correspondents contributed to a multiauthored 'reporters' log' to cover the Iraq war, and since then BBC journalists have often kept online diaries or reporters' logs. Alastair Leithead has written several of these while embedded with military units in Afghanistan and Jeremy Bowen wrote a blog-style diary during the conflict in Gaza in 2009. Defence and Security Producer Stuart Hughes started his own personal blog outside of the BBC, while Robin Lustig and Mark Urban cover defence and security issues on their BBC blogs, the former as part of his work for *World Tonight*, the latter since June 2008 as Defence and Diplomatic Editor for *Newsnight*. A number of BBC correspondents, however, have been asked to write blogs by BBC management, but have refused on the grounds of the sensitivity of their beat, their adherence to the BBC's values and particularly the time commitment of updating a blog regularly. Future BBC defence and security correspondents might view blogging differently, more in keeping with Nick Robinson and Robert Peston, who have used their blogs to 'give shape' to their journalism.

Microblogging on platforms such as Twitter also reduces the expectation to provide substantial quantities of content while offering correspondents more focused and relevant interactions. Twitter has undoubtedly come to be regarded as an important aspect of the BBC's online offering. By 2012, the BBC's main news account—@BBCBreaking—had more than 4 million followers and the statistics from Twitter accounts of individual BBC journalists are monitored on internal dashboards. A number of the BBC's foreign correspondents have started updating Twitter accounts as a way of disseminating short news updates online including Alastair Leithead from Thailand; Security Correspondent Frank Gardner, who began tweeting in November 2010; and Middle East Editor Jeremy Bowen since May 2011.

World Affairs Producer Stuart Hughes also uses a Twitter account to regularly break defence and security stories—a development perhaps foretold by the use of his personal blog to report breaking news from Iraq in 2004. The provision of Twitter updates from conflict zones and in the aftermath of terror attacks remains a technical challenge, but global connectivity continues to improve and the provision of short immediate fragments of news delivered in a microblogging format will undoubtedly be an aspect of future war and terror reporting.

At a peak of interest in blogs at the BBC, Giles Wilson's asserted that they should not be seen as a 'panacea': 'they're great at what they do but they're not magic'.[174] In particular, the BBC's reporters' blogs have failed to realise Kevin Anderson's vision of 'news as conversation'. The final stage in the process was a retreat from using blogs as a 'conversational' tool to conduct a 'dialogue' with the audience. Although Robert Peston says he has benefited from the feedback on his blog, he and other BBC journalists rarely reply to comments and do not have time to read them all. Cricket Correspondent Jonathan Agnew says he abandoned his BBC blog because of the 'appalling comments' he was receiving. In part, blog comments simply do not scale when applied to the BBC's large audiences for blogs. In 2009, Aaron Scullion believed the Corporation needed to improve the value of comments both for the BBC's journalists and their audiences but argued that it was 'not feasible, in most instances, to do the level of interactivity that people expect of us'.[175] Eighteen months later, then Assistant Editor for News blogs Alan Connor wondered whether the media business had reached 'the end of stage one of the comment experiment in news'.[176] Whatever the limitations of online comments, however, abandoning them altogether does not appear to be an option for the BBC—a publicly funded Corporation with a mandate to represent the views of the nation and increasingly, the world. In 2011, the BBC adopted a new approach which distributes comments more widely across the website, introduces ratings for comments and includes a feature for showcasing 'the best' comments as chosen by BBC editors.

This chapter has focused on reporters' blogs, but blogs which are relevant to news output have evolved into four main forms at the BBC—individual correspondent or reporter blogs, the editors' blog, programme blogs and 'live blogging' in the form of live text commentary. The following chapter considers the development of programme blogs as a means of encouraging a more interactive relationship between BBC journalists and their audience.

6 'Can You Teach Granddad How to Dance?'

Involving the Audience on BBC Programme Blogs

Susan Robinson's correspondence with editors in the US in 2005 illustrated that a number of journalists believed journalism was 'now a dialogue rather than a monologue'.[1] Journalists had always received a limited level of feedback from their audience through letters and phone calls, but email communication, reactions on blogs and comments on forums significantly increased the volume of information they received about their journalism. The culture of journalism was already changing prior to the emergence of blogs, but the development of programme blogs at the BBC was an attempt by journalists to help facilitate communication with their audience. In 2008, Anna McGovern, who was working on new blogging proposals at the World Service, said a programme blog was 'not a column' or 'a diary'; it is 'about interacting with your audience in a very direct and rich way'.[2] Blogging opened up a public dialogue with the 'audience', providing journalists working on television and radio programmes with a space to explain decisions and reveal the thinking behind their journalism. It was an exercise in transparency and accountability, an attempt to establish a basis of trust.[3] A blog also offered a way for displaying additional content, promoting TV and radio shows and engaging with new audiences online. Feedback through comments on blogs could become part of the newsgathering process providing case studies, new story suggestions, follow-up coverage and alternative angles.

In 2008, the BBC's College of Journalism identified several programmes which were regarded as pioneering the use of programme blogs: the *PM* programme and its sister programme *iPM* on Radio 4, the BBC's *World Have Your Say* (*WHYS*) programme on the World Service and *Newsnight* broadcast on BBC Two. Using examples from stories concerning war and terrorism this chapter assesses how *Newsnight* and *WHYS* use bloggers in their content and how their journalists use programme blogs. Based on interviews, observations and an analysis of blog content this chapter examines the extent to which the 'people formerly known as the audience'[4] have become involved in the BBC's coverage of conflict and assesses the experience of journalists in audience engagement.

NEWSNIGHT

Background

Newsnight was first broadcast on 30 January 1980. The programme's founding editor, George Carey, felt there was a gap in the news programme market.[5] The aim was to produce a current affairs television programme which made viewers think again by making sense of the day's news stories, explaining current events in detail and holding the powerful to account. In *Uncertain Vision,* Georgina Born argues that this approach meant the programme reconceived impartiality in the 1990s by 'knowingly' acknowledging that their antagonism to power and focus on holding politicians to account necessarily involved 'opportunistic alliances with other interests and agendas'.[6] The show attempted to broaden debate by including marginalised groups and voices to 'widen the representational circle'.[7] In a piece for the BBC website defining the programme's mission in 2005, Editor Peter Barron[8] argued that *Newsnight* was a programme for 'alternative news' that aimed 'always to question the way things are'.[9] One producer describes *Newsnight* as having a slightly more rebellious approach than the BBC's other news programmes and likes 'to poke a bit of fun at the news'.[10] By the time it began a programme blog in 2006, *Newsnight* had an established journalistic brand and an existing audience with expectations of how the programme should be broadcasting.

Incorporating Bloggers in *Newsnight*'s TV Programme: Salam Pax

Previous chapters have demonstrated that the BBC first began to use blogs in their coverage of war and terrorism during the war in Iraq. The introduction to the book started with an overview of the incorporation of Salam Pax's blog into the BBC's journalism. The Baghdad Blogger collaborated with Guardian Films to produce a series of short documentaries which were aired on *Newsnight.* The first of these was shown in July 2003, and 19 were shown up to 2007.[11] The films were about 12 minutes in length and offered snapshots of life in Iraq as the country's residents struggled to maintain their everyday lives in the midst of the invasion and the subsequent insurgency. The blogger provided *Newsnight* with 'a way of doing eyewitness pieces from Iraq'.[12] The films won the Royal Television Society award for innovation in 2005. The judges said the series of films 'took us to places and people in Iraq which could not be reached by other coverage'.[13]

Salam Pax's incorporation into *Newsnight*'s coverage was initially an alliance of the amateur and the professional; an example of what the editor of *The Guardian,* Alan Rusbridger, has described as the 'mutualisation' of journalism.[14] Citing a series of films for the 1997 General Election in which '"ordinary people"' authored films, former *Newsnight* Editor George

Entwistle believes the Salam Pax films were 'not a departure in terms of the general grammar of Newsnight'.[15] The blogger's continued involvement, however, meant that his status as an 'amateur' was quickly undermined. Previously critical of the traditional media on his blog, Salam Pax had nevertheless begun to act as a freelance journalist and media pundit.[16] He continued to contribute to *Newsnight*'s content, writing a blog post in 2008 and appearing on the programme's 'Review' segment to discuss a BBC and HBO film about Saddam Hussein.[17] *Newsnight* continued to refer to Pax, regardless of his substantial experience in traditional journalism by 2008, as the 'Baghdad Blogger'.

The inclusion of Iraqi bloggers in *Newsnight*'s content was exceptional rather than representative of *Newsnight*'s approach to coverage of conflict. There were few notable uses of bloggers to cover the war in Afghanistan, and blogs were not incorporated into *Newsnight*'s coverage of the conflict in Gaza studied in Chapter 8, except for a passing mention in a feature about the 'media war'. It is also apparent that in the field of defence and security, bloggers do not yet appear to have become media pundits to the same extent as several high-profile political bloggers. *Newsnight* has interviewed several political 'bloggers' such as Paul Staines (Guido Fawkes), Iain Dale and Arianna Huffington.

The *Newsnight* Programme Blog: 'Talk About Newsnight' and 'From the Web Team'

Paul Mason and Peter Barron pioneered the use of blogs at *Newsnight*. The previous chapter discussed how Paul Mason's *Newsnight* blog for the G8 summit in 2005 was one of the catalysts for the development of blogging at the BBC. At the end of July 2006, Paul Mason handed over his blog to the *Newsnight* Web team, and the blog was relaunched. Rather than being Mason's personal blog, it became Talk About Newsnight, a group blog for *Newsnight* journalists which included posts from various members of the programme team. The Web team began providing details of what was coming up on the programme, and they were also responsible for organising 'online feedback' and making the blog more interactive.[18] On 19 June 2008, there was another evolution of *Newsnight*'s blog offering. Michael Crick, Peter Barron, Mark Urban and Paul Mason[19] began updating individual blogs.[20] The changes also gave *Newsnight* journalists updating the website their own dedicated blog—'From the Web Team'.

Occasionally, *Newsnight* allowed people from outside the BBC to contribute blog posts. For several weeks in March and April 2007, Salam Pax hosted a segment on the blog titled A Window on Iraq. It included several contributions from Ahmad, a Baghdad student, who posted audio entries and two video pieces by British Padres serving in Basra. *Newsnight* aimed to use these posts 'to gain some perspective on the situation across the country'.[21]

The Audience and Agenda Setting

Initially, the *Newsnight* programme blog was not used as a way of involving the audience in the news agenda. Blog posts written by the Web team in 2006 simply provided a short introduction to the items that *Newsnight* was intending to cover on the programme that evening. They were usually published at around 18h00. Blog commenters were invited to offer their thoughts and opinions on the subjects in the programme, and it provided a place for viewers to respond to the output on television. Only rarely was it evident that their views had any impact on *Newsnight*'s running order.

From October 2007, *Newsnight* made a more concerted effort to include the audience in the news-making decision process by offering blog readers and subscribers to a *Newsnight* email the opportunity to have a say in the construction of the programme. Editor Peter Barron had the idea for this 'experiment in audience participation' after returning from a blogging conference. Each day the Web team would publish an email on the programme blog which previously had been circulated by the duty output editor to *Newsnight* journalists. The email detailed potential stories for the evening's programme, and by placing it on the blog *Newsnight* was inviting its audience to participate in deciding the running order. Peter Barron was 'pleased' with the first day of the experiment.[22] He noted that the team had included a 'cancer story' as a result of a comment on the blog which highlighted the publication of a World Cancer Research Fund report.[23]

Barron believed that asking a community of viewers who engaged with the blog and the daily email for their views on *Newsnight*'s coverage was 'entirely appropriate' on the grounds that they were probably 'diehard viewers'.[24] Several blog commenters welcomed the opportunity to participate, offering suggestions and praising *Newsnight* for an 'excellent idea':[25]

> Wow! We have an interactive Newsnight. There are so many channels that let the viewer decide what they want to see, but it's the first time I've seen it done for a news programme, and I love it.[26]

In part, Peter Barron viewed sharing *Newsnight*'s prospects as an exercise in transparency, and ultimately, the programme's journalists retained their gatekeeping role.[27] On the first day of the experiment, Barron informed blog readers that the following day, *Newsnight* would be showing 'a long film from Mark Urban in Pakistan whether you like it or not'.[28] For the most part, commenters on the blog merely helped journalists 'form' existing 'thoughts' about what to cover on the programme. The following prospects post from March 2008 was typical of the nature of the invitation to participate:

> We have a live interview with Tony Blair's former Chief of Staff Jonathan Powell. We plan a wider discussion as well. Which guests would you like on and what questions would you like asked? . . . Iraq will dominate

the programme, but what other suggestions have you got? We should clearly keep an eye on the National Security plan to be announced in the Commons, and the McCann story.[29]

Moreover, some blog readers did not have any desire to participate in the editorial process. In response to a blog post in November 2007 asking what viewers wanted to see on the programme, 'Rich' said that he paid his 'licence fee to watch' *Newsnight*. He hoped that it was 'produced by a team of experts' and did not want be 'solicited for questions to put to your guest' or asked for 'advice on what issues to discuss in your programme'.[30] Similarly, 'Hannah' wanted 'experts' to select the news on her behalf based on their 'wider knowledge of current affairs':

> I don't want my news to be interactive; I want it to be accurate, considered, balanced, and give me an indication of the important issues affecting the world today. I don't want news that simply panders to the agenda of those who shout loudest. I don't have time to keep up with everything and make decisions about what is and is not important; that's your job![31]

Despite these concerns, Barron's experiment became a regular feature of the *Newsnight* programme blog until October 2008. There was a period of 13 months between October 2008 and November 2009 during which the Web team reverted to simply writing one blog post informing readers what was going to be on the programme. But from November 2009, the *Newsnight* Web team started updating the blog twice every day again: once in the morning, outlining the initial prospects for the show, and then later in the afternoon, when the details of the programme had been finalised.

Interacting with *Newsnight*'s Audience

Editor Peter Barron had also established blogging at *Newsnight* in an attempt to 'get people to have a deeper relationship with the programme'.[32] In conjunction with the website, Barron hoped the blog would develop into 'a community' where fans of the programme could 'spend time', 'talk to each other' and 'complain about things'. It was notable that his successor, Peter Rippon, was the editor responsible for the award-winning *PM* blog and the listener-led *iPM* programme on Radio 4. He was also keen to develop *Newsnight*'s online offering. In an interview for *The Independent*, Rippon talked about 'exploring online options' for *Newsnight* and 'carrying on the conversation' online.[33]

Newsnight's level of engagement on the blog, however, has been mixed. In August 2006, one of their first experiments solicited the audience's views on an alleged airline plot. On that occasion, *Newsnight* asked blog readers for their thoughts on the news that British security services had thwarted a plot to explode as many as 10 transatlantic flights. The post posed five questions:

1. how close were we to 'mass murder on an unimaginable scale'?
2. have the security services found any explosives?
3. why did the police decide to swoop today?
4. were they members of a foreign terror cell or were they British-born?
5. how will this change the way we fly? Will we have to get used to flying without any hand luggage?[34]

Newsnight asked blog readers if they had any answers to those questions or had further questions they would like the team to investigate. The post had attracted more than 150 comments by the time Paul Mason replied to the blog commenters several days later. Mason noted that there was 'a wave of cynicism' among blog commenters around the level of the terrorist threat and the ability of the police to thwart potential plots. Some commenters also alleged the airline plot was staged by the British state. As a consequence, reporter Michael Crick was tasked with exploring 'the mood of scepticism that is tangibly out there' while the rest of the *Newsnight* team attempted to stand up further details about the story.[35]

The reaction to the story on the blog was mentioned in *Newsnight*'s television programme on 11 August 2006, prompting one commenter to argue that debate on the blog had been misrepresented:

Tonight's program[me] gave the impression that all contributors were very sceptical about the very existence of a terrorist threat and even managed to cite 'Norman' who thought the real terrorists are the Israelis. Frankly, it seems more reasonable to be suspicious of the BBC and its motives than the existence of terrorists in our midst.[36]

Another commenter nevertheless applauded 'Newsnight for their scepticism and bravery in reporting what has been said on the blog'.[37]

Very occasionally *Newsnight* used the blog as a way of encouraging interaction between the audience and their journalists or a guest and the audience. In March 2007, Diplomatic Editor Mark Urban hosted a question and answer session about US strategy in Iraq.[38] After a special 25-minute report asking what went wrong in Iraq, Urban agreed to reply to commenters writing 10 personal responses to questions posted on the *Newsnight* blog covering a variety of issues. Notably, one of Urban's replies included a reference to a portion of an interview with Sir Jeremy Greenstock[39] that Urban 'did not have time to broadcast'.[40]

A little more than a year later, *Newsnight* invited blog commenters to submit questions to then foreign secretary David Miliband in relation to a speech he was delivering on the future of a low-carbon economy in Britain.[41] The programme blog received 175 comments in two days. During a live interview, Jeremy Paxman put questions submitted by 'Graham Nick-son' and 'LarsonsMum' to the foreign secretary.[42] Miliband also agreed to answer nine further questions from *Newsnight* commenters directly on the blog briefly, addressing the UK government's humanitarian response to a cyclone in Burma, its support for a two-state solution to the Israel–Palestine conflict and its policy towards Zimbabwe.

In both these instances, engagement with blog commenters meant a broader range of topics were covered by *Newsnight* than would have been possible with only the television programme as an outlet. Mark Urban was able to tackle issues that he had not chosen to incorporate in his original film about Iraq, while Miliband answered questions that were unrelated to climate change. A few blog commenters were also afforded limited direct access to Urban and Miliband. Urban personally addressed questions raised by his report on the programme blog, while Jeremy Paxman was seen to be bringing the concerns of the audience to David Miliband live on air.

These interactions, however, remained exceptional rather than regular features of the Newsnight blog. Occasionally blog posts revealed that *Newsnight* appreciated the feedback it received through emails and comments on the blog as a consequence of its regular pleas for the audience to tell journalists what they thought about a news story. Barron thanked commenters for their story suggestions in October 2007[43] and mentioned several regular commenters in a blog post in April 2008.[44] *Newsnight*'s Web team would also sometimes express their gratitude to contributors for their thoughts and comments. But more often, *Newsnight* allows its blog commenters to debate among themselves, and the Web team rarely replies individually to those who have posted on the blog.

Promoting *Newsnight* and Reaching Online Audiences

After the blog became From the Web Team in June 2008, engagement with the *Newsnight* blog community became more sporadic. In March 2009, *Newsnight* producer Ian Lacey said the blog was not currently being used to foster a community as the Web team did not have the 'time and resources' to engage with people.[45] He said *Newsnight* would be considering how to increase the level of interactivity on the blog but described the main role of the Web team as 'promoting Newsnight's content on other parts of the BBC website and the Web'. Another *Newsnight* producer said that the blog was 'not really being used to engage' with people and that the programme viewed blogging more as 'a broadcast format than a forum'.[46]

The *Newsnight* blog has been used extensively to preview and promote what is coming up in the TV programme. Exclusives, special programmes and reports have often been highlighted on the *Newsnight* blog in advance such as a Gordon Corera exclusive on al-Qaida in November 2006,[47] Alastair Leithead's 'powerful film' from Afghanistan in May 2007[48] or a special programme on the 'war on terror' on 11 September 2008.[49] Sometimes, the blog was used as a teaser for content which was due to be revealed on the TV programme. In June 2010, the Web team told blog readers, 'We are leading on a Newsnight exclusive tonight. It's under wraps at the moment so you'll have to tune in at 10.30pm for details'.[50]

By 2008, *Newsnight*'s blog previews had become more multimedia often including edited clips of longer reports. The 'war on terror' programme preview mentioned earlier, for example, included a 52-second clip of an interview with US Army General David Petraeus. This was a way of extending the reach of *Newsnight*'s content enabling those people who never watch the TV transmission to access the programme online. *Newsnight* was also keen to direct traffic to its own blog and website from the BBC's homepage.[51] At a time when it is perceived that consumers want their media 'on demand' and are less interested in appointment television,[52] it enabled *Newsnight* to be 'a journalistic brand that is open all hours'.[53]

In February 2009, *Newsnight* created a Twitter account—@BBCNewsnight.[54] The majority of tweets are promotional directing followers to *Newsnight* reports or online content. The *Newsnight* account also tends to retweet Twitter users who mention *Newsnight* in a tweet rather than retweeting other information. *Newsnight* do occasionally use the account in a more interactive capacity to try to contact people for the programme, to solicit views on news topics or to reply to basic queries. But *Newsnight*'s Web team producer, Sarah McDermott, describes the main purpose of Twitter as for promoting *Newsnight*'s website content and for informing online audiences what will appear on the television programme.[55] The nature of the 'conversation' around the news is limited.

The End of the Experiment with Audience Participation?

Newsnight was one of the pioneers of the use of blogs to cover war and terrorism, extensively incorporating Salam Pax into its coverage and attempting several experiments in audience participation. In 2011, former Editor Peter Barron recalled that 'back in 2005 and 2006 things were changing so fast that it was possible to try out a new thing almost every week'.[56] The *Newsnight* programme blog and Twitter feed, however, have retreated from experiments in audience participation since the programme blog was relaunched in 2008. Although *Newsnight* appears to appreciate the feedback it receives from blog comments, emails and Twitter users, it has retained a firm grasp on its gatekeeping role. The *Newsnight* audience has been solicited to help journalists 'form' their 'thoughts', but only occasionally are they seen to directly influence the journalism which is produced.[57] *Newsnight* has undoubtedly changed the way it 'relates to the audience'[58] and regular commenters appear to appreciate a platform to discuss the *Newsnight* programme with other viewers even if individual replies to comments are rare.[59] However, the extent to which *Newsnight* has developed a 'swift and informal' conversation between the audience and the programme is limited.[60]

An internal video feature for the BBC College Journalism website claimed that *Newsnight* 'has consistently pushed at the boundaries between traditional and new journalism'.[61] But pushing at one boundary meant pulling at the other; while some *Newsnight* staff members such as Paul Mason and Peter Barron were enthusiastic about the integration of audience contributions into *Newsnight*'s content, others such as presenter Jeremy Paxman have expressed scepticism about its value.[62] Barron's successor as editor, Peter Rippon, was responsible for involving the audience in BBC content at *PM* and *iPM* on Radio 4, but admits he has mixed views about blogging:

> I was very excited about it when I started, expecting to have a sophisticated conversation, but a lot of the commenting has been disappointing. It's more like school yard graffiti.[63]

Commenters on the *Newsnight* blog have also been divided over *Newsnight*'s experiments in participatory journalism. Although a number of commenters valued the opportunity to contribute, several others argued that including User Generated Content or asking for the thoughts of the audience represented the 'dumbing down' of a serious news programme. Having paid the licence fee, some commenters wanted journalists to set the agenda, make news selections and formulate questions to the powerful on their behalf. Not all *Newsnight* viewers believed the 'journalist's job' was to 'ensure every opportunity to have "amateur" input at every stage of the process'.[64]

There are also practical considerations which forestall greater audience participation and interactivity. *Newsnight* producers working for the Web team say they do not currently have the time or the resources to foster and pursue engagement with a community of *Newsnight* viewers who comment on the blog. Problems of scale and the level of audience feedback are long standing and were identified as early as 2004 at the BBC in research conducted by Neil Thurman.[65] Currently the promotion of *Newsnight* as a journalistic brand both internally and externally takes precedent over actively encouraging audience participation. Although *Newsnight*'s latest experiment with Twitter is 'a really useful way to find contributors' and 'get feedback from opinion formers', 'on the whole', *Newsnight* uses Twitter to 'tell people about things that are coming up on the programme' and 'to promote the content' on the website.[66]

In 2011, Editor Peter Rippon described *Newsnight*'s 'focus in the digital space' as 'getting more eyes on our content beyond the linear programme on BBC Two at 2230'.[67] He said that this had been the 'main push over the past two years, rather than using new technology for interactivity'.[68] One *Newsnight* producer suggested that interactivity was simply not part of the organisational 'mindset': 'The BBC doesn't do interactivity. It's a broadcaster. It's like trying to teach a granddad how to dance'.[69] Interactivity was never part of *Newsnight*'s initial remit and adding that element to their existing output proved problematic. The *WHYS* programme, however, used audience involvement as a starting point.

WORLD HAVE YOUR SAY

Background

WHYS was first broadcast on the BBC World Service on 31 October 2005, but the programme aimed to be more than merely an hour-long radio show broadcast every weekday at 18h00.[70] Ambitiously, Editor Mark Sandell hoped to facilitate a '24-hour' 'global conversation' around the news by producing a programme 'where the audience genuinely sets the agenda'.[71] In his previous job at Radio 5 Live, Sandell had helped pioneer audience-centred programmes by devising Nicky Campbell's phone-in show, which sought to broaden both the news agenda and the range of voices that were broadcast on BBC radio. He brought the philosophy to WHYS when World Service bosses commissioned him to start a new, more interactive radio programme.[72] A programme blog soon became a central part of WHYS's operation, enabling listeners to suggest topics for the radio programme and debate issues long after they had been aired. Unlike Newsnight, WHYS was building audience expectations almost entirely from scratch when it began a programme blog. It was notable that the first WHYS team included journalists recruited from outside the World Service and with experience in online journalism such as Kevin Anderson, Ros Atkins, Fiona Crack and Peter van Dyk.[73]

Setting the Agenda for the Show

Usually the WHYS radio programme hosts a daily debate about one or more topics which are capturing the world's attention. In the morning, the WHYS team scours the blogosphere, news aggregator sites, Twitter and the 'most read' or 'most emailed' sections of media websites in an attempt to ascertain what the world is talking about. The team also considers suggestions left by commenters on the WHYS blog. To encourage further contributions, one journalist writes a blog post highlighting several stories which are candidates to be aired on the day's show. At about noon, WHYS journalists meet to choose which topic the audience is most likely to want to hear discussed on air. Members of the audience have taken part in these meetings, either on the phone or in person when the show has been on the road. In May 2009, WHYS also started providing Twitter updates on the progress of the meeting inviting Twitter users to help the team decide what to discuss. Once one or more topics have been chosen, the team formulates a key question or questions to provoke debate.

Although the WHYS team, therefore, still retains the final say over which topic is aired on the radio, Mark Sandell's aim is that the audience should tell his journalists what they want to talk about rather than journalists asking the audience for their thoughts on a predetermined news story or issue. Ascertaining the top story of the day is not a case of looking at the front pages of other news media or consulting the BBC's central news diary but of asking what issue is encouraging discussion or capturing people's imagination. Sandell described *WHYS* as 'the least-tied [programme] to a centralised news agenda within the World Service'.[74]

Producer Kate McGough said this approach meant that some 'big stories' which were reported by the rest of the media were not always covered by *WHYS*. She noted that the Thailand airport protests at the end of November 2008 did not attract a 'huge groundswell of opinion', while people were not always keen to discuss 'massive headline news' in Zimbabwe.[75] On other occasions, Mark Sandell observed that interaction with the *WHYS* community has led the team to cover stories before other BBC programmes and media outlets such as the cartoon controversy which erupted after a Danish newspaper published satirical images of the prophet Muhammad.[76] The *WHYS* audience has also posed some 'really uncomfortable questions',[77] leading to programmes discussing whether the death penalty is essential to combating terrorism and the extent to which Muslims are responsible for solving Islamist terrorism.

Placing listeners and blog readers at the heart of the editorial process shifted the emphasis of the role of the journalist from one of direct interrogator to facilitator of the audience's questions. In November 2008, *WHYS* invited a Taliban spokesperson onto the show to discuss the war in Afghanistan. The show was prerecorded, and Security Correspondent Frank Gardner was invited to pose questions to the Taliban spokesperson. But Gardner did not formulate the questions himself; he asked the questions that *WHYS* listeners had posted on the programme blog. The audience was driving the agenda; Gardner was acting as an experienced mediator of their concerns. He noted that there were some 'hard questions to be put to the Taliban—not from me as a journalist but from the listeners': 'it was extraordinary to be putting together an ex-US Serviceman who had fought in Afghanistan and putting his question directly to his enemy'.[78]

Programme Making with Blogs: Search and Verification

The main task of BBC producers on *WHYS* is finding guests to appear on the radio show. After the noon editorial meeting, a member of the *WHYS* team writes another blog post informing blog readers of the topic they have decided to discuss. This post usually highlights issues around the question or asks blog readers for contributions on the subject. A daily email is also sent out to several thousand subscribers informing them which topic will be debated.[79]

Editor Mark Sandell differentiates his programme from others on the World Service: 'we set out to TRY to reflect what people are talking about and leave the "wider context" to our sister programmes like Newshour'.[80] Although *WHYS* does not exclude official representatives or what might be described as 'powerful' sources altogether, the programme aims to provide a platform for '"real people"'.[81] The team discovered that blogs were a useful way to track down this sort of potential guest. Several WHYS journalists said that they used Google blog search to find bloggers who were talking about the topic of the day. They also bookmarked useful blogs on a range of issues so they could come back to them in the future. Deputy Editor Chloe Tilley, for example, found a blog written by the mother of a soldier fighting in Iraq. The mother contributed to one of WHYS's programmes, and Tilley regularly visited her blog afterwards when she thought the mother's perspective might be relevant to a WHYS programme.

During the Mumbai attacks in November 2008, WHYS journalists were also experimenting with using Twitter to find guests. Kate McGough said it was the first time the team had made significant use of Twitter, noting that one producer was tasked with focussing on finding voices from the micro-blogging service.[82] Tom Hagler said he was particularly 'impressed' by the ability to find people tweeting about Mumbai by searching a hashtag. In a breaking news situation in the future, he said he would use the microblog-ging service 'straight away'.[83] Twitter has since become a regular way for WHYS to find guests to appear on the show. The programme updates a Twitter account—@BBC_WHYS—and asks Twitter users if they would like to contribute.[84]

Once bloggers or Twitter users are contacted, the nature of WHYS means that the verification process is relatively straightforward. The programme aims to reflect a range of personal perspectives on a topic or an issue, not to provide a factual account of an event. Producers are trying to contact people who have an opinion on an issue and are 'not mad' or 'going to defame or libel anyone'.[85] They are 'checking that they are sensible people who you can put live on a radio programme'.[86] Kate McGough noted that although she could not always guarantee that people who said they were in Mumbai were actually there, 'it didn't really matter too much because we wanted people's responses to the events from around the world as well'.[87] WHYS journalists are looking for a range of voices in order to encourage a lively debate and fulfil the BBC's commitment to impartiality. WHYS does not, therefore, always ascertain whether guests are 'telling the truth' before they put them on air. Nevertheless, Chloe Tilley emphasised that the programme's presenter is responsible for ensuring that guests do not offer their opinions as facts: 'If we need facts, we speak to experts and it is also the presenters job to ensure if an opinion is presented as a fact, that is quickly rectified'.[88]

In addition to searching other blogs, the WHYS team receive text mes-sages, phone calls and comments on their own blog. Blog comments and tweets directed at WHYS's Twitter account will be read out on air by the presenter or a producer, but some people will also be invited to elaborate on air as part of the radio programme. Ros Atkins said tapping into WHYS's community in this manner is 'revelatory'.[89] Rather than 'phone-bashing' and 'going through contacts', it enabled him as a programme maker to contact people who 'he might never otherwise have reached'.

Building a Community around Transparency and Impartiality

Mark Sandell believes the blog is fundamental to the programme's aim of building a community around *WHYS*. Initially the blog was a vehicle for transparency and openness. A move in this direction had already been occurring for some time as a consequence of broader changes in media culture and at the BBC had been accelerated by the fall-out from the Hutton Report in 2004. Director of Global News Richard Sambrook, who was embroiled in the dispute with the government, said he came to realise that

> lifting the lid on our journalism . . . showing people why we make the decisions we make and how we work and why we work in certain ways is as important to the product as the outcome itself in retaining people's trust.[90]

Sandell had a similar mindset. He described his experience at Radio 5 Live as a good training ground in transparency where journalists were not afraid to admit mistakes and explain decisions. The *WHYS* blog provided an outlet for Sandell and the team to communicate similar concerns with their audience. As editor, Sandell wrote blog posts where he admitted he had made the wrong editorial decision or apologised for a show with severe technical problems. Ros Atkins said he had written posts explaining why he had decided to present the show in a certain way. Both Atkins and Sandell respond regularly to comments written by blog commenters, particularly on posts of this nature. Atkins believes this approach 'transforms' *WHYS*'s relationship with its audience.[91]

This level of engagement with the audience required a considerable effort on the part of *WHYS*. Blogging required a shift in tone in order to 'open yourself into a dialogue', talking with the audience rather than at them. Ros Atkins implied that this was different from the tone he adopts when he is presenting other World Service programmes such as *World Today* and *Newshour*. Atkins also believes it is 'difficult to overstate the commitment of having a blog': 'it's a lot of little actions. It's checking every ten minutes to see if there is a comment directed at you and taking two minutes to respond'.[92] He describes constantly updating it as a 'labour of love'.

A recognisable community began to emerge around the blog, and the *WHYS* team continued to develop the blog as 'a market square where everyone meets to talk about the news'.[93] Regular contributors emerged as keystones of the community, driving stories and programmes by posting on the *WHYS* blog. One was Lubna, a medical student living in Baghdad. In March 2008, she wrote on the blog that she had almost been killed by a roadside bomb in the Iraqi capital. Within 10 minutes, Ros Atkins claimed that other regulars on the blog were sending her messages and talking about general issues around Iraq. 'Before you know it', Atkins said, 'you could be looking at a programme that you wouldn't otherwise have thought about doing'.[94]

Nevertheless, Sandell said managing the community around the blog had thrown up unexpected difficulties, and he described his oversight of the blog as necessarily strict. When the blog first went live, Sandell said he was willing to accept almost any comments on the blog. By 2008, *WHYS* had developed a set of house rules for contributors to the blog encouraging short relevant comments. The aim was to engender conversation rather than provide a space for irrelevant musings or essays on a topic: '[w]hat we won't publish are comments that would work better on the op-ed pages of a newspaper than on a blog'.[95] Through not publishing comments, encouraging relevant comment and Sandell's interventions on the blog, *WHYS* attempted to train the community contributing to the blog.[96]

Pushing the Boundaries of Audience Involvement and Impartiality at the BBC

WHYS has tested both the BBC's written and unwritten rules on a number of occasions. For Helen Boaden, the BBC's Director of News, the Neil Report in 2004 reaffirmed that BBC editors would remain the gatekeepers of news.[97] By involving the audience in the editorial process and encouraging his journalists to take their lead from the audience's conversations, Mark Sandell challenged the traditional BBC formula.

A particularly bold experiment in the empowerment of the audience was the decision to allow 'trusted members of the community' to moderate the *WHYS* blog.[98] Permitting external moderation by people outside the BBC had practical benefits for *WHYS* because it meant the blog could be continuously updated even when the team in London was asleep. Mark Sandell retained overall control, but he took a significant risk; the head of World Service News and Current Affairs was reluctant to allow this form of external moderation on the grounds that it would amount to temporarily handing over control of an aspect of BBC content.[99] At first, the project was relatively successful, but Sandell came under additional '(understandable) pressure from people higher up the BBC food chain' when he was forced to ban one of the moderators who '"lost it" one night'.[100] *WHYS* persevered with a number of committed external moderators but Sandell began to spend too much time sorting out 'boring bickering' and 'petty disputes'. He felt the blog had become intimidating for visitors, and he regretfully ended the experiment after 'a blindingly idiotic dispute' saw a 'valued newcomer . . . clear off in disgust'.

WHYS also decided that the BBC's commitment to impartiality did not mean that their journalists should be seen as 'anonymous dead hand figures who are moderating the debate'.[101] Impartiality at the BBC was born out of the reporting of the General Strike in 1926.[102] Since then, BBC journalists have not been allowed to reveal their biases or political persuasions in their journalism. Traditionally, this has also extended to all aspects of a BBC journalist's personal views. Even though some BBC correspondents and radio presenters have become well-known personalities, most BBC journalists in the past have revealed very little about their interests, and some BBC journalists and producers have been essentially invisible to the general public. The BBC News website, for example, still does not always identify the BBC journalist who has written a news story.

Areas of the BBC, however, have been experimenting with a more personal approach. Influenced by an article by Jeff Jarvis in which he argued that journalists would gain more trust if they were open about their political affiliations,[103] Ros Atkins asked the *WHYS* audience, 'Would you trust the even-handedness of WHYS more if, for instance, you knew if I voted for Tony Blair or not?'[104] 'Tongue-in-cheek', Atkins said he had suggested revealing his political standpoint on the blog to *WHYS*'s 'most senior news editor' earlier in the week: 'she allowed herself a wry smile before saying, "[D]on't you dare".'[105] Atkins did not publish his voting preferences but nevertheless encouraged the *WHYS* team to write blog posts about their previous work, their media consumption and their news interests.[106] He was working on the principle that if journalists gave 'a little bit' of themselves, they would receive valuable contributions from members of the audience in return.[107]

'We've Heard the News from the BBC, Now it's Your Turn'[108]

WHYS's radio programme operates within the parameters of finding different voices to offer their experiences, opinions and points of view on events or issues. The networked nature of blogging allows journalists to tap into online communities discussing topics or issues. Unlike Mark Fishman's justice reporter in *Manufacturing the News*, *WHYS* journalists consciously avoid relying on a narrow source base built on 'a knowledge of how the social world is bureaucratically organised', whereby 'information sources almost exclusively have a formally organised, governmental bureaucratic character'.[109] In order to access alternative sources, the *WHYS* team make use of blogs because they provide an easily accessible, searchable and ultimately powerful 'map' of relevant voices for any topic.[110] Blogs, Twitter and, more generally, global communications technology afford journalists usually working from London simultaneous virtual 'geographic proximity' to sources all over the world.[111]

In addition to searching for the blogs of others, participating in the blogosphere helps *WHYS* draw interested parties to their blog who subsequently contribute to the journalistic process. The *WHYS* blog is a 'market square', albeit it one hosted by the BBC, where people can discuss news issues, suggest topics for debate and set the news agenda. From the conversations on the blog, *WHYS* has built, encouraged and harnessed a community.[112] To aid this process the blog provides the audience with a window on *WHYS* journalists and their journalism; a place where journalists explain news decisions, admit mistakes and describe how they produce the programme.

WHYS's approach to news is an example of an attempt to shift the emphasis of journalistic authority[113] and, thus, the basis of trust between the journalist and the audience. Mark Sandell is adamant that journalists do not have 'ownership of the news' and that they should not present listeners with an 'All-Bran' news diet, whereby journalists tell their audience what is good for them and expect them to consume it.[114] Sandell believes journalists should respond to the interests of the audience, while Ros Atkins thinks journalists need to adopt a different, more open tone in order to engage them in dialogue.[115] Rather than being based on knowledge, *WHYS*'s authority is founded on openness, transparency, impartiality and *WHYS*'s commitment to facilitating debate and discussion around the news from a variety of perspectives. *WHYS* aims to act as 'the facilitator rather than the gatekeeper'.[116]

WHYS's vision has not always sat comfortably alongside the rest of the World Service which in many places retains a much more traditional journalistic culture based on knowledge and expertise. Sandell believed 'there was a real sense of antipathy towards WHYS from within the building about what on earth "ordinary" people have to add to the news agenda',[117] while Tilley suggested that the difference between *WHYS* and other parts of the BBC was 'massive'.[118] In part, this is because the World Service Newsroom, for example, and *WHYS* have different goals. Whereas the former is primarily seeking to establish a factual narrative of an event, the latter is more interested in the debate and conversation around that event. But Mark Sandell argues that these are not mutually exclusive noting that *WHYS*'s network of contributors and contacts altered the World Service Newsroom's approach during the coup in Thailand and the 50th anniversary in 2006 of the Hungarian Uprising.[119] In 2008, he was nevertheless concerned that *WHYS*'s approach had not influenced the World Service sufficiently:

At the moment we're still at a stage where anything audience related comes through us, when in fact it should be in the DNA of every single programme here. What better source to bring to your news meetings than what you think the audience is talking about and engaged in.

There are limitations to *WHYS*'s efforts to reconfigure the relationship between the journalist and the audience. It is important to note that *WHYS* journalists only engage with a 'community' of at most thousands based on the blog, the daily email and *WHYS*'s Twitter account rather than the radio programme's 'audience' of millions.[120] The extent of the dialogue between journalists and their audience is thus limited; the conversation around the news primarily occurs among members of the audience. *WHYS* journalists also retain control of the programme and the blog. Journalists take issues suggested by the audience and 'frame questions' to provoke debate.[121] The parameters of both the programme and the blog are still set by journalists, and they ultimately take the final decision about the issues which are discussed on the radio programme. The limits of audience empowerment were perhaps discovered most clearly when an experiment allowing external moderators from the audience to manage *WHYS*'s online community ultimately proved unworkable due to the 'idiocy' of a minority.[122] *WHYS* does not, therefore, abdicate responsibility for BBC journalism nor does it sit outside the BBC's values. However, its emphasis on allowing the audience to drive the agenda and its commitment to openness and transparency has challenged the journalistic culture of the BBC particularly within the context of the World Service.

COMPARING *NEWSNIGHT* AND *WORLD HAVE YOUR SAY*

A programme blog was believed to be a useful way to encourage bloggers and other individuals to contribute to BBC journalism. *WHYS* incorporates bloggers and commenters into its programmes far more often than *Newsnight*. In part, this is because the programmes have different aims. The former is a phone-in programme broadcasting opinion and reaction to news events from around the world. Bloggers are regularly contacted by the *WHYS* team because they can be relatively easily located using simple Web searches. *WHYS* is particularly interested in reflecting the viewpoints of 'real people', and the blogosphere provides journalists with a map of relevant voices[123] for any topic which they are featuring on the radio programme. The Internet and mobile phone communications technology have also enabled journalists to have virtual 'geographic proximity' to sources all over the world.[124]

Newsnight is broadcast for a UK domestic audience and attempts to provide analysis on the day's top stories. *Newsnight* journalists regularly bid for high-profile politicians, organisational representatives and experts to appear as guests on the show. The tendency to choose sources who are believed to be informed and knowledgeable is mirrored in *Newsnight*'s choice of bloggers. *Newsnight* incorporates bloggers who are deemed to have an authoritative opinion because of their particular experience or position. Salam Pax effectively became an 'expert' on the war in Iraq, and most of the bloggers interviewed on *Newsnight* are part of an emergent media elite whose blogs have become high profile. This is seen more clearly in the area of politics where a number of bloggers have become part of the cadre of media pundits consulted for their opinions on political stories.

Both *Newsnight* and *WHYS* have used programme blogs as a way of extending the reach of their journalistic brands. Rather than being confined to an hour-long radio or television show, a programme blog has allowed journalists to reach new audiences online and encourages listeners and viewers to engage with their broadcast coverage. In a 24/7 media age, a programme blog reaches nontraditional audiences and provides a space for devoted followers to continue conversations about the news and the programme before, during and after a show has been broadcast.

Journalists at *Newsnight* and *WHYS* have invited blog readers to become part of the news production process asking them to suggest topics to cover on the programme, pose questions for guests and provide feedback. *WHYS* also regularly features people who have commented on the blog in their radio programme. In the field of war and terrorism, bloggers and blog commenters have been able to provide their perspectives of conflict through the BBC's programme blogs and suggest angles which might be deemed unusual or particularly controversial such as *Newsnight*'s coverage of the cynical response to the police's interception of an alleged airline plot in 2006 or various debates on *WHYS* around terrorism.

WHYS in particular can be seen as a programme which has attempted to shift the journalistic culture away from a knowledge-based authority towards one established on openness, transparency and the programme's role as host of a moderated debate. *WHYS* acts as a facilitator of discussion, and the blog provides a place where a *WHYS* community can contribute to making a news programme and debate issues in the news. When *WHYS* do have special guests, such as representatives from organisations or 'experts' on the show, they allow callers to speak to them directly and read out comments left on the blog to further debate. *Newsnight* adopts this position more rarely such as the occasion when questions received through blog comments were put directly to the foreign secretary David Miliband.

Newsnight has generally retained its traditional role as gatekeeper of the programme. Blog readers and subscribers can contribute to the process of deciding on the day's news agenda, but it is notable that even when Editor Peter Barron was enthusiastically pursuing this idea, the output editors would still begin by putting up a blog post which highlighted their key issues of the day. At *WHYS*, however, the parameters of the programme established by Editor Mark Sandell mean the audience, or at least an engaged community around the programme, is encouraged to act as the gatekeeper of the programme as far as possible. Sandell implores his journalists to ask themselves what the world is talking about as a starting point for their journalism.

Newsnight encountered more resistance from its audience to its experiments in audience participation than did *WHYS*. First broadcast in 1980, *Newsnight* already had existing audience expectations of the programme. *Newsnight*'s blog and experiments in audience participation were additions to a long-standing appointment television programme whereas *WHYS* was established in 2005 on the basis that audience contributions would drive the programme and with a programme blog placed at the centre of its production process at an early stage. It is notable that although some commenters on the programme blog welcomed *Newsnight*'s experiments in interactivity, others felt it undermined *Newsnight*'s reputation for its analysis of news events. A number of commenters on *Newsnight*'s blog wanted professional journalists to make news judgements on their behalf and did not want to participate in most, or indeed any, of the stages of the news process. *Newsnight*'s journalists were also divided over the value of incorporating audience contributions in their journalism. *Newsnight* consequently retreated from some of its experiments, and then Head of TV News Peter Horrocks suggested that audiences should not 'expect to see a huge amount of UGC [user-generated content] on Newsnight in the future'.[125] Ultimately, *Newsnight*'s current use of their programme blog supports Anna Maria Jönsson and Henrik Örnebring's conclusion that 'direct user involvement in news is minimal' and that interactivity is more often illusory than regularly empowering.[126]

WHYS has more fully explored how far journalists could hand the news over to their audience discovering limitations in the process. Editor Mark Sandell found that the 'idiocy of a minority' scuppered his attempts to allow 'trusted members' of the *WHYS* community to moderate the programme's blog. He also noted that individuals who had become disaffected with the BBC's commenting rules and who had established similar blogs away from *WHYS* had not been particularly successful. Professional journalists still have a role to play even when they are encouraging a news community to own and contribute to the programme as much as possible.[127]

Both programmes also discovered that maintaining a programme blog was a significant commitment of time and resources particularly when it came to engaging with blog commenters. Given the Corporation's substantial audiences it is only meaningful to talk about interaction with a smaller community of viewers and listeners who are particularly interested in a programme. Even then, engaging in 'dialogue' or 'conversation' requires significant commitment over time. Journalists working for *WHYS*, *Newsnight* and other areas of the BBC are being asked both to produce radio and television programmes and interact with the audience. BBC programme makers have said they stay late to respond to audience comments.[128] One journalist who had worked on *WHYS* said she did not read comments left on the programme blog because she was too busy answering the phone and collating material to be broadcast on air.[129] *Newsnight*'s Web team members said they simply did not have the time to engage with people commenting on the blog and that the blog's main purpose was to promote *Newsnight*'s content both within and outside the Corporation.

In 2008, then Communities Editor Tom van Aardt believed that a shift in journalistic culture was taking place across the Corporation: 'we are changing from just broadcasting to actually interacting and having a conversation with the people'.[130] A move towards meaningful dialogue, interactivity and engagement with an audience potentially transforms the journalistic process. The experience of both *WHYS* and *Newsnight*, however, demonstrates that achieving this aim is time-consuming and difficult to achieve for programmes which broadcast to audiences of hundreds of thousands.

In particular, *Newsnight*'s experimentation with a form of journalism which included more audience contributions emphasises the difficulties of grafting new approaches onto old models. The inclusion of the audience was not always popular with *Newsnight* staff, interactivity required substantial input from journalists, and some viewers felt the programme's existing strengths were being sacrificed. Since Editor Peter Barron left the programme in 2008, *Newsnight* has retreated from some of its experiments with audience participation. Barron argues that this should not be viewed as failure, but simply as the nature of experimentation in a 'constantly changing and evolving' medium.[131]

Barron's successor, Peter Rippon, has viewed the 'main focus in the digital space' as increasing *Newsnight*'s audience by offering content online. *Newsnight* currently uses its blog primarily to extend the reach of its journalistic brand and promote its content. In 2011, Rippon said that 'the most interesting interactive area' was through *Newsnight* viewers discussing the programme on Twitter while watching it on television; the emergence of 'dual screening' is making television a virtual 'collective experience'.[132] 'Interactivity', however, is most usually a facilitation of conversations among members of the audience rather than a dialogue between journalists and their audience.

WHYS benefited from being launched in 2005 with a remit to put the audience at the heart of its journalism. The programme views the news as a conversation and conversation as news. *WHYS* journalists believe their approach broadens the news agenda and enables them to harness the journalistic potential of an engaged audience to produce radio programmes. In the context of the World Service, which has based its journalistic reputation on authority, knowledge and expertise, *WHYS*'s more transparent approach did not always sit comfortably with senior editors, and it has pushed at the boundaries of the BBC's journalistic culture. The programme's commitment to openness through a blog tested existing practices around maintaining control of BBC content, the extent to which BBC journalists revealed their personal views and the gatekeeping role of the journalist.

Part IV

7 'Live Blogging' Terror
The BBC's Coverage of the Attacks on Mumbai

Between the 26 and 28 November 2008, the Indian city of Mumbai was the victim of a coordinated terror attack. Ten men aiming to disrupt political reconciliation between India and Pakistan began a campaign of killing which included Indian citizens at Mumbai's main railway station, Indian and foreign guests at two of the city's iconic hotels and Jews at the headquarters of an orthodox Jewish organisation. The attack, which continued for more than 60 hours while Indian security forces undertook room by room clearances of the occupied buildings, left 174 dead and hundreds wounded.[1] India had witnessed more deadly attacks at the hands of militants in the past. In 1993, 257 people had died in 13 bomb blasts across the city and in 2006, 209 people had been killed after seven bombs exploded on a Mumbai train.[2] The attacks in 2008, however, were dubbed 'India's 9/11'—it was recognition that this event had similarly 'mesmerised the world's media'.[3]

So far this book has considered how BBC journalists use blogs as sources of information to inform their journalism and how they responded to the blogging challenge by writing their own blogs, both in the form of reporters' blogs and programme blogs. The final two chapters focus on the consequences of these developments for BBC content. In the first of two case studies, this chapter explores how BBC journalists used a 'live blog' format during the Mumbai attacks as a reporting tool to quickly convey breaking news to an online audience. The chapter explores the extent to which a digitally connected audience contributed to the BBC's online coverage of a major terror attack and whether the live blogging format is facilitating an increase in the representation of nonofficial sources in the news.

The BBC's 'live blog' or live text updates of the Mumbai attacks proved popular both with audiences and industry analysts. The coverage of the Mumbai attacks drew the third-highest number of unique users to the BBC News website in a single day in 2008.[4] On Thursday 27 November the website registered 6.8 million unique users. On both 27 and 28 November the single-most-read webpage on the BBC website was the respective Mumbai live update page.[5] In 2009, the BBC's online coverage received the internet award from the Online News Association for breaking news. The judges described the BBC's 'breaking news blog' as a 'one-stop shop' with a lot of 'primary source information' and praised the live blog 'for being comprehensive, up-to-date and for the way it incorporated social media'.[6]

The Mumbai live pages sparked debate, both internally and externally, about the integration of blogs and particularly Twitter updates into the BBC's coverage of a major news event. Writing in *The Independent,* Tom Sutcliffe argued that the BBC's live updates were 'the apotheosis of citizen journalism, with Mumbai bystanders shoulder to shoulder with BBC staff in bringing the latest news to a world audience'.[7] He described this approach as a 'worrying development' and urged the BBC not to blur 'the boundary between twittering and serious reporting'. Acknowledging, if not accepting, Sutcliffe's criticism, the Editor of the BBC News website, Steve Herrmann, recognised that the BBC was 'still finding out how best to process and relay such information in a fast-moving account'.[8] Reporting the news with a sense of immediacy placed pressure on the BBC's often cautious approach to journalism particularly in the context of a major terror attack. Concerns ranged from the extent to which BBC journalists should fact check the information in rolling updates to the personal security of the guests contacting the BBC while the attack was in progress.

This chapter is based on a mixture of methods. At its heart is a content analysis of the BBC's live updates of the Mumbai attacks providing a picture of which sources of information BBC journalists cited. In order to understand their experience of the 'live blogging' news process, BBC journalists were observed updating the page on 27 November for a period of approximately six hours from 14h00 until 20h00 and interviews were conducted with some of these journalists after the event. Finally, internal documents were accessed which collated some of the BBC's own reflections on its coverage of Mumbai.

Before considering the details of the BBC's live updates pages, it is worth placing it in the context of media coverage of Mumbai and briefly outlining the main events of the 60-hour crisis.

BACKGROUND TO THE MUMBAI ATTACKS

The attack on Mumbai was allegedly planned and directed by 'one of the most powerful militant groups in South Asia'—Lashkar-e-Taiba (LeT).[9] According to Stephen Tankel, the primary aim of the assault was to destabilise relations between India and Pakistan, disrupt the peace process and strengthen the position of hardliners in both countries.[10]

The 10 men responsible for the attacks on Mumbai set sail from the Pakistani city of Karachi and landed in the southern part of the city shortly after 21h00 local time on 26 November 2008. According to the Indian government, two of the gunmen—Mohammed Ajmal Amir Kasab and Ismail Khan—travelled to the Chhatrapati Shivaji Terminus (CST) railway station.[11] They fired indiscriminately on passengers, mostly Indian citizens, and threw hand grenades, killing 58 and injuring 104. Khan was killed at a police road block; Kasab was captured. The latter was the only gunman to survive the attacks.[12]

Two other gunmen, Hafiz Arshad and Naser, travelled to the Leopold Café. They briefly sprayed the café with rifle fire and threw a grenade, killing at least 10 people before running to the Taj Mahal Hotel. Here they joined up with two other militants who had already attacked the hotel.

Shoaib and Javed had entered the main lobby of the Taj Mahal Hotel at 21h38 killing at least 20 people.[13] In conjunction with Arshad and Naser they moved to the sixth floor of the Heritage wing. The hotel was set on fire. Local police cordoned off the hotel area before Indian Marine Commandos arrived on the scene. The following morning, members of India's National Security Guard (NSG) assumed control of the operation to rescue guests trapped inside, many of whom had locked themselves in their rooms. The building was finally cleared almost 60 hours after the gunmen had entered.

At the Oberoi-Trident Hotel, Abdul Rehman Chotta and Fahadullah had begun their killing spree at 22h00 in the main entrance of the Trident wing of the hotel. Moving to the Oberoi wing they attacked the restaurant and detonated two improvised explosive devices before holding guests as hostages in the upper floors. NSG commandos did not clear the hotel until the afternoon of 28 November.

A final pair of gunmen had arrived at Nariman House, a five-storey building belonging to the Chabad Liberation Movement, an orthodox Jewish organisation. At around 22h25, Babar Imran and Nazir began firing, gained access to the building and took several hostages. The police exchanged fire with the gunmen throughout the night and into 27 November. On 28 November, National Security Guard (NSG) commandos were dropped onto the terrace from helicopters. Five hostages, both gunmen and one NSG commando were killed.

The attacks, which left 174 people dead and several hundred wounded,[14] had significant consequences. In India, the security response was widely criticised[15] and diplomatic relations between India and Pakistan were damaged.[16]

MEDIA COVERAGE

The Mumbai crisis unfolded live in real time across Indian and international media outlets. Like their governmental counterparts, the Indian media were heavily criticised for what was regarded as a catalogue of significant failings. An article for the *Christian Science Monitor* highlighted that television coverage showed dead bodies, images of trapped hostages and ongoing commando and police operations. Interviews revealed the locations of hostages at the Taj Mahal Hotel and one station, the article said, also 'aired a telephone conversation with one of the 10 gunmen'.[17]

The security implications were made plain by the Indian government's release of transcripts of mobile phone intercepts apparently showing that the gunmen were communicating with operatives. Abdul Rehman, one of the gunmen at the Oberoi Trident, was informed by an operative that the media had been comparing his actions to 9/11.[18] A second call from an operative confirmed that 'everything is being recorded by the media. Inflict the maximum damage'.[19] In July 2009, BBC *Newsnight* translated a telephone call to a gunman in Nariman house demonstrating that the operatives had detailed information on police positions.[20] Richard Watson, the BBC *Newsnight* correspondent who investigated the attacks for the programme, believed spotters on the ground were more likely to be the source of such detailed information, but Indian police maintained the operatives were using media coverage to help orchestrate the attacks.

Speaking in December 2008, Indian Navy Admiral Sureesh Mehta said there were tactical implications for rescue operations if they were recorded 'minute by minute'.[21] He alleged that live footage was broadcast of the commando drop from helicopters at Nariman house on 28 November, arguing that the gunmen 'were in live contact with their masters, who were telling them what the channels were reporting'. This prompted a formal statement from NDTV in defence of their broadcasting, stating that the TV coverage of the operation in question had been broadcast on NDTV India with a 25-minute delay and on its webstream channel NDTV 24×7 with a 45-minute delay.[22]

The BBC's coverage of Mumbai was not scrutinised as significantly as the Indian media although similar issues might be raised. At 00h10 (GMT) on 27 November, BBC *World News* broadcast an interview with Andreas Liveras, a British businessman who was trapped at the Taj Mahal Hotel. Liveras had already said he was in a salon at the hotel during the interview but was then asked again for his location by the presenter, Matt Frei:

FREI: 'Andreas, where are you right now?'

LIVERAS: 'I'm in the salon in the hotel.'

FREI: 'Right. And you're hiding somewhere?'

LIVERAS: 'No no, we're not hiding. We are locked in here . . .'[23]

This section of the interview was also posted on the BBC website at 01h22[24] and transcribed for a separate online eyewitness piece which was published nine minutes later.[25] At 13h56, the BBC reported that one British national had been killed during the attacks.[26] He was subsequently named as Andreas Liveras.

It is not possible to link the death of Andreas Liveras to the interview, but one BBC journalist at the time described the incident as 'quite worrying'.[27] A senior BBC editor was concerned that the Corporation did not sufficiently consider the security implications of speaking to people who were trapped in the hotels and suggested that the BBC would have been far more cautious if the same event had happened in the UK.[28]

ONLINE MEDIA COVERAGE

This study has previously identified terror attacks as occasions when the 'audience' has contributed significantly to coverage of a news event.[29] The specific circumstances of the Mumbai attacks also favoured the integration of compelling eyewitness accounts. The social and economic background of the majority of the guests staying at two of Mumbai's most expensive hotels meant a number of trapped guests had access to smart mobile phones or BlackBerrys. Although many could not leave their hotel rooms for fear of encountering the gunmen, they were not directly supervised by the militants facilitating opportunities to contact media outlets.

By 2008, the use of blogs and social networking sites in media coverage was no longer unusual. A variety of informal media sites, such as Ground Report and Mahalo, helped provide news information on Mumbai.[30] Mumbai Metblogs, a general blog about life in Mumbai, began to provide updates about the attacks[31] while a blog called Mumbai Help offered useful phone numbers and contact information for concerned friends and relatives.[32] Blogger Manish Vij started a live blog on the Ultrabrown website,[33] as did Arun Shanbhag, a 46-year-old US resident, who was visiting his parents in Mumbai at the time of the attacks.[34] The latter included images Shanbhag had taken of the Leopold Café, the burning Taj Mahal Hotel and commandos landing on the terrace of Nariman House.[35] Flickr images of the streets of Mumbai were also posted by Vinukumar Ranganathan and were used by CNN, the BBC and other major broadcasters.[36] Nevertheless, according to online communities expert, Gaurav Mishra, who monitored online coverage from 'citizen journalists', original first-hand reporting by so-called citizen journalists on blogs, Flickr and YouTube was limited.[37] Mishra described Ranganathan as an exception along with bloggers Amit Varma, Sonia Faleiro, Rahul Bhatia and Arun Shanbhag. Longer online formats were less useful than were microblogging sites such as Twitter, which Mishra believed was 'the best source for real time citizen news on the Mumbai terrorist attacks'.[38]

Twitter proved to be a major player in the coverage of Mumbai. CNN estimated that 80 messages were being uploaded to Twitter via text message every five seconds. Mishra suggested that Twitter was the 'de facto source for on-ground intelligence for mainstream media' and 'citizen journalists on-site in Mumbai' became 'in-demand pundits overnight'.[39] CNN incorporated a number of Twitter messages in a round-up of eyewitness accounts,[40] while the BBC used 22 Twitter updates in its live updates page and as an early warning system for other news lines.

In an attempt to provide news to online audiences as quickly as possible, a number of traditional media organisations, such as *The Guardian,* the *New York Times* and the BBC began 'live blogging' the crisis, aggregating information and providing links to other online sources. The live blog format allowed journalists to provide a rolling account of the latest information from

Mumbai. Using a long-established journalistic technique—attribution—and the power of the hyperlink, journalists could present a lot of information quickly without individually fact checking each detail and retaining the illusion of journalistic authority.

THE BBC'S MUMBAI LIVE UPDATES PAGE

Live updates had been used regularly by the BBC to cover football matches and other sporting events. Although the format has never officially been described as a 'live blog' by the BBC, the short, time-stamped entries and the adoption of an increasingly light-hearted and 'chatty' tone resembled the blogging genre. News events had been covered in a similar style although the tone tended to remain more serious. During the onset of the Iraq war in 2003, the BBC collated short updates from BBC reporters and correspondents covering the US-led invasion.[41] Although they did not have the scope of the Mumbai live updates page, more basic time-stamped updates were also used by the BBC to chronicle the siege of a school in Beslan, Russia in September 2004 and the terror attacks on London in July 2005. Kevin Anderson kept a more explicit 'weblog' of the US election in 2004 which did adopt a more informal approach[42] and two years later, Alfred Hermida was credited with writing the 'first "live event" blog' from a two-day media conference.[43] It was not until 2008, however, that the BBC began using live-event webpages which 'dynamically updated' whereby a BBC website user would no longer have to keep refreshing a Web browser to update the page.[44] This format was trialled during the BBC's coverage of the 2008 Olympics in Beijing and was used between August and November 2008 to report the US presidential election.[45] Because of technical difficulties the BBC's Mumbai coverage did not use the dynamically updating format, but the live updates page was far more ambitious than the BBC's time-stamped coverage of the Beslan school siege or the London bombings. The Mumbai live updates pages represent a significant evolution in the way the BBC reported a major terror attack online.

Steve Herrmann, the BBC News website Editor, came up with the idea of covering the Mumbai attacks using a live updates page at a BBC World News online editorial meeting on 27 November around 08h00.[46] The first shots were fired by gunmen just before 17h00 (GMT) on 26 November, and so the attacks had been in progress for approximately 15 hours already. The live page was started because there was 'almost incessant breaking news',[47] and it was a 'good way' of 'showcasing events as they unfolded, minute by minute'.[48] Steve Herrmann was confident that there would be significant developments during the day[49] and he also had sufficient staff at his disposal even if resources were stretched.[50] The BBC began the live page at 09h15.[51]

THE NEWS PROCESS AND SOURCES OF INFORMATION

During the day, there were usually two journalists working on the updates at BBC News online's world desk. One was tasked with 'writing as much copy as possible' by monitoring radio, TV and wire reports.[52] His focus was the main news lines and his ability to write in shorthand enabled him to quickly transcribe quotes from sources that were broadcast on TV channels, such as the comments of Mumbai blogger Amit Varma to BBC *World News* at 15h20 and Indian Army Officer General Huda to local TV stations at 15h29 on 27 November.[53]

His copy was fed to the second journalist who was responsible for updating the page as well as collecting material from other sources: BBC correspondents, reporters and programmes, the User Generated Content (UGC) hub and comments on blogs and Twitter. The second journalist checked for grammar and spelling mistakes, running a 'second pair of eyes' over updates before they were published and he was also adding images and video content. He had access to wire pictures through a piece of software called Elvis. For audio and video, he could embed material which had already been cut and edited by the BBC's On Demand media team. The two journalists also had support from other areas of the BBC newsroom. A third person on the BBC News world online desk was occasionally sending relevant material to support them, while a South Asia specialist on the UGC hub, Samanthi Dissanayake, was searching for information on blogs, Twitter and social networks like Orkut.[54] The journalists could also call on the services of a colleague working on the South Asia desk in Delhi. She was watching the Indian channel NDTV and emailing the journalists with new information. One of the journalists claimed that this enabled the BBC to beat the wires on news lines[55] and it was recommended that this sort of monitoring should be implemented in future live updates pages concerning foreign news.[56]

Technical Difficulties

At 15h20 on 27 November, the two journalists noticed that they were having difficulties updating the live page. 'Technology is still an issue—it's always an issue', one of the journalists noted.[57] He described the BBC's computer server as 'excruciatingly slow'.[58] He phoned technical support who informed him that it was a BBC-wide problem. In the meantime, he was told that he should try to persevere with the live updates. By 16h00, the two journalists had been unable to publish information on the website for around 35 minutes but were still working on updates which they would save for publication later. According to one of the journalists, the emergency system also failed and technicians had to reboot the server. Although the problem was being gradually resolved, by 18h00 only the updates up to 17h00 had been published; the 'live' page was still about an hour behind undermining journalists' efforts to provide up-to-the-minute news. It was not until 15 minutes later that updates were appearing almost immediately on the BBC webpage.

Editorial Direction and Audience Comment

Earlier in the afternoon on 27 November the journalists working on the desk received a message from BBC editors who had been reviewing the updates. The editors told them to shorten the length of the individual entries, to focus on events which were happening rather than comments and to include more updates from bloggers and tweeters. One of the journalists said he was receiving this sort of direction from Steve Herrmann and Adam Curtis, then Editor of World News online, at regular intervals usually via emails.[59] He noted that at midmorning on 28 November he was probably sent a similar missive to the one he had received the previous afternoon. Editors were particularly keen to incorporate blog and Twitter comments and to make sure updates were no longer than five lines long.

Very brief ad hoc editorial meetings were also held at other points to keep everybody informed and to discuss issues which arose. Notably, on 27 November, meetings were held in response to problems with the BBC's computer server at 17h20 and to discuss coverage of the death of British businessman Andreas Liveras at 18h20.

Attribution, Fact Checking and Verification

The aim of the live text updates page was 'to get information out as quickly as possible' using short 'snippets'.[60] 'Breaking news was a priority', but it had to be held in tension with the 'BBC mantra of always accuracy ahead of speed'.[61] In order to provide information at speed without compromising the BBC's accuracy, all factual claims on the live updates page were reported with the 'usual caveats'. 'Attribution', whereby a journalist acknowledges the source of a piece of information, was 'key'.[62] During the reporting of the Mumbai attacks, attributing information to sources acted as a mechanism which enabled journalists to provide up-to-the-minute updates on the situation without checking all the factual details themselves. There was a shift away from the usual BBC practice of verifying information using two sources and then publishing. Instead, journalists would publish information which would be attributed to a source and would then verify it as more information was received: 'we attribute it and then if it turned out to be wrong you'd put that right—if it turns out in later reports that it's not true'.[63] One of the journalists described the updates as 'a print version of TV rolling news'. He noted that journalists working on the page consequently included 'more conjecture' and reported 'a lot of things that usually you would put in a lot of calls to firm up'.

Certain information was nevertheless still thoroughly checked before it was published even if it was attributed to a source. The death of British businessman Andreas Liveras was flagged up as a news flash, but it was not published in the live updates until a journalist on another desk had verified the information, shouting 'that's confirmed' to inform the journalists on the live updates page. Although fact checking the content of what sources had to say was limited, there was general checking of the updates for spelling and grammar and potentially harmful material—both to the audience and the BBC. Updates were read and reread before they were published. The spelling of words or individuals was occasionally verified by copying and pasting the relevant word into a Google search bar and checking the spelling against websites which came up in Google's search results. It is notable that for these minor details the journalist felt able to rely on what has been described as the 'algorithmic authority' of a search engine.[64]

The system of having two journalists meant that usually updates were read by both journalists, although staffing changed overnight. At 18h20 on 27 November the two journalists who had been running the live updates came to the end of their shift. The BBC News online world desk has fewer resources overnight, and the two-man team was replaced by one journalist who was tasked with continuing the live updates. He was told to 'scale it [the live updates] down a bit',[65] and the content analysis following shows that the pages were consequently more sparsely updated. Interestingly, the incoming journalist asked whether he should be following the BBC practice of not reporting information without having confirmation from two sources or whether he should just quote the source.[66] As there was nobody else allocated to double-check his updates, he asked a nearby journalist, who was also writing the main online articles, to 'sub over his shoulder'.

The two journalists who had contributed to the page on the 27 November returned the following day. One arrived around 05h00 and proceeded to update the page by himself. The second journalist arrived at 08h00. They handed over to the night team on the evening of the 28 November. On the morning of 29 November a different team took over but the updates were halted after an entry at 10h04 by which time the immediate crisis in Mumbai had finally come to an end.

Experience and Learning on the Job

The use of live updates in news was in its infancy and the journalists working on the Mumbai page had limited experience of covering a news event in this manner. One of the journalists updating the page had worked with Politics Reporter Justin Parkinson on a live event page for the US election. A freelancer from the UK desk was completely new to the genre. There was a particular lack of experience in using information posted on Twitter. One of the journalists working on the updates admitted that he knew very little about Twitter before Mumbai.[67] Another, who arrived for the late shift on the 27 November, was informed by a colleague that he should be incorporating tweets in the live updates page, but he had never used the microblogging website.[68] These journalists, however, could call on the expertise of Samanthi Dissanayake, who was working on the UGC hub. She was feeding tweets and blogs through to the journalists to be incorporated on the page.[69] An internal document outlining advice and guidance for live update pages produced in the aftermath of the attacks nevertheless noted that it would be helpful for journalists updating live pages to spend some time fully understanding the purpose and functions of Twitter.[70]

ANALYSING THE CONTENT OF THE BBC'S MUMBAI LIVE UPDATES

Observing BBC journalists at work provided an insight into the experience and challenges of live blogging a major terror attack, but how did this format affect the content of the BBC's online journalism? In order to ascertain which sources journalists incorporated and the extent to which blogs and digital sources were integrated into the BBC's coverage a content analysis was performed. The BBC's live updates pages on the Mumbai crisis for 27, 28 and 29 November were accessed online.[71] Several basic features of each update were recorded including the format of each update (text, image, video), the length of the text in each update (excluding links) and whether the update linked to other websites.

The live updates pages were then coded for sources of information at two levels.[72] First, the sources cited by the BBC were coded as individuals, organisations or groups of people based on the primary reason they had been cited in the live updates—whether written or assumed. A 'source' was interpreted in its 'journalistic sense' to mean the origins of a piece of information used by a journalist.[73] Twelve categories were identified:[74]

1. BBC Correspondents, Reporters and Outlets
2. Indian Media
3. Foreign Media and Other Media
4. News Agencies
5. Official Sources—Indian
6. Official Sources—Foreign
7. Experts
8. Eyewitnesses
9. Directly Connected Commenters
10. Audience Commenters
11. Gunmen/Alleged Attackers
12. Other

An 'audience commenter' was defined as an individual who apparently had no direct involvement in the news story. This included expatriates who may have been deeply affected by the story but were not directly involved.

Directly connected commenters were defined as either being in Mumbai and thus were at, or near, the scene of the event or were relatives or as other individuals directly involved in the story who were not acting in an official capacity for a government or business. 'Eyewitness' was defined as an individual who had seen or heard the attacks taking place or who was trapped in the hotels or at Nariman House. As with all coding of this nature, problems were encountered when classifying sources.[75]

The sources cited by the BBC were also coded separately for mentions of a digital or online source of communication (email, blog, Twitter etc). This two-level approach to coding avoids a weakness of previous research which has conflated the 'individual or organisational source' and the 'source of communication'. For example, it would be a mistake to code the inclusion of a 'Twitter user' in the BBC's updates as an alternative or nonofficial source when Twitter has been adopted by a wide range of official media and nonofficial actors. This method also means the nature of the digital communication sources cited by the BBC can be assessed in relation to the first level of coding, revealing which actors were using digital and online means to communicate with the BBC.

MULTIMEDIA AND HYPERTEXT? TEXT, AUDIO, VIDEO AND LINKS

For all the multimedia potential of the online medium, the live blogging format was primarily used by the BBC to deliver significant quantities of written information and 'live *text* updates' is an accurate description of the nature of the BBC's web offering on these pages. On 27 November, BBC journalists wrote 119 individual updates, at an average of 50 words for each update and 6,008 words in total. On 28 November, they wrote 144 updates, at an average of 41 words, totalling 5,862 words. Including the 17 updates written on the 29 November before the live updates page was halted at 10h04, BBC journalists contributed 280 updates from start to finish, totalling 12,284 words at an average length of 44 words for each update. The paradox of the live blogging news genre is that while short individual updates inevitably provide minimal context, taken together, a live updates page produces a far more detailed raw account of a news event than do the BBC's online news articles, which usually contain between 500 and 1,000 words.

Although text dominated the live updates pages other forms of media content were present. There were three pictures on 27 November page, eight on 28 November and one, at the top of the page, on 29 November. All of these photos were attributed to news agencies with the exception of one photo on 28 November which had been taken by Vinukumar Ranganathan ('Vinu'), a blogger and Flickr user. In addition to these main news photos, small icons were used to indicate whether an update had been written by a BBC correspondent or had been sourced electronically from an email, a blog or via Twitter.

Table 7.1   27–29 November 2008: Links to webpages in
BBC live updates

	Number Cited	% of Total Links
BBC Video	9	31
BBC Article	1	3
Twitter	15	53
Blogs	3	10
Flickr	1	3
Total	29	100

The live updates pages also included audio and video content, although the former was very limited with only one piece of embedded audio appearing on the pages for the duration of the attacks. It was a recorded interview with British lawyer Mark Abell who described escaping the Oberoi Trident after being trapped in his hotel room on 28 November. The BBC made more use of video content. Videos which were embedded on the live updates page were also hosted on separate BBC webpages. Those used by the live updates team were initially embedded on the page but were subsequently replaced with a link to the page hosting the video content. This was deemed necessary by the BBC to ensure the page loaded quickly and, on 27 November at least, to combat difficulties with the BBC server.[76] Thus, on 27 November, no video remains embedded on the page, but there are six links to video content hosted on other BBC pages. On 28 November, three video clips remain embedded on the page and there are three links to videos hosted elsewhere on the BBC website. No video content was present on 29 November page.

The BBC did not generally link out to other sources of information. In contrast to *The Guardian*'s live online coverage, where 46 links appear between 08h15 and 18h30 on 27 November alone,[77] the BBC's live update pages include only 29 links across the 49-hour period.[78] Slightly more than a third of the links were to the BBC's own content: nine to video content hosted on other BBC pages and one more to a BBC online article documenting eyewitness accounts. There were three links to websites described as blogs by the BBC, one to the photostream of Flickr user Vinukumar Ranganathan and fifteen links to the microblogs of Twitter users. These results are displayed in Table 7.1.

ATTRIBUTED SOURCING

The content analysis demonstrated that the BBC's journalism was very clearly sourced. The 280 updates contained explicit or implicit references to 410 sources of information ranging from the BBC's own reporting, media sources and news agencies, government officials, eyewitnesses, bloggers and Twitter users. There were only a handful of updates—nine in total—where there was no mention of a source of information. One of the BBC journalists working on the updates said that the information contained in these updates would have been confirmed by two separate news agency sources.[79] In other words, apart from updates sourced to BBC reporting there were only nine other occasions when all the information in an update was so firmly established that the BBC would have been content to take full responsibility for the information conveyed.

BBC journalists said they attributed extensively in order to cope with the volume of material without verifying every detail prior to publication. According to Herbert Gans, attribution enables a journalist to not 'have to worry about reliability (and validity), the assumption being that once a story is "sourced" their responsibility is fulfilled and audiences must decide whether the source is credible'.[80] Rather than verifying information by accessing it from two different sources and then publishing it, BBC journalists published first using attribution and then sought to verify from other sources. This is a feature of live rolling TV news, but in the online environment this approach was pioneered by bloggers. In these circumstances, the audience is invited to be part of a collaborative partnership in an unfolding news situation in which they could expect corrections and clarifications. In the networked journalism model they are also expected to make a greater contribution to the reporting of an event.

SOURCES OF INFORMATION

The BBC did include the contributions of the people formerly known as the audience in their live updates coverage of the Mumbai attacks, but it is clear that the Corporation still relied heavily on its traditional newsgathering machine, the reporting of other media organisations, 'official sources' and 'authorised knowers' (Tables 7.2–7.5). The journalists working on the live updates pages cited BBC colleagues—correspondents, reporters or other BBC programmes—as sources of information on 68 (18%) occasions in total. News agencies and traditional media organisations also featured strongly; they were cited 43 (10%) and 79 (20%) times, respectively, by the BBC. Indian government, state government, police, military, security officials and company officials accounted for 61 (15%) sources and their foreign counterparts, 67 (16%; Table 7.5).

Nonofficial sources of information were represented in the BBC's live updates of the Mumbai attacks. The alleged attackers or gunmen were cited as a source of information during the live update pages but never by the BBC directly. Interestingly, Lashkar-e-Taiba—the organisation allegedly responsible for the attacks—is mentioned only once in the context of a Press Trust of India news agency report stating that a member of the organisation had

Table 7.2   27 November 2008: Sources cited in BBC live updates

	Category	Number Cited	% of Total Sources
1.	BBC Correspondents, Reporters and Outlets	30	15
2.	Indian Media	25	13
3.	News Agencies	25	13
4.	Foreign Media and Other Media	7	4
5.	Official Sources—Indian	28	14
6.	Official Sources—Foreign	31	15
7.	Expert	9	5
8.	Eyewitness	13 (3 email)	7
9.	Directly Connected Commenter	3 (1 blog)	2
10.	Audience Commenter	11 (2 blog, 9 Twitter)	6
11.	Gunmen/Alleged Attackers	5 (1 email)	3
12.	Other	5	3
	Total	192	100

Table 7.3   28 November 2008: Sources cited in BBC live updates

	Category	Number Cited	% of Total Sources
1.	BBC Correspondents, Reporters and Outlets	34	17
2.	Indian Media	35	17
3.	News Agencies	13	7
4.	Foreign Media and Other Media	12	6
5.	Official Sources—Indian	28	14
6.	Official Sources—Foreign	36	17
7.	Expert	6	3
8.	Eyewitness	9 (2 blog)	5
9.	Directly Connected Commenter	6 (3 email, 2 Twitter)	3
10.	Audience Commenter	10 (4 email, 6 Twitter)	5
11.	Gunmen/Alleged Attackers	1	1
12.	Other	9	5
	Total	199	100

Table 7.4　29 November 2008: Sources cited in BBC live updates

	Category	Number Cited	% of Total Sources
1.	BBC Correspondents, Reporters and Outlets	4	21
3.	News Agencies	5	26
5.	Official Sources—Indian	5	26
9.	Directly Connected Commenter	1 (1 Twitter)	5
10.	Audience Commenter	4 (4 Twitter)	21
	Total	**19**	**100***

*Rounding accounts for missing 1%.

Table 7.5　27–29 November 2008: Sources cited in BBC live updates

	Category	Number Cited	% of Total Sources
1.	BBC Correspondents, Reporters and Outlets	68	18
2.	Indian Media	60	15
3.	News Agencies	43	10
4.	Foreign Media and Other Media	19	5
5.	Official Sources—Indian	61	15
6.	Official Sources—Foreign	67	16
7.	Expert	15	4
8.	Eyewitness	22 (3 email, 2 blog)	5
9.	Directly Connected Commenter	10 (3 email, 1 blog, 3 Twitter)	2
10.	Audience Commenter	25 (4 email, 2 blog, 19 Twitter)	6
11.	Gunmen/Alleged Attackers	6	1
12.	Other	14	3
	Total	**410**	**100**

been captured.[81] Eyewitnesses were cited on 22 occasions representing 5% of the total cited and directly connected commenters were cited 10 (2%) times (Table 7.5). These accounts were sourced by a variety of means including emails to the BBC, on Twitter, through BBC reporting and in other media and news agency reporting.

In contrast, 'audience comment' was entirely facilitated through electronic communication from emails, on blogs or via Twitter. Journalists were able to use the ease of communication in a networked society to provide

Table 7.6 27–29 November 2008: Digital sources cited in BBC live updates

	Number Cited	% of Total Cited
Email to BBC	10	26
Blogs	5	13
Twitter	22	58
Flickr	1	3
Total	38	100

'colour' from the 'former audience' at speed. The 'people formerly known as the audience'[82]—'audience commenters'—accounted for 6% of the sources cited. During the crisis, senior BBC editors were encouraging journalists to include more contributions from the audience and to source information through Twitter and blogs in order to provide a more rounded picture of the event and to access the 'public mood'.[83]

Twitter was already demonstrating how it would replace longer form blogs as a more useful tool in a breaking news situation even though some of the journalists updating the page had little experience of using the microblogging website. BBC journalists cited five blogs or bloggers during the crisis but included references to 22 Twitter updates (Table 7.6). Samanthi Dissanayake, who was primarily responsible for collecting blog posts and Twitter updates in her role on the UGC hub, noted that individuals who might previously have written longer blog posts were updating Twitter accounts instead.[84] She claimed they usually wrote blog posts after the crisis was over.

In the broad context of news journalism, the extent of change in sourcing practices should not be overemphasised. In Table 7.7, categories 1 through 4 are grouped together as 'media' sources, categories 5 through 7 as 'official sources and authorised knowers' and categories 8 through 11 are collated as

Table 7.7 27–29 November 2008: Official, nonofficial and media sources cited in BBC live updates

	Number Cited	% of Total Sources
Media (categories 1–4)	190	46
Official Sources and 'Authorised Knowers' (categories 5–7)	150	37
Non-official Sources (categories 8–11)	64	16
Other (12**)	6	1
Total	410	100

**Eight sources were redistributed from Category 12 (Other): Seven to 'official sources and authorised knowers' and one to 'nonofficial sources'.

'nonofficial sources'. Category 12—Other—was redistributed on a case-by-case basis into media, official, nonofficial or a new 'other' category. In sum, BBC and media sources were cited on 190 occasions—46% of the total sources cited. Official sources and 'authorised knowers' on 150 occasions—37% of the total. And 'nonofficial' sources on 64 occasions—16%. (Table 7.7). Although there are significant problems with a comparison to Leon Sigal's content analysis of news sources in 2,850 stories in the *New York Times* and the *Washington Post* between 1949 and 1969, it is interesting to note that his research demonstrated that nonofficial sources accounted for 16.5%.[85]

Compared with the BBC's previous use of similar live update formats, however, there has been a significant increase in the number of eyewitness and nonofficial sources included. In the immediate aftermath of the London bombings in 2005, the BBC news website team began updating a webpage titled London blasts: At a glance. The page was far more basic than the Mumbai live pages in 2008, but was similar in style and consisted of 55 time-stamped updates reporting developments during the day. Official sources dominated accounting for 68% of the sources cited; only four eyewitnesses were included, and in total nonofficial sources represented only 7%.[86] In the context of the BBC's approach to live updates pages, the level of nonofficial sources included had more than doubled from 7% in 2005 to 16% by 2008.

REFLECTING IN THE AFTERMATH: ACCURACY, TWITTER AND THE LESSONS OF MUMBAI

On 27 November, the BBC's live updates team reported several pieces of information that demonstrated how difficult it is to achieve accuracy when reporting a breaking-news situation. One of the aims of the ten Lashkar-e-Taiba attackers and their handlers based in Pakistan was to create confusion about the number of operatives in Mumbai.[87] At 09h15, the BBC quoted 'officials' who said four had been killed and nine arrested. At 15h29, Maj. Gen. R. K. Huda was reported as saying there were 10 to 12 attackers in total. At 16h06, the BBC cited the Press Trust of India which claimed that '20 to 25 gunmen' had arrived in Mumbai. At 20h32, a tweet from 'SDMike' in San Diego was included which questioned the figures: 'Approx 25 terrorists entered Mumbai. Where all of them? Approx 9 killed and a few captured. Where are the rest?' BBC correspondents also had to amend initial judgements. Mark Dummett, stationed outside the Taj Mahal Hotel, suggested that the siege was over at 09h15 on 27 November. The following day, the BBC's Nik Gowing was reporting gunfire and troop movements inside the hotel. Various sources of information, therefore, might have attracted criticism, but it was one erroneous Twitter update which proved to be the focus of attention in the aftermath.

Writing in *The Independent*, Tom Sutcliffe felt the juxtaposition of the reports of the BBC's professional journalists with Twitter updates was a 'worrying development'.[88] He admitted to being lured by the immediacy of the BBC's updates but was disturbed by 'the almost Platonic conjunction of message and means'—a reference to the use of short updates to report the news and the BBC's incorporation of tweets on the page. He suggested Twitter updates could not be trusted. While a journalist would incur professional penalties for providing false information, a 'Twitterer owes no duty except to their own impressions and their own state of mind'.

Concerns were not limited to external commentators. The BBC's own Technology Correspondent, Rory Cellan-Jones, highlighted that a tweet the BBC had used on 27 November had no basis in fact.[89] The tweet alleged that the Indian government had asked people to stop using Twitter:

> 1108 Indian government asks for live Twitter updates from Mumbai to cease immediately. 'ALL LIVE UPDATES—PLEASE STOP TWEETING about #Mumbai police and military operations,' a tweet says.[90]

Compared to other tweets the BBC used, this tweet was unusually poorly attributed—it did not provide a link or even mention the Twitter user who had posted the information. Writing on his BBC blog, Cellan-Jones said he could find no evidence that any 'official source' from the Indian government had ever made such a request.[91] He said the line had been sourced by the BBC from a blog post written by Lloyd Shepherd, who was then working for Channel 4 as Head of Future Media Solutions.[92] Shepherd had merely highlighted the tweet on his blog and suggested that 'for all sorts of reasons, this seems to be significant'.[93]

One of the journalists working on the updates said the tweet was passed to him for inclusion as 'something that was plausible and interesting'.[94] It turned out to be the sort of 'unfounded speculation' that the BBC Trust's Neil Report had warned journalists to avoid in 2004.[95] It was notable that the erroneous Twitter update was not given to the journalists updating the live pages through the UGC hub which was the procedure for most tweets that were included. After the Mumbai attacks, the UGC hub's role in verifying information on social networks,[96] and 'checking tweets for authenticity before publication'[97] was reemphasised.

In a post on the Editors' blog discussing the BBC's live updates coverage of Mumbai, Steve Herrmann, the Editor of News online, suggested that the BBC should have checked the veracity of the tweet and conceded that the Corporation had 'learnt a lesson'.[98] He said the BBC would not have included the tweet in one of its regular online news stories differentiating the format from the live updates page. During an unfolding story, Herrmann argued there was value in 'simply monitoring, selecting and passing on the information we are getting as quickly as we can'.[99] Such an approach meant journalists could not be expected to verify every detail, but would thoroughly attribute leaving 'some of the weighing up of each bit of information and context' to the audience.

Herrmann's post was at least partly an exercise in public relations. More practically, BBC journalists who had worked on the updates were collating advice and guidance on how to run live update pages based on their experiences. In an internal document written in the aftermath there was a section on the use of Twitter which suggested that BBC journalists would be more stringent in future live updates pages.[100] It noted that Twitter updates contained 'a lot of unsubstantiated rumour' and 'accusations as to who was responsible for the attacks', while it was not clear whether tweets about Mumbai were being provided by eyewitnesses or people who were simply commenting on media reports.[101] Consequently, blog posts and Twitter updates should be treated in a similar manner to other audience material: 'eyewitness claims and pictures must be verified' and 'any content being used as fact must be verified'. The document advised journalists to use Twitter as a source of atmosphere and 'public mood' rather than factual information.

In particular, the BBC wanted to avoid repeating the Mumbai error by deciding not to report the actions of a government authority based on a Twitter update unless they had checked the information with the relevant authority. The advice of Peter Horrocks, then head of the BBC Newsroom, was highlighted:

> The emerging distinction we are drawing with Twitter is around how inherently credible the eyewitness information is. So a Twitterer who says 'I've heard shots being fired' or 'We're all feeling angry' could be used un-checked. But an assertion from Twitter about someone else or the action of an authority (e.g. that Twitter was being shut down) should be checked.[102]

There were, then, significant issues with using Twitter as a source of information. The microblogging service did, however, provide journalists with some useful leads. The internal document offered an example of how 'unsubstantiated rumour' on Twitter might become 'news'.[103] During the crisis, the BBC's overnight team was alerted to the possibility that a number of Jews had been taken hostage at Nariman House. The 'rumour' was monitored 'over 30–40 minutes online and was eventually stood up', enabling the BBC to publish the story before the news agencies. This was cited as an example of the sort of Twitter update which should be investigated before being published so that the BBC could eventually 'use it with confidence—and still be quick'.

THE LIVE BLOG: A COLLABORATIVE NEWS FORMAT FOR A NETWORKED WORLD

Mumbai was not the first 'live' online coverage of a major terror attack, but Web-based communication had developed considerably since the 9/11 attacks in 2001. Online publication had become straightforward and ubiquitous—the potential for the 'people formerly known as the audience' to publish at a click of a button rapidly sped up the news cycle. According to Nik Gowing, the 'information pipelines facilitated by the new media can provide information and revelations within minutes', triggering an 'almost merciless, competitive rush to fill the media space'.[104] The practices of bloggers also played their part in accelerating news journalism. A number of early successful blogs which challenged the traditional media, particularly in the fields of politics and technology, began publishing whatever information they had and invoking other bloggers and readers to verify the details.[105] The emergence of simple blogging software and other publishing tools—particularly web forums and social networks—meant news and information was increasingly being published by individuals who did not necessarily have any regard for the existing rituals of journalistic publication. They broke news faster than did journalists undertaking traditional fact checking which potentially posed a significant threat to one of the key pillars of journalism's cultural and economic capital. The widespread adoption of live blogging by the traditional media in various guises is a way of directly addressing this challenge online by providing the latest information first and by encouraging web users to access their webpages during live news events.

This chapter, in its very subject matter, demonstrated that the BBC has adopted this approach for online news and that the blogging genre has had an influence on the way the Corporation covers a major terror attack. The format of the BBC's live updates page borrows from short blog-style updates, whereby the most recent piece of information appears at the top of the page. Rather than follow the structures of traditional print journalism which prioritised information according to what was deemed most important in the course of a day,[106] on these pages the emphasis has shifted towards prioritising that which has occurred most recently. Journalists' preference for immediacy is not new,[107] but a sense of 'liveness' facilitated by constantly updated webpages represents a significant departure for the presentation of news online. BBC editors actively seek to provide a live experience online for their audience.[108] News is presented as a flow or stream of information which requires greater participation from the reader in interpreting context and accuracy,[109] and provides a space, however limited, for them to participate in an unfolding story.

According to Peter Horrocks, then Head of the BBC Newsroom, increased communication with the audience during the Mumbai crisis 'brought immediacy—and newsmaking UGC—from the moment the story broke', but he also noted that it 'posed new questions about how we [the BBC] use that material including Twitter comments in our online live commentary'.[110] Live updates, by which journalists are expected to condense, sift, manage and republish information from a variety of sources, undoubtedly places pressure on the BBC's values. The use of live updates transports some of the problems of live television to the online medium. Indeed, one journalist described the live text updates as 'a print version of TV rolling news'.[111] The

BBC included various pieces of contradictory information about the number of gunmen involved in the attacks and published an erroneous rumour suggesting that the Indian government had called for Web users to stop providing live updates on Twitter. It is evidence that accuracy can be sacrificed in the rush to publish information.

Traditionally, BBC journalists have aimed to 'get the news first' but not at the expense of 'getting the news *right* first'. The BBC's 2005 Editorial Guidelines stated that 'accuracy is more important than speed',[112] but the 2010 edition allowed for more flexibility: 'due accuracy is more important than speed'.[113] It was notable that during the coverage of Mumbai 'breaking news was a priority' and that journalists were proud to have regularly 'beaten the wires' to the news.[114] According to one journalist working on the updates, there was also some loosening of usual editorial procedures:

> You still temper yourself and go through a similar editorial process [but] I think you can get away with a lot. In a sense, because we're allowed to, you can legitimately put one source as long as you attribute it properly. You wouldn't normally do that.[115]

In order to distance the Corporation from factual claims made in the updates, the BBC sought to clearly attribute each piece of information and to a more limited extent use the hyperlink particularly when referencing Twitter accounts. Time-pressed journalists have always attributed information to their sources, and it is recognised by one experienced correspondent as an 'old trick at the BBC'.[116] However, the journalistic shift towards 'live' online updates reinforces the importance of this traditional journalistic routine.[117] In the context of live blogging, attribution facilitates the rapid publication of news updates and the presentation of an 'unconfirmed' breaking news story, while distancing the BBC from responsibility for the accuracy of the news and information. Journalists are able to publish first and verify later: an approach pioneered online by a number of bloggers. Only more serious news updates—such as the possible death of a named individual—are more thoroughly verified prior to publication. The widespread adoption of attributed sourcing for breaking news online and the publication of the extent to which a piece of information has been verified could be viewed as the new strategic rituals of a more transparent online journalism.[118] The BBC's authority as a news organisation, therefore, is no longer presented as if it were based exclusively on the knowledge and expertise of their journalists: live updates invited the 'former audience' to be a collaborative partner in attempting to report and understand a major terror attack.[119]

The contribution of 'the people formerly known as the audience'[120] to the BBC's live blogging coverage of Mumbai was significant and was facilitated by the speed of digital communication. According to Peter Horrocks, Mumbai was 'an event where people . . . have used new technology to communicate on a scale we've never seen before'.[121] The journalists working on the

BBC's UGC hub searched for and selected audience comment through email, on blogs, via Twitter and on social networking sites like Orkut to provide 'colour' and to represent the 'public mood'. The experience of Samanthi Dissanayake on the UGC hub, who noted that Indians were using the micro-blogging service rather than longer-form blogs, and the fact that over four times as many Twitter updates were included in the BBC's live updates pages than blogs, illustrates the emerging importance of Twitter as a tool used by journalists to access breaking news stories.

An increase in the number of 'nonofficial' sources, eyewitness accounts and contributions from the 'people formerly known as the audience' in the BBC's live updates should not be overstated in the broader context of news journalism, but it should be considered significant in comparison with the BBC's approach to this increasingly important online news format. In 2005, nonofficial sources represented only 7% of the total cited in the BBC's At a Glance live updates page for the London bombings. For the Mumbai attacks in 2008, this figure had risen to 16%, and the shift is confirmed by a comparison with the BBC's live updates coverage of Anders Behring Breivik's killing spree in Norway in 2011,[122] when the percentage of non-official sources was 20%. The increase was partly due to the BBC's decision to begin a live blog much sooner after the initial bomb blast in Oslo than they had done during the Mumbai crisis. BBC journalists covering Breivik's attack for the live updates page consequently included more eyewitness accounts (11%)—particularly facilitated by email—than their colleagues covering Mumbai (5%) who were already receiving reports from a BBC reporting team at the scene by the time they began publishing. Eyewitnesses may not have been 'taking over the news'[123] at the BBC but they were undoubtedly playing a more important role in the BBC's live updates cover-age by 2011 than they were in 2008 or 2005.[124] Over the same period, the live updates format has become a far more prominent aspect of the BBC's broader online coverage for major news events, and a 'live' online offering is regarded by senior editors and managers as central to the future of the Corporation's news website.

This chapter has demonstrated how the BBC has adopted a 'new style of journalism'[125] which draws on the conventions of blogging and incorporates the voice of the audience but is understood by BBC journalists in the context of existing practices whether in terms of a print version of live television or through the more widespread application of the journalistic ritual of attribu-tion. It has documented an emerging shift in the nature of the BBC's online journalism whereby digitally connected eyewitnesses, bystanders and other interested parties are quickly incorporated into a rolling news story, playing a more important role in making, disseminating and commenting on the news.

The following chapter, a case study of one week of the war in Gaza in 2009, broadens the exploration of how the BBC incorporates blogs into its reporting by considering its online, TV and radio coverage.

8   Reporting Conflict
War in Gaza and the Limits of the News Revolution

A month after the attacks on Mumbai, war returned to the Middle East. On 27 December 2008, the Israeli Air Force launched a series of airstrikes on the Gaza Strip. The Israeli government said it was responding to rockets fired at towns in Southern Israel by Hamas militants in the territory. Apparently intent on delivering a serious blow to the Hamas movement in Gaza, Israel Defense Forces (IDF) began a ground operation in the New Year, surrounding Gaza City in the north and entering Khan Younis in the south. Despite international pressure for an end to the fighting and the passing of a UN Security Council Resolution demanding an immediate ceasefire on 8 January, the war continued for another 10 days. Estimates for the number of Palestinians killed during the conflict range from 1,166 to 1,444.[1] The Israeli Ministry of Foreign Affairs said 13 Israelis died during the three-week operation including three civilians in southern Israel.[2]

During the hostilities, Israel conducted a concerted information campaign. In 2006, critics had deemed that Hezbollah had controlled the narrative of the Second Lebanon War through the manipulation of foreign journalists and had emerged as 'the master of the new media message'.[3] In contrast, Israel's democratic openness was adjudged to have led to a proliferation of mixed messages and unclear goals.[4] Fewer than three years later, Israel provided foreign journalists covering Operation Cast Lead with information packs on arrival, text message updates during the war and tours of towns in southern Israel hit by rocket fire. Israel also prohibited international journalists from covering the conflict from inside Gaza on the grounds that the area of operations was too dangerous for reporters. They gathered instead on a hilltop on the Israeli side of the Gaza border, plying the 24-hour news machine with images of military activity. Israel could not, however, prevent images of civilian casualties being beamed across the world. Reporters based in Gaza provided material for international media organisations while the UN and nongovernmental organisations (NGOs) continued to operate, telling the stories of those on the ground.

An 'information war' was also waged online. The IDF launched a hastily conceived digital media campaign including a blog, a YouTube channel and a Twitter feed[5] while unaffiliated Internet campaigns such as that orchestrated by the Jewish Internet Defense Force also spread the Israeli message.[6] A few Gazans, journalists and NGO activists updated blogs directly from inside the conflict zone despite the difficulties in accessing electricity and Internet connections. More generally, the conflict was debated around the Arab blogosphere, and Israeli bloggers discussed the progress of the war in English and Hebrew. This media context provides an interesting backdrop for a comparative exploration of the coverage of the Gaza conflict available on blogs and from the BBC.

Some bloggers began covering conflict because they were dissatisfied with aspects of traditional media coverage of conflict. A blog was an outlet for individuals to convey their experiences, set their own agendas, offer an alternative perspective, publish their own images and interact with other bloggers. Academics suggested that blogs offered a different news style to the traditional media. Stuart Allan argued that news on blogs tended to be more personal, raw and unpolished,[7] a style of news that Melissa Wall describes as 'postmodern', 'emphasising personalisation, audience participation in content creation and story forms that are fragmented and interdependent with other websites'.[8] As the blogosphere has merged with online news media various areas of convergence can be identified. The previous chapter, for example, demonstrated that the BBC's live blog of the Mumbai attacks was to a certain extent 'unpolished' and encouraged 'audience participation' in the construction of content.

This chapter explores the extent to which the BBC's coverage of Gaza was influenced by blogging. It thus identifies areas in which the BBC was willing to collaborate with bloggers or adopted a similar approach to covering conflict, but it also demonstrates that the BBC's editorial principles fundamentally limited the impact of blogs on their journalism. It analyses the extent to which the blogging format was adopted by the BBC; whether the themes covered by the BBC were influenced by those on blogs; what impact a personal, subjective blogging voice has on the style of the BBC's war reporting; if bloggers' use of language and images has been adopted by the BBC; and how far bloggers have become a feature of BBC coverage.

METHODS: SELECTING BLOGS, BBC CONTENT AND TIME

A sample of blogs was selected on the basis of categories of blogs which might be of interest to a working journalist identified in Chapter 1.[9] They include a blog written by an eyewitness and independent journalist (Sameh A Habeeb), blogs written by activists (Tales To Tell, In Gaza and Ghazzawiyya), an Israeli military blogger (The Muqata blog), a diasporic or 'bridge-blogger' (Gaza Mom),[10] an official military blog (IDF Spokesperson), and specialists and academics (Yaacov Lozowick and Juan Cole). It was not possible to find a frontline Israeli military blog although the author of A Soldier's Mother included conversations with her son who was fighting in the conflict. An English-language Hamas blog was also not identified. Nevertheless, the sample contains a wide range of representations of the conflict, and blogs in this sample were featured in a variety of media organisations. A short description of each blog in the sample follows.

IDF Spokesperson[11]

IDF Spokesperson was an official blog run by the IDF. It was set up on Boxing Day 2008, a day before the start of Israeli airstrikes on Gaza. The blog provided formal summaries of the day's events, other press releases and embedded video from the IDF's YouTube channel.

The Muqata Blog[12]

The Muqata blog was started in 2005 by 'Jameel', a Jewish settler who had lived in Chomesh, Gaza, before the Israeli withdrawal. The blogger says his aim was to promote *aliya* or ascension to Israel by promoting the 'love of Israel, the land of Israel, and aspiration of living in Israel to the JBlogosphere'. During the Gaza crisis, the blog provided dozens of rolling time-stamped updates on the conflict.

Yaacov Lozowick's Ruminations[13]

Israeli author and historian Yaacov Lozowick wrote *Right to Exist: A Moral Defense of Israel's Wars* and was former Director of Archives at Yad Vashem, Israel's memorial to the Holocaust. He updated his blog more frequently during the Gaza crisis, in part as a way of dealing with his son's deployment to the battlefield. He rarely mentioned his son, however, and more usually criticised media coverage of the war.

A Soldier's Mother[14]

The author of 'A Soldier's Mother' was living in the West Bank settlement of Maaleh Adumim during the conflict. She describes herself as an Israeli 'not by birth but most definitely by choice'. Her blog was started in 2007 just before her son, 'Elie', entered the army. He was called up to fight in Gaza, and her posts often discussed her feelings about his deployment.

Gaza Mom[15]

Laila El-Haddad is a Palestinian from Gaza City. She describes herself as 'a journalist', 'a blogger', 'a mother', 'a Muslim' and 'a Media Activist'. Her work as a journalist has appeared in a variety of media outlets including Al Jazeera English, (for whom she worked as a reporter in Gaza between 2003 and 2006). During the sample period, she was based in the United States, but her blog posts relayed several of her telephone conversations with her parents living in Gaza.

Tales to Tell[16]

Sharyn Lock had arrived in Gaza by boat, dodging the Israeli navy's sea blockade in August 2008. Her blog documented her time in Gaza as a volunteer for the International Solidarity Movement (ISM). ISM is 'a Palestinian-led movement committed to resisting the Israeli occupation of Palestinian land using nonviolent, direct-action methods and principles'.[17] The organisation aims to provide international protection by living alongside Gazans and to give them a voice by publishing their stories.

In Gaza[18]

Born in Michigan and raised in Canada, Eva Bartlett had been banned from entering Israel for 10 years in early 2008, but arrived in Gaza with other ISM volunteers by boat.[19] Like Lock, she used her blog to document Palestinian stories and volunteered with medics working for the Palestinian Red Crescent Society (PRCS).

Gaza Today[20]

Sameh A Habeeb, an independent Palestinian journalist, was based in Gaza and had previously worked for the Ramattan Press Agency. His blog offered short, numbered updates of incidents in Gaza on a daily basis. He said he often had to risk his life travelling to find electricity and an Internet connection. He claimed he received death threats because of his blog.

Ghazzawiyya[21]

During the Gaza conflict, Ghazzawiyya or Moments in Gaza acted as a group blog which was maintained by Nader Houella. The two main contributors during this period were Natalie Abou Shakra, a Lebanese woman working with the ISM and professor Dr Said Abdelwahed, who was in Gaza at the time, but said he was based in the department of English at Al-Azhar University in Cairo.

Informed Comment[22]

Informed Comment is written by Juan Cole, Professor of History at the University of Michigan. He has been blogging about the Middle East since 2002.

These blogs were analysed over five days between 5 and 9 January and were compared with BBC coverage over the same period. The following BBC radio coverage was selected for analysis: Radio 4's 06h00 and 18h00 news bulletins; Radio 5 Live's news bulletins at 06h00, 12h00 and 17h00; Radio 4's *PM* programme; and the *World Have Your Say* (*WHYS*) programme on the World Service. With regards to television, the *Ten O'Clock News* and the *Newsnight* programme were selected, and online the BBC's main news articles and blog posts on Gaza were analysed.[23]

The five days between 5 and 9 January was the first week that the BBC was running their usual schedule after the Christmas and New Year holidays. This period also proved to be an eventful week in the war. After a series of air strikes from 27 December, an Israeli ground offensive had begun on Saturday 3 January. The IDF pushed into Zeitoun and Gaza City in the north and towards Khan Younis in the south over the weekend. Diplomatic pressure was also placed on Israel to halt the offensive after two major incidents in which Gazan civilians were killed. The first was an Israeli attack on 6 January near al-Fakoura school, run by the United Nations Relief and Works Agency for Palestine Refugees in the Near East (UNRWA). The second concerned accusations emanating from the International Committee of the Red Cross (ICRC) and the United Nations High Commissioner for Human Rights that Israeli forces had failed to meet their obligations under the Geneva Convention with regard to the evacuation of wounded Gazans in the Zeitoun area.

THE ADOPTION OF THE BLOG FORMAT BY THE BBC

For bloggers in this sample, the blog was usually their main publication outlet and often their only one. Multiple posts by bloggers on a single day were not uncommon and because of their particular interest in the Gaza conflict, posts rarely wavered from covering the war. For the BBC, the blogging format complements their existing output, and it was notable that the BBC's use of blogging to cover Gaza was far from comprehensive. Jeremy Bowen did keep a regular diary for the BBC news website while he was reporting from the Israeli border which drew on the blogging format. But across the official BBC blog network blogging was sporadic. Notably, the BBC decided not to start a 'live blog' to cover Gaza as they had done for the Mumbai attacks and as other news organisations did during the conflict.

For the BBC's blogging correspondents, it was one issue among many they covered that week. On 5 January, Justin Webb's *Ten O'Clock News* two-way discussion about Gaza included the URL of his blog flashing up on screen, and the audience might have expected to find out more about the issue on his BBC blog.[24] Between 5 and 9 January, the North America Editor's TV appearances discussed US involvement in diplomatic moves to end the conflict and the potential impact of a change of presidency on the Gaza crisis,[25] but his blog posts concerned 'America's greatness' and the imminent appointment of Leon Panetta as head of the Central Intelligence Agency

(CIA). Webb did not write about Gaza on his blog during the whole of January. There were several other posts scattered across the BBC's blogs which discussed the Gaza conflict,[26] but BBC presenter Robin Lustig was the only BBC blogger who wrote more than one post on the conflict between 5 and 9 January. The Jerusalem Bureau Chief, James Stephenson, also considered the frustration of not being able to access Gaza in a post for the Editors' blog.[27]

In addition to the BBC's individual bloggers, Gaza occasionally featured on the BBC's programme blogs. *Newsnight* used a blog post to trail its coverage of the conflict on its television programme,[28] while the Radio 5 Live Breakfast team uploaded the audio of a conversation between an Israeli and a UK-based Palestinian onto its blog.[29] In these instances, blogs were being used as a way of bringing content to a wider audience whether by encouraging online readers to tune in to TV or by expanding the reach of radio by posting audio online. Similarly, the BBC's *WHYS* team uploaded videos of a television version of the show to their blog so that Web users could access the special programme.

The *WHYS* team, however, was unusual in the way it consistently covered the Gaza conflict on its blog and also engaged with commenters. A daily *WHYS* blog post acted as a starting point for discussion which fed into their radio shows. In this period, *WHYS*'s blog posts introduced topics on Israel's right to defend itself, the experience of war for young people in Gaza and Israel, the propaganda war, the impact of global reaction on Israel's foreign policy and whether the conflict was exacerbating divisions in other parts of the world. Editor Mark Sandell, who believes that the *WHYS* community should have a stake in the editorial process, also wrote a post titled 'Help Needed', which asked for the community's views on how to best avoid unnecessarily long contributions from radio guests in the context of discussing an emotive conflict.[30] Sandell's commitment to engagement is demonstrated by the fact that he commented on this post five times in response to suggestions on the issue and several times to commenters who were debating whether there was a point when 'Israel loses the right to defend itself'.[31]

THEMES AND NEWS AGENDAS

Analysing the extent to which the BBC has adopted the blogging format is more straightforward than ascertaining the influence that blogs have on the themes present in BBC coverage and the news agendas of BBC journalists. No clear picture emerges from current academic research. Adopting a quantitative approach, Jure Leskovec et al. found that only 3.5% of stories appear dominantly in the blogosphere before being taken up by the traditional media.[32] Based on a content analysis of articles in the *New York Times* and the *Washington Post*, Marcus Messner and Marcia Watson DiStaso argue, however, that blogs and the traditional media are increasingly influencing one another's news agendas.[33] In order to attempt to offer an insight into whether the themes present on blogs were having an impact on the BBC's coverage of Gaza this section is guided by Greg Philo's and Mike Berry's approach to thematic analysis.[34]

There were several prominent common themes present in blog posts and the BBC's coverage between 5 and 9 January. These were the progress of the Israeli offensive, the military and political strategies of the two combatants, civilian suffering and the humanitarian crisis in Gaza, the prospects for a ceasefire and longer-term peace and the media coverage of the war. There were also some references to the origins of the conflict, although these accounts usually began no earlier than the economic blockade imposed by Israel after Hamas took control of the Strip in June 2007 or the breakdown of the previous ceasefire agreement in November 2008.[35] In both blogs and the BBC's coverage, there was much discussion of who was to blame for civilian casualties particularly after the Israeli attack near an UNRWA school on 6 January. Israeli bloggers and voices in BBC coverage accused Hamas of using 'human shields' and storing weapons in civilian buildings, a line which was repeated several times on the IDF Spokesperson blog.[36] Israel's critics argued that the ground offensive was a disproportionately heavy-handed response. Spokespeople for the UN and UNRWA in BBC coverage emphasised the shortage of basic food and medical supplies, pressed for humanitarian aid and argued that nowhere in Gaza was safe for civilians because they were unable to legally flee over the Israeli or Egyptian borders.

There were, however, several notable differences in the nature of the themes covered on the BBC and on blogs. Bloggers tended to pay more attention to general media coverage of the war than did the BBC. In part, this was because they blogged about their own interactions with the media. On her Gaza Mom blog, Laila El-Haddad posted a piece which reflected on her joint interview for CNN with her father in Gaza, while the author of A Soldier's Mother informed readers of a conversation with an Italian journalist who had contacted her.[37] A number of journalists had left comments on blogs asking the blogger to contact them for an interview, and the Ghazzawiyya blog put up a list of links to traditional media articles that had mentioned the blog.[38] Some bloggers and commenters were also keen to discuss the nature of media coverage on the war in order to criticise it and occasionally to praise the blogosphere for its perceived superiority. For Yaacov Lozowick media criticism formed a central feature of his postings in this period, and he was particularly fond of attacking the BBC and *The Guardian* newspaper.[39]

Although the BBC reported the media angle of the war, the proportion of coverage devoted to it was far less significant. The BBC included more material on the wider global impact of the conflict than did the bloggers in this sample. For bloggers, the prospects of a ceasefire and the negotiations surrounding them were rarely discussed; the BBC, on the other hand, often covered international diplomatic efforts to end the conflict. A broad range of viewpoints was considered in this context and the BBC carried pieces considering the positions of Israel, the West Bank, Iran, Egypt, Syria, the United States and the United Kingdom vis-à-vis the conflict. BBC journalists discussed the diplomatic initiatives of the United States, the EU, Arab leaders and the Quartet, represented by former UK prime minister Tony Blair. The BBC's broader lens also meant it covered issues which had been caused as a consequence of the conflict including anti-Semitic attacks in Europe,[40] a rise in oil prices[41] and the possible radicalising effect of the conflict on Muslims in the UK and in Arab countries.[42] With the exception of *WHYS*, there was little evidence, therefore, that blogs were particularly influencing the BBC's news agenda.

It is possible that more engagement with the blogs in the sample might have altered the BBC's coverage and enabled journalists to report some stories sooner than they did. On 4 January, 21 members of Wa'el al-Samouni's family were killed in an Israeli attack in Zeitoun.[43] The incident was mentioned by blogger Sameh A Habeeb as breaking news on 5 January. ISM bloggers Lock and Bartlett also posted about the incident on a number of occasions during the week. That is not to say that blogs were significantly ahead of the breaking-news cycle: according to Haaretz an AP reporter had interviewed survivors of Zeitoun on 5 January;[44] Sharyn Lock says one of the victims was interviewed on TV the same day;[45] and the Israeli human rights organisation B'Tselem issued a press release about Zeitoun on 6 January saying they had been in contact with the al-Samouni family.[46]

The BBC, however, did not begin reporting the events in Zeitoun until 8 January, when the ICRC issued a press statement expressing their frustration at Israeli forces blocking access to the area. It appears that it was only at this stage that Rushdi Abu Alouf, a BBC reporter based in Gaza, travelled to Al Quds hospital to speak to members of the al-Samouni family. Their responses were documented in an article published on the BBC website around 07h30 on 9 January. A comment on one of Sharyn Lock's posts suggests some of her blog readers had noted the time lag between reports of Zeitoun appearing on Lock's blog and the BBC's coverage of the story: 'we are hearing about the house of horrors in Zeitoun, even the BBC are talking about it'.[47] Although BBC journalists might not have been able to rely on bloggers for the facts, they still could have used blogs as an additional source to research the Zeitoun story. Instead, the BBC's news agenda was being driven by the ICRC press release.

THE PERSONAL STYLE

If the influence of blogs on BBC journalists' choice of themes and news agenda appears limited, the blogging genre has had an impact on the BBC's style of journalism online. Although not applicable to the IDF Spokesperson blog, the Muqata blog and Sameh A Habeeb's blog, a number of bloggers in this sample tended to have a personal focus. These bloggers 'relied heavily on personalisation'[48] reflecting on the consequences of the conflict for themselves, their family or friends or colleagues.

Several blogs in the sample resembled personal diaries—a common blogging genre. The author of A Soldier's Mother primarily used her blog as a way of expressing her fears for the safety of her son, 'Elie', in combat. Similarly, Laila El Haddad's blog tended to be personal, documenting her phone conversations with her parents in Gaza and a speech she gave at a vigil at Duke University in North Carolina.[49]

The blogs written by ISM members Eva Bartlett and Sharyn Lock were a mixture of the stories of the Palestinians they met and their own personal experiences of being in Gaza. Several of their posts resembled traditional media feature articles. They were written in the first person, but the bloggers were keen to relay the stories of the Palestinians on the ground. Interestingly, although they often dealt with the tragic, there was room for references to the dark humour which sustained some Palestinians in Gaza through the conflict.[50]

These more personal accounts, however, were not exclusively available on blogs in the sample; the BBC also adopted the personal diary format. During the Gaza conflict, Hatem Shurrab, an aid worker in Gaza with the British-based charity, Islamic Relief Worldwide, kept a diary for the BBC. Despite difficulties with electricity and Internet access he managed to provide regular updates for a month from the beginning of Israeli air attacks on 27 December 2008.

The BBC's Middle East Editor, Jeremy Bowen, also wrote a diary for the BBC website, sometimes writing updates on his BlackBerry smartphone from the back of a car or in occasional breaks in a hectic schedule.[51] The content Bowen wrote for the diary overlapped with the work he was doing for television and radio, but he used it as an opportunity to provide additional reflections which would not fit into a broadcast piece. On a number of occasions, Bowen discussed in more detail the workings of the 'news machine', highlighting the limitations of acting as a journalist without access to the story.[52] He emphasised, for example, that he could provide audiences with more detail about the funeral of an IDF soldier than he could about the images of a man kissing his dead son in Gaza:

> I can tell you that Nitai Stern had hundreds of friends and family at his funeral. But I don't even know the name of the poor heartbroken man in Gaza, or of his dead wife, and his dead children.[53]

The nature of these personal diaries on the BBC website differed from blogs. They were edited in the BBC house style, and the text of the BBC's Gaza diaries was more closed than that available on blogs: there was nowhere for the audience to comment on them, nor were there any hyperlinks to other websites.

IMPARTIALITY AND SUBJECTIVITY

Writing in 2005, Melissa Wall argued that 'the opinionated voice is a hall-mark of blog writing'.[54] A blog does not have to be opinionated, but the expectation that it should be was a fundamental stumbling block for the BBC's adoption of blogging. During the Gaza conflict, BBC presenter Robin Lustig demonstrated how BBC bloggers could write a post in an unasham-edly opinionated manner and still retain their obligation to uphold the Cor-poration's commitment to impartiality. Taking a 'look at the world through someone else's eyes', Lustig wrote from a Palestinian perspective first:

> You want to know what it's like in Gaza at the moment? It's Hell on earth . . . Since the day I was born, I have lived in a stinking, rotten prison, with no freedom and no dignity . . . The rockets? Sure, fire rockets at the Israelis. Let them feel how it hurts when children are killed, when you live every day in fear. Let them learn how it feels to be a Palestinian . . .[55]

And then he considered what an Israeli might be feeling:

> You want to know why Israel is attacking Hamas in Gaza? . . . Do you know how many rockets they have fired at us since we left Gaza? How many times they have tried to send suicide bombers into Israel to kill us in our shopping malls and our bus stations? Have you any idea what it feels like when your neighbours are terrorists?[56]

These views would usually be represented through a contributor to a BBC programme not articulated by a BBC journalist. Hence, Lustig made sure that his blog readers were aware that the post did not represent any of his own standpoints:

> Let there be no misunderstanding: these are not my views, but based on my experience of more than 20 years reporting from and about Israel and Palestine, I'm pretty sure they're the views of a great many Palestin-ians and Israelis.[57]

The post attracted hundreds of comments.

Lustig had managed to tap into a subjective style without sacrificing his necessarily impartial approach to journalism as a BBC journalist and in the sample the BBC seemed to have fulfilled its commitment to impartial, accurate and 'objective' journalism. A more open approach by BBC journal-ists about how they conduct their journalism and occasional, usually trivial revelations about their personal lives did not extend to their voicing their personal opinions on the Gaza conflict. 'Lifting the lid'[58] on the BBC's jour-nalism only provided a small glimpse into the inner workings of the BBC's news process and the editorial decisions of its journalists. Their individual biases, agendas and thoughts about what they were covering were not visible in the BBC's content. If the BBC had heeded calls for transparency to form a new cornerstone of objectivity in the Internet era,[59] then it would have resulted in a fundamental reorientation of their journalism.

The contrast with bloggers in the sample is stark; they were often open about their personal biases and agendas. Yaacov Lozowick, for example, regularly criticised the media in his blogs posts in this period. He openly admitted his 'lowish opinion of journalists wasn't formed this week' and that his assertion that a blogger called Meryl Yourish based in Richmond, Virginia, was doing 'a far better job' than the BBC's Middle East Editor Jeremy Bowen was formed, in part, as a consequence of his own 'prejudices'.[60]

The ISM bloggers were members of an organisation which aimed to provide 'a voice with which to non-violently resist an overwhelming military occupation force' and believed 'the Palestinian struggle is not accurately reported by the mainstream corporate media'.[61] They were actively attempting to influence traditional media coverage of the war and provide an alternative perspective.

The Muqata blog went one step further, overtly positioning itself as a combatant in an information war. In a post on 5 January the Muqata blog stated, 'We're doing our part, to help with the war on the information front, while the IDF does it's [*sic*] job in Gaza'.[62] Two days later the Muqata bloggers also suggested IDF radio could not be trusted:

> We need to be as forceful as possible in our media reporting on behalf of Israel. Our soldiers in Gaza do not need to be stabbed in the back by IDF radio—they need our full and total support, and not hearing interviews with the head of the Shifa hospital [in Gaza].[63]

The Muqata authors were openly taking up the blog as a digital weapon in a media war against a perceived enemy[64] and calling out 'information traitors' from within their own ranks.

LANGUAGE

Conscious subjectivity was also apparent with regard to the language used by bloggers. With the exception of Gazan blogger Sameh A Habeeb, who chose to refer to Hamas fighters as 'Palestinian militants', no effort was made by bloggers to adopt balanced, fair or neutral language to describe the conflict. One of the authors of Ghazzawiyya, a Lebanese woman called Natalie Abou Shakra, regularly described Israeli forces as the 'Zionist death machine of war and terror'.[65] Clearly identifying with the cause of the Gazans she wrote, 'we are not going to give in to Israel . . . to those modern day crusaders. Either martyrdom or victory . . . Samidoun, samidoun! We shall not be humiliated'.[66]

Scottish ISM worker Sharyn Lock tended to be more moderate in tone, but she pointedly referred to the IDF as the Israeli Occupation Force, or the IOF, and referred to dead members of the al-Samouni family as *shaheed* or martyrs. The Muqata blog regularly described Palestinian combatants as 'Hamas terrorists'. The IDF Spokesperson blog referred variously to Hamas terrorists, militants and operatives. On Laila El-Haddad's blog, commenters engaged in a debate about who they regarded to be the 'terrorists' in the situation.[67]

The BBC has strict guidance concerning the language used by their journalists, and the Corporation is particularly careful to avoid using the word *terrorist* in news reports. The Editorial Guidelines identify the term as 'a barrier rather than an aid to understanding'[68] and recommend 'words which specifically describe the perpetrator such as "bomber", "attacker", "gunman", "kidnapper", "insurgent" and "militant"'. The BBC's use of language in relation to the Israeli-Palestinian conflict had also been criticised for 'imprecision and inconsistency' in a report for the Governors published in 2006.[69] The findings led to the development of a new Middle East style guide for journalists and the BBC was generally consistent in its use of language between 5 and 9 January 2009. BBC journalists, for example, almost always used the word *militants* to describe Hamas fighters. When bloggers and other voices were incorporated into BBC coverage, however, they were represented in their own words. The subjective voice was evident on the BBC website through bloggers' round-ups and similar online features. Israeli Michael Hessler, for example, was quoted on the BBC website as saying, '[T]here are probably plenty of nice Gazan people being used by Hamas terrorists as human shields'.[70]

IMAGES

Donald Matheson and Stuart Allan observe that the 'image of war is suddenly out of the hands of the political marketer or the cautious editor' and is now also communicated by soldiers, citizens and activists.[71] The bloggers in this sample embedded their own photos and videos into their posts and displayed imagery by third parties. Although there were no blogs in the sample in which images dominated, all the bloggers with the exception of Yaacov Lozowick included at least one picture or video between 5 and 9 January.

Several blogs were providing images from the conflict they had produced themselves. Although he did not publish them directly on his blog, Sameh A Habeeb was updating a Picasa account with photos from Gaza. A collection of his photos of children in Gaza was used by Sky News on its website.[72]

ISM volunteers Lock and Bartlett also illustrated their posts with photos. They captured images of injured men, women and children in ambulances and hospitals, bread queues inside Gaza, ruined buildings and the daily lives of PRCS medics. Bartlett recorded some short segments of video which she posted on her blog. These clips provided an embedded glimpse of what life as a medic was like in Gaza. In a post on 5 January, she uploaded a video of a man receiving treatment as he was being transferred from Beit Hanoun to Shifa Hospital in an ambulance. On the blog, Bartlett said the man had been shot in the face. Compared to the images presented by the BBC, these videos were raw, unedited and unpackaged. No attempt was made to 'balance' them with other images either within the same blog post or across several blog posts.

There were several images of children whose suffering as an 'innocent' party was deemed particularly unjust by bloggers. One such photo, taken on a mobile phone and posted on the Ghazzawiyya blog, showed a man grieving over three dead Palestinian children. The blog post was titled 'Israel's new target for today: families' and simply said, 'What have they done wrong to deserve this?'[73] The author of A Soldier's Mother addressed the issue of the portrayal of children in the media in a blog post on 7 January. She argued that media images of injured Palestinian children were not representative of the conflict:

> The news is filled with them today and they can easily sway you to think that all of the situation in the Middle East comes down to a picture.[74]

Although she stated that it was 'horrible, truly tragic, unacceptable and wrong . . . to have a child die', she wanted to undermine the idea that all Palestinian children were 'innocent' casualties by posting a series of photos of them armed with weapons. One showed a child holding a grenade; another depicted a youth with an explosive device strapped to his body. Other photos showed children holding rifles or dressed in military uniform. The blogger provided no information regarding the origin of the photos, when they were taken or if they were all pictures of Palestinian children. It is highly unlikely that these images would have been shown by the BBC at any stage during the conflict, and they were certainly not present in the BBC material studied in this chapter.

The Muqata blog also included pictures that would not be seen on the BBC website such as one image which they claimed was a Hamas 'propaganda' picture of a sniper who had been killed in Gaza on 6 January.[75] As self-styled participants in a media war the blog's authors were keen to challenge the veracity of images, reporting that various bloggers had started an investigation into whether one news photo was an example of 'fauxtography'.[76]

The BBC's approach to images was fundamentally different to bloggers in the sample. The Corporation's commitment to impartiality was an important consideration in its use of imagery. The use of images by the BBC directly linked the Israeli offensive with civilian casualties and Gazans' suffering. The BBC's TV coverage and online stills showed helicopters firing missiles, flares lighting up the night sky, military vehicles and smoke coming from Gaza. Often they were followed in TV reports by images from Gaza of bombed-out buildings, ambulances, wounded Gazans in hospitals and Palestinian funerals.[77] These images were 'balanced' by Hamas rocket attacks and Israeli civilians taking cover in towns such as Sderot near the Gaza border.[78] The BBC's *Ten O'Clock News* on 6 January also included images of Prime Minister Ehud Olmert visiting injured soldiers in an Israeli hospital, and the BBC covered the funerals of Israeli military casualties.[79]

The Corporation did not have access to images of Hamas fighters who had gone into hiding after the start of the offensive and were necessarily fighting a guerrilla campaign. It meant there was no identifiable visual source of Israeli suffering other than trails of smoke in the sky identified as Hamas rocket attacks, nor, more importantly, was there any visual evidence that Hamas militants were using 'human shields'. As a consequence, the BBC attempted to balance pictures with words or words with pictures. The claims of Israeli spokespeople that civilian suffering was primarily being caused by Hamas's use of human shields, for example, was visually contradicted by pictures of Israeli military hardware bombing Gaza. Indeed, Matt Prodger, presenting a segment called the 'War of Words' for BBC *Newsnight*, concluded that while the Israeli spokespeople dominated the words, the pictures of civilian suffering emanating from the Palestinian side 'were doing all the talking'.[80]

The BBC's approach was also different to bloggers and commenters in the sample. There was little concern openly expressed for the privacy of the victims or the potential distress to their online audience caused by shocking images. A number of commenters, nevertheless, deemed that bloggers were showing them 'the truth' in a way that the traditional media were not. One commenter thanked Eva Bartlett for her regular blog updates on the grounds that 'the coverage of the BBC and others in the UK is not giving the full picture of the atrocities being committed'.[81] Bloggers might well have decided not to publish images which they deemed too graphic, but they did not attempt to warn audiences about graphic imagery like the BBC does.

The Corporation's journalists 'worry about' 'viewers' feelings' and 'the privacy of victims'[82]—concerns which are documented in the BBC's Editorial Guidelines.[83] Jeremy Bowen noted that Western media organisations were 'more squeamish' than were their Arab counterparts but suggested that the BBC broadcasted more graphic images than during the Balkan wars in the 1990s. While images available on the blogs in the sample tended to be more graphic than those present on the BBC website, the *Ten O'Clock News* did show a number of sequences of injured and dead Gazans in the aftermath of attacks and in hospitals.

Some of the images available on blogs in the sample could have been incorporated in BBC coverage. Eva Bartlett's videos were not present in the BBC's television content, for example, but they perhaps could have been integrated into a BBC news report in the way that many mobile phone videos were from Iran during the election crisis of 2009 and from Libya in 2011. The lack of amateur video in the BBC's news reports was notable. This can, perhaps, be explained by the fact that the BBC did have access to pictures from Gaza despite the Israeli ban on journalists accessing the Gaza Strip. Jeremy Bowen said both Reuters and APTN were providing footage to the BBC, and Gazan-based BBC journalists were also filming material.

SOURCES AND VOICES

Research suggests that most bloggers rely heavily on traditional media organisations, such as the BBC, for their information.[84] The Muqata bloggers, Juan Cole and Yaacov Lozowick all used traditional media reports. The Muqata blog aggregated information from other media sources providing links to articles from *The International Herald Tribune*, the *Washington Post, The Guardian, The Jerusalem Post* and Fox News and included references to IDF radio, Press TV and Channel 2 Israel TV. Yaacov Lozowick took a keen interest in media coverage of the war and regularly linked to articles and blog posts. Juan Cole also often used media reports as the basis for his commentary on the Gaza conflict.

These blogs would have been of less interest to the BBC because they were using sources which their journalists could already access. In particular, it was not necessary to incorporate the IDF Spokesperson blog into the BBC's coverage because journalists could interview Israeli spokespeople directly. There were a number of bloggers in the sample, however, who were speaking to a variety of people on the ground in Gaza, offering alternative angles and perspectives which the BBC might not have been able to easily contact.

The ISM bloggers based in Gaza regularly spoke to members of the PRCS and other Gazan civilians. These provided the ISM workers with the access which some foreign journalists had been denied. Bartlett, for example, interviewed eyewitnesses who had seen medic Arafa Hani Abd al Dayem killed on 4 January.[85] Similarly, Sameh A Habeeb said he relied primarily on contacts on the ground. The sources of his information are not always clear from his blog posts but in an interview for *The Indypendent* he stated that he called doctors at hospitals, listened to local radio stations and spoke to people in the 'humanitarian field' and 'the media world'.[86]

Laila El-Haddad was also relaying first-hand experience of life inside Gaza through her blog posts. She spoke to her parents in the territory, using her conversations as interviews for her blog posts, and helped traditional media journalists to contact other people living in Gaza.[87]

Blogs in this sample did offer limited access to the voices of Israeli soldiers through their parents' blogs. Yaacov Lozowick only briefly mentioned his son's military service,[88] but the author of A Soldier's Mother wrote regularly about the life of her son, 'Elie'.[89] Blog readers had access to small snapshots of Elie's life and general mood. Elie was still mediated by his mother rather than by a military censor. On 8 January, Elie's reaction to the attack near an UNRWA school was documented: '"What did they want us to do? They were firing mortars from there? Why didn't the UN stop them?"'[90] He also commented on the introduction of a daily three-hour ceasefire by Israel to allow food and medical supplies into Gaza: '"We're doing it to show the world . . . so they see that we aren't fighting the people."'

Given the potential for these bloggers to provide journalists with access to perspectives and accounts on the ground in Gaza, it was surprising that only two bloggers from the sample were mentioned in BBC output in this period. On 7 January, the BBC website posted snippets of commentary on Gaza.[91] It included a link to a piece by Nancy Kanwisher in *The Huffington Post* and noted that Juan Cole had commented on Kanwisher's piece on his Informed Comment blog. Two days before, the BBC had included a quote from Sharyn Lock. She was described as 'an activist with the ISM, a Palestinian-led organisation which campaigns against Israel's actions'.[92] There was no mention of Lock's blog, and it appears that the quote was taken from a telephone interview conducted by the BBC during the night of 4 January.[93] The fact that a source was a blogger was not always mentioned in BBC content.

Other bloggers did feature on the BBC website which produced several round-ups of civilian voices and eyewitnesses. On 4 January, the BBC published a webpage with three accounts from civilians in Gaza although there is no mention of any of these accounts being sourced through blogs. Two days later, the BBC added an article by BBC Monitoring titled 'Israeli blogs back Gaza operation'.[94] The piece included extracts from bloggers on Israblog[95] and The Marker Café,[96]—both written in Hebrew—and contributions from several English-language blogs including Shiloh Musings,[97] Jews Sans Frontieres[98] and Zionist Conspiracy.[99] The BBC noted that generally Israeli bloggers backed the Gaza offensive. Although some sympathised with the suffering of Palestinian civilians, most believed Israel's actions were justified in the face of Hamas rocket attacks.

Indeed, there remained limits on the range of views expressed in BBC coverage even if a variety of voices were represented. It was unusual to hear dissenting voices—either an Israeli who opposed the Gaza invasion[100] or a Palestinian who blamed Hamas. For example, in an article for the BBC website on 9 January, the four Israelis interviewed all said they supported the offensive.[101] It might be the case that it was difficult for the BBC to obtain dissenting minority views. Alan Johnston stated in his backgrounder for *Newsnight* that Hamas has 'severe critics' in Gaza, but they would not speak out publicly. A similar lack of range is also a weakness of the blog sample used in this chapter, but an article in *The Guardian* by Lisa Goldman suggests that other voices might have been accessed. A number of prominent Israeli Hebrew-language bloggers supported the Hadash Party during the February election and openly discussed their opposition to the Gaza war.[102]

Evidence of bloggers influencing the BBC's radio or TV coverage was rare. There was a notable pattern to the BBC's use of sources between 5 and 9 January. In news bulletins, official sources tended to dominate. Radio 4 News at 06h00 and at 18h00 exclusively used interview clips from individuals acting in an official capacity. In contrast, Radio 5 Live bulletins did include some audio from civilians living in Gaza and Israel. In five programmes, the *Ten O'Clock News* only rarely quoted individuals who would not be deemed to be 'official sources' including a relative of an IDF soldier, four unnamed Palestinians, an anonymous Israeli and a Bedouin guide. *Newsnight* did not feature bloggers in any of their programmes. This was surprising given that it has more airtime than the *Ten O'Clock News* to represent different points of view, included several bloggers in its coverage of the Iraq war and inter-viewed a number of political bloggers in the past. Radio 4's *PM* programme also did not interview any bloggers in this period.

The *WHYS* programme was exceptional in its approach. As noted in Chapter 6, Editor Mark Sandell tries to differentiate his programme from others available on the World Service by placing less emphasis on 'official sources'. When *WHYS* has official representatives or experts on the pro-gramme the aim is to allow other listeners to question guests or debate with them rather than the programme's presenter asking all the questions. During their shows on Gaza, the programme did use 'experts'—journalists, academics and politicians—as studio guests on several occasions, but *WHYS* also invited a blogger, Sunny Hundal, to participate in a similar role.[103] The programme also aired a wide range of voices from around the world.

THE LIMITS OF THE INFLUENCE OF BLOGGING ON THE BBC'S COVERAGE OF GAZA

The impact of blogs on the BBC's coverage of the Gaza war can be seen in three main areas. First, the BBC incorporated the personal narrative into its journalism by commissioning the blog-style diaries written by BBC corre-spondent Jeremy Bowen and aid worker Hatem Shurrab. BBC bloggers also adopted a more informal style in their coverage of Gaza, even if posting on the subject was sporadic. Although it was exceptional, Robin Lustig's blog post, in which he imagined himself as an Israeli and as a Palestinian, was an interesting experiment in how a BBC journalist could employ a highly opinionated voice and yet remain within the confines of the BBC's commit-ment to impartiality.

Second, bloggers were an important aspect of various articles on the BBC news website. Bloggers Sharyn Lock and Juan Cole featured in BBC News online articles and there were several round ups in which various bloggers outside the sample were incorporated. These bloggers offered a personal perspective on the conflict that provided a richer understanding of how indi-viduals experienced war.

Third, the BBC journalists running *WHYS* consciously looked to the blogosphere and commenters on their blog to shape their news agenda. The *WHYS* blog was used as a way of encouraging debate and conversation around the Gaza news story which influenced their radio and television coverage. A number of bloggers and voices from all over the world appeared on their programme representing a broad range of views. In this sense *WHYS* can be viewed as a BBC programme which encourages and facilitates the co-creation of their journalistic content.

More generally, however, the chapter has demonstrated the fundamental limitations of the impact of blogs on the BBC's journalism. The BBC's news values and its news agenda remain relatively unchanged. Bloggers in the sample tended to chronicle the consequences of the conflict for their friends, family, colleagues or, if they were based in Gaza, the people who they met in the conflict zone. By contrast, the BBC offered audiences a broader understanding of the 'big picture' and the impact of the conflict on a variety of people and countries. In particular, the BBC delivered a range of international coverage evident in its reporting of the diplomatic initiatives for peace and the prospects for a ceasefire.

Viewed through the lens of the resulting content, the incorporation of blogs or bloggers into BBC broadcast news was not substantial. With the exception of the *WHYS* programme, bloggers and blogs were not a visible feature of radio and television output. It is notable that the BBC benefits from the number of people who directly engage with the organisation and its content. The fact that the IDF Spokesperson blog did not figure is not surprising given the BBC's access to numerous Israeli government and military spokespeople.

Blogs are merely one method of contacting sources. Matthew Eltringham, then Head of Interactivity, noted that during the Gaza conflict a number of people also contacted the BBC directly by email: 'for much of the crisis this has been one of the main ways we have been getting voices—text and audio—out of the Strip'.[104] The limitations of time and space in TV and radio mean that even if an interviewee was a blogger a BBC report might not have an opportunity to mention that fact. For example, Sharyn Lock was interviewed for BBC radio and appeared in a news website article, but her blog was not referenced.

In the sample, the BBC's established editorial guidelines around its use of language and its commitment to balance and impartiality were not compromised. Unless they were representing the opinions of another party, the BBC was consistent in its use of 'neutral' language and attempted to balance the imagery it showed as much as possible. Consequently, the BBC often juxtaposed images representing civilian distress from Gaza with Israeli voices which claimed that these were being caused by the deployment of 'human shields' by Hamas. The BBC accessed imagery from inside Gaza through APTN and Reuters. Its sensitivity to 'the need to be compassionate and to avoid any unjustified infringement of privacy' meant any graphic images it showed were prefaced with warnings.[105] On the BBC News website, the images shown were less graphic than those shown by bloggers, who demonstrated that they were less 'cautious editors' than BBC News online journalists.[106]

Bloggers were more concerned with representing unedited realities of war than worrying about offending potential audiences. A number of images found on blogs in the sample, such as the unverified images of armed children,[107] would probably be 'judged unshowable'[108] by the BBC and certainly not without significantly more context and explanation. The BBC *Ten O'Clock News*, however, did show imagery which was as graphic as some of the images available on blog posts, including severely injured civilians. Bloggers such as Eva Bartlett and Sharyn Lock were also able to upload their own raw, unedited footage of what they were seeing, acting as eyewitnesses on the ground in places the BBC might not have been able to access. These videos were not present in the BBC sample, but they could have been incorporated into BBC coverage in the way that videos were used to form news reports from the Iran election crisis in 2009 and the conflicts in Syria and Libya in 2011. Perhaps most notably in the latter case when the BBC showed graphic amateur footage of the killing of the Libyan leader Muammar Gaddafi.[109]

The BBC might also have used blogs in the sample to report what was happening in Zeitoun earlier than 9 January. The attack in the area was reported by several blogs as early as 5 January. It appears that the BBC waited until the ICRC issued a press release before following up the story. These are areas where the BBC could have collaborated with the bloggers in the sample, and it was surprising that there was not more use of these blogs by the BBC given that they were featured in other traditional media outlets.

The particularly sensitive nature of the Israeli–Palestinian conflict for the BBC might explain their caution in using blogs. The BBC's journalism in the Middle East had already come under intense scrutiny before the conflict. A 2004 report written by senior journalist Malcolm Balen exploring whether BBC coverage of the Israeli–Palestinian conflict was biased has never been published.[110] Two years later, a report for the BBC governors documented 'identifiable shortcomings, particularly in respect of gaps in coverage, analysis, context and perspective and in the consistent maintenance of the BBC's own established editorial standards'.[111] Later in January 2009, the BBC inadvertently became an angle of the Gaza conflict story for refusing to show an aid appeal by the Disasters Emergency Committee for the children of Gaza.[112] Jeremy Bowen noted that one of the reasons the BBC had not yet sanctioned a blog for him as Middle East Editor was partly because of the potential that it might be hijacked by interest groups.[113]

Perhaps more importantly, however, this chapter emphasises the importance of the live blog or live text commentary as a format for incorporating blogs and Twitter updates in the BBC's journalism. The decision not to update a live blog—which may come to be regarded as exceptional in the light of how often the BBC now uses live pages—meant fewer blogs and Twitter updates were incorporated online. *The Guardian* website's live blog in the same period, for example, included links to blog posts by both Laila El-Haddad and the author of A Soldier's Mother, among a number of others.[114]

This chapter acts as an important counterpoint to previous chapters which have tended to highlight areas of change. It demonstrated that, for the most part, blogs did not influence the broad basis of the BBC's journalism.

WHYS's coverage of Gaza, which offered the most comprehensive attempt to 'co-create content' with the audience and engage in a 'news conversation' remained unusual when compared with the rest of the BBC's content. Other aspects of blogging were grafted onto the BBC's existing editorial approach. The adoption of a 'personal' 'blogging' style through BBC blogs and diaries complemented the more 'distant' and detached news reporting on the BBC news website. The content generally remained similar—it is simply delivered in a more personal style[115] and is an attempt to extend a BBC journalists' personal voice into the online medium as a method of showcasing their authority and expertise.

The incorporation of bloggers into BBC coverage supplemented the Corporation's online news reporting. Several commenters on blogs in the sample said they had turned to blogs because they provided the 'true link to the story' in Gaza,[116] or 'have an immediacy—and a humanity—that those written by most broadcast journalists lack'.[117] BBC journalists addressed this weakness by incorporating the authentic voices of some bloggers into their online coverage alongside more traditional news reporting. This 'complementarity' could have been more fully exploited by the BBC through the integration of more blogs in the sample into their coverage of Gaza.[118]

While bloggers, therefore, have the opportunity to present their own narratives of conflict on the Web and exist alongside large news organisations in a pluralistic media landscape, the BBC has not been led to abandon an understanding of journalism based on impartiality and 'objectivity'. The BBC's long-established news culture remains relatively unchanged in the face of blogging. News bulletins were still dominated by official sources of information, and there was no significant impact on news agendas. When bloggers were incorporated they tended to be those who articulated the war in an existing media frame evident in the way that Israeli bloggers included by the BBC all supported the invasion. There was little room for dissenting voices which might have revealed a more complex situation. The inherent structural limitations of TV and radio were also not conducive to the visible inclusion of bloggers,[119] and the main use found for blogs by the BBC's radio and TV programmes appears to be marketing news and transferring audiences from one platform to another. Robin Lustig's stylistically 'subjective' blog post was made to fit a principle of impartiality which balanced two opposing viewpoints. The convergence of blogs and the traditional media is limited, and bloggers do not currently fundamentally threaten the BBC's role as an important mediator of conflict in a more diverse news network.[120]

The conclusion places these findings alongside those of previous chapters when considering the impact widespread online publication by the 'former audience' has had on the BBC's coverage of war and terrorism. It also discusses how the challenges of blogs have been reconciled with the BBC's approach to journalism and identifies existing tensions which are likely to affect the BBC's working practices and the content of the BBC's journalism in the future.

Conclusion
The Two Faces of Janus—The Future of Journalism

The impact of blogging on the BBC's coverage of war and terrorism in the first decade of the 21st century can be represented by the two faces of Janus, the Roman god of gatekeepers and doors, of beginnings and ends, who faces both forwards into the future and backwards into the past. The incorporation of blogging into the BBC's journalism represented a significant organisational leap and was part of a wider ongoing cultural shift in the presentation of news and the BBC's relationship with its audience. The use of blogs as reporting tools and the inclusion of blogs in BBC output points towards a future for journalism which includes the 'people formerly known as the audience' as essential contributors to a collaborative news process.[1] Blogging has undoubtedly influenced how BBC journalists produce news stories online and to a lesser extent on radio and television. The BBC's incorporation of blogging, however, has been grafted onto the Corporation's existing approach to journalism—the new face has been cast onto the old. Where blogs have pressured the BBC's values or exposed weaknesses in editorial procedures, the BBC initially reaffirmed the rigour of its traditional journalistic standards. But the practices and values of some bloggers have also led to shifts in the BBC's approach to journalism evident in a reevaluation of aspects of the BBC's understanding of impartiality, accountability and accuracy.[2]

This book has demonstrated that identifying the distinctiveness of blogs as an online genre is increasingly difficult. Blogging software now provides the engine for more complex websites and it is possible to argue that people 'blog' on social networking sites such as Facebook and in large group forums. Many have turned to the shorter-form microblogging available on platforms such as Twitter. The ability to feed a blog into Twitter, include Twitter updates on blogs and comment on the forum-like conversations which appear below YouTube videos demonstrates that Internet genres are merging. In addition, corporations, militaries, governments and the media have all entered the blogosphere or include features on websites which resemble blogs. If blogs were not a 'delimited category' in 2004,[3] they were even less so by the second decade of the 21st century. Blogging has become a ubiquitous method of presenting news and information online. While the blog genre might eventually dissolve as it merges and evolves in tandem with other Web genres,[4] an array of features synonymous with blogging such as straightforward, low-cost publication, the personal voice, streams of news, the hyperlink, networks of information and the participation of the 'audience' will continue to contribute to journalism in the 21st century.

Mark Tremayne identified three stages of the traditional media's response to the emerging opportunities presented by blogs and the challenges they posed to their news operation and output. First, they attacked blogs; second, they learnt how to 'take advantage of active citizen-readers to generate a better product' and third, they embraced blogs by writing their own and hiring bloggers.[5] Through the lens of the BBC's coverage of war and terrorism, this book has focussed on the second and third stages. It has thus assessed how the BBC has adopted blogs as a reporting tool and analysed how journalists use blogs as sources of information in their journalism.[6]

BLOGS AS SOURCES AND THEIR IMPACT ON THE BBC'S JOURNALISM

BBC journalists who have incorporated blogs into their journalism on a regular basis have embedded themselves in online communities. Rather than emphasise the individual pursuit of news, they view journalistic autonomy as more collaborative both with their colleagues and with the audience.[7] Their success in harnessing blogs and bloggers was a consequence of a decision to actively participate—they write their own personal blogs, update their own Twitter accounts and have made numerous contacts through the Web. They have become what some academics have described as Distributed[8] or Networked[9] journalists. By developing a visible online presence they are known nodes in overlapping online networks attracting interest and information from sources and contacts. Chris Vallance's collaboration with a blogger in Iraq to help him report the Awakening Movement in 2007 offers an example of war reporting at the BBC which resonates with Jeff Jarvis's and Charlie Beckett's vision of 'Networked Journalism'[10] or Alan Rusbridger's assertion that journalism is becoming 'mutualised'.[11] Vallance, the professional, worked with an 'amateur'—a blogger known as Last of Iraqis. The latter recorded his own audio in Iraq, helping Vallance produce a story he would never otherwise have been able to access.

As part of a 'networked information economy' which includes the 'reorganisation of the public sphere',[12] blogs have enabled the views of many more individuals and communities to be heard. These new perspectives, voices, opinions and reactions have also appeared in the BBC's journalism. They have proved especially valuable in the aftermath of terror attacks where those affected have felt compelled to write about their experiences. In July 2005, BBC journalist Alan Connor collated blog posts discussing the London bombings, while Rachel North, who survived one of the blasts, wrote a blog for the BBC website. Blogs have also been more prominent in stories where a perspective on a news event is difficult to access due to the limitations placed on media coverage by the dangers of conflict or the restrictions of a state government. The story of the Iraq war, more dangerous than any previous conflict for journalists,[13] was accessed through the blog posts of Iraqis and US soldiers. When the BBC covered Burma in 2007,[14] stories concerning China,[15] the Iran election crisis in 2009, or the conflict in Syria in 2011, blogs, YouTube videos and Twitter feeds became more important to the BBC. In these circumstances, the BBC's own ability to access and publish a news story through traditional means had been impaired because of safety concerns, bans on journalists, interference with the BBC website or electronic jamming of a satellite. Digital sources of information became more important as a means to tell the story or fulfil the BBC's impartiality remit. One BBC journalist suggested that these stories represent 'probably the closest you get to a breaking news situation where blogs are an official kind of source'.[16] More generally, it is no longer unusual to find material produced by 'amateurs' and published online being incorporated into the BBC's coverage of war and terrorism, whether on radio, TV or the news website.

The BBC's incorporation of blogs into their journalism played a part in a wider cultural shift within the BBC towards an impartiality based on representing a broader spectrum of views rather than merely juxtaposing two opposing viewpoints.[17] The desire to reflect a greater diversity of voices was not new at the Corporation: A.P. Ryan, who was made Controller of News in 1942, believed that 'official' news alone was not adequate for the public and that the BBC should produce journalism based on 'a variety of sources'.[18] Nevertheless, the Internet has facilitated unprecedented opportunities that make fulfilling this long-held aim more achievable. In conjunction with the media space offered by the BBC website, the Corporation has used blogs to offer coverage of war and terrorism which is more 'multiperspectival'.[19] According to the BBC Trust, the One Day in Iraq project in 2005, which included a number of Iraqi and US military bloggers, presented 'varied fragments' from a spectrum of sources to provide 'an illuminating picture of daily life' in the country.[20] The two case studies in this book demonstrated that this approach remains an important feature of the BBC's online reporting of war and terrorism. The BBC's coverage of Gaza incorporated a number of bloggers in articles on the BBC website to access a variety of Israeli and Palestinian voices. The chapter on Gaza highlighted how these authentic personal voices complement a more distanced, neutral and detached style of news reporting.

During the BBC's live blogging coverage of the Mumbai terror attacks, these voices appeared directly alongside those of BBC journalists and official sources. The live updates page reflected 'reactions not just from high officials, but from citizens in various walks of life'.[21] Incorporating audience material can also be viewed as a method of mitigating the potential threat posed by a shift in the power relation between the journalist and the audience.[22] Although the proliferation of individual online publishers offers the prospect of a decline in the traditional media's importance in the media landscape, news organisations have responded by curating, organising, selecting and editing these accounts. By combining this approach with traditional news reporting, the BBC retains an important and relevant cultural role in the dissemination of news and information.

In order to include audience contributions in its online coverage of war and terrorism, the BBC has adopted live text commentary or live blogging. The format is used to present news online not as a traditional packaged news narrative but as an emerging continuous stream of news information. A live blog is a way for journalists to represent a 'networked society'[23] in which digital technology has enabled individuals to practice many-to-many communication which is simultaneous without being contiguous.[24] It is an example of a 'space of flow'[25] designed to facilitate networked news. BBC journalists writing the live updates page can be seen as producing the 'first draft of journalism'[26] rather than 'the first draft of history'. The live text updates of the Mumbai attacks—the first time the BBC covered a major terror attack in this manner—provides a baseline study which can be used to assess the impact of online news on the BBC's coverage of war and terrorism in the future. Publishing rolling online coverage of a terror attack transferred some of the problems of live television into the online medium. The competitive nature of news online whereby publishing information at speed is necessary in order to remain most relevant in the media landscape meant BBC journalists dispensed with the practice of having two separate sources for a news line. Instead, they tended towards publish first, verify later—an approach pioneered by bloggers. This shift was nevertheless conceptualised in the context of established journalistic values. Updating the page was conceived not as 'blogging' but as producing a text version of live television. In order to maintain the BBC's commitment to accuracy, the Corporation adopted a widespread and consistent policy of attributing information to its source as a means to distance the organisation from the accuracy of the content in the updates.

The tensions between old and new approaches were evident in the inclusion of a Twitter update which reported an inaccurate factual claim about the Indian government although the BBC's reporting from other sources of information might also have been scrutinised. In the immediate aftermath, BBC journalists reemphasised the importance of verification and accuracy. Drawing on existing guidance established for the use of audience material by the User Generated Content (UGC) hub, an internal document offering advice on updating live text commentary pages stated: 'Twitter and blogs should be considered and treated in the same way as UGC coming in directly to us'.[27] The document also stated that Twitter and blogs should be used for atmosphere and mood while eyewitness claims and pictures' and 'any content being used as fact' 'must be verified'. Since then, the BBC has reevaluated its approach to verification in response to a media environment where anybody with access to an Internet connection can publish information online.

The 2004 Neil Report for the BBC recommended that in order to fulfil its commitment to 'truth and accuracy' the Corporation should 'avoid unfounded speculation' and be 'honest and open' about what it did not know.[28] Increasingly the emphasis is on the latter rather than the former. In 2011, Assistant Editor of Social Media Development Matthew Eltringham articulated this new approach by identifying a 'line of verification'.[29] On the 'light side' of the line is material which is deemed to be accurate by the BBC, confirmed by two independent sources. On the 'dark side' of the line are 'rumour, gossip, facts and factoids' circulating on the Internet.[30] Previously the 'dark side' would be neither reported by the BBC nor acknowledged by their journalists, but increasingly the BBC engages with a variety of unconfirmed reports. Eltringham argued that the BBC's role should be to investigate leads in an open manner, informing the audience of what is not verified while working to confirm the veracity of information which is being discussed online.

For the most part, BBC journalists still see this verification process through the lens of existing journalistic practices.[31] BBC journalists talk in terms of cross-referencing, contacting bloggers via email or telephone and relying on their 'instincts to identify the wheat from the chaff'. They tend to describe their treatment of blogs as though it were any other source. They require corroborating evidence, must perform thorough checks and 'need to work with bloggers in the same way' that they 'work with [other] sources'.[32] Although some journalists have developed a specialist set of skills,[33] the emphasis on traditional practices was initially also necessary to reassure sceptical editors that journalists' use of blogs was in line with the BBC's rigorous approach to other sources of information. The journalistic ritual of 'triangulation' whereby a 'tip-off' found on a blog is 'stood up' by consulting other sources remains durable.

OVERCOMING THE CHALLENGES OF BLOGS AS SOURCES

In order to harness the potential of blogs given the volume of information available to them, the BBC's working practices have had to become more collaborative. The newsroom itself has become more 'internally networked',[34] particularly evident in the positioning of the UGC hub at the centre of the BBC's operation since 2008. The UGC hub scours blogs and social networks for potential news stories, verifies the accuracy of audience material and distributes it to news programmes around the BBC. Since January 2010, the hub has been managed by a Social Media Editor—a new editorial role. As the rise of 'mass self-communication'[35] has increased in the form of blogs and other genres, the demand for sifting, organising, aggregating and curating material has grown. The significant staff resources that the BBC dedicates to these tasks is an acknowledgement that UGC is 'here to stay as a major component of news coverage'.[36] UGC hub journalists act as professional 'redactors'[37] or human search engines in an era when automation is improving but cannot yet be taught the elusive and ever-shifting concept of 'news value'. Although an awareness of the potential of blogs and social media platforms is now commonplace across the newsroom, the time-consuming nature of finding journalistic needles in digital haystacks means that the role of redaction so far has often been the domain of both formal and informal specialists at the BBC.

Indeed, this book highlights that finding and verifying information on blogs is not always straightforward for BBC journalists who are also contributing output for news stories.[38] Herbert Gans argues that the incentive to produce multiperspectival news is limited by the requirement of efficiency in producing the news.[39] For defence and security correspondents and online journalists reporting breaking news on the website, the inefficiency of blogs as sources of information was a central difficulty. Journalists were concerned that longer form blogs do not supply sufficiently regular, newsworthy information at the necessary speed. Unsurprisingly, BBC correspondents reporting conflict and terrorism on the ground rely on local contacts rather than blogs. But even for correspondents reporting stories from London, the pace of the news cycle, the volume of information they are receiving and the number of outlets for which they are expected to provide content mean they do not have time to search for blogs and verify the information they find there.

Journalists encountered difficulties with multiauthored forums such as the Army Rumour Service because it was not always straightforward to identify anonymous contributors,[40] while official blogs, such as those offered by the Ministry of Defence (MoD) would not reveal anything a journalist did not already know. Correspondents tend to rely on background briefings and off-the-record conversations to source stories. Frank Gardner identifies a 'sliding scale' in defence and security whereby those who know most speak least in public.[41] In short, while they are aware there is plenty of interesting material on the Web, in an age of 'information overload', much time can be wasted in a futile search for 'new facts'—the hard currency of a news story.

Journalists writing the BBC's main news articles online paradoxically have the least opportunity to incorporate blogs in their journalism. The expectation placed on them to 'churn out' news stories for the website based primarily on wire reports and the work of fellow BBC journalists leaves them little time to investigate the blogosphere for alternative angles. It was also apparent that their editors were wary of reporting information which was not already on the wires; reporting a story emerging on an unknown blog might be deemed to be too much of a risk.

This book highlights that, although there were exceptions, initially there was a fundamental lack of engagement with tools which might help a journalist access relevant Web material in a timely manner. In 2007 and 2008, some journalists did use RSS feeds, Netvibes, Google Reader or Twitter to monitor blogs, but they were in the minority. Most tended to bookmark relevant pages in a Web browser. More complicated strategies which might make use of networks on social bookmarking sites, online software such as Yahoo Pipes or the development of code for accessing and filtering information online were not identified. This should not necessarily be interpreted as a lack of interest, ability or desire on the part of journalists, more a consequence of the shortage of time available to invest in learning new skills while producing daily news.[42] In 2009, the College of Journalism launched a pan-BBC social media course to address this skills gap,[43] but BBC journalists have also relied on the informal dissemination of news practices and the experience they gained from incorporating digital media content into major news stories such as the Iran election crisis in 2009 and the Arab Spring in 2011. There has been a much broader uptake of online tools and the development of Web skills at the BBC which will continue to be necessary if the Corporation is to fulfil its remit of acting as a 'trusted guide to the Web' and increasingly to the world as the boundaries between 'real' and 'virtual communities' continue to dissolve.[44] In particular, Twitter has been adopted as a tool to track breaking news and source information by a wide range of journalists across the BBC.

Twitter acts as an 'early warning radar' for journalists. It is 'an awareness system' which allows them to monitor the 'ambient journalism' produced by the former audience.[45] BBC journalists describe it as a 'news wire' enabling them to detect new events and information. A 140-character limit on Twitter updates encourages brevity and allows a journalist to monitor thousands of accounts. Updates are easy to search, tweets mentioning specific events can be collected around hashtags, and individuals can update accounts remotely from mobile phones. In a world where people are increasingly connected to a digital network, BBC journalists thus benefit from an unprecedented virtual 'geographic proximity' to hundreds,[46] or even thousands of sources, by which they are able to quickly and continually monitor news and information in real time.

If journalists' 'overriding aim' is 'efficiency',[47] then it is understandable that Twitter has, in many respects, replaced longer-form blogs as the most useful online digital tool to cover breaking news. Accessing sources of information online through Twitter is more efficient for journalists than sifting through blog posts. Moreover, as BBC UGC hub journalist Samanthi Dissanayake noted during the Mumbai attacks in 2008, bloggers began updating their Twitter accounts first and writing blog posts later: 'people sometimes just don't update a blog until after an event. It's so different to when I first started looking at blogs, years ago when they were always updating and they were writing a blog post every few hours'.[48] World Affairs Producer Stuart Hughes, who began using Twitter in May 2010, says he has a markedly different experience of accessing new stories using the microblogging service than through longer-form blogs. While he was not convinced that he has ever found a story from a blog, he claims that he discovers 'as many stories through Twitter' as he does 'through the newspapers or the wires'.[49] He says Twitter is having a 'massive effect' on the BBC newsroom.[50]

Communication tools like Twitter and developments in mobile communication technology, such as the smartphone, tablets, laptop computers, wireless Internet access and increasingly sophisticated portable video cameras, have the potential to liberate more journalists from the newsroom. So far the Internet has encouraged the development of 'glocalised journalists' at the BBC, who have benefited from global access to sources online but have been tethered to their desks in London as a consequence. These technological and broader societal trends, however, point to a potential future of 'networked individualism' whereby connections between individuals are less oriented around the location of an individual and more around the individual person.[51] This might free more journalists to access sources, collate digital material, work collaboratively and distribute the news as part of a looser networked news organisation which is less dependent on a physical newsroom.

BLOGS, THE JOURNALIST'S SOURCES AND THE LIMITS OF MULTIPERSPECTIVAL NEWS AT THE BBC

A revolution in access to the means of publication and simple widespread distribution of information through digital networks has, therefore, enabled nonofficial sources of information to more easily capture the attention of journalists. Previously, a journalist's knowledge of the social world was dependent on its bureaucratic organisation—a perspective they transmitted to their audience. Blogs and social networks enable journalists to access another picture of the social world, informed by the active participation of the audience. A hierarchical bureaucratic society provided journalists with a 'map of relevant knowers' which consisted of governmental and organisational sources.[52] Although they are still of fundamental importance, a journalist is no longer entirely dependent on 'these structural locations to provide for the continuous detection of events'.[53] In a 'networked society',[54] the journalist's map is complemented by a network of digitally connected sources.

The Internet facilitates a phenomenon that allows for the rapid emergence of nonofficial sources into public view in specific circumstances—most evident in this book in the context of terror attacks when eyewitnesses played a key role in news coverage. Their impact on the news, however, tends to be fleeting rather than sustained. Paradoxically, on occasions where a blogger's access to the news becomes more regular it might be necessary to reevaluate the status of a source of information as their role changes in a relatively short time. Salam Pax, for example, was initially an anonymous blogger whose blog was quoted with many caveats in 2003, but several years later he was treated by the media as an expert authority on the war in Iraq. For a time, his opinions on the progress of the war in Iraq were reported as news. Since the drawdown of US and British involvement in Iraq from 2009, he has largely disappeared from the news agenda.

Various factors continue to limit the extent of the 'democratisation' of the BBC's news content. Throughout this book, it has been acknowledged that increasingly a blog or a Twitter feed should not simply be conceptualised as an alternative, a nonofficial or a new source of information. BBC Defence and Security Correspondents, for example, tended to access 'old sources' in 'new bottles'[55]: academics or experts who have begun updating blogs on their particular specialty. A comparison of the BBC's live blogging coverage of the lone gunman attacks in Norway in 2011 with the Mumbai study in Chapter Seven demonstrates that whereas in 2008 Twitter updates included by the BBC were all written by members of the 'former audience', three years later this number had fallen to 34%. In 2011, nearly half of the Twitter updates the BBC included in their coverage of the incident in Norway had been written by other journalists. Indeed, Twitter's impact on the newsroom has been driven, in part, by the adoption of the format by journalists, media organisations and official sources as a method of conveying news and information—a process that mirrored the uptake of blogs by governments, corporations and militaries outlined in Chapter 1.

Initially sceptical of the importance of the Internet, and then ponderous in adapting largely vertical organisational structures to an instantaneous communications environment,[56] official sources of information are now bringing significant budgets and resources to the challenge of presenting news and information in a more diverse media landscape. Official sources remain 'serious about media relations',[57] and their array of news management techniques has been updated for the new media landscape. Digital media campaigns conducted by official sources on blogs, Twitter, Facebook and YouTube not only aim to influence journalists at media organisations by providing regular access to content at speed for a 24/7 news cycle, but also seek to bypass the journalist's 'secondary role' in reproducing and potentially reinterpreting news events by publishing directly to online audiences.[58] Furthermore, the economic and political pressures facing journalists have not disappeared in the information age, while hierarchies of power are reasserting themselves online through direct and indirect censorship.[59] Existing social structures have also been transferred into the online environment and new structures of informational power are being created around access to the Internet, online engagement and the development of social networks online.

The inclusion of content from official sources is particularly maintained by the fact that, for the most part, journalists' understanding of 'newsworthiness' remains largely unchanged. The pronouncements and actions of powerful official sources are usually still privileged as more consequential and therefore more newsworthy than are nonofficial sources. The impact of the 'former audience' is significant in the coverage of terror attacks and during political crises when foreign governments are deemed to be operating a wide-ranging policy of censorship, but in the context of day-to-day defence and security stories, nonofficial blogs and bloggers are generally accessed to provide reaction, comment and opinion on news stories rather than to provide the factual basis for a narrative. BBC journalists producing defence and security stories continued to implicitly index stories to 'the dynamics of governmental debate' evident in the requirement for 'a legitimating backdrop of official voices':[60] a military blogger was not regarded as a suitable commenter for a television package for the *Ten O'Clock News* bulletin, while journalists working on the BBC news website usually required an official level of comment for 'straight' news articles. Although an index of sources is matched to an index of content at the BBC—the same military blogger might be suitable for use in a feature for the news website or for inclusion in a radio programme like *World Have Your Say*—significant remaining barriers nevertheless limit the extent to which traditional media content has become multiperspectival and therefore the extent to which 'the public' accesses 'an ever-widening array of news sources'.[61]

BBC REPORTERS' BLOGS

Expressing some of the concerns which have also prohibited more extensive use of blogs as sources, defence and security correspondents have not embraced blogs as a tool to report stories online. Although a number of BBC journalists, such as Business Editor Robert Peston and Political Editor Nick Robinson, placed their blogs at the centre of their working processes, their colleagues in defence and security have only engaged in blogging sporadically. Stuart Hughes's Blog from Northern Iraq was a personal blog unconnected with the BBC's official output, although it offered a template for how a dedicated defence blog might be made to work before he stopped blogging in 2007. Mark Urban regularly keeps a blog called War and Peace for BBC *Newsnight*, but his posts usually resemble the analysis pieces which he would have written previously for the BBC website.

At various times, BBC reporters have contributed to reporters' logs or diaries, such as during the invasion of Iraq in 2003, Alastair Leithead's updates while embedded with military units in Afghanistan and Jeremy Bowen's diary on the Gaza conflict. These blogging ventures have enabled journalists to offer a more personal perspective on their situation within a news story, particularly in the context of the BBC's presentation of news online.[62] They have also been used as a vehicle for accountability and transparency—a way of 'lifting the lid' on the BBC's journalism.[63] Jeremy Bowen's diary from Gaza explained the frustrations and the subsequent impact on his journalism of his lack of access to the conflict area. The Editors' blog has been used to explain how the BBC reports casualties from Afghanistan[64] and the Corporation's use of language around the subject of 'terrorism'.[65]

Defence and security correspondents, however, have turned down opportunities to write blogs on a more regular basis. They view blogging merely as an additional outlet for content to which they could not devote sufficient time. Frank Gardner noted that a blog would require most attention during periods when he was 'flat out' providing content for other BBC news programmes. Correspondents were also concerned that a blog would have to be disingenuous if it were to protect contacts and sources. They believed that the area of war and terrorism was too 'sensitive', 'raw' or 'controversial', that blog comments might become hijacked by interest groups and that it would be difficult to write a blog without making it opinionated. One correspondent suggested that he was 'too old', implying that blogs might be adopted by the next generation of defence and security correspondents.

Following the lead of Chief Political Correspondent Laura Kuenssberg, Twitter has also emerged as a platform for the BBC's defence and security reporters to use when disseminating news online. Stuart Hughes regularly uses Twitter to break defence and security news, while security correspondent Frank Gardner started updating an account in November 2010. Although limited in the area of defence and security, through blogs and on Twitter, BBC journalists have become individual news portals magnifying their personal influence and increasing their importance to a more distributed BBC news brand.

BBC PROGRAMME BLOGS

Like many news organisations the BBC used blogs to 'distribute content and interact with their audience, mixing vertical and horizontal communication modes'.[66] This book has explored how the World Service's *World Have Your Say* (*WHYS*) programme has attempted to use contributions by blog commenters as a starting point for its journalism. *WHYS* was established in 2005 as a forum for debate and with a mission to act as a facilitator of audience participation in news discussions. *WHYS* journalists have not relinquished their gatekeeping role, but by placing the audience at the centre of their editorial decision-making process, news selections are made in collaborative partnership with members of the audience. This approach encourages a discussion of a diverse range of perspectives on war and terrorism and can be seen as an attempt to shift journalistic authority away from one founded on the knowledge of the journalist to one underpinned by transparency, openness and the facilitation of discussion around the news.

Interactivity through programme blogs, however, was not straightforward to achieve. *Newsnight* struggled to adapt its existing journalistic remit for serious news analysis to a perceived culture of the Web. Grafting the face of 'new' media onto 'old' journalistic models proved problematic. Initially, *Newsnight* was at the forefront of BBC experiments in involving the audience in their journalism including broadcasting the Salam Pax films, starting Paul Mason's blog for the G8 summit in 2005, running an 'Oh My Newsnight' video competition and using its blog as a way of providing space for additional debate with journalists and guests. But since 2008, the programme has used its blog and Twitter feed primarily as a promotional tool and as a way of reaching online audiences with the *Newsnight* brand. In part, this was a response to a reaction of a section of *Newsnight*'s existing audience who felt the programme's remit for serious news journalism and analysis was being diluted by the involvement of the audience, but it was also a consequence of *Newsnight*'s existing journalistic culture and a perceived lack of resources.

THE FUTURE OF JOURNALISM: CALLING
ON THE PAST TO FACE THE FUTURE

Blogging has contributed to a trend whereby news online has become characterised by immediacy, transparency, the curation of relevant digital material, instant collaboration and interactive engagement. In order to adapt to these developments, the BBC has both reaffirmed its traditional editorial standards but also reconceived aspects of its approach to journalism. It explains why Kevin Marsh, the Executive Editor of the BBC College of Journalism, could claim that 'blogging has done more to change the way in which journalists work . . . than possibly anything else thus far',[67] while Director-General Mark Thompson maintained that a blog post is a 'carefully balanced' 'piece of, essentially, broadcast journalism'—'fact-checked' by a 'senior editorial manager'.[68] Working out the future of journalism at the Corporation will continue to be a process whereby the challenges of new developments in the media landscape will be articulated and addressed through existing editorial principles even when practices and values are consequently significantly reevaluated.

Blogging has played a role in a relatively rapid shift towards the 'live' feel and functionality of the World Wide Web. When questions were raised by critics over the extent of editorial oversight on the BBC's reporter blogs and the speed at which they were updated, the BBC described blogs as no different to any other piece of 'broadcast journalism'[69] with rigorous editorial procedures including a 'second pair of eyes' and a blog team to check copy.[70] A journalist's Twitter updates do not have to be checked before they are published, but an editor is monitoring them and would inform the journalist if a correction is necessary. Notably, when correspondents use Twitter to report a story for the BBC their output is being treated editorially in a manner which 'replicates live broadcasting' reinforcing the thesis that the challenges of new communication technology are being met by recourse to existing practices and editorial values.[71] The rapidly updated and evolving online medium, however, continues to test the BBC's editorial practices and standards. In May 2012, Social Media Editor Chris Hamilton apologised for the BBC's illustration of an alleged massacre by a progovernment militia in the Syrian town of Houla with a photo which had been 'circulating on Twitter'. Despite triggering the BBC's 'process for checking user-generated content' which included obtaining 'some information pointing to its veracity', the picture was subsequently found to have been taken during the war in Iraq nearly a decade earlier.[72]

Because it has become instantly alterable and updateable, the Web has facilitated a shift in emphasis in online news: where previously it was always presented as a processed package, now it is also presented as a packaged process. As previously discussed in the context of the Mumbai attacks, accuracy has been pressurised by live blogging the news and near-immediate online publishing in much the same way that it has been by rolling television news. A move away from verification before publication online in favour of 'publish first, verify later' was reconciled with the BBC's commitment to accuracy through the adoption of extensively attributing to sources. For live blogging journalists, more transparent sourcing facilitates the quick publication of unconfirmed reports by distancing a media organisation from immediate responsibility for the accuracy of the news and information. The 'verification of facts' remains 'a professional accomplishment',[73] but one which stands alongside the presentation of an 'unconfirmed' picture of breaking news. The practices of consistently publishing attributed news lines and informing audiences of the extent to which information has been verified can be viewed as manifestations of transparency as a new 'strategic ritual' in online journalistic practice.[74]

Some bloggers had challenged journalists' adherence to objectivity through a conscious embrace of subjectivity.[75] By revealing some of their own biases and limitations, they exposed a lack of openness about the process of journalism and the difficulties of reporting news objectively. In response, BBC editors believe building trust in their journalism requires an approach which combines authority and expertise with a willingness to explain the editorial quandaries and limitations of the journalistic process. Blogs have provided BBC journalists with the space to explain how and why they are making news decisions. They have also played a part in a broader initiative in the post-Hutton era of deconstructing some of the performative illusions of the authoritative news product.

Increased transparency at the BBC has been limited by the tension between openness and the Corporation's commitment to impartiality, which had been based on journalists not revealing their political positions and personal preferences. Calls for greater transparency and attempts to build more open relationships between journalists and the audience using blogs led BBC journalists to question how open they could be about their own biases. This issue was consciously explored by the *WHYS* programme on its blog and is often inadvertently highlighted by BBC journalists writing their own personal blogs outside the BBC and updating their personal Twitter accounts.

The extent to which BBC content could become personal in tone was also relevant to the BBC's reporters' blogs which were regarded by some critics as opinionated punditry. The BBC says it has never used blogs written by correspondents as a vehicle for the personal opinions of its journalists, but a 'personal tone' or 'authenticity of voice' which characterises some BBC blogs has illuminated a grey area between 'personal opinion' and 'professional judgement'. Although BBC News Blogs Editor Giles Wilson acknowledges that there is 'a theoretical risk' of engaging with an informal and 'slightly unguarded' genre, he maintains that the content of BBC blogs is 'informed expert analysis based on the evidence'.[76] He compares blog content to that found in two-ways for the *Ten O'Clock News* in which a BBC correspondent will offer analysis on a news story. The BBC blog network and other technological advances are regarded as facilitating the BBC's long-established brand of 'professional journalism'.[77]

THE FUTURE OF JOURNALISM: COLLABORATIVE WAR AND TERROR REPORTING

The BBC's blogs have not always achieved their aim of facilitating a more interactive relationship with the audience. Kevin Anderson's 2005 report on blogging for the BBC was titled News as Conversation.[78] He believed that if the BBC successfully undertook Tremayne's two stages of adapting to the blogging challenge by incorporating blogs as sources and embracing blogging, then the BBC would become an active participant in an online conversation. By engaging with commenters, it was hoped that BBC journalists would be able to harvest news stories, build relationships with trusted audience members and use the knowledge of the audience to improve their journalism.[79] There was some success evident in programmes such as *PM/ iPM* and *WHYS* where 'home grown' blogging initiatives were combined with an 'outward looking approach' which sought to reflect and join other conversations that were taking place around the Web.[80] Comments on blogs have also provided BBC journalists with alternative angles on news stories, helpful feedback, leads to follow up and informed reaction.

News as conversation, however, proved problematic as the BBC's blogs were undermined by their own success. When blogs were first established, they initially attracted a number of informed specialists who contributed to 'incredibly high-value discussions' in blog comments,[81] but an informal conversation with a few blog commenters quickly became overwhelmed by a noisy audience. Those written by Business Editor Robert Peston and Political Editor Nick Robinson, for example, have hundreds of thousands of readers and hundreds of comments presenting an intractable problem.[82] Comment moderation was time-consuming and expensive, leading to a move to a new registration system for commenters and the outsourcing of comment moderation for news blogs to an external company called Tempero in April 2008.

Senior Product Manager Aaron Scullion notes that journalists are still expected to read through the comments that Tempero clears for moderation,[83] but the direct link between journalist and commenter has been broken. While Peston and Robinson may have time to skim through some of the comments they receive, finding value in comments became difficult for hard-pressed journalists and replies to commenters from journalists are exceptionally rare. Yochai Benkler has described blogs as facilitating a 'weighted conversation'[84] to acknowledge the salience of the blogger over the commenter, but BBC news bloggers often do not engage in a conversation with commenters at all. The 'conversation' on BBC blogs usually takes place exclusively among blog commenters without the active participation of the BBC blogger, and the limitations of blog comments have been aired in public by some of the Corporation's most senior blogging journalists.

In 2011, the BBC embarked on a new experiment which allowed website users to comment on news stories across the BBC website rather than limit comments to blogs and other pages such as the Have Your Say forum. BBC editors select the best comments to display in a featured icon, while website users are able to rate comments 'up' or 'down'.[85] There was some criticism of the BBC's decision to limit comments to 400 characters.[86] The incorporation and representation of the 'collective intelligence'[87] of the audience on the BBC's website remains a 'live issue',[88] and the democratising potential of a shift in journalism from 'a one-way discourse to a two-way dialogue'[89] often remains unfulfilled.

If conversation is difficult to achieve, collaboration[90] has become an important feature of the BBC's journalism. Journalism has often been a collaborative exercise between the journalist and other actors, but the collaboration was cumbersome and highly limited. Digital communication has made journalism instantaneously collaborative. Each stage of the news process has the potential to be influenced by blogs or their offspring. Twitter has become an indispensable source of news and information for journalists; blogs provide a useful tool for reporting news online; social networks and online forums offer the opportunity to tap into the knowledge and experience of dedicated online communities; feedback and potential new angles can be accessed from comments and responses.

In particular, this book has documented how blogs and bloggers have contributed to a more collaborative approach to war reporting: Salam Pax worked with *Newsnight* to provide an insight into Iraq and bloggers regularly featured in the Corporation's online coverage of the conflict, BBC journalists incorporated audience material of the London bombings and chronicled the reaction of bloggers to the attacks, the BBC used blogs and Twitter updates in their coverage of terror in Mumbai and activists' YouTube videos provided the BBC with frontline footage of the conflicts in Libya and Syria. A shift to a more instantly collaborative journalism has led to changes in the newsgathering process and the presentation of news online. Curating digital material produced by the former audience is increasingly important evident in the establishment of the UGC hub at the Corporation, while the BBC's live updates pages display news as a curated process rather than as a packaged story.

This book has shown, however, that the BBC has retained a dominant role in collaborative news partnerships in the context of war reporting. An examination of the BBC's reporting of Gaza found no significant evidence that news agendas or the themes which the BBC covered were particularly influenced by blogs. The BBC's TV and radio coverage of the conflict rarely featured bloggers or material created by the audience. News bulletins in particular continued to be dominated by official sources of information and even in programmes with more airtime, such as Radio 4's *PM* programme and *Newsnight*, no bloggers were featured. In the context of a conflict which has attracted particular attention to the BBC's journalism in recent years, the BBC may have been especially cautious. It appears that more audience material was used by the BBC when covering the Arab Spring in 2011. A *Ten O'Clock News* report on the conflict in Libya by John Simpson in March 2011, for example, included two sequences of amateur video footage, while the difficulties for journalists in accessing the conflict in Syria have meant that the BBC has often included material provided by Syrian activists uploaded onto YouTube. Nevertheless, a wide-ranging content analysis performed as part of a BBC Trust report into the Arab Spring found that in over 90% of BBC news items, no UGC content was present.[91] Indeed, the BBC's coverage of the Gaza conflict highlighted clear boundaries between the BBC's approach to covering conflict and that of bloggers. The BBC's broad journalistic aim—its attempt to achieve, impartial and 'objective' journalism—remained unchanged. With the notable exception of the BBC's approach to accuracy, the BBC's commitment to these values has tended to dictate the terms of 'the kind of uneasy truce' which has been brokered between their journalism and the 'collective intelligence' of digital publication.[92]

THE FUTURE OF JOURNALISM: THE TENSIONS BETWEEN THE TWO FACES OF JOURNALISM

The BBC faces a future where the practices of journalists will evolve with new communication tools and 'the people formerly known as the audience'[93] will collaborate in the process of journalism. At the Corporation, however, another face draws on the experience of the past. Perhaps inevitably at an organisation with culturally ingrained values, new processes of journalism and the contributions of the audience have been grafted onto existing understandings of the practices and standards of BBC journalism. Where the adoption of blogging has exposed potential weaknesses, the BBC has reaffirmed its commitment to the principles of the organisation's long-established brand of journalism.

This book has illuminated the areas of tension within an emerging model of journalism which is 'neither purely networked nor purely traditional, but is rather a mutualistic interaction between the two'.[94] The practices and values of some bloggers including their conscious subjectivity, their presentation of news as a transparent process rather than a finished product and an approach which placed publication before verification have contributed to the reevaluation of certain aspects of the BBC's commitment to impartiality, transparency, accountability and accuracy. New opportunities online mean impartiality is increasingly conceived as presenting a variety of perspectives rather than as an emphasis on balancing a few alternatives as dictated by the limits of broadcast news. A renewed emphasis on transparency and accountability means BBC journalists have attempted to lift the lid on how the BBC does its journalism. Finally, the BBC's approach to accuracy has been reconsidered in light of the increased speed and ease of publication online.

Tensions between the face of the past and the face of the future remain. Publishing information at speed tests the BBC's commitment to accuracy. Reporting objectively in a personal tone cannot lead to the subjective reporting available in the blogosphere. Developing trust in the BBC's journalism is dependent on a balancing act between a new transparent approach and their journalists continuing to conceal their opinions on matters of public controversy.

THE IMPACT OF BLOGGING ON THE BBC'S COVERAGE OF WAR AND TERRORISM

This book has shown that the BBC initially struggled to recognise the challenges and opportunities of blogs. Regarded as an outlet for bloggers' opinionated musings, journalists often dismissed blogs as irrelevant to the practice of professional journalism and incompatible with the BBC's values. The adoption of blogs both as sources of information and as a feature of BBC content was driven by a number of experiments and individual initiatives at various levels of the organisation. BBC journalists broke with existing procedures to start a number of projects before the organisation decided it needed to provide a more coherent framework through which journalists could engage with blogging.

The impact is evident in two significant institutional changes: first, the establishment of the UGC hub which recognised the importance of audience contributions to the future of journalism and, second, the launch of the blog network—a collaborative and occasionally fraught cross-divisional BBC project. These developments helped blogs, Twitter and social networks to become a standard set of sources for BBC journalists, and although there were technical difficulties and ongoing editorial challenges, BBC blogs became regular features of the Corporation's online news offering.

The BBC did test the limits of utilising blogs and casting the face of 'new' media onto 'old' journalistic models has not always been successful. Time pressures, providing news for multiple outlets, the perceived risk of using blogs and the problem of information overload meant journalists did not always access blogs as sources. The UGC hub and a number of unofficial specialists were often left to harness their journalistic potential. Some of these issues were addressed by microblogging, and Twitter is emerging as a journalist's tool of choice for accessing newsworthy material online. The BBC also discovered that applying concepts of 'community' and 'conversation' to much larger audiences has been fundamentally problematic.

The BBC blog network was retrenched in 2011 as several infrequently updated BBC blogs were cut back and many of the others moved to a new format known as 'correspondent pages'.[95] In the process, the term 'BBC News blog' is likely to be lost or at least significantly diminished in prominence, bringing this stage of the BBC's experimentation with the format to an end. But the BBC's news content online will continue to be organised around the individual personalities of BBC correspondents—the 'crown jewels'[96] of BBC News—in order to enhance the authority of the BBC brand.

The adoption of blogging has consequently led to a more personal style of journalism in the BBC's online coverage, both in their own reporters' use of diaries, blogs and Twitter accounts and in the inclusion of audience experience. The BBC News website's use of live text commentary or live blogging to report war and terror has emerged as a significant new approach enabling the BBC to incorporate a selection of material from a digitally connected audience at speed. Material published by soldiers, citizens, activists, governments and militaries and made available on a variety of evolving online media platforms will continue to be included in the BBC's journalism in the future. By providing images and accounts of conflict and terror attacks they will blur the boundaries of who reports war and terror in the 21st century. These developments point to a more collaborative approach to reporting war and terror online whereby the personal tone—the expert views of the BBC's defence and security correspondents on one hand and the authentic voices of those experiencing conflict on the other—will complement the BBC's existing impartial and objective approach to covering conflict.

Appendix A
Code Book for Content Analysis of BBC's Mumbai Live Updates

Source Cited: Individuals, People or Groups of People

1. **'BBC Correspondent'** or **'Reporter'** or **'Outlets'**. BBC journalist or programme.

2. **'Indian Media'**—Indian news organisations and journalists.

3. **'Foreign Media'** and **'Other Media'**—Media outside India and uncategorised media organisations and journalists.

4. **'News Agencies'**—Press Trust of India, Reuters, AP, AFP, etc

5. **'Official Sources—Indian'**. For example, Prime Minister, Foreign Minister, State Minister, "officials", Indian Government, Police, Military, National Security Guards, Indian company official acting in official capacity—i.e., not an eyewitness account.

6. **'Official Sources—Foreign'**. For example, World Leader, President, Prime Minister, Foreign Minister, "officials", Company official, government, UK spokesperson)

7. **'Expert'**. Commenter included for expertise in a certain area.

8. **'Eyewitness'**. Individuals who had seen or heard the attacks or who were trapped in hotels in Mumbai.

9. **'Directly Connected Commenter'**. In Mumbai but not an eyewitness or somebody who has another direct connection to the events. E.g. a relative of somebody who has died. Not members of the diaspora who are commenting from afar. (See below)

10. **'Audience Commenter'**. Individual commenting on the news who has no direct involvement in the story even if they are expatriates with a strong interest.

11. **'Gunmen'** or **'Alleged Attackers'**.

12. **'Other'**. Religious spokesperson, Cricket, uncategorised.

'LEVEL TWO' CODING

Source of Communication Cited: Method of Verbal or Written Communication

1. 'Email' sent to BBC. Includes BBC website users filling in a 'post form' at the bottom of a BBC webpage which are emailed through to BBC journalists.

2. 'Blog'.

3. 'Twitter'.

4. 'Other'. Statement, TV address, government data, press conference, etc.

Appendix B
A Note on Methodology

Rather than pursuing one or two methodological approaches, I adopted a variety of methods in an attempt to broaden the scope of the book and to provide a firmer basis for the development of theoretical conclusions. The aim was to employ 'a wide range of interconnected interpretative practices' as part of an inductive process to develop theory from research.[1] During the course of the research, I deployed a broad tool set including semistructured interviews, focus groups, participant observation, 'progressive theoretical sampling' and content analysis. Although the methods used in each chapter are highlighted, this note critically analyses these techniques and explains in more detail the rationale behind the approaches adopted. It also reflects on my role as a researcher and reflexively considers the impact of my research decisions on the resulting book.[2]

A MIXED-METHODS APPROACH

Uwe Flick observes that 'the use of multiple methods, or triangulation, reflects an attempt to secure in-depth understanding of the phenomenon in question',[3] adding 'rigour, breadth, complexity, richness and depth to any inquiry'.[4] A mixed methods approach often refers to the application of both quantitative and qualitative research methods to an inquiry. Although arguments against mixing qualitative and quantitative approaches have been expressed from an epistemological standpoint, a more technical understanding of qualitative and quantitative research emphasises the strengths of data collection and analysis arising from a combination of approaches.[5]

Chapter 7 of this book, which studied the BBC's live updates of the Mumbai attacks undoubtedly, benefitted from combining a quantitative content analysis with data obtained from qualitative approaches. Bernard Berelson defines content analysis as a 'research technique for the objective, systematic and quantitative description of the manifest content of communication'.[6] The technique is mainly used to examine texts, documents and particularly mass media items.[7]

The BBC's live updates of the Mumbai attacks provided a defined and manageable sample for quantification in order to explore the nature of the sources used by the BBC in their journalism.[8] The reliability of the findings would have been strengthened by independent coding by other researchers.[9] I am confident, however, that the study is reproducible with access to Chapter 7 and the code book provided in Appendix A. The decision to study sources as identified modes of communication (Twitter, blog, statement, etc.) and named sources as individuals or organisations (Prime Minister, police, eyewitness, etc.) is particularly important in ensuring that the results can be compared with future research. The findings could inform comparative studies on live updates pages at other news organisations or the BBC's coverage of other events using the format.

A straightforward content analysis of the BBC's live updates page covering the attacks on Mumbai would have been valuable. It would not, however, have illuminated journalists' decision-making process when selecting sources, while relying solely on frequency counts of sources mentioned might have led to inadequate interpretations. In the context of my research into the Mumbai attacks, for example, nine of the BBC's updates on the pages provided no source of information. Whereas a researcher relying on content analysis alone might conclude that this demonstrated that these updates were poorly sourced, I discovered through interviews[10] that these were the only occasions when BBC journalists had two independent sources for a piece of information. This finding fundamentally alters the interpretation of the data.

I believe, therefore, that my observations of BBC journalists at the time, my interviews with BBC journalists after the event and that my access to internal editorial documents produced in the aftermath substantially increased the rigour, depth and validity of the inquiry into the BBC's use of liveblogging to cover the attacks on Mumbai.

I otherwise employed a qualitative approach throughout the book, but emphasised the deployment of a variety of research methods. Parts of Chapters 2 and 3, for example, covered similar areas of ground, but whereas the former was based primarily on a historical account of the BBC's Web and broadcast content, the latter focussed on interviews with BBC journalists. I was able, therefore, to capture the historical development of the BBC's adoption of blogs as sources and provide a more 'current' perspective on the BBC's engagement with blogs.

PARTICIPANT OBSERVATION AT THE BBC

My preference for multiple methods was also a consequence of my decision to adopt participant observation as a method of inquiry. Norman Denzin defines participant observation as 'a field strategy that simultaneously combines document analysis, interviewing of respondents and informants, direct participation and observation, and introspection'.[11] It is a logic process of inquiry that is flexible, open-ended and opportunistic.[12] The aim is to gain a deeper understanding of human meaning and interaction between members of a community in a particular setting. Participant observation is an iterative process whereby the nature of the inquiry is constantly subject to redefinition through interaction in the field.

The conventional sense in which I acted as a participant observer was in relation to the BBC. The project was a joint venture funded by the Arts and Humanities Research Council and the BBC.[13] The Corporation afforded significant access to BBC meetings, journalists and newsrooms. I had a BBC building pass and was informally attached to the College of Journalism and the World Affairs Unit. The BBC was inevitably interested in making use of the findings.

The BBC is a large and complex organisation. It quickly became apparent that even BBC journalists who had been at the Corporation for many years were not fully aware of many aspects of the BBC's structure and operation. Although I began with the intention of gaining a broad understanding of the BBC as a field, therefore, it was not practical to undertake a comprehensive set of descriptive observations.[14] Instead, I decided to proceed to a more focussed set of observations of areas within the BBC. I selected the World Affairs Unit, the BBC News website, the BBC World Service Newsroom, *World Have Your Say*, *Newsnight* and *iPM/PM*. These locations provided range in terms of media platform (TV, radio and online), news format (bulletins and programmes) and experience of journalism and using blogs. The selection of these sites thus enabled me to access multiple perspectives on the impact of blogging on the BBC's coverage of war and terrorism.

R.L. Gold identified four roles available to the participant observer ranging from 'complete participant' to 'complete observer'.[15] At the BBC, I tended to operate in the two roles between these extremes—as a 'participant as observer' or as an 'observer as participant'. I tried to build relationships over the four-year period with journalists and news programmes, very occasionally helping them produce BBC content[16]—an approach which tends towards the 'participant as observer' role. However, I also interviewed some journalists once without any further contact except for publication approval—more in line with the 'observer as participant' role. The fluid nature of my participation and observation meant that I did not fit neatly into any category, and it is perhaps more helpful to see participant observation as a less rigid 'continuum' from 'complete outsider' to 'complete insider'.[17] The model offered by Gold and Junker suggests that participation would have an adverse affect on observation,[18] but I would agree with Danny Jorgensen that in practice 'skilled and self-conscious investigators' 'are able to participate, intensively and extensively at the same time they are experiencing and observing the world around them'.[19]

Acting as a participant observer, I was able to access a variety of perspectives and standpoints. In particular, I formed an understanding of the internal culture of BBC newsrooms including institutional frustrations and challenges that would not always be brought up so readily in more formal semistructured interviews or in public. My regular presence within the

organisation over a period of four years was conducive to building a trusting relationship with BBC journalists. It also provided opportunities for
research that might not have been envisaged at the start of the study such as
the impromptu focus groups discussed below.

My role as a participant observer at the BBC raised three main issues
which I reflected on regularly throughout the project.

First, it was important to reflexively consider how to use material ethically. Most BBC journalists were aware of my research and my intent to use
material for the study, although occasionally it was not practical at larger
meetings or in open plan offices to inform every BBC journalist of the reason
for my presence. I nevertheless contacted all journalists if I wanted to use
a quote which was attributed to them and presented journalists with unat-
tributed quotes which may or may not have been related to them when I felt
it was possible they might have been identified.

Second, I had to ensure that I was aware of the potential consequences of
'going native' by subsuming the viewpoints of those I was studying. Uwe Flick
notes that 'going native' can be used as an instrument for gaining insights into
the field of study but emphasises that researchers must not lose 'their critical
external perspective'.[20] As I was not usually performing a role as a journalist,
it was easier to retain a sense of distance, and often I was able to control the
extent of my participation. I nevertheless did occasionally experience what
Herbert Gans describes as an 'internal tug of war' whereby a researcher must
assess the nature of his or her 'spontaneous participation'.[21]

In December 2008, for example, I was present during an editorial meeting
with *World Have Your Say* (*WHYS*) for one of their radio shows. I was intending not to participate in the meeting, but was invited to offer my opinion on
what topic should be covered on the programme. I felt I could not refuse the
invitation to contribute and had to quickly consider how I should respond.
One of the potential topics concerned terrorism, and it would have been beneficial for me to put forward an argument for that topic to be discussed. I decided,
however, that if I were acting as a *WHYS* journalist, (which I had in effect been
invited to do) then another topic—concerning the economy—would make for
a stronger programme. I decided to be open to the meeting about the personal
advantages of *WHYS* covering terrorism, before expressing my view that acting as a journalist I felt the show should cover the economic topic.

Given the generosity of journalists in offering their time, I believe this
open and reflexive approach is a more satisfactory solution than is Gans's
suggestion that researchers must usually refuse to offer advice or help in
order to maintain their neutrality.[22] Although a researcher should be aware
not to become too involved, I would argue that refusing to offer occasional
help or advice altogether similarly affects a researcher's neutrality and has
as an impact on the quality of the data collected. Persistent obstinacy could
precipitate a potential breakdown of trust.

Third, I was concerned not to unduly influence my own research question
and undermine the validity of the book. I was aware, for example, that BBC

staff read my blog posts. Occasionally, I could identify a blog post having a direct impact on certain areas of the BBC. In one blog post, I highlighted that a piece written by Mark Urban for his blog had been copied directly as an analysis piece for the website (or vice versa), undermining the stated aim of the BBC to provide alternative content on its blogs. I subsequently received an email from a member of BBC staff working on the blog team. He informed me that he had taken action to inform relevant parties that blog copy should be unique. There may have been other consequences as a result of my contact with journalists and my blog posts which are far harder to trace. However, the size of the BBC and the fact that the sum of my participation in the production of the BBC's journalism was exceptionally small meant that I certainly did not influence the BBC's practices to an extent that would invalidate the findings of the book.

PARTICIPANT OBSERVATION AS A BLOGGER

I also adopted a form of participant observation through my decision to write my own blogs as part of the project. Jill Walker Rettberg argues that the 'best way to understand blogging is to immerse yourself in it'.[23] Initially, becoming a blogger was a reasonable way to introduce myself to the world of blogging, but increasingly I adopted it as an integral research method. Only by fully engaging in the blogosphere—tracking developments on other blogs, updating my own blog and interacting with other blogs—could I claim to have a deep understanding of the blogosphere necessary for an approach based on 'progressive theoretical sampling' (see the following discussion). The potential problem with this approach was that I would naturally settle on a narrow range of blogs based around my own interests but as highlighted above I used interviews with BBC journalists and interactions with bloggers to broaden the range of blogs I accessed.

I also consciously acted as a journalist, attempting to use my own blog as an outlet for news stories that I had sourced using blogs. Through this process I experienced some of the opportunities, frustrations and challenges of using blogs as sources of information which informed some of my interview questions to BBC journalists. The blog also formed a useful archive of information relevant to the project and rather than being an entirely internal record, it was open to challenge, comment and addition.[24] A number of commenters on the blog provided valuable new directions for research.

INTERVIEWS AND FOCUS GROUPS

Alan Bryman notes that participant observation in a large organisation can limit the researcher's access to a range of 'people, incidents and localities'.[25] Although I often interviewed people from the areas I was observing, I also broadened the scope of the inquiry by interviewing BBC journalists from outside these locations, including a few individuals who had left the Corporation.

The main tranche of interviews aimed to explore BBC journalists' use of blogs documented in Chapters 3 and 4. These were semistructured to facilitate comparison between the responses given by journalists at the BBC and explored a variety of themes in relation to the project as outlined at the beginning of Chapter 3.[26] Several pilot interviews were conducted in order to identify additional areas of inquiry. More generally, in the context of a fast-moving period of change in the media landscape, it was necessary to be flexible, reflexive and critical in light of new developments. Twitter was rarely discussed in early interviews in 2007, but by 2009 the microblogging tool was becoming an increasingly prominent theme.

Some interviews were unstructured in nature. I mainly employed this mode of interview when I was seeking to access information relevant to the historical narrative of the development of blogging at the BBC or when I was seeking to clarify specific matters of fact or interpretation in the case studies. There were also numerous occasions when I informally interviewed people as part of observations at the BBC. I occasionally emailed questions to BBC journalists.

I also collected data from several focus groups. The use of focus groups was a not preplanned research strategy but opportunities to conduct them emerged as the project progressed. These focus groups, therefore, were not structured and were used as a means of 'exploration rather than strict comparability'.[27] In 2008, for example, the BBC organised 'BEEB Camp'—an internal 'unconference' for BBC journalists—where the participants set the agenda for sessions. This proved to be an excellent opportunity for me to lead an unscheduled focus group on blogging at the BBC. Small focus groups were also conducted with World Service journalists and Defence and Security producers. These focus groups particularly helped to highlight differences of opinion on the nature of blogs and BBC journalists' approaches to using them as sources of information. Data collected from the focus groups contributed to my reflections on interview questions and to the body of evidence presented in Chapters 3 and 4.

SELECTING A BLOG SAMPLE

The main methodological difficulty I encountered was finding a suitable approach to select blogs for analysis in Chapters 1 and 8. Thomas Johnson and Barbara Kaye note that 'the internet does not provide a reliable mechanism to randomly sample the entire online population or smaller subgroups such as blog users'.[28] Their work into the credibility of war blogs was based on an online survey of several thousand blog users which led to difficulties generalising from their results. Perhaps more importantly, analysing thousands of blogs was beyond the scope of the book.

As outlined in Chapter 1, I decided to adopt David Altheide's method of 'progressive theoretical sampling'[29] to identify the categories of a war and terror blogosphere. I sought to develop a deep understanding of the topic to enable me to select categories of blogs that are more theoretically or conceptually relevant than using a simple method of random sampling.[30] By acting as a 'participant-observer' in the blogosphere and guided by the theory of new media commentators and academics, I aimed to identify different categories of war and terrorism blogs over time rather than being "trapped" by a preset list of categories.[31] The resulting sample was not statistically grounded but it was systematically selected with reference to existing literature on blogging. The set of categories identified in Chapter 1 also formed the basis of my selection of blogs for my case study of Gaza in Chapter 8.

Melissa Wall used this sampling method to select news blogs that covered the Iraq war.[32] However, I felt it was necessary to develop Wall's method, as she does not appear to have had any method for externally verifying the categories. When Janet Finch and Jennifer Mason used a similar approach to identify a representative interview sample they exchanged emails, researchers notes and conversations to generate a documented process by which the categories were discussed, adjusted and finally selected.[33]

Wall does not document a similar process. Unlike Finch and Mason, she appeared to be carrying out her research alone. I was also working alone, but I used interviews with BBC journalists, interactions with other bloggers and subscriptions to more than 300 blogs as well as sites which curated blogs from a variety of sources. This created a reflexive and systematic process by which to continuously judge the validity of my sample. Research and literature on blogging was also developing during the research period and my adoption of Ethan Zuckerman's category of 'bridgeblogger' was a consequence of his 2008 article.[34] Accessing these external reference points improved the validity of the resulting selection of categories.

Weaknesses remain with this approach for selecting blogs. The resulting sample was not statistically representative of all war and terror blogs and the focus was necessarily on English-language speaking blogs—a significant limitation. In Chapter 8, I noted that the resulting sample of blogs covering the Gaza conflict tended to exclude moderate voices that might have been present in the Hebrew blogosphere. It is not possible, therefore, to generalise from Chapter 1 and Chapter 8 as to the nature of all blogs concerning war and terrorism. In a limited sense, however, these chapters do offer an understanding of the types of relevant blogs available to a BBC journalist during the period of the research.

COLLECTIVE REFLEXIVE FLEXIBILITY: AN APPROACH FOR 'A RUNAWAY WORLD'

The media landscape is in the midst of a period of fundamental upheaval. Tracking, monitoring and archiving developments on the Web in a new era of information overload is a significant challenge for researchers attempting to document, understand and analyse the changing face of the online world.

Journalists' working practices have also evolved significantly in the first decade of the 21st century as they have adopted a variety of Web-based tools and new technological devices to help them conduct journalism. In an attempt to meet these challenges, I adopted a collective, flexible and reflexive approach.

First, I attempted to harness the 'collective intelligence' of bloggers, journalists and academics through open and interactive online engagement,[35] writing hundreds of blog posts during the project which were open to comment. One of my blogs became a working archive documenting debates within the media industry about blogging and the BBC's engagement with blogs. The other blog considered how militaries, governments and other parties were using blogs in the context of war and terrorism.

I also deployed a variety of methods in order to provide a broad range of perspectives on the research question. A flexible approach to the inquiry meant I drew on methods and approaches from several disciplinary backgrounds including media studies, the social sciences and history. Rather than adopt a single methodological approach, I used an array of techniques in an attempt to add depth and rigour to the research.

Finally, I remained flexible and reflexive throughout the research process to ensure that I was tracing developments in the media and considering the impact of my decision to act as a participant observer on the results of the inquiry. The academic literature on blogging advanced considerably during the period of study; early interview schedules had to be revised to account for the emergence of tools such as Twitter; journalists were contacted regularly during the period in order to assess how newsroom practices were evolving; and my own role as a researcher within the BBC was constantly scrutinised.

There will always be weaknesses with the printed book format as a method for capturing a media landscape in flux, but the collective, flexible and reflexive approach I have outlined offers a potential template that could be critiqued and developed further in future research. Moreover, I believe there is academic and public value in the production of a fixed document which provides a broad snapshot of an important period of the BBC's engagement with blogging in the context of war and terrorism.

Notes

NOTES TO THE INTRODUCTION

1. S. Pax, *Where is Raed?*, http://dear_raed.blogspot.com/, (4 Dec 2007).
2. S. Allan, *Online News*, (Open University Press, 2006), p. 110.
3. BBC, 'Life in Baghdad via the Web', 25 Mar 2003, http://news.bbc.co.uk/1/hi/technology/2881491.stm, (4 Dec 2007).
4. I. Katz in Pax, *Salam Pax: The Baghdad Blog*, (Atlantic Books, 2003), p. xi.
5. Ibid., p. xii; 'G' is Ghaith Abdul-Ahad, who subsequently won awards for his reporting from Iraq.
6. J. Naughton, 'Breakthrough with the Baghdad Blogger', *The Observer*, 14 Sep 2003, http://observer.guardian.co.uk/business/story/0,,1040861,00.html, (4 Dec 2007).
7. B. Cammaerts and N. Carpentier, 'Blogging the 2003 Iraq War: Challenging the ideological model of war and mainstream journalism?', *Observatorio*, 3 (2), (2009).
8. Y. Benkler, *The Wealth of Networks: How social production transforms markets and freedom*, (Yale University Press, 2006), pp. 216–217.
9. M. Castells, *Communication Power*, (Oxford University Press, 2009), p. 4.
10. A. Bruns, 'News Blogs and Citizen Journalism: New directions for e-journalism' in K. Prasad (ed.), *e-Journalism: New media and news media* (BR Publishing, 2009), pp. 101–126.
11. M. Scammell, 'The Internet and Civic Engagement: The Age of the Citizen-Consumer', *Political Communication*, 17 (4), (2000), pp. 351–355.
12. Benkler, *Wealth of Networks*, p. 10.
13. D. Gillmor, *We the Media: Grassroots journalism by the people, for the people*, 2nd Ed., (O'Reilly, 2006), p. xxiv: 'Tomorrow's news reporting and production will be more of a conversation or a seminar'.
14. Castells, *The Information Age: Economy Society and Culture, Vol. 1: The rise of the network society*, 2nd Ed. (Blackwell, 2000).
15. A. Giddens, *Runaway World*, 2nd Ed. (Profile, 2002).
16. For example, A. Briggs, *The History of the British Broadcasting in the United Kingdom*, Vols. 1–5 (Oxford University Press); G. Born, *Uncertain Vision*, (Secker and Warburg, 2004).
17. D. Bennett, 'The number of staff employed by the BBC', *Mediating Conflict*, 24 May 2011, http://mediatingconflict.blogspot.com/2011/05/number-of-staff-employed-by-bbc.html.
18. Gillmor, *We the Media*, pp. 124, 131.
19. J. Markoff in S. Rosenberg, *Say Everything: How blogging began, what it's becoming and why it matters*, (Crown, 2009), p. 269.

20. A. Hermida, 'The BBC goes blogging: Is "Auntie" finally listening?', http://online.journalism.utexas.edu/2008/papers/Hermida.pdf, (1 Aug 2008) and 'The blogging BBC: Journalism blogs at "the world's most trusted news organisation"', *Journalism Practice*, 33 (2009), pp. 1–17.
21. P. Bourdieu, *On Television*, tr. by P. Parkhurst Ferguson, (The New Press, 1998), p. 7.
22. P. Knightley, *The First Casualty: The war correspondent as hero, propagandist and myth-maker*, (Andre Deutsche Ltd, 2003); S. Moeller, *Compassion Fatigue: How the media sell disease, famine, war and death*, (Routledge, 1999).
23. R. Clutterbuck, *The Media and Political Violence*, (Macmillan Press, 1981).
24. S. Carruthers, *The Media at War*, (Palgrave Macmillan, 1999); D. Kellner, *Media Spectacle and the Crisis of Democracy: Terrorism, war, and election battles*, (Paradigm Publishers, 2005); Knightley, *The First Casualty*.
25. Allan, *Online News*; P. Seib, *Beyond the Front Lines: How the news media cover a world shaped by war*, (Palgrave MacMillan, 2004); H. Tumber and F. Webster, *Journalists Under Fire: Information war and journalistic practice*, (Sage, 2006).
26. Recent general surveys include D. Matheson and S. Allan, *Digital War Reporting* (Polity Press, 2009), and A. Hoskins and B. O'Loughlin, *War and Media: The emergence of diffused war*, (Polity Press, 2010).
27. J. Hartley, 'Communicative Democracy in a Redactional Society: The future of journalism studies' *Journalism*, 1 (1), 2000, p. 45.
28. S. Allan, 'The Culture of Distance: Online reporting of the iraq war' in S. Allan and B. Zelizer (eds), *Reporting War: Journalism in wartime*, (Routledge, 2004), p. 358.
29. M. Wall, "Blogs of War': Weblogs as news', *Journalism*, 6 (2), 2005; M. Wall, 'Blogging Gulf War II', *Journalism Studies*, 7 (1), 2006.
30. S. Allan and B. Zelizer, 'Rules of Engagement: Journalism and War' in S. Allan and B. Zelizer (eds), *Reporting War: Journalism in wartime* (Routledge, 2004), pp. 3–6; K. Sanders, *Ethics and Journalism*, (Sage, 2003).
31. D. Altheide, *Qualitative Media Analysis*, (Sage, 1996), pp. 33–35.
32. For the duration of the project, I updated two blogs and a Twitter feed. On many occasions, I acted as a journalist attempting to use blogs and social media tools to source and report stories. This participative approach was regarded as a key research method enabling me to experience the frustrations and opportunities of using blogs and other digital media tools as journalistic sources.
33. Hermida, 'The BBC goes blogging'.
34. *WHYS* programmes also appear occasionally on BBC World TV.
35. The *WHYS* programme was a notable exception.
36. M. Thompson in J. Townend, 'BBC director-general on social media use: 'You can't take BBC cloak off at will', Journalism.co.uk, 21 May 2009, http://www.journalism.co.uk/news-events-awards/bbc-director-general-on-social-media-use—you-can-t-take-bbc-cloak-off-at-will/s14/a534512/, (11 Nov 2010).
37. Castells, *Rise of the Network Society*.
38. M. Fishman, *Manufacturing the News* (University of Texas Press, 1980), p. 51.
39. H. Gans, *Deciding What's News*, 2nd Ed. (Northwestern University Press, 2004), pp. 304–334.
40. P. Lévy, *Collective Intelligence: Mankind's emerging world in cyberspace*, tr. Robert Bononno, (Perseus Books, 1999).
41. H. Jenkins, 'The Cultural Logic of Media Convergence', *International Journal of Cultural Studies*, (7) 1, (2004), p. 35.
42. By Jorn Barger. S. Rosenberg, *Say Everything*, pp. 78–79.

43. S. Herring et al, 'Longitudinal Content Analysis of Blogs: 2003–4' in M. Tremayne (ed.), *Blogging, Citizenship and the Future of Media*, (Routledge, 2007).
44. Technorati.com, http://www.technorati.com/about/.
45. Allan, *Online News*, p. 46.
46. J.W. Rettberg, *Blogging*, (Polity Press, 2008), pp. 26–30.
47. Herring et al, 'Analysis of Blogs: 2003–4' and Z. Papacharissi, 'Audiences as Media Producers: Content Analysis of 260 Blogs' in M. Tremayne (ed), *Blogging, Citizenship and the Future of Media* (Routledge, 2007), pp. 15, 35; R. Blood, "Weblogs: A History and Perspective", *Rebecca's Pocket*, 7 Sep 2000, http://www.rebeccablood.net/essays/weblog_history.html, (22 Feb 2008).
48. M. Cornfield et al., *Buzz, Blogs and Beyond*, Pew Internet and American Life Project, 17 Sep. 2004, http://195.130.87.21:8080/dspace/bitstream/123456789/557/1/Buzz,%20Blogs,%20And%20Beyond.pdf (3 May 2008), p. 3.
49. Tremayne, *Blogging*, pp. x–xi.
50. J. Merelo and B. Prieto, *Blogosphere Community Formation, Structure and Visualisation*, http://webdiis.unizar.es/~ftricas/Articulos/Blogosphere%20community%20formation.pdf, (1 Aug 2008).
51. J. Kelly and B. Etling, 'Mapping Iran Online Public', The Berkman Center for Internet and Society, 6 Apr 2008, http://tinyurl.com/4ht9y4, (31 July 2008).
52. Bruns, 'Is there an Australian Blogosphere', *Snurblog*, http://snurb.info/node/864, 20 Aug 2008, (5 Sep 2008).
53. J.B. Singer, 'The Political J-Blogger: "Normalising" a new media form to fit old norms and practices', *Journalism*, 6 (2), (2005), p. 179.
54. The Drudge Report was more of a website than a blog. Rosenberg, *Say Everything*. pp. 82–85.
55. Lott subsequently stepped down prompting the *New York Post* to declare the 'Internet's First Scalp'. Allan, *Online News*, pp. 78–83.
56. Ibid., pp. 96–98.
57. D. Matheson, 'Weblogs and the Epistemology of the News: Some trends in online journalism', *New Media & Society*, 6 (4), (2004), p. 452.
58. C. Beckett, 'Blogs are dead, long live blogging', *Polis Director's Blog*, 31 Mar 2011, http://www.charliebeckett.org/?p=4241, (31 Mar 2011).

NOTES TO CHAPTER 1

1. R. Cellan-Jones, 'Is blogging dead?', *dot.life*, 22 Oct 2008, http://www.bbc.co.uk/blogs/technology/2008/10/is_blogging_dead.html, (23 Oct 2008).
2. P. Boutin, 'Twitter, Flickr, Facebook Make Blogs Look So 2004', *Wired*, 20 Oct 2008, http://www.wired.com/entertainment/theweb/magazine/16–11/st_essay, (3 June 2010).
3. Ibid.
4. D. Altheide, *Qualitative Media Analysis*, (Sage, 1996), pp. 33–35.
5. S. Rosenberg, *Say Everything: How blogging began, what it's becoming and why it matters*, (Crown, 2009), pp. 1–5.
6. M. Castells, *Communication Power*, (Oxford University Press), pp. 54–56; C. Shirky, *Here Comes Everybody: How change happens when people come together*, 2nd Ed., (Penguin, 2009), p. 77.
7. D. Matheson and S. Allan, *Digital War Reporting* (Polity Press, 2009), p. 29.
8. Rosenberg, *Say Everything*, pp. 110, 112–113.
9. J. Simpson, *A Mad World, My Masters*, (Macmillan, 2000), pp. 256, 266.

10. Matheson and Allan, *Digital War Reporting*, pp. 42–45.
11. J.D. Lasica, 'Conveying the War in Human Terms', *American Journalism Review* (June), (1999).
12. S. Allan, 'The Culture of Distance: Online Reporting of the Iraq War' in S. Allan and B. Zelizer (eds) *Reporting War: Journalism in wartime*, (Routledge, 2004), p. 357.
13. Rosenberg, *Say Everything*, pp. 1–4.
14. Katz in Pax, *Salam Pax: The Baghdad Blog*, (Atlantic Books, 2003), p. ix.
15. R. Sambrook, 'Citizen Journalism and the BBC', *Nieman Reports,* Winter, (2005); S. Outing, The 11 Layers of Citizen Journalism, *Poynter Online*, 13 June 2005, http://www.poynter.org/content/content_view.asp?id=83126, (25 Feb 2008).
16. J.D. Lasica, 'Blogs and Journalism Need Each Other', *Nieman Reports*, 57 (3), (2003). pp. 70–74.
17. S. Allan, 'Citizen Journalism and the Rise of "Mass Self-Communication": Reporting the London Bombings', *Global Media Journal* (Australian Edition), 1 (1), (2007), pp. 1–20.
18. J. Schuster, *Iraqi Bloggers Central*, http://jarrarsupariver.blogspot.com/, (15 June 2010).
19. Global Voices, 'About', http://globalvoicesonline.org/about/, (15 June 2010).
20. N. Petrov, 'Images amateurs des attentats de Moscou', *Les Observateurs* (France) 24, 29 Mar 2010, http://observers.france24.com/fr/content/20100329-russie-attentat-metro-moscou-video-victime-terrorisme, (29 Mar 2010).
21. M. Mohan, '30 minutes in the life of an "On the Scene Reporter"', *Best Engaging Communities,* 26 July 2008, http://bestengagingcommunities. com/2008/07/26/30-minutes-in-the-life-of-an-on-the-scene-reporterb.aspx, (29 July 2008).
22. Mukund Mohan, Technology Entrepreneur, Email Correspondence, 17 June 2010.
23. Samanthi Dissanayake, BBC Senior Broadcast Journalist, Interview, 26 Jan 2010.
24. Matheson and Allan, *Digital War Reporting*, pp. 78–83.
25. C. Allbritton, 'Q&A', *Back to Iraq*, 7 April 2003, http://www.back-to-iraq. com/page/109, (16 July 2010).
26. A. Monck with M. Hanley, *Can You Trust the Media?*, (Icon Books, 2008), pp. 77–82.
27. Allbritton, 'I am not a blogger', *Back to Iraq,*3 Sep 2007, http://www.back-to-iraq.com/2007/09/i-am-not-a-blogger.php, (9 Aug 2010).
28. D. Betz, 'The Virtual Dimension of Contemporary Insurgency and Counter-insurgency', *Small Wars & Insurgencies*, 19 (4), (2008), pp. 525–526.
29. For example, M. Yon, 'Bullshit Bob', *Michael Yon Online,*25 Sep 2009, http://www.michaelyon-online.com/bullshit-bob.htm, (25 Sep 2009).
30. Krikorian, 'Conflict Resolution and Education', *Onnik Krikorian in Armenia*, 6 Dec 2008, http://frontlineclub.com/blogs/onnikkrikorian/2008/12/conflict-resolution-and-education.html (8 Jan 2011).
31. S. Wilson in M. Wells, 'Confessions of an NGO media minder', *BBC College of Journalism*, 12 July 2010, http://www.bbc.co.uk/journalism/blog/2010/07/ negotiating-haiti-with-my-medi.shtml, (16 July 2010).
32. See www.oxfamblogs.org.
33. See http://www.msf.org.uk/blogs.aspx.
34. N. Fenton disagrees. She says Internet-based media are simply used to deliver what traditional media organisations are 'crying out for—news that conforms to established news criteria and provides journalistic copy at little or

no cost'. See N. Fenton, 'NGOs, New Media and the Mainstream News' in N. Fenton (ed), *New Media, Old News: Journalism and democracy in the digital age*,(Sage, 2010), p. 166.

35. N. Davies, *Flat Earth News*, (Chatto & Windus, 2008), pp. 99–105.
36. M. Wall, 'Blogging Gulf War II', *Journalism Studies*,7 (1), (2006), pp. 111–126.
37. M. Burden, *The Blog of War: Front-line dispatches from soldiers in Iraq and Afghanistan*,(Simon & Schuster, 2006).
38. C. Buzzell, *My War: Killing time in Iraq*,(Penguin, 2005), p. 115.
39. Lt. Col. Barry Venable in C. Cooper, 'Army Blogger's Tales Attract Censors' Eyes', *Wall Street Journal*, 9 Sep 2004.
40. M. Gallagher, *Kaboom: Embracing the suck in a savage little war*, (Da Capo Press, 2010), pp. 142–45.
41. 'Sensei Katana', 'A letter to Ms Rice', 10 Feb 2008.
42. MoD Press Officer, Interview, 29 Apr 2008.
43. US Army, 'Operations Security', *AR530–1*,2007.
44. MoD, 'Contact with the Mediaand communicating in public', *DIN03–006*, Aug 2007.
45. HQ, Multi-National Corps—Iraq, *MNC-I Policy #9*,6 Apr 2005.
46. Maj. E.L. Robbins, 'Muddy Boots IO', *Military Review*,Sep-Oct 2007.
47. US Corps, 'IMMEDIATE BAN OF INTERNET SOCIAL NETWORKING SITES', 3 Aug 2009.
48. Deputy Secretary of Defense, 'Responsible and Effective Use of Internet Capabilities', *DTM-09–026*,25 Feb 2010.
49. J. Anderson, 'The rise and fall of a military blogger', *Army Times*, 8 Dec 2009, http://www.armytimes.com/offduty/technology/offduty_blogger_120809/, (22 Dec 2009).
50. 'Laughing_Wolf', 'An open letter to Secretary Gates', *Blackfive.net*,17 Dec 2009, http://www.blackfive.net/main/2009/12/an-open-letter-to-secretary-gates-joint-chiefs-and-senior-leadership.html#comment-6a00d8341bfadb53ef0120a75d5ca0970b, (20 Dec 2009).
51. 'MsMarti', 'Milblogs Go Silent', *War on Terror News*,http://waronterrornews. typepad.com/home/2009/12/milblogs-go-silent.html#more, (22 Dec 2009).
52. Cammaerts and Carpentier, 'Blogging the 2003 Iraq War: Challenging the ideological model of war and mainstream journalism?', *Observatorio*, 3 (2), (2009), pp. 1–23.
53. S. Haugbolle, 'From A-list to Webtifada, Developments in the Lebanese Blogosphere 2005–2006', *Arab Media and Society*, 1 (Spring), (2007), p. 9.
54. Ibid., p. 17.
55. C. Fadda-Conrey, 'Writing Memories of the Present Alternative Narratives about the 2006 Israeli War on Lebanon', *College Literature*,37.1 (Winter), (2010), p. 161.
56. Haugbolle, 'A-list to Webtifada'.
57. E. Zuckerman, 'Meet the bridgebloggers', *Public Choice*, 134, (2008), pp. 47–65.
58. Beirut Journal, http://beirutjournal.blogspot.com.
59. Z. Harb, 'The July 2006 War and the Lebanese Blogosphere: Towards an alternative media tool in covering wars', *Journal of Media Practice*,10 (2&3), (2009), pp. 255–258.
60. W. Ward, 'Uneasy Bedfellows: Bloggers and mainstream media report the conflict in Lebanon', *Arab Media and Society*, 1 (Spring), (2007).
61. Ibid.
62. Haugbolle, 'A-list to Webtifada', p. 1.
63. Fadda-Conrey, 'Writing Memories', p. 161.

64. Ibid., p. 162.
65. Wall, 'Blogging Gulf War II'.
66. 1Lt. A. Bonanno, Email Correspondence, 5 Nov 2008. A ramp ceremony is a short parade which takes place when a deceased soldier is carried onto the ramp of a transport plane for his or her final trip home.
67. N. Meo, Email Correspondence, 1 Dec 2008.
68. Meo, Email Correspondence, 6 Nov 2008.
69. Bonanno in T. Steward, 'The Power of the Milblogs, Meo Update #3', Bouhammer.com, 30 Oct 2008, http://www.bouhammer.com/2008/10/the-power-of-the-milblogs-meo-update-3/, (3 Nov 2008).
70. J. Kinniburgh and D. Denning suggested that 'information strategists can consider clandestinely recruiting or hiring of prominent bloggers . . .' in 'Blogs and Military Information Strategy', *Joint Special Operations University*, Report 06–5, 2006.
71. Editor's Note in Capt. S. Alvarez, 'Centcom Team Engages Bloggers, *American Forces Press Service*, 2 Mar 2006, http://www.defense.gov/news/newsarticle.aspx?id=15287, (23 July 2010).
72. Maj. S. Alvarez, Email Correspondence, 16 July 2010.
73. At least 27 were created in this period.
74. Angela Gassett, Weber Shandwick/US Army Accessions Command, Email Correspondence, 14 July 2010.
75. J. Holt, Senior Strategist for Emerging Media for the Department of Defense, in D. Bennett 'Tracing the first official US military blogs', *Reporting War*, 7 July 2010, http://frontlineclub.com/blogs/danielbennett/2010/07/official-us-military-blogs.html, (7 July 2010).
76. Lt. Col. P. Swiergosz, 'Welcome!', *Task Force Mountain*, 18 Aug 2008, http://www.taskforcemountain.com/mountain-sound-off/19-blog/365-mnd-cpao, (6 July 2010).
77. Maj. Gen. M. Oates, *Sexual Assault in the Army*, Task Force Mountain, 9 Apr 2009, http://www.taskforcemountain.com/mountain-sound-off/19-blog/3151-sexual-assault-in-the-army, (9 Apr 2009).
78. Maj. Gen. K. Bergner, 'MG Bergners Welcome', *Army Live*, 7 Apr 2009, http://armylive.dodlive.mil/index.php/2009/04/mg-bergners-welcome/, (6 July 2010).
79. MoD, 'About the UK MoD News blog', *Defence News Blog*, http://www.blogs.mod.uk/about.html, (7 July 2010).
80. Alex Ford ('RAF Airman'), Personal Correspondence, 19 Aug 2010.
81. Major Paul Smyth, Email Correspondence, 17 April 2011.
82. Smyth, Email Correspondence, 17 April 2011.
83. It was started in March 2009.
84. Smyth, Interview, 5 June 2009.
85. MoD Press Release, 'British Forces Blogging From the Frontline', 1 July 2010.
86. A DDoS attack is launched from a multitude of compromised computer systems. These are used to flood a website server with an unbearable number of messages simultaneously forcing it to close down.
87. Ministry of Foreign Affairs of Georgia, 'Cyberattacks disable Georgian websites', 11 Aug 2008, http://georgiamfa.blogspot.com/2008/08/cyber-attacks-disable-georgian-websites.html, (13 Aug 2008).
88. M. Akhvlediani, 'The Fatal Flaw: The media and the Russian invasion of Georgia', *Small Wars & Insurgencies*, 20 (2), (2009), p. 379.
89. S. Korns and J. Kastenberg, 'Georgia's Cyber Left Hook', *Parameters*, XXXVIII, (4, Winter), (2008–2009), pp. 60–76.
90. N. Shachtman, 'Info Wars: Pentagon could learn from Obama, Israel', *Danger Room, Wired*, 25 Feb 2009, http://www.wired.com/dangerroom/2009/02/info-war-pentag/#ixzz0tCEfeYqx, (9 July 2010).

91. J. Michaels 'Cellphones put to 'unnerving' use in Gaza', *USA Today*, 13 Jan 2009, http://www.usatoday.com/tech/wireless/2009–01–13-gazaphones_N. htm, (9 July 2010).
92. Shachtman, 'Info Wars'.
93. Air Chief Marshal Sir S. Dalton in K. Sengupta, 'Head of the RAF says British Forces must embrace internet technology', *Belfast Telegraph*, 16 Feb 2010, http://www.belfasttelegraph.co.uk/news/local-national/head-of-the-raf-says-british-armed-forces-must-embrace-internet-technology-14683953. html?#, (3 Mar 2010); Lt. Gen. W. Caldwell IV, D. Murphy and A. Menning, 'Learning to Leverage New Media', *Australian Army Journal*, 6 (3), (2009), pp. 133–146.
94. Lindy Kyzer, Former Social Media Manager for the US Army said, 'The notion of feedback, conversation, and independent, candid voices took a while.' See L. Kyzer in D. Bennett 'Tracing the first official US military blogs', *Reporting War*, 7 July 2010, http://frontlineclub.com/blogs/danielbennett/2010/07/official-us-military-blogs.html, (7 July 2010).
95. Stuart Hughes, BBC World Affairs Producer, Email Correspondence, 1 July 2010.
96. Maj. P. Smyth, 'Blogging from the battlefield', *Social Media for the Military*, 31 Jan 2012, http://militarysocialmedia.posterous.com/blogging-from-the-battlefield, (2 Feb 2012).
97. D. Drezner and H. Farrell, 'Web of Influence', *Foreign Policy Magazine*, 1 Nov 2004.
98. Arms Control Wonk, http://www.armscontrolwonk.com/.
99. Kings of War, http://kingsofwar.org.uk/.
100. The Small Wars Journal, www.smallwarsjournal.com.
101. Abu Muqawama, www.cnas.org/blogs/abumuqawama. Previously at www.abumuqawama.blogspot.com.
102. A. Bacevich, 'The Petraeus Doctrine', *Atlantic Magazine*, October 2008, http://www.theatlantic.com/magazine/archive/2008/10/the-petraeus-doctrine/6964/1/, (13 July 2010).
103. C. Griffin, 'Small Wars, Big Ideas', *Armed Forces Journal*, October 2007, http://www.armedforcesjournal.com/2007/10/3022382, (14 July 2010).
104. W. McCants et al, 'About', *Jihadica*, http://www.jihadica.com/about/, (13 July 2010).
105. The blog was started in May 2005. Richard North, Email Correspondence, 4 Aug 2009.
106. C. Brooker, 'Tories Must Call for Inquiry into Snatch Land Rover Scandal', *The Telegraph*, 16 Nov 2008, http://www.telegraph.co.uk/comment/columnists/christopherbooker/3563538/Tories-must-call-for-inquiry-into-Snatch-Land-Rover-scandal.html, (13 July 2010).
107. W. Lowrey and J. Burleson Mackay, 'Journalism and Blogging': A test of a model of occupational competition', *Journalism Practice*, 2 (1), (2008).
108. Cammaerts and Carpentier, 'Blogging the 2003 Iraq War'.
109. Lowrey, 'Mapping the journalism-blogging relationship', *Journalism*, 7 (4), (2006), p. 493.

NOTES TO CHAPTER 2

1. J. Raynsford, 'Blogging—the new journalism?', Journalism.co.uk, 25 Mar 2003, http://www.journalism.co.uk/5/articles/5604.php, (4 Dec 2007).
2. B. Thompson, 'Is Google too powerful?', *BBC*, 21 Mar 2003, http://news.bbc.co.uk/1/hi/technology/2786761.stm, (3 Jan 2008).

3. BBC Editorial Guidelines, http://www.bbc.co.uk/guidelines/editorialguidelines/edguide/editorialvalues/, (28 July 2008).
4. K. Anderson, *BBC Blogs: News as conversation*, 2005, p. 5.
5. J. Rosen, 'Bloggers vs Journalists is over', *PressThink*, 21 Jan 2005, http://journalism.nyu.edu/pubzone/weblogs/pressthink/2005/01/21/berk_essy.html, (27 Nov 2007).
6. H. Gans, *Deciding What's News*, 2nd Ed. (Northwestern University Press, 2004), pp. 304–34.
7. W. Gieber and W. Johnson, 'The City Hall beat: A study of reporter and source roles', *Journalism Quarterly*, 38 (3), (1961), pp. 289–97.
8. W.L. Bennett, 'Toward a Theory of Press-State Relations in the United States', *Journal of Communication,* 40 (2), (1990), p. 103.
9. E.S. Herman and N. Chomsky, *Manufacturing Consent: The political economy of the mass media*, (Pantheon, 1988), p. 18.
10. Ibid., pp. 19–25.
11. P. Bourdieu, *On Television*, tr. P. Parkhurst Ferguson (New Press, 1998), p. 69.
12. Ibid., pp. 69–70.
13. G. Tuchman, *Making News: A study in the construction of reality*, (The Free Press, 1980), p. 81.
14. M. Fishman, *Manufacturing the News*, (University of Texas Press, 1980), p. 44.
15. Gans, *Deciding What's News*, p. 119.
16. Ibid., p. 117.
17. P. Golding and P. Elliott, 'Making the News (Excerpt)', in H. Tumber (ed) *News A Reader*, (Oxford University Press, 1999), p. 115.
18. N. Davies, *Flat Earth News*, (Random House, 2008), pp. 118, 121–122.
19. R.W. McChesney, 'The Problem of Journalism: A political economic contribution to an explanation of the crisis in contemporary US journalism', *Journalism Studies*, 4 (3), (2003), p. 324.
20. S. Hall et al., *Policing the Crisis: Mugging, the state, and law and order*, (Macmillan, 1978), p. 58.
21. Ibid., p. 57.
22. Ibid., pp. 57–59.
23. D. Hallin, *The "Uncensored War": The media and Vietnam*, (University of California Press, 1989), p. 163.
24. Ibid., p. 73.
25. Gans, *Deciding What's News*, p. 116.
26. Ibid., p. 128.
27. Ibid., pp. 128–131.
28. Fishman, *Manufacturing the News*, p. 51.
29. Ibid., p. 52.
30. Gans, *Deciding What's News*, p. 130.
31. L.V. Sigal, *Reporters and Officials: The organisation and politics of newsmaking*, (D.C. Heath & Co., 1973), p. 5.
32. P. Schlesinger and H. Tumber, *Reporting Crime: The media politics of criminal justice*, (Oxford University Press, 1994), p. 182.
33. Ibid., p. 271.
34. Ibid., pp. 166–170.
35. Gans, *Deciding What's News,* p. 116; Schlesinger and Tumber, *Reporting Crime*, p. 24; M. Schudson, *The Sociology of News*, (W. W. Norton & Co, 2003), p. 54.
36. R.V. Ericson, P.M. Baranek and J.B.L. Chan, *Negotiating Control: A study of news sources*, (University of Toronto Press, 1989).
37. Ibid., p. 378.

38. J. Harrison, *News*, (Routledge, 2006), p. 142.
39. H. Molotch and M. Lester, 'News as Purposive Behavior: On the strategic use of routine events, accidents, and scandals', *American Sociological Review*, 39 (1), (1974), pp. 107.
40. Ibid., p. 108.
41. E. Goldenberg, *Making the Papers: The access of resource-poor groups to the metropolitan press*, (D.C. Heath & Co., 1975).
42. T. Gitlin, *The Whole World is Watching: Mass media in the making and unmaking of the New Left*, (University of California Press, 1980); P. Manning, *News and News Sources: A critical introduction*, (Sage, 2001).
43. Hallin, *The "Uncensored War"*, p. 163.
44. Bennett, 'Toward a Theory of Press-State Relations', p. 106.
45. Ibid., p. 107.
46. Hallin, *The "Uncensored War"*, p. 117.
47. Gans, *Deciding What's News*, pp. 125–126.
48. Fishman, *Manufacturing the News*, p. 45.
49. J. Pavlik, *Journalism and New Media*, (Columbia University Press, 2001), p. 24.
50. Gillmor, *We the Media: Grassroots journalism by the people, for the people*, 2nd Ed. (O'Reilly Media Inc., 2006), p. xxv.
51. J. Bardoel and M. Deuze, 'Network Journalism: Converging competences of media professionals and professionalism', *Australian Journalism Review*, 23 (2), (2001), pp. 91–103.
52. Castells, *Communication Power*, pp. 70–71.
53. Gans, *Deciding What's News*, p. 125.
54. Fishman, *Manufacturing the News*, p. 51.
55. Ibid., p. 52.
56. J. Shulevitz, 'THE CLOSE READER; At Large in the Blogosphere', *New York Times*, 5 May 2002, http://www.nytimes.com/2002/05/05/books/the-close-reader-at-large-in-the-blogosphere.html, (26 Oct 2011).
57. M. Messner and M. Watson Distaso, 'The Source Cycle: How traditional media and weblogs use each other as sources', *Journalism Studies*, 9 (3), (2008), p. 453.
58. R. MacKinnon, 'Blogs and China Correspondence: How foreign correspondents covering China use blogs', Paper for the World Journalism Education Congress (WJEC), Sep 2007, p. 18.
59. Ibid., p. 13.
60. P. Bradshaw, 'Blogging journalists: pt.2: Blogs and news ideas: "The canary in the mine"', *Online Journalism Blog*, 15 Oct 2008, http://onlinejournalismblog.com/2008/10/15/blogging-journalists-pt2-blogs-and-news-ideas-the-canary-in-the-mine/, (15 Oct 2008). He received 200 responses from 30 different countries.
61. N. Newman, 'The Rise of Social Media and its Impact on Mainstream Journalism', *Reuters Institute for the Study of Journalism*, (2009), p. 5.
62. Pavlik, *Journalism and New Media*, p. 92.
63. Ibid., p. 24.
64. Gillmor, *We the Media*, p. xxv.
65. Shirky, *Here Comes Everybody: How change happens when people come together*, 2nd Ed. (Penguin, 2009), p. 66.
66. Gillmor; *We the Media*, p. xxiv; Pavlik, *Journalism and New Media*, p. 136.
67. Castells, *Communication Power*, p. 421.
68. Ibid., p. 302.
69. Pavlik, *Journalism and New Media*, p. 95.

70. N. Gowing, "Skyful of Lies' and Black Swans: The new tyranny of shifting information power in crises', *Reuters Institute for the Study of Journalism*, (2009), p. 1.
71. A. Phillips, 'Old Sources: New Bottles' in N. Fenton (ed), *New Media, Old News: Journalism and democracy in the digital age*, (Sage, 2009), p. 101; Chapter 1 highlighted how 'new bottles' in the form of blogs have been adopted by official sources in the area of war and terrorism.
72. Thurman, 'Forums for Citizen Journalists? Adoption of user generated content by online news media', *New Media & Society*, 10 (1), pp. 23–24.
73. I. Hargreaves, *Journalism: Truth or Dare*, (Oxford University Press, 2003), p. 27; Born, *Uncertain Vision*, (Secker and Warburg, 2004), p. 379.
74. Born, *Uncertain Vision*, p. 379.
75. Ibid., p. 31.
76. A. Briggs, *A History of Broadcasting in the United Kingdom, Vol I: The birth of broadcasting*, (Oxford University Press, 1961), p. 330.
77. Ibid.
78. J. Seaton, *Power without Responsibility: the press, broadcasting and new media in Britain*, 6th Ed., (Routledge, 2003), p. 119.
79. Born, *Uncertain Vision*, p. 33.
80. M. Thatcher, Speech to the American Bar Association, 15 July 1985, http://www.margaretthatcher.org/speeches/displaydocument.asp?docid=106096, (15 May 2008).
81. P. Gilbert, 'The Oxygen of Publicity: Terrorism and reporting restrictions' in A. Belsey and R. Chadwick (eds), *Ethical Issues in Journalism and the Media*, (Routledge, 1992).
82. F. Welch, 'The 'broadcast ban' on Sinn Fein', *BBC*, 5 Apr 2005, http://news.bbc.co.uk/1/hi/uk_politics/4409447.stml, (5 Sep 2008).
83. R. Lindley, *Panorama: Fifty years of pride and paranoia*, (Politico's Publishing, 2002), pp. 346–347.
84. Simpson, *A Mad World*, pp. 249–286.
85. A. Gilligan in Rt. Hon. The Lord Hutton, Report of the Hutton Inquiry, Jan 2004, http://www.the-hutton-inquiry.org.uk/, (1 May 2008).
86. Hutton, Report of the Inquiry.
87. M. Thompson, Director-General of the BBC (2004–2012), quoted in T. Douglas, 'What does the Neil Report mean?', *BBC*, 23 June 2004, http://news.bbc.co.uk/1/low/entertainment/3833771.stm, (28 July 2008).
88. Hutton, Report of the Inquiry.
89. Born, *Uncertain Vision*, p. 456.
90. G. Davies, 'These threats to the BBC are serious and sinister', *The Telegraph*, 27 July 2003, http://www.telegraph.co.uk/opinion/main.jhtml?xml=/opinion/2003/07/27/do2701.xml, (9 May 2008).
91. R. Neil et al., The Neil Report: The BBC's journalism after Hutton, (June, 2004), p. 4.
92. Ibid., p. 5.
93. Ibid., p. 6.
94. Thompson, 'Is Google too powerful?'.
95. M. Smartt cited in Raynsford, 'Blogging: The new journalism?'.
96. C. Nuttall, 'Back Orifice is child's play say virus firms', *BBC*, 13 July 1999, http://news.bbc.co.uk/1/hi/sci/tech/392526.stm, (16 Mar 2009).
97. M. Ward, 'A blog for everyone', *BBC*, 22 July 2003, http://news.bbc.co.uk/1/hi/magazine/3078541.stm, (16 Mar 2009).
98. BBC, 'The year in issues: the role of the blog', 29 Dec 2004, http://news.bbc.co.uk/1/hi/world/4092611.stm, (16 Mar 2009).

99. BBC, 'Go Digital 2003 Archive', 19 Feb 2003, http://news.bbc.co.uk/1/hi/technology/2780097.stm, (16 Mar 2009).

100. The BBC Producer Guidelines were established in 2000 and were superseded by the Editorial Guidelines in 2005. These were updated in 2010.

101. BBC Producer Guidelines, Part Two: Accuracy, 2000, p. 43.

102. A. Rice, 'Baghdad blogger: "Elections our only hope"', *BBC*, 12 Oct 2004, http://news.bbc.co.uk/1/hi/programmes/newsnight/3733104.stm, (25 May 2008).

103. P. Wood, 'Heated debate over white phosphorus', *BBC*, 17 Nov 2005, http://is.gd/pqWS (21 July 2008).

104. Ibid.

105. J. Cobb, et al. 'The fight for Fallujah', *Bnet.com,* http://is.gd/pqPm, (26 Mar 2009). M. Kraft, 'US Marine comes forward', *Insomnia*, 8 Nov 2005, http://is.gd/pqQR, (22 July 2008).

106. G. Zamparini, http://www.thecatsdream.com/.

107. Reynolds, 'White phosphorus: weapon on the edge', *BBC*, 16 Nov 2005, http://news.bbc.co.uk/2/hi/americas/4442988.stm, (16 Mar 2009).

108. Paul Wood, BBC Middle East Correspondent, Email correspondence, 16 Mar 2009.

109. Reynolds, 'White phosphorus'.

110. R. Sambrook, Internal BBC Blog, 13 Jan 2005.

111. Kevin Anderson joined the BBC in Oct 1998 and was BBC News Online's first full-time reporter outside of the United Kingdom based in Washington, DC. Anderson says he was late to blogging, but he was an early Internet adopter and had experience of the new media scene in the United States. He left the BBC in 2006.

112. Anderson, *BBC Blogs: News as conversation*, 2005.

113. Kevin Anderson, Former BBC journalist, Interview, 16 June 2008.

114. Anderson, *BBC Blogs*, p. 1.

115. Ibid., pp. 2–3.

116. BBC, 'One Day in Iraq', 7 June 2005, http://news.bbc.co.uk/1/hi/world/middle_east/4613849.stm, (16 May 2008).

117. Anderson, *BBC Blogs*, p. 10.

118. Anderson, 'So what is this "blogging" anyway?', *BBC*, 7 June 2005, http://www.bbc.co.uk/fivelive/programmes/upallnight_blog/20050607.shtml, (16 May 2008).

119. Anderson, 'Blogs offer taste of war in Iraq', *BBC*, 30 Dec 2005, http://news.bbc.co.uk/1/hi/technology/4555590.stm, (25 May 2008).

120. Anderson, Interview, 16 June 2008.

121. Reynolds, 'White phosphorus'.

122. Reynolds, 'Bloggers: an army of irregulars', *BBC*, 9 Feb 2006, http://news.bbc.co.uk/1/hi/world/4696668.stm, (19 May 2008).

123. Neil et al., The Neil Report, p. 7.

124. J. Bridcut, 'From Seesaw to Wagon Wheel: Safeguarding impartiality in the 21st Century', *BBC Trust Report*, 2007.

125. BBC, 'Iraqi bloggers react to the violence', 21 Dec 2006, http://news.bbc.co.uk/1/hi/talking_point/6194329.stm, (25 May 2008).

126. BBC, 'Iraqi bloggers react to execution', 12 Jan 2007, http://news.bbc.co.uk/1/hi/talking_point/6228785.stm, (25 May 2008); BBC, 'Round up of Iraqi bloggers', 4 May 2007, http://news.bbc.co.uk/1/hi/talking_point/6612983.stm, (25 May 2008).

127. BBC, 'Round-up of Iraqi bloggers'.

128. BBC, 'Kenyan bloggers at home and abroad', 4 Jan 2008, http://news.bbc.co.uk/1/hi/talking_point/7171284.stm, (7 Jan 2008).

129. Vivienne Sands, Head of Emerging Media, BBC Monitoring, 1 Sep 2008.
130. Ibid.
131. A. Burnett, 'Alternative views', *The Editors*, 5 Mar 2008, http://www.bbc.co.uk/blogs/theeditors/2008/03/alternative_views.html, (21 May 2008).
132. 'Life must go on in Gaza and Sderot', http://gaza-sderot.blogspot.com/, (21 May 2008).
133. Burnett, 'Alternative views'.
134. S. Herrmann, 'SuperPower: BBC and Global Voices', *The Editors,* 8 Mar 2010, http://www.bbc.co.uk/blogs/theeditors/2010/03/superpower_bbc_and_global_voic.html, (8 Mar 2010).
135. Global Voices, www.globalvoicesonline.org.
136. BBC Blogworld, http://www.bbc.co.uk/blogs/blogworld/.
137. P. Coletti, 'Blogworld on TV', *BBC Blogworld*, 17 Feb 2010, http://www.bbc.co.uk/blogs/blogworld/2010/02/blogworld_on_tv.html, (10 Dec 2010).
138. Chris Vallance, BBC Senior Broadcast Journalist, Interview, 28 Jan 2008.
139. Ibid. See Chapter 3.
140. D. Jimenez, 'With mobiles and internet, protesters battle to keep world's eyes on Burma', *The Guardian*, 29 Sep 2007, http://www.guardian.co.uk/world/2007/sep/29/burma.topstories32, (26 May 2008).
141. S. Holmes, 'Burma's cyber-dissidents', *BBC,* 26 Sep 2007, http://news.bbc.co.uk/1/hi/world/asia-pacific/7012984.stm, (25 May 2008).
142. BBC, 'Iran asks BBC reporter to leave', 22 June 2009, http://news.bbc.co.uk/1/hi/8111638.stm, (7 Dec 2010).
143. Herrmann, 'Social Media in Iran', *The Editors*, 16 June 2009, http://www.bbc.co.uk/blogs/theeditors/2009/06/social_media_in_iran.html, (16 June 2009).
144. P. Horrocks 'Stop the Blocking Now', *The Editors*, 14 June 2009, http://www.bbc.co.uk/blogs/theeditors/2009/06/stop_the_blocking_now.html, (14 June 2009).
145. Trushar Barot, BBC Senior Broadcast Journalist, Interview, 16 Sep 2009. In June 2010, he became Assistant Editor of the UGC hub.
146. BBC, 'Shot UK soldier was TA volunteer', 17 Nov 2009, http://news.bbc.co.uk/1/hi/uk/8364923.stm, (18 Nov 2009).
147. Bridge Afghanistan, http://bridgeafghanistan.blogspot.com/.
148. Silvia Costeloe, BBC Broadcast Journalist (UCG hub), Email Correspondence, 6 Dec 2010.
149. BBC, 'Blog reveals Afghanistan medic Karen Woo's dedication', 7 Aug 2010, http://www.bbc.co.uk/news/uk-10903737, (7 Aug 2010).
150. K. Woo, *Explorer Kitten in Afghanistan*, http://explorerkitteninafghanistan.blogspot.com/, (7 Aug 2010).
151. Outing, '11 layers of citizen journalism'; Allan, 'Citizen Journalism and the Rise of Mass Self-Communication', *Global Media Journal*, Australian Edition, 1 (1), (2007), p. 1; S. Bowman and C. Willis, 'The Future is Here, But Do Media Companies See It?', *Nieman Reports*, Winter 2005, http://www.nieman.harvard.edu/assets/pdf/Nieman%20Reports/backissues/05winter.pdf, (28 July 2008).
152. Gillmor, *We the Media*, pp. 136–157.
153. Bowman and Willis, 'The Future is Here', p. 7.
154. A comprehensive study of the UGC Hub was completed in 2008. C. Wardle and A. Williams et al., 'UGC@theBBC: Understanding its impact upon contributors, non-contributors and BBC News', 2008, http://www.bbc.co.uk/blogs/knowledgeexchange/cardiffone.pdf, (3 Nov 2009). See also J. Harrison, 'User-Generated Content and Gatekeeping at the BBC Hub', *Journalism Studies*, 11 (4), (2010), pp. 243–256.

155. M. Eltringham, 'UGC five years on', *BBC College of Journalism*, 6 July 2010, http://www.bbc.co.uk/journalism/blog/2010/07/ugc-five-years-on.shtml, (6 July 2010).

156. V. Taylor, 'Profile', *LinkedIn*, No Date, http://www.linkedin.com/pub/vicky-taylor/6/138/658, (6 July 2010); Eltringham, 'UGC five years on', *BBC College of Journalism*, 6 July 2010, http://www.bbc.co.uk/journalism/blog/2010/07/ugc-five-years-on.shtml, (6 July 2010).

157. Sambrook, 'Citizen Journalism and the BBC', *Nieman Reports*, Winter 2005, http://www.bbc.co.uk/journalism/blog/2010/07/ugc-five-years-on.shtml, (28 July 2008), p. 14; Eltringham, 'UGC five years on'.

158. J. Day et al., 'We had 50 images in an hour', *The Guardian*, 11 July 2005, http://www.guardian.co.uk/attackonlondon/story/0,16132,1525911,00.html, (18 Oct 2007).

159. Sambrook, 'Citizen Journalism', p. 14.

160. A. Connor, 'Blogs on the bombs', *BBC,* 11 July 2005, http://news.bbc.co.uk/1/hi/4672195.stm, (22 Nov 2010).

161. R. North, 'Coming together as a city', *BBC,* 15 July 2005, http://news.bbc.co.uk/1/hi/uk/4670099.stm, (22 Nov 2010).

162. Research by M.T. Hänska-Ahy and R. Shapour, in 'Who's Reporting The Protests', *Journalism Studies*, 13, (2012), http://dx.doi.org/10.1080/14616 70X.2012.657908, demonstrates that BBC Persian and Arabic journalists felt 'far more comfortable and effective integrating UGC into their news output' in 2011 than in 2009.

163. Sambrook, 'Are Foreign Correspondents Redundant?', *Reuters Institute for the Study of Journalism*, 2010.

164. Appointed in Nov 2009, Gubbay's Social Media Editor role began in Jan 2010. He left the BBC in June 2011. Chris Hamilton was appointed as his successor.

165. BBC Press Release, 'BBC News appoints Alex Gubbay as first Social Media Editor', 16 Nov 2009, http://www.bbc.co.uk/pressoffice/pressreleases/stories/2009/11_november/16/gubbay.shtml, (19 Nov 2009).

166. M. Hockaday in 'BBC News appoints Alex Gubbay'.

167. Anderson, *BBC Blogs*, p. 6.

168. Ibid., p. 10.

169. R. Allman, 'What's iPM?', *BBC,* 12 Oct 2007, http://www.bbc.co.uk/blogs/ipm/2007/10/whats_ipm_1.shtml, (19 May 2008).

170. J. Tracey, 'Like all good things . . .', *iPM,* 15 Mar 2010, http://www.bbc.co.uk/blogs/ipm/ (28 Apr 2011).

171. E. Mair, 'Got a sentence of news for us?', PM, 25 Jan 2011, http://www.bbc.co.uk/blogs/pm/2011/01/got_a_sentence_of_news_for_us.shtml, (28 Apr 2011).

172. See Chapter 6.

173. BBC, 'WHYS FAQS', http://worldhaveyoursay.wordpress.com/whys-faqs/, (2 Aug 2008).

174. BBC, 'Bloggers on WHYS', http://worldhaveyoursay.wordpress.com/whys-faqs/bloggers-on-whys/, (2 Aug 2008).

175. R. Atkins, Presenter, BBC *WHYS*, Global News Blogging Masterclass, 17 Mar 2008.

176. Atkins, Blogging Masterclass.

177. D. Hayward, Head of the Journalism Programme, BBC College of Journalism, Interview, 21 Apr 2008.

178. R. Hamman, Former BBC Senior Broadcast Journalist, Email Correspondence, 15 Mar 2011.

179. RSS stands for Really Simple Syndication, RDF Site Summary or Rich Site Summary. RSS was developed to keep track of the rapidly increasing number of blogs. Subscribing to an RSS feed means a blog reader will be sent a message alerting them to new blog posts. For a summary of the origins, see Rosenberg, *Say Everything: How blogging began, what it's becoming and why it matters*, (Crown, 2009), pp. 207–9.
180. Claire Wardle, Freelance Consultant for the BBC College of Journalism, Interview, 5 Jan 2010.
181. Ibid.
182. Wardle, Personal Correspondence, 8 Dec 2010. The course was not mandatory.
183. Ibid.
184. Horrocks, 'Value of citizen journalism', *The Editors*, 7 Jan 2008, http://www.bbc.co.uk/blogs/theeditors/2008/01/value_of_citizen_journalism.html, (7 Jan 2008).
185. Bridcut, 'From Seesaw to Wagon Wheel'.
186. Horrocks, 'Value of citizen journalism'.

NOTES TO CHAPTER 3

1. Chris Vallance, BBC Senior Broadcast Journalist, Interview, 28 Jan 2008.
2. A. Gahran in Anderson, *BBC Blogs: News as conversation*, 2005, p. 5.
3. BBC Journalist, Interview, 2008.
4. Jamillah Knowles, BBC Broadcast Journalist, Interview, 25 May 2009. Knowles left the BBC in 2012 to become UK Editor of The Next Web. She continued to present Outriders for BBC Radio 5 Live.
5. See also S. Rosenberg, *Say Everything: How blogging began, what it's becoming and why it matters*, (Crown, 2009), p. 13.
6. Knowles, Interview, 25 May 2009.
7. Vallance, Interview, 28 Jan 2008.
8. BBC World Affairs Producers and Researchers, Focus Group, 12 Nov 2008.
9. BBC Correspondent, Interview, 2009.
10. Joe Boyle, BBC Broadcast Journalist, Interview, 23 Mar 2009.
11. Vallance, Interview, 28 Jan 2008.
12. Adam Blenford, BBC Senior Broadcast Journalist (News Online), Interview, 24 Mar 2009.
13. Arms Control Wonk, http://www.armscontrolwonk.com.
14. Gordon Corera, BBC Security Correspondent, Interview, 14 Dec 2007.
15. Rob Watson, BBC Defence and Security Correspondent (World Service), Interview, 3 Mar 2009; Small Wars Journal, http://smallwarsjournal.com/; Long War Journal, http://www.longwarjournal.org/; Counterterrorism Blog, http://counterterrorismblog.org.
16. World Affairs, Focus Group, 2008.
17. Ibid.
18. BBC News Online Journalist (a), Interview, 2009.
19. Corera, Interview, 14 Dec 2007.
20. Blenford, Interview, 24 Mar 2009.
21. World Affairs, Focus Group, 2008.
22. Blenford, Interview, 24 Mar 2009.
23. BBC Journalist, Interview, 2007.
24. BBC Correspondent (b), Interview, 2008.
25. Claire Wardle, Freelance Consultant for the BBC College of Journalism, Interview, 5 Jan 2010.

26. Wardle, Email Correspondence, 8 Apr 2011.
27. Blenford, Interview, 8 Apr 2011.
28. C. Beckett, *SuperMedia: Saving journalism so it can save the world*, (Blackwell, 2008), pp. 55, 58.
29. Knowles, Interview, 25 May 2009.
30. Caroline Wyatt, BBC Defence Correspondent, Interview, 14 Nov 2008.
31. Watson, Interview, 3 Mar 2009.
32. Vallance, Interview, 28 Jan 2008.
33. BBC World Service Journalists, Focus Group, 23 May 2008.
34. Jeremy Bowen, BBC Middle East Editor, Interview, 2 June 2009.
35. Corera, Interview, 14 Dec 2007.
36. Alison Baily, BBC Researcher, Interview,12 Nov 2008.
37. World Affairs, Focus Group, 2008.
38. H. Gans, *Deciding What's News*, 2nd Ed., (Northwestern University Press), pp. 129–131.
39. Corera, Interview, 14 Dec 2007.
40. G. Sick, *Gary's Choices*, http://garysick.tumblr.com/, (5 Nov 2009).
41. Bowen, Interview, 2 June 2009.
42. D. Levy, *Prospects for Peace*, www.prospectsforpeace.com, (5 Nov 2009).
43. Corera, Interview, 14 Dec 2007.
44. J. Lewis, 'Who are these people', *Arms Control Wonk*, http://armscontrolwonk.com/about, (25 Feb 2011).
45. Gordon Corera, BBC Security Correspondent, Email Correspondence, 11 Apr 2011.
46. Rosenberg, 'Much ado about blogging', *Salon.com,* 10 May 2002, http://dir.salon.com/story/tech/col/rose/2002/05/10/blogs/index.html, (31 Oct 2007). Rosenberg's italics. It is interesting that Rosenberg highlights 'time-strapped reporters'; in Chapter 4, BBC journalists identify time constraints as a reason why they do not use blogs as sources.
47. Stuart Hughes, BBC Defence and Security Producer, Interview, 14 Dec 2007. (His title has been World Affairs Producer since 2010).
48. Hughes, Interview, 14 Dec 2007.
49. Vallance, Interview, 28 Jan 2008.
50. Blenford, Interview, 24 Mar 2009.
51. Vallance, Interview, 8 Mar 2011.
52. The Twitter accounts of news wires may contribute to the observation that Twitter is faster.
53. Hughes, World Affairs Producer, Interview, 14 June 2010.
54. Blenford, Email Correspondence, 2 Dec 2010.
55. Hughes, Email Correspondence, 29 Jan 2011.
56. ENPS is a piece of software designed by the Associated Press which provides all BBC journalists with news and information from news agency sources and other BBC journalists. It is also used to produce TV and radio programmes.
57. Hughes, 'Newsgathering for social media—a case study', BBC College of *Journalism*, http://www.bbc.co.uk/journalism/blog/2011/04/newsgathering-for-social-media.shtml, 1 Apr 2011.
58. Hughes, Email Correspondence, 29 Jan 2011.
59. Boyle, Interview, 23 Mar 2009.
60. BBC Editorial Guidelines, Section 3: Accuracy: Gathering Material, 3.4.4, 2010, http://www.bbc.co.uk/guidelines/editorialguidelines/page/guidelines-accuracy-gathering-material.
61. Ibid., User Contributions in News Output: Guidance in Full, 2010, http://www.bbc.co.uk/guidelines/editorialguidelines/page/guidance-user-contributions-full.

62. Ibid., Section 3: Accuracy, 3.4.4.
63. Ibid.
64. Ibid., Internet Research: Guidance in Full, 2010, http://www.bbc.co.uk/guidelines/editorialguidelines/page/guidance-internet-research-full.
65. Ibid., Section 3: Accuracy, 3.4.3.
66. Ibid., User Contributions in News Output.
67. Thirty-six per cent did not reveal their name or used a pseudonym; B. Etling et al., 'Mapping the Arabic Blogosphere: Politics, Culture and Dissent', Berkman Center for Internet & Society, June 2009, http://cyber.law.harvard.edu/sites/cyber.law.harvard.edu/files/Mapping_the_Arabic_Blogosphere_0.pdf, (24 Aug 2009), p. 36.
68. Blenford, Interview, 24 Mar 2009.
69. Wyatt, Interview, 14 Nov 2008.
70. Krassimira Twigg, BBC Broadcast Journalist (News Online), Interview, 31 Mar 2009.
71. Blenford, Interview, 24 Mar 2009.
72. Knowles, Interview, 25 May 2009.
73. J. Harrison, *News,* (Routledge, 2006), pp. 144–145.
74. This was the case in the BBC's coverage of the use of white phosphorus in Iraq in 2005 in Chapter 2.
75. BBC Journalist, Interview, 2009.
76. Ibid. This has methodological implications for researching journalists' use of blogs as sources of information. In particular it highlights one of the weaknesses of content analyses of media output.
77. Last of Iraqis, http://last-of-iraqis.blogspot.com.
78. E. Mair, BBC Presenter, BBC Radio 4 *iPM* programme, 24 Nov 2007.
79. Ibid.
80. Vallance, Interview, 28 Jan 2008.
81. Anderson, Interview, 16 June 2008; The "Sunni Triangle" was an area to the west and north of Baghdad, the heartland of the Sunni insurgency in Iraq.
82. Vallance, Interview, 28 Jan 2008.
83. World Service, Focus Group, 23 May 2008
84. After B. Wellman, 'Little Boxes, Glocalisation and Networked Individualism', *Revised Papers from the Second Kyoto Workshop on Digital Cities II, Computational and Sociological Approaches*, 2001.
85. A. Murray, 'The hazards of war reporting from the other side of the world', *Ici, leguape*, 31 Oct 2011, http://www.leguape.com/journalism/the-hazards-of-war-reporting-from-the-other-side-of-the-world, (1 Nov 2011).
86. Murray, 'BBC processes for verifying social media content', *BBC College of Journalism*, 18 May 2011, http://www.bbc.co.uk/blogs/blogcollegeofjournalism/posts/bbcsms_bbc_procedures_for_veri, (18 May 2011).
87. Murray, 'The hazards of war reporting'.
88. Audience research conducted as part of the BBC Trust's report on the coverage of Arab Spring noted that respondents 'potentially influenced by the contribution of social media . . . often referred to the perceived rawness of footage as being indicative of accuracy'. E. Mortimer, 'A BBC Trust report on the impartiality and accuracy of the BBC's coverage of the events known as the "Arab Spring"', *BBC Trust*, June 2012, p. 65.
89. World Service, Focus Group, 23 May 2008; Boyle, Interview, 23 Mar 2009. The latter point mentioned specifically by Vallance, Interview, 28 Jan 2008.
90. Barot, Senior Broadcast Journalist, Interview, 16 Sep 2009. In June 2010, he became Assistant Editor of the UGC hub.
91. Barot, Interview, 16 Sep 2009. He said the wires were using their own sources which were different from the Twitter accounts that the BBC were accessing.

92. Boyle, Interview, 23 Mar 2009.
93. R. Sambrook in L. Oliver, 'UGC offering authenticity despite restrictions in Iran, says BBC's Richard Sambrook', Journalism.co.uk, 17 June 2009, http://www.journalism.co.uk/news/ugc-offering-authenticity-despite-restrictions-in-iran-says-bbc-s-richard-sambrook/s2/a534793/, (17 June 2009).
94. S. Allan, 'Reweaving the Internet: Online news of September 11' in B. Zelizer and S. Allan, (eds), *Journalism After September 11*, (Routledge, 2002), pp. 119–140.
95. Anderson, Interview, 16 June 2008.
96. World Service, Focus Group, 23 May 2008.
97. Boyle, Interview, 23 Mar 2009.
98. Hughes, Interview, 14 June 2010.
99. Ibid.
100. World Service, Focus Group, 23 May 2008.
101. Ibid.
102. Olivia Cornes, Senior Broadcast Journalist (News Online), Interview, 14 November 2007.
103. World Service, Focus Group, 23 May 2008.
104. Boyle, Interview, 23 Mar 2009.
105. World Affairs, Focus Group, 12 Nov 2008.
106. Wyatt, Interview 14 Nov 2008.
107. Frank Gardner, BBC Security Correspondent, Interview, 3 Dec 2008.
108. Wyatt, Interview, 14 Nov 2008; Gardner, Interview, 3 Dec 2008.
109. Beckett, *SuperMedia*.
110. J. Jarvis, 'Networked journalism', *Buzz Machine*, 5 July 2006, http://www.buzzmachine.com/2006/07/05/networked-journalism, (5 Nov 2009).
111. They may very well not be amateurs. BBC correspondents specifically like to access the blogs of experts.
112. Knowles, Interview, 25 May 2009. Knowles argues that journalism has, for the most part, learnt to 'step down from its pedestal'.
113. M.S. Granovetter, 'The Strength of Weak Ties', *American Journal of Sociology*, 78 (6), (1973), pp. 1360–1380: 'weak ties, often denounced as generative of alienation are here seen as indispensable to individuals' opportunities and to their integration into communities'.
114. Knowles, Interview, 25 May 2009.
115. Vallance, Interview, 28 Jan 2008.
116. M. Eltringham, Assistant Editor of Interactivity, Social Media Global News Event, 16 Sep 2008. He became Editor of the BBC College of Journalism in May 2011.
117. Knowles, Interview, 25 May 2009.
118. She was speaking in the context of carrying audio recording equipment when reporting.
119. Knowles, Interview, 25 May 2009.
120. Knowles, Email Correspondence, 12 Dec 2010.
121. Knowles, Interview, 25 May 2009.
122. Eltringham, Social Media Global News Event, 16 Sep 2008.
123. Hermida, 'From TV to Twitter: How Ambient News Became Ambient Journalism', *Media and Culture Journal*, 13 (2), (2010), http://journal.media-culture.org.au/index.php/mcjournal/article/viewArticle/220 (Accessed 10 July 2010).
124. Bennett, 'A Twitter Revolution in Breaking News' in J. Mair and R. Keeble (eds), *Face the Future: Tools for the modern media age*, (Abramis, 2011), pp. 63–73.
125. Granovetter, 'Strength of Weak Ties', pp. 1360–1380.

126. Tuchman, *Making News: A study in the construction of reality*, (The Free Press, 1980), p. 25.
127. Bardoel and Deuze, 'Network Journalism', pp. 91–103; J. Jarvis, 'Networked journalism', *Buzz Machine*, 5 July 2006, http://www.buzzmachine.com/2006/07/05/networked-journalism, (5 Nov 2009).
128. Phillips, 'Old Sources: New bottles', p. 100.
129. Wardle and Williams et al., 'UGC@theBBC: Understanding its impact on contributors, no-contributors and BBC News,' http://www.bbc.co.uk/blogs/knowledgeexchange/cardiffone.pdf, (3 Nov 2009), p. 45.

NOTES TO CHAPTER 4

1. B. McNair, 'What Is Journalism?' in H. De Burgh (ed.), *Making Journalists*, (Routledge, 2005), p. 39; N. Gowing, '"Skyful of Lies" and Black Swans: The new tyranny of shifting information power in crises', *Reuters Institute for Journalism*, 2009, pp. 27, 29.
2. The BBC's Editorial Guidelines describe reporting conflict as a 'special responsibility', Section 11: War, Terror and Emergencies, Introduction, 2010, http://www.bbc.co.uk/guidelines/editorialguidelines/page/guidelines-war-introduction.
3. R. Keeble, *Ethics for Journalists*, (Routledge, 2001), pp. 97–109.
4. R. Clutterbuck, *The Media and Political Violence*, (Macmillan Press, 1981).
5. P. Knightley, *The First Casualty: The war correspondent as hero, propagandist and myth-maker*, (Andre Deutsche Ltd., 2003); S. Allan and B. Zelizer, 'Rules of Engagement: Journalism and war' in S. Allen and B. Zelizer (eds) *Reporting War: Journalism in wartime*, (Routledge, 2004), p. 4; J. Simpson, *A Mad World, My Masters*, (Macmillian, 2000), pp. 249–286; J. Kampfner, *Blair's Wars*, 2nd Ed. (Free Press, 2004), p. 46.
6. P. Hammond, 'Humanizing War: The Balkans and beyond', in S. Allan and B. Zelizer (eds), *Reporting War: Journalism in wartime* (Routledge, 2004), pp. 174–187.
7. K. Sanders, *Ethics and Journalism,* (Sage, 2003), p. 99; K. Adie, *The Kindness of Strangers*, (Headline, 2002), p. 286.
8. Allan and Zelizer, 'Rules of engagement', pp. 3–21.
9. Paul Adams, BBC World Affairs Correspondent, Interview, 7 Nov 2008.
10. Rob Watson, BBC World Service Defence and Security Correspondent, Interview, 3 Mar 2009.
11. There is competition for stories among correspondents within the BBC. Individualism allows journalists to develop their own original ideas for stories, but it perhaps also means they are less willing to engage in a social media world which arguably thrives on a culture of sharing and crowdsourcing.
12. Gardner, Interview, 3 Dec 2008.
13. Bowen, Interview, 2 June 2009.
14. Watson, Interview, 3 Mar 2009.
15. Jeremy Bowen, BBC Middle East Editor, Interview, 2 June 2009.
16. Richard Sambrook, BBC Director of Global News (2004–2010), Reuters 'News of the World' Panel, 16 June 2009.
17. Ibid.
18. Alastair Leithead, BBC Asia Correspondent, Interview, 28 May 2009.
19. Bowen, Interview, 2 June 2009.
20. G. Born, *Uncertain Vision*, (Secker and Warburg, 2004), p. 404.
21. McNair 'What Is Journalism?', p. 39.
22. Bowen, Interview, 2 June 2009.
23. Gardner, Interview, 3 Dec 2008.

24. BBC Correspondent (b), Interview, 2008.
25. Kate Robinson, Assignments Editor of Home Newsgathering, Interview, 19 June 2009.
26. BBC Senior Editor, Nov 2007.
27. H. Gans, *Deciding What's News*, 2nd Ed. (Northwestern University Press, 2004), p. 128.
28. Gordon Corera, BBC Security Correspondent, Interview, 14 Dec 2007.
29. Gardner, Interview 3 Dec 2008.
30. Hughes, Interview, 14 Dec 2007.
31. Corera, Interview, 14 Dec 2007.
32. Caroline Wyatt, BBC Defence Correspondent, Interview, 14 Nov 2008.
33. Watson, Interview, 3 Mar 2009.
34. Gardner, Interview, 3 Dec 2008.
35. Ibid.
36. P. Adams, 'China diary: Astonishing ambition', *BBC Online*, 26 Feb 2008, http://news.bbc.co.uk/1/hi/world/asia-pacific/7265490.stm, (27 Aug 2009).
37. Adams, Interview, 7 Nov 2008.
38. Stuart Hughes, BBC Defence and Security Producer, Interview, 14 Dec 2007.
39. Stuart Hughes, World Affairs Producer, Interview, 14 June 2010.
40. Gardner, Interview, 3 Dec 2008.
41. BBC Journalist, Interview, 2009. This should not be generalised. Areas of radio at the BBC and the World Service are highly tech savvy and responsible for significant innovation.
42. BBC Correspondent (b), Interview, 2008.
43. BBC Correspondent (a), Interview, 2008.
44. Wyatt, Interview, 14 Nov 2008.
45. Corera, Interview, 14 Dec 2007; Wyatt, Interview, 14 Nov 2008; BBC World Service Journalists, Focus Group, 23 May 2008.
46. Corera, Interview, 14 Dec 2007.
47. Gardner, Interview, 3 Dec 2008.
48. Jeremy Bowen, BBC Middle East Editor, Interview, 2 June 2009.
49. I did not give BBC journalists a definition of a blog prior to interviews but explored their understanding of blogs during questioning.
50. Wyatt, Interview, 14 Nov 2008.
51. Watson, Interview, 3 Mar 2009.
52. P. Clifton, 'News Interactive and the Re-Organisation', 2007: the financial pressures were a 'reduced licence fee and big efficiency targets requiring savings of 25% over five years'. In the five-year period, 190 posts were due to be axed in the Newsroom Department, some 20% of the existing workforce.
53. The Web is a medium where seconds are deemed to matter. In May 2006, Pete Clifton noted an improvement in load times of the website on News Interactive's internal blog: 'New research on the speed to access some of the big news sites highlighted what a fantastic job we are now doing in this area. Our site came on top with a load time of 0.85secs to beat the likes of ITV and Sky (1.63secs), while Reuters was back at more than six seconds.' P. Clifton, 'Pete's weekly update', *BBC News Online Intranet*, 5 May 2006.
54. BBC News Online Journalist (a), Interview, 2009.
55. Adam Blenford, BBC Senior Broadcast Journalist (News Online), Interview, 24 Mar 2009.
56. BBC News Online Journalist (b), Interview, 2009.
57. N. Davies, *Flat Earth News,* (Chatto & Windus, 2008), pp. 69–73.
58. BBC News Online Journalist (c), Interview, 2009.
59. AP, 'BBC Marks Tenth Anniversary With ENPS', 9 Sep 2006, http://www.enps.com/press_releases/101/bbc_marks_tenth_anniversary_with_enps, (13 Aug 2009).

60. Joe Boyle, BBC Broadcast Journalist (News Online), Interview, 23 Mar 2009.
61. World Service, Focus Group, 23 May 2008.
62. Ibid.
63. Blenford, Interview, 24 Mar 2009.
64. Boyle, Interview, 23 Mar 2009; World Service, Focus Group, 23 May 2008.
65. Blenford, Interview, 24 Mar 2009.
66. Boyle, Interview, 23 Mar 2009
67. Ibid.
68. Blenford, Interview, 24 Mar 2009.
69. Ibid.
70. The previous chapter identified contradictions in approach dependent on whether journalists were trying to report a significant breaking news crisis. World Service, Focus Group, 23 May 2008.
71. Boyle, Interview, 23 Mar 2009.
72. BBC News Online Journalist (a), Interview, 2009.
73. Blenford, Interview, 24 Mar 2009.
74. Adam Blenford, BBC Senior Broadcast Journalist, Email Correspondence, 2 Dec 2010. A phenomenon observed by A. Hermida in 'From TV to Twitter: How ambient news became ambient journalism', *Media and Culture Journal*, 13 (2), (2010).
75. Blenford, Email Correspondence, 2 Dec 2010.
76. See Stuart Hughes's comments in Chapter 3.
77. Bowen, Interview, 2 June 2009.
78. Adams, Interview, 7 Nov 2008.
79. Gardner, Interview, 3 Dec 2008.
80. Bowen, Interview, 2 June 2009.
81. Gardner, Interview, 3 Dec 2008. This was in the context of a question about Foreign Secretary David Miliband's blog, and the blog established by the Georgian Foreign Ministry during the Russo-Georgia War in 2008.
82. Gardner, Interview, 3 Dec 2008.
83. Corera, Interview, 14 Dec 2007.
84. Ibid.
85. Chris Vallance noted that by 2011, Twitter had been adopted by a significant number of his colleagues. Vallance, BBC Senior Broadcast Journalist, Interview, 8 Mar 2011.
86. Gardner, Email Correspondence, 24 Mar 2011.
87. BBC Executive Producer, Internal BBC Event, 2008.
88. Jonathan Baker, Deputy Head of Newsgathering (2006–10), *War Reporting—Where does a journalist's duty lie?*, St Bride's Church, London, 9 April 2008. In March 2010, he became Head of the BBC College of Journalism.
89. S. Costeloe in J. Stray, 'Drawing out the Audience: Insider the BBC's User-Generated Content Hub', *Nieman Journalism Lab*, 5 May 2010, http://www.niemanlab.org/2010/05/drawing-out-the-audience-inside-bbc%E2%80%99s-user-generated-content-hub/, (4 May 2011).
90. G. Born, *Uncertain Vision* (Secker and Warburg, 2004), p. 5.
91. There has been a row about rigging phone votes on the popular children's television programme *Blue Peter*; an apology for using inaccurately edited footage of the Queen; the resignation of the controller of Radio 2, Lesley Douglas, after complaints about the broadcasting of a prank phone call by Jonathan Ross and Russell Brand to actor Andrew Sachs; and widespread criticism of the BBC's decision not to show an aid appeal for the children of Gaza on behalf of the Disasters and Emergencies Committee in January 2009.
92. Wyatt, Interview, 14 Nov 2008.

93. World Service, Focus Group, 23 May 2008.
94. Wyatt, Interview, 14 Nov 2008.
95. Adams, Interview, 9 Nov 2007.
96. BBC News Online Journalist (a), Interview, 2009.
97. Alexis Akwagyiram, BBC News Online Journalist, Interview, 4 Mar 2009.
98. BBC News Online Journalist (a), Interview, 2009.
99. Corera, Interview 14 Dec 2007.
100. Kate Robinson, Assignments Editor of Home Newsgathering, Interview, 19 June 2009.
101. World Affairs, Focus Group, 2008.
102. Blenford, Interview, 24 Mar 2009.
103. Adams, Interview, 7 Nov 2008.
104. Beckett, *SuperMedia*, p. 63.
105. BBC Correspondent (a), Interview, 2008; BBC Correspondent (b), Interview, 2008.
106. Blenford, Interview, 24 Mar 2009.
107. Blenford, Interview, 24 Mar 2009; Corera, Interview 14 Dec 2007; Hughes, Interview, 14 Dec 2007.
108. Blenford, Interview, 24 Mar 2009.
109. Twitter Statistics for 2010, *Sysomos*, 2010, http://sysomos.com/insidetwitter/twitter-stats-2010, (19 Dec 2010).
110. Blenford, Email Correspondence, 2 Dec 2010.

NOTES TO CHAPTER 5

1. M. Tremayne (ed), *Blogging, Citizenship and the Future of Media*, (Routledge, 2008), p. xvi.
2. W. Lowrey, 'Mapping the Journalism-Blogging Relationship', *Journalism*, 7 (4), pp. 477, 493.
3. S. Robinson, 'The Mission of the J-Blog: Recapturing journalistic authority online', *Journalism*, 7 (1), (2006b), p. 65.
4. S. Allan, *Online News*, (Open University Press, 2006), p. 108.
5. Robinson, 'Mission of the J-Blog', p. 65.
6. Quoted in N. Thurman, 'Forums for Citizen Journalists? Adoption of user generated content initiatives by online news media', *New Media & Society*, 10 (1), (2008), p. 146.
7. D. Matheson 'Weblogs and the Epistemology of the News: Some trends in online journalism', *New Media & Society* 6 (4), (2004), p. 449.
8. J. Stone, *Pan-BBC Blog Trial*, 14 Nov 2005, p. 3; Hermida, 'The BBC goes blogging: Is "Auntie" finally listening?', http://online.journalism.utexas.edu/2008/papers/Hermida.pdf, (1 Aug 2008), p. 2.
9. Allan, *Online News*, p. 35; D. Gillmor, *We the Media: Grassroots journalism by the people, for the people*, (O'Reilly Media Inc., 2006), p. 131.
10. Sambrook in C. Willis and S. Bowman, 'Interview with Richard Sambrook, Director of the BBC Global News Division', *Hypergene Media Blog*, 11 Apr 2005, http://www.hypergene.net/blog/weblog.php?id=P266, (14 Apr 2011).
11. Hermida, 'BBC goes blogging', p. 8.
12. M. Belam, Former Senior Development Producer (2004–2005), 'Blogging at the BBC: Part 2', *Currybetdotnet*, 12 Dec 2007, http://www.currybet.net/cbet_blog/2007/12/blogging_at_the_bbc_2.php, (2 Feb 2009).
13. Scotblog, *BBC Scotland*, http://www.bbc.co.uk/scotland/webguide/scotblog/whatis.shtml, (5 May 2008).

14. 'Blogging and the BBC', *BBC Scotland Interactive*, May 2005.
15. Ibid. Island Blogging closed at the end of January 2009.
16. According to Euan Semple, 'DigiLab was set up by a committee whose aim was to introduce new ways of doing things . . . Our brief was to talent spot new technologies that may be of interest to the BBC.' Euan Semple, Former Manager of BBC DigiLab, Email Correspondence, 2 Mar 2011.
17. Euan Semple, Internal BBC Blog, 12 June 2002.
18. Belam, 'Blogging at the BBC: Part 1', *Currybetdotnet*, 11 Dec 2007 http://www.currybet.net/cbet_blog/2007/12/blogging_at_the_bbc_1.php, (16 Jan 2009).
19. Belam, 'Blogging at the BBC: Part 8', *Currybetdotnet*, 20 Dec 2007, http://www.currybet.net/cbet_blog/2007/12/blogging_at_the_bbc_8.php, (2 Feb 2009).
20. Ibid.; Nick Reynolds, Senior Advisor, Editorial Policy, Interview, 14 May 2008. By 2011, Reynolds was Social Media Executive in BBC Online.
21. Kevin Anderson, *BBC Blogs: News as conversation*, 2005, p. 15.
22. Lucy Hooberman, Former BBC Innovation Executive, Interview, 8 Apr 2011.
23. For example, see N. Robinson, 'The Campaign Today', *BBC,* 14 May 2001, http://news.bbc.co.uk/vote2001/hi/english/newsid_1329000/1329471.stm, (2 Feb 2009).
24. Giles Wilson, BBC News Blogs Editor, Global News Masterclass, 17 Oct 2007.
25. Robinson, 'The Beauty of Blogging', *Nick Robinson's Newslog*, 5 Dec 2005, http://www.bbc.co.uk/blogs/nickrobinson/2005/12/the_beauty_of_b.html, (5 May 2008).
26. Wilson, 'What is newslog?', *Nick Robinson's Newslog*, 5 Dec 2001, http://news.bbc.co.uk/1/hi/uk/1692330.stm, (5 May 2008).
27. Ibid.
28. Wilson, Global News Masterclass, 17 Oct 2007.
29. Wilson, 'What is newslog?'.
30. P. Mason, 'A balance sheet of the blog', *Newsnig8t,* 12 July 2005, http://paulmason.typepad.com/newsnig8t/2005/07/a_balance_sheet.html, (13 Jan 2009).
31. Peter Barron gained permission at 'a high level executive breakfast'. See P. Mason, *Newsnig8t,* 'The blog goes live!', 16 June 2005, http://paulmason.typepad.com/newsnig8t/2005/06/the_blog_goes_l.html, (13 Jan 2009).
32. Mason, 'A balance sheet of the blog'.
33. Nick Reynolds, Interview, 14 May 2008.
34. Ibid.
35. Tana Umaga is a former All Black rugby union captain.
36. Jem Stone, Executive Producer, Social Media at BBC Audio & Music, Interview, 9 July 2008.
37. Aaron Scullion, who worked under Giles Wilson, says there was 'a really big drive' to get Nick Robinson blogging. Scullion, Senior Product Manager, Future Media and Technology, Interview, 7 May 2008.
38. Robinson quoted in O. Gibson, '"I'm more than just a chirpy northerner"', *The Guardian,* 5 Sep 2005, http://www.guardian.co.uk/media/2005/sep/05/broadcasting.mondaymediasection, (13 Jan 2009).
39. Anderson, 'Blogging the US Election XIII', *BBC,* http://news.bbc.co.uk/1/hi/world/americas/3984453.stm, (13 Jan 2009).
40. Belam, 'Blogging at the BBC: Part 9', Currybet.net, http://www.currybet.net/cbet_blog/2007/12/blogging-at-the-bbc-part-9—-t.php, (13 Jan 2009).
41. Ibid. Belam describes Pete Clifton as one of the 'prime movers in getting the BBC to adopt a formal blogging platform'.
42. Anderson, *BBC Blogs*, p. 1.

43. P. Clifton, 'BLOG BAN', *BBC*, 29 July 2005, http://news.bbc.co.uk/1/hi/
    magazine/4727579.stm, (13 Jan 2009).
44. Richard Sambrook, BBC Director of Global News (2004–2010), Interview,
    11 July 2008.
45. Hooberman, Interview, 8 Apr 2011.
46. Lucy Hooberman, BBC Innovation Executive, Internal Blogging Wiki, 20 Oct
    2005.
47. Stone, Interiew, 9 July 2008.
48. Internal Blogging Wiki, 20 Oct 2005; Stone, Interview, 9 July 2008. He notes
    that 'the current technology that we had—Island Blogging, some of the other
    forums—wasn't very good.'
49. Internal Blogging Wiki, 20 Oct 2005.
50. Crsstal was never fully developed and eventually shelved. In some documen-
    tation it is spelt 'Crystal'.
51. Jem Stone, *Pan-BBC Blog Trial*, 14 Nov 2005.
52. Ibid., p. 3.
53. Movable Type. The BBC stopped using Movable Type for News blogs in Apr
    2011.
54. Stone, *Blog Trial*, pp. 3, 5.
55. Hooberman, Blogging Wiki, 20 Oct 2005.
56. Stone, Interview, 9 July 2008.
57. Nick Robinson's blog was launched at the end of November 2005 before the
    new technology was ready. It was initially hosted on Typepad with a masked
    URL so it looked like part of the BBC website.
58. R. Hamman, 'What's the Purpose of TV and Radio Blogs?', *BBC Pods and
    Blogs*, 15 Nov 2006, http://www.bbc.co.uk/blogs/podsandblogs/2006/11/
    whats_the_purpose_of_tv_and_ra.shtml, (14 Jan 2009).
59. Stone, Interview, 9 July 2008.
60. Scullion, Interview, 7 May 2008.
61. Ibid.
62. Scullion, Interview, 7 May 2008; Stone, Interview, 9 July 2008.
63. In January 2007, Evan Davis and Robert Peston both started blogs.
64. Scullion, Interview, 7 May 2008.
65. Stone, 'Dear PM blog readers', *PM*, 8 Feb 2007, http://www.bbc.co.uk/blogs/
    pm/2007/02/dear_pm_blog_readers.shtml, (16 Jan 2009).
66. Stone, Interview, 9 July 2008; More than £22.5 million had been spent devel-
    oping and maintaining BBC iPlayer by July 2010: FOI Request, *What Do They
    Know*, http://www.whatdotheyknow.com/request/36229/response/95657/
    attach/3/RFI20100757%20final%20response.pdf, (15 January 2009).
67. Stone, Interview, 9 July 2008.
68. Ibid.
69. Sambrook, Interview, 11 July 2008.
70. Ibid.
71. Anderson, *BBC Blogs*, p. 10.
72. B. Thompson, 'Is Google too powerful?', *BBC*, 21 Mar 2003, http://news.
    bbc.co.uk/1/hi/technology/2786761.stm, (3 Jan 2008).
73. M. Smartt cited in J. Raynsford, 'Blogging—the new journalism?', *Journal-
    ism.co.uk*, 25 Mar 2003, http://www.journalism.co.uk/5/articles/5604.php
    (4 Dec 2007).
74. D. Harris, 'BBC Blogs: Qualitative Research Debrief', *BBC MC&A Audience
    Research*, Sep 2006.
75. Robin Hamman reported to Jem Stone. Hamman, who left the BBC in 2008,
    was a central point of contact for the BBC's blogs and was responsible for the

everyday running and editorial direction of the trial. His role working on the blog trial was never formalised with an official BBC job title. Individual divisions, such as News and Sport, were responsible for the day-to-day editorial direction and content of news and sport blogs.

76. Hamman, 'Purpose of TV and Radio blogs?'.
77. Mason, 'A balance sheet of the blog'.
78. Hamman, 'Purpose of TV and Radio blogs?'.
79. Hughes, Interview, 14 Dec 2007.
80. Anderson, *BBC Blogs,* p. 15.
81. Harris, 'BBC Blogs: Qualitative Research'.
82. Robinson, 'The Beauty of Blogging'.
83. Sambrook, Interview, 11 July 2008.
84. Scullion, Interview, 7 May 2008.
85. R. Peston, BBC Future of Journalism Conference, 26 Nov 2008.
86. R. Peston, BBC Global News Masterclass, 12 July 2010.
87. K. Marsh, Executive Editor of BBC College of Journalism (2006–2011), *News Rewired Conference,* London, 14 Jan 2010.
88. Peston, Global News Masterclass.
89. Giles Wilson, Editor BBC News blogs, Interview, 3 Nov 2010.
90. A. Budd et al, *Report on the Independent Panel for the BBC Trust on the Impartiality of BBC Business Coverage,* April 2007, p. 18, para. 2.18.
91. Ibid. The report also criticised several Five Live presenters.
92. P. Preston, 'Danger lurks for BBC's bloggers', *The Observer,* 12 Oct 2008, http://www.guardian.co.uk/media/2008/oct/12/bbc-blogs-richard-peston, (16 Oct 2008).
93. S. Glover, 'Pontificating Mr Peston, self-indulgent bloggers, and why the BBC should stop putting opinion before facts', *The Daily Mail,* 28 Dec 2008, http://www.dailymail.co.uk/debate/article-1101744/Stephen-Glover-Pontificating-Mr-Peston-self-indulgent-bloggers-BBC-stop-putting-opinion-facts.html, (2 Feb 2009).
94. BBC journalists are not permitted to offer their 'personal views' on matters of 'public-policy', 'political or industrial controversy' or on 'controversial subjects', but senior journalists can provide their 'professional judgement'. BBC Editorial Guidelines, Section 4: Impartiality, Personal View Content, 4.4.31, 2010, http://www.bbc.co.uk/guidelines/editorialguidelines/page/guidelines-impartiality-personal-view/.
95. Robin Lustig, BBC World Tonight Presenter, Interview, 21 Oct 2008.
96. H. Boaden, 'BBC blogs are in good hands', *Letter to The Observer,* 19 Oct 2008, http://www.guardian.co.uk/theobserver/2008/oct/19/27, (19 Oct 2008).
97. M. Mardell in Radio 4 Feedback, 'The role of the BBC's news blogs', 27 Oct 2008, http://www.bbc.co.uk/blogs/theeditors/2008/10/the_role_of_the_bbcs_news_blog.html, (10 Nov 2008).
98. Wilson, 'Why blogs matter to the BBC', *The Editors,* 29 Dec 2008, http://www.bbc.co.uk/blogs/theeditors/2008/12/why_blogs_matter_to_the_bbc.html, (2 Feb 2009).
99. The controller of Radio 2, Lesley Douglas, resigned after complaints about the broadcasting of a prank phone call by Jonathan Ross and Russell Brand to actor Andrew Sachs. According to an article in the BBC's internal newspaper, 'extra layers of paperwork' were introduced after the Ross/Brand affair, causing 'strong resentment' and 'incomprehension'. 'Compliance' [with the BBC's editorial procedures] was a key topic at the BBC's Festival of Journalism in January 2009. See S. Hillier, 'Are you compliant or are you just ticking a box', *Ariel,* 20 Jan 2009.

100. Giles Wilson, BBC News Blogs Editor, Future of Journalism Conference, 26 Nov 2008.
101. Ibid.
102. Wilson, Interview, 3 Nov 2010.
103. BBC Editorial Guidelines, Section 4: 4.4.31, 2010.
104. Wilson, Interview, 3 Nov 2010.
105. Blog Guidelines, No Date. The questions include 'Is what a blogger is saying sensible? Is it impartial? Are there inadvertent errors there? Are things said which could be more clearly phrased to avoid controversy? Has the blogger said things they wouldn't say on air? Does the piece need balancing, either within this post or in a subsequent one? How will the post look if it was filleted and dressed up in the nationals tomorrow?'
106. M. Thompson in J. Townend, 'BBC director-general on social media use: "You can't take BBC cloak off at will"', *Journalism.co.uk*, 21 May 2009, http://www.journalism.co.uk/news-events-awards/bbc-director-general-on-social-media-use—you-can-t-take-bbc-cloak-off-at-will-/s14/a534512/ (11 Nov 2010). Thompson was Director-General from 2004–2012.
107. C. Shirky, *Here Comes Everybody: How change happens when people come together*, 2nd Ed. (Penguin, 2009).
108. Anderson, *BBC Blogs*, pp. 11, 15.
109. Wilson, 'New ways into blogs', *The Editors blog*, 17 Apr 2008, http://www.bbc.co.uk/blogs/theeditors/2008/04/new_ways_into_blogs.html, (28 Apr 2008).
110. BBC Management, 'Review of bbc.co.uk: BBC Management's submission to the BBC Trust's review', Dec 2007.
111. Scullion, Interview, 7 May 2008; R. Hamman, '18 Months of Blogs (Part 1)', *BBC Internet Blog*, 12 Nov 2007, http://www.bbc.co.uk/blogs/bbcinternet/2007/11/robin_post_part_i_1.html, (16 Jan 2009).
112. Scullion, Interview, 7 May 2008.
113. P. Barron, 'Blog Problems', *The Editors*, 26 Oct 2008, http://www.bbc.co.uk/blogs/theeditors/2007/10/blog_problems_1.html, (16 Jan 2009).
114. Robin Hamman, Former Senior Broadcast Journalist, Email Correspondence, 15 Mar 2011.
115. Atkins, 'We've Moved', *World Have Your Say Blog*, 28 Nov 2007, http://www.bbc.co.uk/blogs/worldhaveyoursay/2007/11/weve_moved.html#042697, (14 Jan 2009).
116. Stone, Interview, 9 July 2008.
117. Alan Connor, Senior Broadcast Journalist, (Assistant Editor BBC News blogs), Interview, 12 Oct 2010.
118. Blog Guidelines, No Date.
119. Connor, Interview, 12 Oct 2010.
120. Scullion, Interview, 12 Feb 2009.
121. Blog Guidelines, No Date.
122. Scullion, Interview, 12 Feb 2009.
123. Shirky, 'Communities, audiences and scale', www.shirky.com, 6 Apr 2002, http://shirky.com/writings/herecomeseverybody/community_scale.html (10 Aug 2008).
124. Robinson in Bennett, 'Nick Robinson looking for "less abusive debate" on blogs', *Mediating Conflict,* 10 Aug 2010, http://mediatingconflict.blogspot.com/2010/08/nick-robinson-looking-for-less-abusive.html, (10 Aug 2010).
125. J. Agnew in Bennett, 'BBC's cricket correspondent hits blog comments for six', *Mediating Conflict*, 23 Sep 2010, http://mediatingconflict.blogspot.com/2010/09/bbcs-cricket-correspondent-hits-blog.html, (23 Sep 2010).

126. Townend, 'Is the BBC really falling out of love with blogging?, Journalism. co.uk, 4 Mar 2010 http://blogs.journalism.co.uk/editors/2010/03/04/is-the-bbc-really-falling-out-of-love-with-blogging/, (4 Mar 2010).
127. Wilson, Interview, 3 Nov 2010.
128. Scullion, Interview, 12 Feb 2009.
129. M. Eltringham in Bennett, '#Newsrw: BBC considers introducing Daily Mail-style comment system', *Mediating Conflict*, 28 June 2010, http://mediatingconflict.blogspot.com/2010/06/newsrw-bbc-considers-introducing-daily.html, (28 June 2010).
130. Hermida, 'BBC goes blogging', pp. 13–15.
131. Ibid., p. 7.
132. Hughes, Interview, 12 Dec 2007.
133. Ibid.
134. Hughes quoted in J. Dube, 'Behind the Scenes: BBC's Stuart Hughes' "Blog exclusive"', *CyberJounalist.net*, 30 June 2004, http://www.cyberjournalist. net/news/001429.php, (2 Feb 2009).
135. Hughes, *Beyond Northern Iraq*, 14 Mar 2004, http://stuarthughes.blogspot. com/2004/03/i-had-planned-to-give-regular-updates.html, (16 Jan 2009).
136. Hughes, 'BLOGGING EXCLUSIVE—MUST CREDIT BEYOND NORTH-ERN IRAQ', *Beyond Northern Iraq*, 28 June 2004, http://stuarthughes. blogspot.com/2004/06/blogging-exclusive-must-credit-beyond.html, (2 Feb 2009).
137. Hughes quoted in Dube, 'Behind the Scenes'.
138. X. Jardin, 'News of early Iraq Power handover broken by a blog', *Boing Boing*, 28 June 2004, http://www.boingboing.net/2004/06/28/news-of-early-iraq-p.html, (2 Feb 2009).
139. Hughes quoted in Dube, 'Behind the Scenes'.
140. Although some of his blog posts were used as online articles.
141. There were also personal factors in his decision.
142. Hughes, Interview, 12 Dec 2007.
143. J. Leyne et al, 'Reporters' Log: Waiting for war', *BBC*, 20 Mar 2003, http:// news.bbc.co.uk/1/hi/in_depth/2864627.stm, (2 Feb 2009).
144. Caroline Wyatt, Defence Correspondent, Interview, 14 Nov 2008.
145. For example: A. Leithead, 'Afghan Conflict: Reporter's Diary', *BBC*, 8 Nov 2006, http://news.bbc.co.uk/1/hi/world/south_asia/6109076.stm, (20 Jan 2009).
146. Wyatt, Interview, 14 Nov 2008.
147. Fiona Anderson, Editor, Coaching, BBC College of Journalism, Email Correspondence, 12 Apr 2011.
148. Wyatt, Interview, 14 Nov 2008.
149. Ibid.
150. Watson, Interview, 20 Jan 2009.
151. Wyatt, Interview, 14 Nov 2008.
152. Gardner, Interview, 3 Dec 2009.
153. He refers to the terror attacks on Mumbai and the seizure of ships off the east coast of Africa in November 2008.
154. Wyatt, Interview, 14 Nov 2008.
155. Jeremy Bowen, Interview, 2 June 2009.
156. Jeremy Bowen, Email Correspondence, 11 Apr 2011.
157. BBC Correspondent, Interview, 2009.
158. Peston, Global News Masterclass.
159. She started tweeting in August 2009 prior to covering the Trades Union Congress in September.

160. Wilson, Interview, 3 Nov 2010.
161. BBC News: Social media guidance, July 2011.
162. BBC News: Official tweeters' guidance, June 2011.
163. Alastair Leithead, Asia Correspondent, Email Correspondence 17 Apr 2011.
164. The 'black shirts' were 'apparently an armed wing' of the 'red shirt' anti-government protest movement. T. Johnston, '"Black shirts" on front line in Thai clashes', *Financial Times*, 17 May 2010, http://www.ft.com/cms/s/0/fdbc3ae8–61a3–11df-aa80–00144feab49a.html#axzz1JsyP2ceu, (18 Apr 2011).
165. Leithead, Email Correspondence, 17 Apr 2011.
166. NPR's Andy Carvin gained particular notoriety for his comprehensive coverage from Twitter sources. Sky News's Tim Marshall used his Twitter account to provide updates from Tahrir square in Cairo, while video journalist Mohamed Abdelfattah, tweeted his arrest by Egyptian authorities.
167. BBC, 'Libya fighting: As it happened', 25 Aug 2011, http://www.bbc.co.uk/news/world-africa-14674119, (28 Aug 2011).
168. BBC, 'Libya protests: Gaddafi says "all my people love me"', 28 Feb 2011, http://www.bbc.co.uk/news/world-africa-12603259, (1 Mar 2011).
169. Wilson, Future of Journalism Conference.
170. Nic Newman, Former Controller, Future Media, Journalism (2007–2010), Email Correspondence, 13 Apr 2011.
171. BBC Senior Editor, 9 Nov 2007.
172. BBC Management, 'Review of bbc.co.uk', p. 17.
173. Thompson in Townend, 'BBC director-general on social media'.
174. Wilson, Future of Journalism Conference.
175. Scullion, Interview, 12 Feb 2009.
176. Connor, Interview, 12 Oct 2010.

NOTES TO CHAPTER 6

1. S. Robinson, 'Gateway or Gatekeeping: The institutionalisation of online news in creating an altered technological authority', *International Symposium on Online Journalism*, 2006, p. 22.
2. Anna McGovern, Producer, World Service Future Media, Global News Masterclass, 17 Mar 2008.
3. According to P. Lee-Wright, 'new media' was used as a new way for journalists to 'weld a relationship with their audience'. Lee-Wright, 'Culture Shock: New media and organisational change in the BBC' in N. Fenton (ed), *New Media, Old News: Journalism & democracy in the digital age*, (Sage, 2010), p. 80.
4. J. Rosen, 'A Most Useful Definition of Citizen Journalism', *PressThink*, 14 July 2008, http://archive.pressthink.org/2008/07/14/a_most_useful_d.html (17 July 2008)'.
5. BBC *Newsnight*, 'A history of Newsnight', http://news.bbc.co.uk/1/hi/newsid_8070000/newsid_8072000/8072060.stm, (2 July 2009).
6. G. Born, *Uncertain Vision*, (Secker and Warburg, 2004), p. 421.
7. Ibid., p. 422.
8. Peter Barron was editor between 2004 and 2008. He left to become Google's Head of Communications and Public Affairs for the UK and Ireland.
9. Barron, 'The Newsnight Mission', *BBC Newsnight*, 23 Jan 2005, http://news.bbc.co.uk/1/hi/programmes/newsnight/newsnight25/4198849.stm, (2 July 2009).
10. BBC *Newsnight* Producer, Interview, 2009.

11. F. Lloyd-Davis, *Studio 9 Films*, No date, http://www.studio9films.co.uk/pages/about.html, (13 August 2010). Fiona Lloyd-Davis was recruited by Guardian Films as a producer to work on the project.
12. George Entwistle, Former BBC *Newsnight* Editor (2001–2004), Interview, 24 Sep 2010.
13. Lloyd-Davis, *Studio 9 Films*.
14. By which 'our readers have become part of what we do'. A. Rusbridger, 'First read: The Mutualised Future is Bright', *Columbia Journalism Review*, 19 Oct 2009, http://www.cjr.org/reconstruction/the_mutualized_future_is_brigh.php, (21 Oct 2009).
15. Entwistle, Interview, 24 Sep 2010. In 2012, Entwistle succeeded Mark Thompson to become Director-General of the BBC.
16. B. Cammaerts and N. Carpentier, 'Blogging the 2003 Iraq War: Challenging the ideological model of war and mainstream journalism?', *Observatorio*, 3 (2), (2009).
17. B. Thornton, 'Newsnight Review, 25 July', *BBC Newsnight*, 25 July 2008, http://www.bbc.co.uk/blogs/newsnight/fromthewebteam/2008/07/newsnight_review_25_july.html, (13 Aug 2010).
18. Mason, 'I get demoted to a category', *Talk About Newsnight*, 8 Aug 2006, http://www.bbc.co.uk/blogs/newsnight/2006/08/i_get_demoted_to_a_category.html, (17 Aug 2010).
19. Mason said his blog subsequently 'gained a new lease of life' as an 'on-the-fly reporting tool for the financial crisis'. Paul Mason, Economics Editor, BBC *Newsnight*, Email Correspondence, 6 Apr 2011.
20. S. Denman, 'Thursday, 19 June, 2008, *From the Web Team*, http://www.bbc.co.uk/blogs/newsnight/fromthewebteam/2008/06/thursday_19_june_2008.html, (17 Aug 2010).
21. Pax, 'Normal for Iraq?', BBC *Newsnight*, 14 Mar 2007, http://www.bbc.co.uk/blogs/newsnight/2007/03/normal_for_iraq.html, (13 Aug 2010).
22. Ibid.
23. 'Doza' in ibid.
24. P. Barron, 'What Do You Want in Wednesday's Programme?', *Talk About Newsnight*, 31 Oct 2007, http://www.bbc.co.uk/blogs/newsnight/2007/10/what_do_you_want_in_wednesdays_programme.html (Accessed 2 Jul 2009).
25. 'Michael Stead' in ibid.
26. 'Mistress76uk' in ibid.
27. Peter Barron, *New Media, New Ways with Audiences, College of Journalism*, 30 May 2008.
28. Barron, 'What do you want in Wednesday's programme?'.
29. D. Kelly, 'Prospects for Wednesday, 19 March', *Talk About Newsnight*, 19 Mar 2008, http://www.bbc.co.uk/blogs/newsnight/2008/03/prospects_for_wednesday_19_march.html, (2 July 2009).
30. 'Rich', 'What do you want this Wednesday', *Talk About Newsnight*, 7 Nov 2007 http://www.bbc.co.uk/blogs/newsnight/2007/11/what_do_you_want_this_wednesday.html, (17 Aug 2010).
31. 'Hannah', 'What do you want this Wednesday', *Talk About Newsnight*, 7 Nov 2007, http://www.bbc.co.uk/blogs/newsnight/2007/11/what_do_you_want_this_wednesday.html, (17 Aug 2010).
32. Barron, *New Media, New Ways*.
33. P. Rippon in M. Bell, '"Newsnight and Paxman are what the BBC is all about"', *The Independent*, 6 Dec 2009, http://www.independent.co.uk/news/media/tv-radio/newsnight-and-paxman-are-what-the-bbc-is-all-about-1834851.html, (17 Aug 2010).

34. D. Pearl, 'Terror questions—do you have answers', *Talk About Newsnight*, 8 Aug 2006, http://www.bbc.co.uk/blogs/newsnight/2006/08/terror_questions_do_you_have_answers.html, (17 Aug 2010).
35. Mason, 'A wave of cynicism hits the blog', *Talk About Newsnight*, 11 Aug 2006, http://www.bbc.co.uk/blogs/newsnight/2006/08/a_wave_of_cynicism_hits_the_blog.html, (17 Aug 2010).
36. 'David' in ibid.
37. 'Andrew' in ibid.
38. M. Urban, 'Iraq—what went wrong? Mark Urban Q&A', *Talk About Newsnight*, 22 Mar 2007, http://www.bbc.co.uk/blogs/newsnight/2007/03/iraq_what_went_wrong_mark_urban_qa.html, (17 Aug 2010).
39. A former British Ambassador to the UN, Sir Jeremy Greenstock was appointed as UK Special Representative for Iraq in 2003.
40. Urban, 'Iraq—what went wrong?'.
41. BBC Newsnight, 'David Miliband on Newsnight', 7 May 2008, http://www.bbc.co.uk/blogs/newsnight/2008/05/david_miliband_on_newsnight.html, (17 Aug 2010).
42. J. Paxman, BBC *Newsnight*, 7 May 2008.
43. Barron, 'What do you want in Wednesday's programme?'.
44. Barron, 'Blogging—a new era', *Talk About Newsnight*, 28 Apr 2008, http://www.bbc.co.uk/blogs/newsnight/2008/04/blogging_a_new_era.html, (2 July 2009).
45. Ian Lacey, BBC *Newsnight* Producer, Interview, 11 Mar 2009.
46. BBC *Newsnight* Producer, Interview, 2009.
47. BBC *Newsnight*, 'Thursday, 16 November, 2006', 16 Nov 2006, http://www.bbc.co.uk/blogs/newsnight/2006/11/thursday_16_november_2006.html, (17 Aug 2010).
48. BBC *Newsnight*, 'Thursday, 31 May, 2007', 31 May 2007, http://www.bbc.co.uk/blogs/newsnight/2007/05/thursday_31_may_2007.html, (17 Aug 2010).
49. L. Freeman, 'Can the "War on Terror" ever be won?', *From the Web Team*, http://www.bbc.co.uk/blogs/newsnight/fromthewebteam/2008/09/can_the_war_on_terror_ever_be.html, (17 Aug 2010).
50. S. McDermott, 'Wednesday, 16 June, 2010', *From the Web Team*, 16 June 2010, http://www.bbc.co.uk/blogs/newsnight/fromthewebteam/2010/06/wednesday_16_june_2010.html, (12 Aug 2010).
51. Verity Murphy, BBC *Newsnight* Producer, Interview, 30 June 2009.
52. The Ofcom Communications Market Report 2010 demonstrates that television consumption remains the most popular form of media in the United Kingdom (225 minutes per day in 2009). Internet use is growing (doubling to 27 minutes per day in 2009).
53. Barron, *New Media, New Ways*.
54. *Newsnight* journalists have also started individual accounts. Economics Editor Paul Mason says he has 'built a network of followers' and uses his Twitter account for journalism, both at the 'input' stage—to source information and as an 'output' for his journalism. Mason, Email Correspondence, 6 Apr 2011.
55. Sarah McDermott, Web Team Producer, Email Correspondence, 16 Mar 2011.
56. Barron, Former *Newsnight* Editor (2004–2008), Email Correspondence, 15 Mar 2011.
57. Barron, 'What do you want in Wednesday's programme?'.
58. Barron, *New Media, New Ways*.

59. Viewers can also discuss *Newsnight* on the programme's Facebook page: BBC Newsnight Facebook Page, http://www.facebook.com/bbcnewsnight.
60. Barron, 'Blogging—a new era'.
61. BBC College of Journalism, *New Media, New Ways,* 30 May 2008.
62. In 2006, *Newsnight* asked viewers to send in two-minute videos that they had shot about a news issue. Five were shown on *Newsnight* that December. At the end of the 30 November programme, Jeremy Paxman promoted the slot by sarcastically highlighting 'our Editor's pathetic pleas for you to send some of us your old bits of home movie and the like so we can become the BBC's version of *Animals Do The Funniest Things*'.
63. Rippon in M. Bell, '"Newsnight and Paxman are what the BBC is all about"', *The Independent*, 6 Dec 2009, http://www.independent.co.uk/news/media/tv-radio/newsnight-and-paxman-are-what-the-bbc-is-all-about-1834851.html, (17 Aug 2010).
64. C. Beckett, *SuperMedia: Saving journalism so it can save the world*, (Oxford, 2008), p. 53.
65. N. Thurman, 'Forums for Citizen Journalists? Adoption of user generated content initiatives by online news media', *New Media & Society*, 10 (1), (2008), pp. 13–14, 17–18.
66. McDermott, Email Correspondence, 16 Mar 2011.
67. Peter Rippon, *Newsnight* Editor, Email Correspondence, 18 Apr 2011. A 'Job Market Mentors' item in April 2011 was consumed online by around 500,000 people. The whole of *Newsnight*'s TV programme was watched by 800,000. Rippon said *Newsnight* 'can add hugely to numbers by making content in a consumable way online'.
68. Rippon, Email Correspondence, 18 Apr 2011.
69. BBC *Newsnight* Producer, Interview, 2009.
70. BBC *WHYS*, 'What's WHYS?', No Date, http://worldhaveyoursay.wordpress.com/whys-faqs/, (29 July 2010).
71. Mark Sandell, Editor BBC WHYS, *New Media, New Ways with Audiences, College of Journalism*, 30 May 2008.
72. Mark Sandell, Editor, BBC *WHYS*, Interview, 10 Dec 2008.
73. BBC *WHYS*, 'About the team', 3 Mar 2006, http://news.bbc.co.uk/1/hi/talking_point/world_have_your_say/4379364.stm, (29 July 2010).
74. Sandell, *New Media, New Ways*.
75. Kate McGough, Broadcast Journalist, BBC *WHYS*, Interview, 4 Dec 2008.
76. Sandell, Interview, 10 Dec 2008.
77. Ibid.
78. Gardner, Interview, 3 Dec 2008.
79. Presenter Ros Atkins started the daily email. He believes that without it 'our blog would definitely suffer'. Atkins, BBC Global News Masterclass, 17 Mar 2008.
80. Sandell, 'Help needed. . .', *WHYS blog*, 6 Jan 2009, http://worldhaveyoursay.wordpress.com/2009/01/06/help-needed/, (6 Jan 2009).
81. Sandell, Interview, 10 Dec 2008. Sandell prefaced his use of the phrase by saying, 'in inverted commas'.
82. McGough, Interview, 4 Dec 2008.
83. Tom Hagler, BBC Senior Broadcast Journalist, *WHYS*, Interview, 11 Dec 2008.
84. BBC WHYS, Twitter Feed, *www.twitter.com/BBC_WHYS*. For example, '@*kiranmanral* Would you like to take part in the programme? How can we contact you? My email is martin.vennard@bbc.co.uk'. BBC_WHYS, Twitter Update, 4 May 2011, http://twitter.com/#!/BBC_WHYS/status/65707937368244224, (6 May 2011).

85. Chloe Tilley, Deputy Editor BBC *WHYS*, Interview, 10 Dec 2008.
86. Tilley, Interview, 10 Dec 2008. *WHYS* journalists will always speak to con-tributors on the phone before they are put on air.
87. McGough, Interview, 4 Dec 2008.
88. Tilley, Interview, 10 Dec 2008.
89. Atkins, BBC Global News Masterclass.
90. Richard Sambrook, BBC Director of Global News (2004–2010), Interview 11 July 2008.
91. Atkins, BBC Global News Masterclass.
92. Ibid.
93. Sandell, *New Media, New Ways*.
94. Atkins, BBC Global News Masterclass.
95. Atkins, 'House Rules on the Blog', *BBC WHYS*, 9 Dec 2005 (this is the date of the post but the rules were written sometime afterwards), http://www.bbc.co.uk/blogs/worldhaveyoursay/2005/12/house_rules_on_the_blog.html, (4 Aug 2010).
96. Sandell, Editor, BBC *WHYS*, Interview, 13 Oct 2008.
97. J. Bridcut, 'From Seesaw to Wagon Wheel: Safeguarding impartiality in the 21st century', *BBC Trust Report*, 2007.
98. Sandell, Interview, 10 Dec 2008. With the exception of this experiment, the *WHYS* blog has been moderated by journalists working on the programme; it is not one of the BBC blogs that is moderated by Tempero, an external company. R. Akins, Email Correspondence, 15 Mar 2011.
99. Sandell, Editor, BBC *WHYS*, 13 Oct 2008.
100. Sandell, 'All good things. . .', *BBC WHYS*, 30 Oct 2008, http://worldhaveyoursay.wordpress.com/2008/10/30/all-good-things/, (29 July 2010).
101. Sandell, *New Media, New Ways*.
102. A. Briggs, *The History of Broadcasting in the United Kingdom, Vol I: The birth of broadcasting* (Oxford University Press, 1961), p. 333; Bridcut, 'From seesaw to wagon wheel', pp. 25–28.
103. J. Jarvis, 'The Objectivity Myth', *The Guardian*, 19 Feb 2008, http://www.guardian.co.uk/commentisfree/2008/feb/19/theobjectivitymyth, (4 Aug 2010).
104. Atkins, 'Would you like to know what I think?', *BBC WHYS*, 21 Mar 2008. http://worldhaveyoursay.wordpress.com/2008/03/21/would-you-like-to-know-what-i-think-about-iraq/, (13 Jan 2009).
105. Ibid.
106. Atkins, 'Who are we?', *BBC WHYS*, 15 April 2008, http://worldhaveyoursay.wordpress.com/2008/04/15/who-are-we/ (4 Aug 2010).
107. Atkins, BBC Global News Masterclass.
108. One of the idents used to introduce *WHYS* after the main news bulletin.
109. M. Fishman, *Manufacturing the News* (University of Texas Press, 1980), p. 44.
110. After Fishman, *Manufacturing the News*, p. 51.
111. After H. Gans, *Deciding What's News*, 2nd Ed. (Northwestern University Press, 2004), pp. 125–126.
112. P. Bradshaw, 'BASIC Principles of Online Journalism: C is for Community & Conversation (pt2: Conversation)', *Online Journalism Blog*, 15 Sep 2008, http://onlinejournalismblog.com/2008/09/15/basic-principles-of-online-journalism-c-is-for-community-conversation-pt1-community/, (8 Aug 2008).
113. See Robinson, 'Gateway or Gatekeeper'.
114. Sandell, Interview, 10 Dec 2008.
115. Atkins, BBC Global News Masterclass.
116. Beckett, *SuperMedia*, p. 52.

117. Sandell, Interview, 10 Dec 2008. Sandell indicated that he would use inverted commas around the word *ordinary*.
118. Tilley, Deputy Editor *WHYS*, 13 Oct 2008.
119. Sandell, Interview, 10 Dec 2008.
120. Shirky argues that communities operate on a many-to-many model and the personal dialogue found there does not scale to audiences which necessarily function using a one-to-many model because of the number of people involved. See C. Shirky, 'Communities, Audiences and Scale', www.shirky.com, 6 Apr 2002, http://shirky.com/writings/herecomeseverybody/community_scale.html (10 Aug 2008).
121. McGough, Interview, 4 Dec 2008.
122. Sandell, Interview, 10 Dec 2008.
123. After Fishman, *Manufacturing the News*, p. 51.
124. Gans, *Deciding What's News*, pp. 125–6.
125. Horrocks quoted by Lee-Wright, 'Culture Shock', p. 86.
126. A.M. Jönsson and H. Örnebring, 'User-Generated Content and the News: Empowerment of citizens or interactive illusion?', *Journalism Practice*, 5(2), (2011), pp. 127–144.
127. Sandell, *New Media, New Ways*.
128. BBC Journalist (a), Audience Interaction Session, BEEB Camp, 28 Nov 2008.
129. BBC Journalist (b), Audience Interaction Session, BEEB Camp, 28 Nov 2008.
130. T. van Aardt, BBC Communities Editor (2008–2009), Audience Interaction Session, BEEB Camp, 28 Nov 2008.
131. Barron, Email Correspondence, 15 Mar 2011.
132. Rippon, Email Correspondence, 18 Apr 2011.

NOTES TO CHAPTER 7

1. BBC, 'Mumbai ttacks: One year on', 25 Nov 2009, http://news.bbc.co.uk/1/hi/world/south_asia/8379828.stm, (7 Jan 2010).
2. A. Rabasa et al., 'The Lessons of Mumbai', *RAND Corporation*, Jan 2009, p. 6.
3. Ibid., p. 1.
4. S. Herrmann, 'Updates: Mumbai, planning, global news. . .', *BBC News Online Intranet*, 1 Dec 2008.
5. On 27 Nov, 1.476 million, and 28 Nov, 1.168 million.
6. BBC, 'BBC website wins major award', 4 Oct 2009, http://news.bbc.co.uk/1/hi/entertainment/8289207.stm, (7 Dec 2009).
7. T. Sutcliffe, 'Twittering on is not the way to provide news', *The Independent,* 2 Dec 2008, http://www.independent.co.uk/opinion/columnists/thomas-sutcliffe/tom-sutcliffe-twittering-on-is-not-the-way-to-provide-news-1047115.html, (8 Dec 2009).
8. Herrmann, 'Mumbai, Twitter and live updates', *The Editors,* 4 Dec 2008, http://www.bbc.co.uk/blogs/theeditors/2008/12/theres_been_discussion_see_eg.html (8 Dec 2009).
9. S. Tankel, 'India's 9/11: How it could happen again', *Foreign Policy*, 24 Nov 2009, http://www.foreignpolicy.com/articles/2009/11/24/indias_911?page=0,0, (10 Dec 2009).
10. Ibid.
11. Indian Government Dossier, 'Mumbai Terrorist Attacks, Nov 26–29, 2008', January 2009. Available at *The Hindu*, http://www.hindu.com/nic/dossier.htm, (10 Dec 2009).

12. Rabasa et al., 'The Lessons of Mumbai'.
13. Indian Government Dossier, 'Mumbai Terrorist Attacks'.
14. BBC, 'Mumbai Attacks: One year on'.
15. BBC, 'Officials quit over India attacks', 30 Nov 2008, http://news.bbc. co.uk/1/hi/world/south_asia/7757122.stm, (7 Jan 2010).
16. Rabasa et al., 'The Lessons of Mumbai'.
17. D. Pepper, 'India's media blasted for sensational Mumbai coverage', *Christian Science Monitor*, 24 Dec 2008, http://www.csmonitor.com/World/Asia-South-Central/2008/1224/p01s01-wosc.html, (11 Dec 2009).
18. Indian Government Dossier, 'Mumbai Terrorist Attacks', p. 52.
19. Ibid., p. 53.
20. R. Watson, 'Mumbai: what really happened', *The Daily Telegraph*, 28 June 2009, http://www.telegraph.co.uk/comment/5661920/Mumbai-What-really-happened.html, (10 Dec 2009).
21. S. Mehta cited by S. Dikshit, 'Navy chief upset with electronic media', 3 Dec 2008, *The Hindu Times*, http://www.hindu.com/2008/12/03/stories/2008120360861300.htm, (12 Jan 2010).
22. NDTV Correspondent, 'NDTV's official response on some questions raised after Mumbai attacks', *NDTV*, 6 Dec 2008, http://www.ndtv.com/convergence/ndtv/mumbaiterrorstrike/Story.aspx?ID=NEWEN20080075514&type=News, (12 Jan 2010).
23. BBC *World News*, 27 Nov 2008.
24. BBC, 'An eyewitness inside the hotel?', 27 Nov 2008, http://news.bbc. co.uk/1/hi/programmes/world_news_america/7751650.stm, (23 May 2011).
25. BBC, 'Witnesses tell of Mumbai violence', 27 Nov 2008, http://news.bbc. co.uk/1/hi/7751423.stm, (23 May 2011).
26. BBC, 'As it happened: Mumbai attacks', 27 Nov 2008, http://news.bbc. co.uk/1/hi/world/south_asia/7752003.stm, (17 Nov 2009).
27. BBC Journalist (a), 27 Nov 2008.
28. BBC Editor, Interview, 2009.
29. See Chapters 2 and 3.
30. GroundReport,http://www.groundreport.com/Media_and_Tech/GroundReport-Connects-Readers-and-News-Outlets-to-/2874909, (7 Jan 2010); Mahalo, http://www.mahalo.com/mumbai-terrorist-attacks, (7 Jan 2010).
31. Mumbai Metblogs, Nov 2008, http://mumbai.metblogs.com/category/terror-attacks/page/4/, (7 Jan 2010).
32. Mumbai Help, Nov 2008, http://mumbaihelp.blogspot.com/2008_11_01_archive.html, (7 Jan 2010).
33. M. Vij, 'Bombay under terrorist attack', http://mars.select-servers.com/~ultrab/posts/bombay-under-terrorist-attack, (7 Jan 2010).
34. AFP, 'Twitter, blogs provide riveting accounts of Mumbai attacks', 28 Nov 2008, http://www.google.com/hostednews/afp/article/ALeqM5gd5KpOLBPELdU7yODAe_rBn0qRJg, (7 Jan 2010).
35. A. Shanbhag, 'Mumbai Blasts: Taj Burning; More pics from terrorist killing', 26 Nov 2008, http://arunshanbhag.com/2008/11/26/mumbai-blasts-taj-is-burning/, (7 Jan 2010).
36. S. Busari, 'Tweeting the Terror: How social media reacted to Mumbai', *CNN*, http://edition.cnn.com/2008/WORLD/asiapcf/11/27/mumbai.twitter/, (7 Jan 2010).
37. G. Mishra, 'Social media & citizen journalism in the 11/26 Mumbai terror attacks: A case study', *Gauravonomics,* 28 Nov 2008, http://www.gauravonomics. com/blog/social-media-citizen-journalism-in-the-1126-mumbai-terror-attacks-a-case-study/, (7 Jan 2010).

38. Mishra, 'Real time citizen journalism in Mumbai terrorist attacks', *Gaura-vonomics*, 29 Nov 2008, http://www.gauravonomics.com/blog/real-time-citizen-journalism-in-mumbai-terrorist-attacks/, (7 Jan 2010).
39. Mishra, 'Social media & citizen journalism'.
40. CNN, 'Witness Accounts of Mumbai Attacks from sites around the Web', 26 Nov 2008, http://www.cnn.com/2008/WORLD/asiapcf/11/26/mumbai.attacks.web.sites/index.html?iref = newssearch, (7 Jan 2010).
41. For example, BBC, 'Waiting for War', 19 Mar 2003, http://news.bbc.co.uk/1/hi/in_depth/2864627.stm, (12 Jan 2010); D. Steven and M. Weston, 'Whose Agenda? The BBC's Reporters' Log on Iraq', 25 Sep 2003, http://ics.leeds.ac.uk/papers/pmt/exhibits/1759/Whose_agenda.pdf, (12 Jan 2010).
42. K. Anderson, 'Blogging the US Election I', *BBC*, http://news.bbc.co.uk/1/hi/world/americas/3726132.stm, (16 Dec 2009).
43. Pete Clifton, 'Pete's Weekly Update', *BBC News Online Intranet*, 5 May 2006; Hermida, *We Media blog*, http://www.bbc.co.uk/blogs/wemedia/, (16 Dec 2009).
44. Horrocks, 'The newsroom—latest news Sept 8th', *BBC News Online Intranet*, 8 Sep 2008. This automatically refreshing format was not used for the Mumbai live updates page initially because there were technical difficulties with making it work on a South Asia webpage template.
45. BBC Journalist, Interview, 13 Dec 2009.
46. Simon Fraser, BBC News Online South Asia Editor, Interview, 26 Jan 2010.
47. BBC Journalist, Interview, 13 Dec 2009.
48. Fraser, Interview, 26 Jan 2010.
49. BBC Journalist, Interview, 13 Dec 2009.
50. Shortly after Mumbai a collation of thoughts by BBC journalists who had contributed to a variety of live pages noted that their operation is 'hugely labour intensive'. Russell Smith (ed.), 'Livepage Guidelines, Full', BBC Internal Document, No Date.
51. 14h45 local time.
52. BBC Journalist, Interview, 13 Dec 2009.
53. Timings of updates on the BBC's web pages.
54. Orkut is a social networking site popular in India and Brazil.
55. BBC Journalist, Interview, 13 Dec 2009.
56. Smith (ed.), 'Livepage Guidelines, Full'.
57. BBC Journalist (a), 27 Nov 2008. He noted that there were also problems throughout the day caused by incorrect HTML/XML code. These took around 15 minutes to spot, and the page would not be refreshed during these periods.
58. BBC Journalist (a), 27 Nov 2008.
59. BBC Journalist, Interview, 13 Dec 2009.
60. BBC Journalist (a), 27 Nov 2008.
61. BBC Journalist, Interview, 13 Dec 2009.
62. BBC Journalist (a), 27 Nov 2008.
63. BBC Journalist, Interview, 4 Feb 2010.
64. Clay Shirky defines 'algorithmic authority' as: 'the decision to regard as authoritative an unmanaged process of extracting value from diverse, untrustworthy sources, without any human standing beside the result saying "Trust this because you trust me."' See Shirky, 'A Speculative Post on the Idea of Algorithmic Authority', *Clay Shirky*, 15 Nov 2009, http://www.shirky.com/weblog/2009/11/a-speculative-post-on-the-idea-of-algorithmic-authority/, (17 Nov 2009).
65. BBC Editor, 27 Nov 2008.

66. BBC Journalist (b), 27 Nov 2008.
67. BBC Journalist, Interview, 13 Dec 2009.
68. The author of the book helped him understand the basics.
69. Samanthi Dissanayake, Senior Broadcast Journalist, Interview, 26 Jan 2010. (At the time of the Mumbai attacks, she was the UGC hub's Asia Specialist working as a Broadcast Journalist).
70. Smith (ed.), 'Livepage Guidelines, Full'.
71. According to the BBC website these pages have not been altered since Saturday 29 November. It should be noted that the BBC did not classify their updates strictly in terms of which date they were written on—the '28 November' page runs from 01h55 on the 28 November until 02h30 on the 29 November. The BBC's classification was retained.
72. As S. Shyam Sundar notes a 'source' has been conceptualised in various ways in communication research. S. Shyam Sundar, 'Effect of Source Attribution on Perception of Online News Stories', *Journalism and Mass Communication Quarterly*, 75 (1), (1998), p. 56.
73. A. Phillips, 'Old Sources: New bottles' in N. Fenton (ed) *New Media Old News: Journalism & democracy in the digital age* (Sage, 2010), p. 89.
74. The resulting code book is Appendix A.
75. For example, it was decided that when the BBC used a quote from a government official given to a news agency, both the government and the news agency should be coded. Although the government official was only being mediated through a news agency, there was assumed to be extra work by the news agency in accessing the source and so the two sources should be coded separately.
76. BBC Journalist (a), 27 Nov 2008.
77. M. Weaver, 'Mumbai siege: Live', *The Guardian*, 27 Nov 2008, http://www.guardian.co.uk/world/2008/nov/27/mumbai-terror-attacks-india2, (17 Nov 2009).
78. Links added after the event which direct Web users between the different days of the live updates were excluded.
79. BBC Journalist, Interview, 13 Dec 2009.
80. H. Gans, *Deciding What's News*, 2nd Ed. (Northwestern University Press, 2004), p. 130.
81. One of the BBC journalists working on the updates said the BBC took care not to engage too heavily in speculation about the identity of the attackers.
82. Rosen, 'The people formerly known as the audience', *PressThink*, 27 June 2006, http://journalism.nyu.edu/pubzone/weblogs/pressthink/2006/06/27/ppl_frmr.html, (12 Jan 2010).
83. BBC Journalist, Interview, 13 Dec 2009.
84. Dissanayake, Interview, 26 Jan 2010.
85. L.V. Sigal, *Reporters and Officials: The organization and politics of newsmaking*, (D.C. Health & Co., 1973), p. 124.
86. These figures can be compared with Table 7.7. It is important to note that eyewitness accounts were included in other BBC website coverage including a dedicated BBC webpage which was linked to from the 'At a Glance' page.
87. S. Tankel, *Storming the World Stage: The story of Lashkar-e-Taiba*, (Columbia University Press, 2011). There were 10 attackers in total.
88. Sutcliffe, 'Twittering on'.
89. Cellan-Jones, 'Twitter—the Mumbai myths', *dot.life*, 1 Dec 2008, http://www.bbc.co.uk/blogs/technology/2008/12/twitter_the_mumbai_myths.html, (8 Dec 2009).
90. Cited in ibid.

91. Cellan-Jones, 'Twitter—the Mumbai myths'.
92. L. Shepherd, 'About Me and This', *I've Said Too Much*, No Date, http://www.lllj.net/blog/?page_id=283, (12 Jan 2010).
93. Shepherd, 'Remember This Day', *I've Said Too Much*, 27 Nov 2008, http://www.lllj.net/blog/?p=555, (8 Dec 2009). Media consultant Amy Gahran attempted to trace the origin of the tweet during 27 November. She was unable to obtain the source of the original tweet or discover with certainty whether the Indian authorities had ever specifically asked for Twitter users to stop using the service. See A. Gahran, Contentious.com, 27 Nov 2008, http://www.contentious.com/2008/11/27/tracking-a-rumor-indian-government-twitter-and-common-sens/, (6 Jan 2010).
94. BBC Journalist, Interview, 13 Dec 2009.
95. Neil et al, The Neil Report, p. 6. See Chapter 2.
96. Smith, 'Livepage Guidelines, Full'.
97. N. Newman, 'The Rise of Social Media and its Impact on Mainstream Journalism,' *Reuters Institute for the Study of Journalism*, 2009.
98. Herrmann, 'Mumbai, Twitter and live updates'.
99. Ibid.
100. One BBC journalist suggested that in subsequent discussions journalists agreed that it would be 'foolish to put anything news-wise from Twitter'.
101. Smith, 'Livepage Guidelines, Full'.
102. Horrocks quoted in ibid.
103. Smith, 'Livepage Guidelines, Full'.
104. N. Gowing, '"Skyful of Lies" and Black Swans: The new tyranny of shifting information power in crises,' *Reuters Institute for the Study of Journalism*, pp. 27, 29.
105. S. Rosenberg describes the work of Josh Marshall, a former journalist, who started the Talking Points Memo blog: 'His work resembled any journalist's except that, rather than waiting to assemble his finds into a polished final report, he posted them as he confirmed them . . . And the very speed and openness of this process meant that any readers with new information could see that if they took the time to send Marshall a note he'd make use of it.' Rosenberg, *Say Everything: How blogging began, what it's becoming and why it matters*, (Crown, 2009), p. 145.
106. T. Harcup, *Journalism: Principles and practice*, (Sage, 2005), pp. 108–112.
107. P. Schlesinger, 'Putting Reality Together: BBC News', in H. Tumber (ed), *News: A reader*, (Oxford University Press, 1999).
108. R. Smith, 'Front page session yesterday', *BBC News Online Intranet*, 1 July 2008.
109. Smith, 'Livepage Guidelines, Full'; Herrmann, 'Mumbai, Twitter and live updates'.
110. Horrocks, 'The Newsroom—latest news'.
111. BBC Journalist, Interview, 4 Feb 2010.
112. BBC Editorial Guidelines, http://downloads.bbc.co.uk/guidelines/editorialguidelines/Legacy_Guidelines/2005-editorial-guidelines-full.pdf, (2005), p. 16.
113. BBC Editorial Guidelines, Section 3: Accuracy, 3.1, http://www.bbc.co.uk/editorialguidelines/page/guidelines-accuracy-introduction, (2010).
114. BBC Journalist, Interview, 13 Dec 2009.
115. Ibid.
116. BBC Correspondent, Interview, 2009.
117. Gans, *Deciding What's News*, p. 130.
118. K. Andén-Papadopoulos and M. Pantti, 'Transparency and Trustworthiness: Strategies for incorporating amateur photography into news discourse'

in Andén-Papadopoulos and M. Pantti (eds), *Amateur Images and Global News*, (University of Chicago Press, 2011), pp. 97–112.

119. In particular, the burden of making sense of the event was shifted; the BBC asked the audience to do more work in interpreting accuracy and context.
120. Rosen, 'The people formerly known as the audience'.
121. Horrocks, 'The Newsroom—latest news', *BBC News Online Intranet*, 8 Dec 2008.
122. BBC, 'As it happened: Norway attacks', 22 July 2011, http://www.bbc. co.uk/news/world-europe-14254705, (22 July 2011); BBC 'As it happened: Norway attacks aftermath', 23 July 2011, http://www.bbc.co.uk/news/ world-europe-14260205, (23 July 2011).
123. Jarvis, 'In Mumbai'.
124. That is not to say that this increase in the percentage of nonofficial sources will inevitably continue. By 2011, Twitter was no longer simply an 'alternative source' providing journalists with access to 'audience comment'. The microblogging service had been adopted by a wide variety of media organisations and official sources and BBC journalists covering the crisis in Norway cited these Twitter accounts far more often than nonofficial sources. Journalists also included less 'audience comment' overall than they had done in 2008.
125. Newman, 'The Rise of Social Media', p. 10.

NOTES TO CHAPTER 8

1. R. Goldstone et al., 'Human Rights in Palestine and the Other Occupied Territories', UN Human Rights Council, 25 Sep 2009, pp. 90–92.
2. Ibid., p. 92.
3. Lt. Gen. W. Caldwell IV, D. Murphy, and A. Menning, 'Learning to Leverage New Media', *Australian Army Journal*, 6 (3), (2009), pp. 133–146.
4. M. Kalb and C. Saivetz, 'The Israeli–Hezbollah War of 2006: The media as a weapon in asymmetrical conflict', *The Harvard International Journal of Press/Politics*, 12 (3), (2007), pp. 43–66.
5. Maj. A. Leibovich in N. Hodge, 'Youtube, Twitter: Weapons in Israel's Info War', *Danger Room*, http://www.wired.com/dangerroom/2008/12/israels-info-wa/#ixzz0oOkUyEts, (19 May 2010).
6. J. York, 'Facebook war continues with group hacks', *Global Voices*, 5 Jan 2009, http://globalvoicesonline.org/2009/01/05/facebook-war-continues-with-group-hacks/, (18 Jan 2010).
7. S. Allan, *Online News*, (Open University Press, 2006), p. 109.
8. M. Wall, '"Blogs of War": Weblogs as news', *Journalism*, 6 (2).
9. Alongside the BBC blogs studied in this chapter, the blogs selected cover each category of Domingo and Heinonen's typology of journalistic weblogs: citizen, audience, journalist and media blogs. D. Domingo and A. Heinonen, 'Weblogs and Journalism: A typology to explore blurring boundaries', *Nordicom Review*, 29 (1), (2008), p. 7.
10. E. Zuckerman, 'Meet the Bridgebloggers', *Public Choice*, 134, (2008), pp. 47–65.
11. IDF Spokesperson, http://idfspokesperson.com.
12. The Muqata Blog, http://muqata.blogspot.com.
13. Yaacov Lozowick's Ruminations, http://yaacovlozowick.blogspot.com.
14. A Soldier's Mother, http://israelisoldiersmother.blogspot.com.
15. Gaza Mom, http://www.gazamom.com.

16. Tales to Tell, http://talestotell.wordpress.com.
17. ISM, 'About ISM', No date, http://palsolidarity.org/about, (20 May 2010).
18. In Gaza, http://ingaza.wordpress.com.
19. P. Bailey, 'Eva Bartlett follows in the footsteps of Rachel Corrie', *Palestine Telegraph*, 16 March 2010.
20. Gaza Today, http://gazatoday.blogspot.com/.
21. Ghazzawiyya, http://gaza08.blogspot.com/.
22. Informed Comment, http://www.juancole.com.
23. Radio and television programmes were accessed using the BBC's online archive available to their journalists. Programmes were not transcribed in their entirety, but the main features of each programme were noted including the use of pictures for TV. More detailed transcription was undertaken when relevant to the themes explored in the chapter.
24. J. Webb, BBC *Ten O'Clock News*, 5 Jan 2009.
25. Webb, *Justin Webb's America*, Jan 2009, http://www.bbc.co.uk/blogs/thereporters/justinwebb/2009/01/, (4 May 2010).
26. For example, J. Reynolds, 'China and Gaza', *James Reynolds' China*, http://www.bbc.co.uk/blogs/thereporters/jamesreynolds/2009/01/china_and_gaza.html, (13 Jan 2010).
27. J. Stephenson, 'Reporting from Gaza', *The Editors*, 6 Jan 2009, http://www.bbc.co.uk/blogs/theeditors/2009/01/reporting_from_gaza.html, (13 Jan 2010).
28. Lacey, 'Monday, 5 January, 2009', *BBC Newsnight*, 5 Jan 2009, http://www.bbc.co.uk/blogs/newsnight/fromthewebteam/2009/01/monday_5_january_2009.html, (13 Jan 2010).
29. N. Brown, 'Two Voices of Loss in Gaza', *5 Live Breakfast*, http://www.bbc.co.uk/blogs/fivelivebreakfast/2009/01/two_voices_of_loss_in_gaza.html, (13 Jan 2010).
30. Sandell, 'Help Needed', *BBC WHYS*, 6 Jan 2009, http://worldhaveyoursay.wordpress.com/2009/01/06/help-needed/, (18 May 2010).
31. Sandell, 'On air: does there come a point when Israel loses its right to defend itself?', *BBC WHYS*, 5 Jan 2009, http://worldhaveyoursay.wordpress.com/2009/01/05/gaza-on-the-ground/#more-3636, (18 May 2010).
32. J. Leskovec, L. Backstrom, and J. Kleinberg, 'Meme-tracking and the Dynamics of the News Cycle', *ACM SIGKDD International Conference on Knowledge Discovery and Data Mining*, 2009, http://cs.stanford.edu/people/jure/pubs/quotes-kdd09.pdf.
33. M. Messner and M. Distaso, 'The Source Cycle: How traditional media and weblogs use each other as sources', *Journalism*, 9 (3), pp. 447–463.
34. G. Philo and M. Berry, *Bad News from Israel*, (Pluto Press, 2004), p. 94–99. The researcher considered 'explanatory themes' underpinning reporting.
35. A period of relative peace began to unravel when Hamas significantly increased rocket firing from Gaza and Israeli forces conducted operations inside the territory.
36. IDF Spokesperson, 'IDF Vlog: Hamas terrorists hide in UN school', *IDF Spokesperson*, 6 Jan 2009, http://idfspokesperson.com/2009/01/06/idf-vlog-hamas-terrorists-hide-in-un-school/, (18 May 2010).
37. A Soldier's Mother, 'Messages to Elie', *A Soldier's Mother*, 5 Jan 2009, http://israelisoldiersmother.blogspot.com/2009/01/messages-to-elie.html, (18 Jan 2010).
38. Ghazzawiyya, 'In Solidarity', 6 Jan 2009, http://gaza08.blogspot.com/2009/01/in-solidarity-spreading-word-around.html, (18 Jan 2010).
39. Y. Lozowick, 'Cycle of Poor Reporting', *Yaacov Lozowick's Ruminations*, 7 Jan 2009, http://yaacovlozowick.blogspot.com/2009/01/other-day-jefferey-goldberg-was-in-blue.html, (18 Jan 2010).

40. BBC PM Programme, 5 Jan 2009; BBC *WHYS*, 9 Jan 2009.
41. BBC, 'Oil price rises on Gaza conflict', 5 Jan 2009, http://news.bbc.co.uk/1/hi/business/7811043.stm, (18 Jan 2010).
42. BBC *PM* Programme, 9 Jan 2009.
43. Goldstone et al., 'Human Rights in Palestine', p. 161.
44. News Agencies, 'UN calls for war crimes', *Haaretz*, 9 Jan 2009, http://www.haaretz.com/news/un-calls-for-war-crimes-probe-into-idf-shelling-of-civil-ian-occupied-building-in-gaza-1.267832, (27 May 2010).
45. S. Lock, 'Jan 4–5: Israel targets Jabalia medic's ambulance, then his funeral', *Tales to Tell*, 5 Jan 2009, http://talestotell.wordpress.com/2009/01/05/sun-4-jan-6pm-mon-5-jan-5pm/, (18 Jan 2010).
46. B'Tselem, '6 Jan. '09: B'Tselem: Evacuate wounded trapped in buildings shelled by Israeli army', 6 Jan 2009, http://www.btselem.org/English/Press_Releases/20090106.asp, (18 Jan 2010).
47. 'Pamela' in Lock, 'Bringing the dead on donkey carts', *Tales to Tell*, 9 Jan 2009, http://talestotell.wordpress.com/2009/01/09/january-789/#comment-166, (14 Apr 2010).
48. Wall, 'Blogs of War', p. 162.
49. L. El-Haddad, 'This is Gaza', *Gaza Mom*, 9 Jan 2009, http://www.gazamom.com/2009/01/this-is-gaza/, (18 Jan 2010). She did also highlight some news items.
50. Lock, 'Jan 6 evening to Jan 7 morning: Be Strong!', *Tales to Tell*, 8 Jan 2009, http://talestotell.wordpress.com/2009/01/08/jan-6-evening-to-jan-7-morning-be-strong/, (18 Jan 2010).
51. Jeremy Bowen, BBC Middle East Editor, Interview, 2 June 2009.
52. Bowen, '5 January: Israel-Gaza border', 5 Jan 2009, *BBC*, http://news.bbc.co.uk/2/hi/middle_east/7811721.stm, (15 May 2009).
53. Bowen, '6 January: Jerusalem', 6 Jan 2009, *BBC*, http://news.bbc.co.uk/2/hi/middle_east/7811721.stm, (15 May 2009).
54. Wall, 'Blogs of War', p. 161.
55. Lustig, 'Gaza points of view', *Robin Lustig: 'Trying to make sense of the world'*, 9 Jan 2009, http://www.bbc.co.uk/blogs/worldtonight/2009/01/gaza_points_of_view.html, (13 Jan 2010).
56. Ibid.
57. Lustig, 'Gaza points of view'.
58. R. Sambrook, BBC Director of Global News (2004–2010), Interview, 11 July 2008.
59. D. Weinberger, 'Transparency is the New Objectivity', *Joho: The Blog*, 17 July 2009, http://www.hyperorg.com/blogger/2009/07/19/transparency-is-the-new-objectivity/, (20 Apr 2011).
60. Lozowick, 'Bloggers vs. Hacks', *Yaacov Lozowick's Ruminations*, 8 Jan 2009, http://yaacovlozowick.blogspot.com/2009/01/bloggers-vs-hacks.html, (18 Jan 2010).
61. International Solidarity Movement, 'About ISM' (n.d.) http://palsolidarity.org/about (20 May 2010).
62. J. Settler, 'Day 10 of the War', *The Muqata blog*, 5 Jan 2009, http://muqata.blogspot.com/2009/01/day-10-of-war-monday-january-5-2009.html, (30 Apr 2010).
63. Settler, 'Day 12 of the War', *The Muqata blog*, 7 Jan 2009, http://muqata.blogspot.com/2009/01/day-12-of-war-wednesday-january-7-2009.html, (30 Apr 2010).
64. D. Matheson and D. Allan, *Digital War Reporting*, (Polity Press, 2009), p. 95.
65. N. Abou Shakra, 'They wait for people to gather at the bomb site', *Ghazza-wiyya*, http://gaza08.blogspot.com/2009/01/natalie-abou-shakra-they-wait-for.html, 5 Jan 2009, (18 Jan 2010).

66. Ibid.
67. 'Dragonfly52', in L. El Haddad, 'Israel's psychological warfare', *Gaza Mom*, 4 Jan 2009, http://www.gazamom.com/2009/01/israels-psychological-warfare/#comment-5091, (13 May 2010).
68. BBC Editorial Guidelines, http://www.bbc.co.uk/guidelines/editorialguidelines/edguide/war/mandatoryreferr.shtml, (13 May 2010).
69. Q. Thomas et al., Report of the Independent Panel for the BBC Governors on Impartiality of BBC Coverage of the Israeli-Palestinian Conflict, April 2006, p. 7.
70. M. Hessler in BBC, 'Israeli voices: When to Stop', 9 Jan 2009, http://news.bbc.co.uk/1/hi/world/middle_east/7820241.stm, (19 May 2010).
71. Matheson and Allan, *Digital War Reporting*, p. 146.
72. Sky News, 'The Innocent Child Victims of the Gaza War', 8 Jan 2009, http://news.sky.com/skynews/Home/The-Innocent-Child-Victims-of-The-Gaza-War/Media-Gallery/200901215199483?lpos=Home_News_in_Picture_Home_Region_0&lid=GALLERY_15199483_The_Innocent_Child_Victims_of_The_Gaza_War, (21 Apr 2010).
73. Ghazzawiyya, 'Israel's target for today: Families', 5 Jan 2009, http://gaza08.blogspot.com/2009/01/israels-target-for-today-families.html, (18 May 2010).
74. A Soldier's Mother, 'The images they show', *A Soldier's Mother*, 7 Jan 2009, http://israelisoldiersmother.blogspot.com/2009/01/images-they-show.html, (18 Jan 2010).
75. Settler, 'Day 11 of the War', *The Muqata blog*, 6 Jan 2009, http://muqata.blogspot.com/2009/01/day-11-of-war-tuesday-january-6–2009.html, (30 Apr 2010).
76. Settler, 'Day 12 of the war', *The Muqata blog*, 7 Jan 2009, http://muqata.blogspot.com/2009/01/day-12-of-war-wednesday-january-7-2009.html (30 Apr 2010).
77. Jeremy Bowen said APTN and Reuters provided most of the footage.
78. For example, BBC *Newsnight*, 5 Jan 2009.
79. BBC *Ten O'Clock News*, 6 Jan 2009.
80. M. Prodger, BBC *Newsnight*, 9 Jan 2009.
81. 'Andy Davies' in E. Bartlett, 'I'll tell you how he died', *In Gaza*, 5 Jan 2009, http://ingaza.wordpress.com/2009/01/05/i%E2%80%99ll-tell-you-how-he-died/#more-1042, (19 Jan 2010).
82. Bowen, 'Bowen diary: Powerless amid pain', *BBC*, 9 Jan 2009, http://news.bbc.co.uk/1/hi/world/middle_east/7811721.stm, (19 Jan 2010).
83. BBC Editorial Guidelines, Section 7: Privacy, Reporting Death Suffering and Distress, 7.4.38, http://www.bbc.co.uk/guidelines/editorialguidelines/page/guidelines-privacy-death-suffering-distress/.
84. Project for Excellence in Journalism, 'New Media, Old Media', 23 May 2010, http://www.journalism.org/node/20621, (26 May 2010).
85. E. Bartlett, 'I'll tell you how he died', *In Gaza*, 5 Jan 2009, http://ingaza.wordpress.com/2009/01/05/i%E2%80%99ll-tell-you-how-he-died/, (18 Jan 2010).
86. S. Habeeb in Z. Hankir, 'Interview with Sameh A Habeeb', *The Indypendent*, 5 Jan 2009, http://www.indypendent.org/2009/01/05/habeeb-interview/, (6 May 2010).
87. El-Haddad, 'Where do you hide?', *Gaza Mom*, 8 Jan 2009 http://www.gazamom.com/2009/01/where-do-you-hide-the-terror-in-gaza-continues/, (18 Jan 2010).
88. Lozowick, 'Tenth of Tevet', *Yaacov Lozowick's Ruminations*, 6 Jan 2009 http://yaacovlozowick.blogspot.com/2009/01/tenth-of-tevet-on-determination-and.html, (23 Apr 2010).
89. The blogger informed readers that 'Elie' was not his real name.

90. A Soldier's Mother, 'And today he sounded . . .', 8 Jan 2009, http://israelisoldiersmother.blogspot.com/2009/01/and-today-he-sounded.html, (23 Apr 2010).
91. BBC, 'Points of view on Gaza', 7 Jan 2009, http://news.bbc.co.uk/1/hi/world/middle_east/7815840.stm, (18 Jan 2010).
92. Lock quoted in BBC, 'Israeli forces split Gaza in two', 5 Jan 2009, http://news.bbc.co.uk/1/hi/world/middle_east/7810804.stm, (18 Jan 2010).
93. Lock mentions on her blog that the BBC was calling her hourly during the night of 4–5 January.
94. BBC, 'Israeli blogs back Gaza operation', 6 Jan 2009, http://news.bbc.co.uk/1/hi/world/middle_east/7814303.stm, (23 April 2010).
95. Israblog, http://Israblog.nana10.co.il.
96. The Marker Café, http://cafe.themarker.com.
97. Shiloh Musings, http://shilohmusings.blogspot.com.
98. Jews sans frontieres, http://jewssansfrontieres.blogspot.com.
99. Zionist Conspiracy, http://www.zioncon.blogspot.com.
100. Exceptionally Professor Avi Shlaim, an Israeli academic, was critical of the offensive during his appearance on *WHYS*. He had written a piece in *The Guardian* in which he described Israel's logic as 'an eye for an eyelash': A. Shlaim, 'How Israel brought Gaza to the brink of humanitarian catastrophe', The Guardian, http://www.guardian.co.uk/world/2009/jan/07/gaza-israel-palestine, 7 Jan 2009, (30 Apr 2010).
101. BBC, 'Israeli voices: When to stop', 9 Jan 2009, http://news.bbc.co.uk/1/hi/world/middle_east/7820241.stm, (18 Jan 2010).
102. L. Goldman, 'If bloggers were representative of the mainstream. . .', *The Guardian*, 3 Feb 2009, http://www.guardian.co.uk/world/blog/2009/feb/03/israel-election-bloggers, (14 Nov 2009).
103. WHYS, 9 Jan 2009. Author of the Pickled Politics blog: http://www.pickledpolitics.com/.
104. M. Eltringham, BBC Head of Interactivity, Email Correspondence, 8 Jan 2009.
105. BBC Editorial Guidelines, Section 7: Privacy, Reporting Death Suffering and Distress, 7.4.38.
106. Matheson and Allan, *Digital War Reporting*, p. 146.
107. These photos might have been accessed from propaganda sites that purport to show imagery of jihadi summer camps. See J. Brachaman and J.J.F. Forest 'Exploring the Role of Virtual Camps', in M. Innes (ed) *Denial of Sanctuary: understanding terrorist safe havens*, (Greenwood Publishing Group, 2007), p. 124. G. Weimann argued that since the Al Aqsa Intifada in 2001 terrorist organisations increased their recruitment of Palestinian children to carry out suicide attacks against Israel. 'Using the Internet for Terrorist Recruitment and Mobilisation' in B. Ganor et al. (eds), *Hypermedia Seduction for Terrorist Recruiting*, (IOS Press, 2007), p. 49.
108. A. Hoskins and B. O'Loughlin, *War and Media: The emergence of diffused war*, (Polity Press, 2010), p. 31.
109. The BBC received hundreds of complaints. A still image was also shown on the BBC website suggesting that there might have been a shift in practices around the publication of graphic images on the website between 2009 and 2011. See Hockaday, 'The Challenges of Reporting Gaddafi's Death', *The Editors*, 21 Oct 2011, http://www.bbc.co.uk/blogs/theeditors/2011/10/the_challenges_of_reporting_ga.html, (2 Nov 2012).
110. J. Sturcke, 'BBC Report on Middle East conflict coverage', *The Guardian*, 11 Feb 2009. http://www.guardian.co.uk/media/2009/feb/11/bbc-middle-east-report-balen, (11 Feb 2009).
111. Thomas et al., Report of the Independent Panel, p. 4.

112. In a BBC blog post, Director-General Mark Thompson explained that in the context of an ongoing story, the BBC could not broadcast an appeal, however 'carefully constructed', without running the risk of damaging the confidence of the public in the BBC's ability to report the story impartially. M. Thompson, 'BBC and the Gaza appeal', *The Editors*, 24 Jan 2009, http://www.bbc.co.uk/blogs/theeditors/2009/01/bbc_and_the_gaza_appeal.html, (24 May 2011).
113. Bowen, Interview, 2 June 2009. Although 'time' was cited as the main factor.
114. M. Weaver, 'Gaza Invasion: Latest News', *The Guardian*, 7 Jan 2009, http://www.guardian.co.uk/news/blog/2009/jan/07/gaza-middleeast, (22 Mar 2011).
115. A conclusion also reached by W. Ward 'Uneasy Bedfellows', p. 12: 'traditional media formats tend to be mimicking blogs in style but not content'.
116. 'Nostos' in L. El-Haddad, 'What do you tell your daughter?', *Gaza Mom*, 6 Jan 2009, http://www.gazamom.com/2009/01/what-do-you-tell-your-daughter/, (18 Jan 2010).
117. 'James Wiegert' in S. Lock, 'Still here . . .', *Tales to Tell*, 8 Jan 2009, http://talestotell.wordpress.com/2009/01/09/still-here/, (18 Jan 2010). Matheson and Allan describe this phenomenon as the 'lure' of 'citizen journalism' in *Digital War Reporting*, p. 147.
118. C. Neuberger and C. Nuernbergk, 'Competition, Complementarity or Integration?', *Journalism Practice*, 4 (3), (2010), pp. 319–332.
119. A conclusion confirmed by a BBC Trust Report into the BBC's coverage of the Arab Spring which found that only a 'small minority' of BBC reports included User Generated Content. See E. Mortimer, 'A BBC Trust report on impartiality and accuracy of BBC's coverage of events as the "Arab Spring",' *BBC Trust*, June 2012, p. 4.
120. M. Castells, *Communication Power* (Oxford University Press, 2009), p. 419.

NOTES TO THE CONCLUSION

1. J. Rosen, 'A Most Useful Definition of Citizen Journalism', *PressThink*, 14 July 2008, http://archive.pressthink.org/2008/07/14/a_most_useful_d.html (17 July 2008).
2. See also Hermida's work: 'The BBC goes blogging: Is "Auntie" finally listening?', http://online.journalism.utexas.edu/2008/papers/Hermida.pdf, (1 Aug 2008), and 'The blogging BBC: Journalism blogs at 'the world's most trusted news organisation', *Journalism Practice*, 3 (3), (2009), pp. 1–17.
3. D. Matheson 'Weblogs and the Epistemology of the News: Some trends in online journalism,' *New Media & Society*, 6 (4), p. 448.
4. C. Beckett, 'Blogs are dead, long live blogging', *Polis Director's Blog*, 31 Mar 2011, http://www.charliebeckett.org/?p=4241 (31 Mar 2011).
5. M. Tremayne, *Blogging Citizenship and the Future of Media*, (Routledge, 2007), p. xvi.
6. This book highlights that at the BBC these two stages occurred concurrently with each stage informing the other. While they have usually been discussed separately during the book for the sake of clarity, they should not be treated as discrete developments.
7. M. Deuze, 'What Is Journalism?: Professional identity and ideology of journalists reconsidered', *Journalism*, 6 (4), (2005), p. 457.
8. Bradshaw, 'A model for the 21st Century Newsroom', *Online Journalism Blog*, http://onlinejournalismblog.com/2007/10/02/a-model-for-the-21st-century-newsroom-pt2-distributed-journalism/, (2 Oct 2007).

9. C. Beckett, *SuperMedia: Saving journalism so it can save the world*, (Blackwell, 2008), p. 58.
10. J. Jarvis, 'Networked journalism', *BuzzMachine*, 5 July 2006, http://buzzmachine.com/2006/07/05/networked-journalism/ (22 Feb 2008); Beckett, *SuperMedia*, p. 46.
11. Rusbridger, Editor of *The Guardian*, 'First Read: the mutualised future is bright', *Colombia Journalism Review*, 19 Oct 2009, http://www.cjr.org/reconstruction/the_mutualized_future_is_brigh.php, (21 Oct 2009).
12. Y. Benkler, *Wealth of Networks: How social production transforms markets and freedom*, (Yale University Press, 2006), p. 217.
13. H. Tumber, 'Journalism and the War in Iraq' in S. Allan (ed.), *Critical Issues in Journalism*, (Open University Press, 2005), p. 374.
14. P. Horrocks, 'The End of Fortress Journalism' in C. Miller (ed), *The Future of Journalism*, (BBC College of Journalism, 2009).
15. BBC World Service Journalists, Focus Group, 23 May 2008.
16. BBC News Online Journalist (a), Interview, 2009.
17. The approach was encapsulated in J. Bridcut, 'From Seesaw to Wagon Wheel: Safeguarding impartiality in the 21st century,' *BBC Trust Report*, 2007.
18. Ryan's view was borne out of the experience of wartime in which the BBC's broadcasts were restricted by the Ministry of Information. See Briggs, *The History of Broadcasting in the United Kingdom, Vol III: The war of words*, (Oxford University Press, 1961), p. 545,
19. H. Gans, *Deciding What's News*, 2nd Ed. (Northwestern University Press, 2004), pp. 304–334.
20. BBC Trust, Annual Report and Accounts, 2005/6, p. 48.
21. Gans, *Deciding What's News*, pp. 313.
22. W. Lowrey, 'Mapping the Journalism-Blogging Relationship', *Journalism*, 7 (4), p. 493.
23. M. Castells, *The Information Age: Economy Society and Culture, Vol. I: The Rise of the network society*, 2nd Ed. (Blackwell, 2000).
24. M. Castells, *Communication Power*, (Oxford University Press, 2009), p. 34.
25. Ibid., pp. 33–36.
26. A. Sparrow, 'Liveblogging the General Election', *The Guardian*, 10 May 2010, http://www.guardian.co.uk/media/2010/may/10/live-blogging-general-election, (10 May 2010).
27. R. Smith (ed.), 'Livepage Guidelines, Full', BBC Internal Document, No Date.
28. R. Neil et al., The Neil Report: The BBC's journalism after Hutton, June 2004, p. 4.
29. Eltringham, 'The line of verification': a new approach to objectivity for social media, BBC College of Journalism blog, 21 Jan 2011, http://www.bbc.co.uk/journalism/blog/2011/01/the-line-of-validation-new-app.shtml, (2 Apr 2011).
30. Ibid. Charlie Beckett was responsible for the idea of a 'light' and 'dark side'.
31. Reinforcing the findings of C. Wardle and A. Williams et al., 'UGC@theBBC: Understanding its impact upon contributors, non-contributors and BBC News', 2008, p. 45, http://www.bbc.co.uk/blogs/knowledgeexchange/cardiffone.pdf, (3 Nov 2009).
32. Vallance, Interview, 28 Jan 2008. His view had not changed in 2011: Vallance, Interview, 8 Mar 2011.
33. S. Costeloe in J. Stray, 'Drawing out the audience: Inside the BBC's user-generated content hub', *Nieman Journalism Lab*, 5 May 2010, http://www.niemanlab.org/2010/05/drawing-out-the-audience-inside-bbc%E2%80%99s-user-generated-content-hub/ (4 May 2011).
34. Castells, *Communication Power*, p. 65.
35. Ibid., p. 4.

36. E. Mortimer, 'A BBC Trust report on the impartiality and accuracy of the BBC's coverage of the events known as the "Arab Spring"', *BBC Trust*, June 2012, p. 70.
37. J. Hartley, 'Communicative Democracy in a Redactional Society: The future of journalism studies', *Journalism,* 1 (1), (2000), pp. 43–44.
38. Costeloe in Stray, 'Drawing out the Audience'.
39. Gans, *Deciding What's News*, p. 334.
40. Although BBC journalists have used forums to source stories.
41. Gardner, Interview, 3 Dec 2008.
42. Wardle, 'Social Media & Journalism: A research critique', *Exploring the impact of digital media on journalism and society*, 23 May 2010, http://clairewardle.com/2010/05/23/social-media-journalism-a-research-critique/, (23 May 2010).
43. Wardle, Interview, 5 Jan 2010.
44. H. Rheingold, *The Virtual Community: Homesteading on the electronic frontier*, (Addison-Wesley, 1993), p. 3.
45. A. Hermida, 'From TV to Twitter: How ambient news became ambient journalism', *Media and Culture Journal*, 13 (2).
46. Gans, *Deciding What's News*, p. 125.
47. Ibid., p. 128.
48. Samanthi Dissanayake, Senior Broadcast Journalist, Interview, 26 Jan 2010.
49. Stuart Hughes, World Affairs Producer, Interview, 25 Aug 2010.
50. Stuart Hughes, BBC World Affairs Producer, Email Correspondence, 29 Jan 2011.
51. B. Wellman, 'Little Boxes, Glocalisation and Networked Individualism', *Revised Papers from the Second Kyoto Workshop on Digital Cities II, Computational and Sociological Approaches*, 2001.
52. M. Fishman, *Manufacturing the News*, (University of Texas Press, 1980), p. 51.
53. Ibid., p. 52.
54. Castells, *The Rise of the Network Society.*
55. A. Phillips, 'Old Sources: New bottles' in *New Media, Old News: Journalism & democracy in the digital age*, (Sage 2010), pp. 87–101.
56. N. Gowing, '"Skyful of Lies" and Black Swans: The new tyranny of shifting information power in crises', *Reuters Institute for the Study of Journalism*, 2009, p. 11.
57. P. Schlesinger and H. Tumber, *Reporting Crime: The media politics of criminal justice*, (Oxford University Press, 1994), p. 271.
58. S. Hall et al., *Policing the Crisis: Mugging, the state, and law and order* (Macmillan, 1978), pp. 57–59.
59. E. Morozov, *The Net Delusion: How not to liberate the world*, (Allen Lane, 2011).
60. W.L. Bennett, 'Toward a Theory of Press/State Relations in the United States', *Journal of Communication*, 40 (2), (1990), p. 108.
61. Gans, *Deciding What's News,* pp. 304–334; Pavlik, *Journalism and New Media*, p. 93.
62. *From Our Own Correspondent* on Radio 4 already offered a similar outlet.
63. Richard Sambrook, BBC Director of Global News (2004–2010), Interview, 11 July 2008.
64. Herrmann and Wyatt, 'Reporting Afghanistan casualties', *The Editors*, 26 Jan 2010, http://www.bbc.co.uk/blogs/theeditors/2010/01/reporting_afghanistan_casualti.html, (26 Jan 2010).
65. Burnett, 'A 'So-Called' War on Terror, *The Editors*, 2 Oct 2006, http://www.bbc.co.uk/blogs/theeditors/2006/10/why_the_socalled_war_on_terror.html, (9 Nov 2010).

66. Castells, *Communication Power*, p. 70.
67. Kevin Marsh, Executive Editor of BBC College of Journalism (2006–2011), News Rewired Conference, 14 Jan 2010.
68. M. Thompson in J. Townend, 'BBC director-general on social media use: "You can't take BBC cloak off at will"', *Journalism.co.uk*, 21 May 2009, http://www.journalism.co.uk/news-events-awards/bbc-director-general-on-social-media-use—you-can-t-take-bbc-cloak-off-at-will-/s14/a534512/ (11 Nov 2010).
69. Ibid.
70. Giles Wilson, Editor BBC News blogs, Interview, 3 Nov 2010.
71. Ibid. Wilson said this approach is used only with correspondents 'who have been properly trained and are familiar with the risks'.
72. C. Hamilton, 'Houla massacre picture mistake', *The Editors*, 29 May 2012, http://www.bbc.co.uk/blogs/theeditors/2012/05/houla_massacre_picture_mistake.html, (29 May 2012).
73. G. Tuchman, *Making News: A study in the construction of reality* (Free Press, 1978), pp. 82–83.
74. Tuchman, 'Objectivity as Strategic Ritual: An Examination of Newsmen's Notions of Objectivty', *American Journal of Sociology*, 77 (4), (1972), pp. 660–679; K. Andén-Papadopoulos and M. Pantti, 'Transparency and Trustworthiness: Strategies for incorporating amateur photography ito news discourse' in K. Andén-Papadopoulos and M. Pantti (eds), *Amatuer Images and Global News*, (University of Chicago Press, 2011), pp. 97–112.
75. Bradshaw, 'Culture Clash: Journalism's ideology vs blog culture', *Online Journalism Blog*, 7 Mar 2011, http://onlinejournalismblog.com/2011/03/07/culture-clash-journalisms-ideology-vs-blog-culture/, (7 Mar 2011). For journalists' professional identification with 'objectivity' see Deuze, 'What Is Journalism?', p. 448.
76. Wilson, Interview, 3 Nov 2010.
77. Thompson in Townend, 'BBC "does not want to be the last PSB standing", says BBC director-general', Journalism.co.uk, 21 May 2009, http://www.journalism.co.uk/news/bbc-does-not-want-to-be-the-last-psb-standing—says-bbc-director-general-/s2/a534508/, (23 May 2009).
78. Kevin Anderson, *BBC Blogs: News as conversation*, 2005.
79. Ibid; Horrocks, 'End of Fortress Journalism'.
80. Vallance, Interview, 8 Mar 2011.
81. Aaron Scullion, Senior product Manager, Future Media and Technology, Interview, 12 Feb 2009.
82. C. Shirky, 'Communities, audiences and scale', www.shirky.com, 6 Apr 2002, http://shirky.com/writings/herecomeseverybody/community_scale.html (10 Aug 2008).
83. Aaron Scullion, Executive Product Manager, Future Media and Technology, Interview, 26 Oct 2010.
84. Benkler, *Wealth of Networks*, p. 217.
85. Gubbay, 'Comments and making our coverage more social', *The Editors*, 18 Mar 2011, http://www.bbc.co.uk/blogs/theeditors/2011/03/comments_and_making_our_covera.html, (21 Apr 2011).
86. A. Tinworth, 'The BBC's revamped blogs are a road crash', *One Man and His Blog*, 14 May 2011, http://www.onemanandhisblog.com/archives/2011/05/the_bbcs_revamped_blogs_are_a_road_crash.html, (14 May 2011). The cost of moderating the comments was a significant factor in the BBC's decision.
87. Lévy, *Collective Intelligence*, p. xxvii-xxviii. As I understand it 'collective intelligence' does not necessarily mean that all of the individual contributions are 'intelligent'.
88. Wilson, Interview, 3 Nov 2010.

89. J. Pavlik, *Journalism and New Media*, (Columbia University Press, 2001), p. 136.
90. Benkler, 'A Free Irresponsible Press', *Harvard Civil Rights-Civil Liberties Law Review*, 2011, p. 66, http://benkler.org/Benkler%20Wikileaks%20CRCL%20Working%20Paper%20Feb_8.pdf, (31 Mar 2011); A. Bruns, 'News Blogs and Citizen Journalism: New directions for e-journalism' in K. Prasad (ed), *e-Journalism: New media and news media*, (BR Publishing, 2009); H. Jenkins, 'Cultural Logic of Media Convergence', *International Journal of Cultural Studies*, 7 (1), p. 36.
91. "UGC" here included among other categories 'mobile phone footage', Facebook and Twitter updates, blogs, other websites, YouTube and email. Surprisingly the study did not include an analysis of the BBC's live pages where this material is more likely to be included. Mortimer, *BBC Trust*, Appendix A, Content Analysis, pp. 55–56.
92. Jenkins, 'Cultural Logic', p. 35.
93. J. Rosen, 'The people formerly known as the audience', *PressThink*, 27 June 2006, http://journalism.nyu.edu/pubzone/weblogs/pressthink/2006/06/27/ppl_frmr.html (12 Jan 2010)..
94. Y. Benkler, 'A Free Irresponsible Press', *Harvard Civil Rights-Civil Liberties Law Review*, p. 68, http://benkler.org/Benkler%20Wikileaks%20CRCL%20Working%20Paper%20Feb_8.pdf, (31 Mar 2011).
95. The BBC also stopped using Movable Type for news blogs.
96. Leading correspondents have been referred to as such by BBC editors and managers.

NOTES TO THE APPENDIX B

1. N. Denzin and Y. Lincoln, *The Sage Handbook of Qualitative Research*, 3rd Ed. (Sage, 2005), p. 4.
2. In the wake of postmodernism, there is 'greater awareness and acknowledgement of the role of the researcher as part and parcel of the construction of knowledge'. A. Bryman, *Social Research Methods*, 3rd Ed. (Oxford University Press, 2008), p. 682.
3. U. Flick, *An Introduction to Qualitative Research*, 2nd Ed. (Sage, 2002), p. 227.
4. Ibid., p. 229.
5. Bryman, *Social Research Methods*, p. 606.
6. B. Berelson, *Content Analysis in Communication Research*, (Free Press, 1952), p. 18.
7. Bryman, *Social Research Methods*, p. 275.
8. Chapter 7 discusses the methodology of the content analysis in some detail including an exploration of initial coding problems and how these were resolved.
9. See K. Krippendorf, *Content Analysis: An introduction to its methodology*, (Sage, 1980), p. 132.
10. My use of interviews is discussed in more detail in the following discussion.
11. Denzin, *The Research Act*, (Prentice Hall, 1989), pp. 157–158.
12. D. Jorgenson, *Participant Observation: A methodology for human sciences*, (Sage, 1989), p. 23.
13. J. Cheek discusses the methodological implications of funded research in 'The Practice and Politics of Funded Qualitative Research' in N. Denzin & Y. Lincoln, *The Sage Handbook of Qualitative Research*, 3rd Ed. (Sage, 2005).
14. See. J.P. Spradley, *Participant Observation*, (Rinehart & Winston, 1980), p. 34.
15. R.L. Gold, 'Roles in Sociological Field Observations', *Social Forces*, 36, (1958), pp. 217–223.

16. For example, I provided a report for Radio Five Live from a military blogging conference and helped *World Have Your Say* produce a radio show.
17. Jorgenson, *Participant Observation*, p. 55.
18. B.H. Junker, *Field Work: An introduction to the social sciences*, (University of Chicago, 1960).
19. Jorgenson, *Participant Observation*, p. 56.
20. Flick, *An Introduction to Qualitative Research*, 4th Ed. (Sage, 2009), p. 229.
21. Gans, 'The Participant-Observer as a Human Being: Observations on the personal aspects of field work', in A. Bryman and R.G. Burgess (eds), *Qualitative Research*, Vol. II, (Sage, 1999), p. 42.
22. Ibid. p. 51; I was similarly open about the advice I offered to a BBC journalist using Twitter during the attacks on Mumbai in Chapter 7, which is documented in a footnote.
23. J.W. Rettberg, *Blogging*, (Polity Press, 2008), p. 1.
24. Historian and blogger Juan Cole argues that the ability to comment on blogs facilitates the 'open-source implementation of the goals of the traditional peer-reviewed journal'. J. Cole, 'Blogging Current Affairs', *The Journal of Contemporary History*, 46 (3), (2011), p. 669.
25. Bryman, *Social Research Methods*, p. 468.
26. Ibid. p. 438.
27. M. David and C.D. Sutton, *Social Research: The basics*, (Sage, 2004), p. 92.
28. Johnson and Kaye, 'Believing the blogs of war? How blog users compare on credibility and characteristics in 2003 and 2007', *Media, War & Conflict*, 3 (3), (2010), p. 328.
29. Altheide, *Qualitative Media Analysis*, (Sage, 1996), pp. 33–35.
30. Ibid., p. 34.
31. Ibid., p. 33.
32. M. Wall, '"Blogs of War": Weblogs as news', *Journalism*, 6 (2), (2005), p. 161.
33. J. Mason and J. Finch, 'Decision Taking in the Fieldwork Process: Theoretical sampling and collaborative working' in A. Bryman and R.G. Burgess, (eds), *Qualitative Research*, Vol. I, (Sage, 1999), p. 295.
34. Zuckerman, 'Meet the Bridgebloggers', *Public Choice*, 134, (2008), pp. 47–65.
35. P. Lévy, *Collective Intelligence: Mankind's emerging world in cyberspace*, tr. Robert Bononno, (Perseus Books, 1999).

Bibliography

PRIMARY SOURCES

Unpublished

Interviews and Informal Conversations

Adams, Paul, BBC World Affairs Correspondent, 9 Nov 2007.
———, BBC World Affairs Correspondent, Interview, 7 Nov 2008.
Akwagyiram, Alexis, BBC News Online Journalist, Interview, 4 Mar 2009.
Anderson, Kevin, Former BBC Journalist, Interview, 16 June 2008.
Baily, Alison, BBC Researcher, Interview, 12 Nov 2008.
Barot, Trushar, Senior Broadcast Journalist, Interview, 16 Sep 2009.
BBC Correspondent (a), Interview, 2008.
BBC Correspondent (b), Interview, 2008.
BBC Correspondent, Interview, 2009.
BBC Editor, 27 Nov 2008.
BBC Editor, Interview, 2009.
BBC Journalist, Interview, 2007.
BBC Journalist (a), 27 Nov 2008.
BBC Journalist (b), 27 Nov 2008.
BBC Journalist, Interview, 2008.
BBC Journalist, 2009.
BBC Journalist, 13 Dec 2009.
BBC Journalist, 4 Feb 2010.
BBC *Newsnight* Producer, Interview, 2009.
BBC News Online Journalist (a), Interview, 2009.
BBC News Online Journalist (b), Interview, 2009.
BBC News Online Journalist (c), Interview, 2009.
BBC Senior Editor, 9 Nov 2007.
BBC Senior Editor, Nov 2007.
Blenford, Adam, BBC Senior Broadcast Journalist (News Online), Interview, 24 Mar 2009.
———, BBC Senior Broadcast Journalist, Interview, 8 Apr 2011.
Bowen, Jeremy, BBC Middle East Editor, Interview, 2 June 2009.
Boyle, Joe, BBC Broadcast Journalist (News Online), Interview, 23 March 2009.
Connor, Alan, Senior Broadcast Journalist, (Assistant Editor BBC News blogs), BBC News blogs, Interview, 12 Oct 2010.
Corera, Gordon, BBC Security Correspondent, Interview 14 Dec 2007.
Cornes, Olivia, Senior Broadcast Journalist (News Online), Interview, 14 Nov 2007
Dissanayake, Samanthi, Senior Broadcast Journalist, Interview, 26 Jan 2010.

Entwistle, George, Former BBC *Newsnight* Editor (2001–2004), Interview, 24 Sep 2010.
Fraser, Simon, BBC News Online South Asia Editor, Interview, 26 Jan 2010.
Gardner, Frank, BBC Security Correspondent, Interview, 3 Dec 2008.
Hagler, Tom, BBC Senior Broadcast Journalist, World Have Your Say, 11 Dec 2008.
Hayward, David, Head of the Journalism Programme, BBC College of Journalism, Interview, 21 Apr 2008.
Hooberman, Lucy, Former BBC Innovation Executive, Interview, 8 Apr 2011.
Hughes, Stuart, BBC Defence and Security Producer, Interview, 14 December 2007.
———, World Affairs Producer, Interview, 14 Jun 2010.
———, World Affairs Producer, Interview, 25 Aug 2010.
Knowles, Jamillah, BBC Broadcast Journalist, Interview, 25 May 2009.
Lacey, Ian, BBC *Newsnight* Producer, Interview, 11 Mar 2009.
Leithead, Alastair, BBC World Affairs Correspondent, Interview, 28 May 2009.
Lustig, Robin, BBC World Tonight Presenter, Interview, 21 Oct 2008.
McGough, Kate, BBC Broadcast Journalist, *World Have Your Say*, Interview, 4 Dec 2008.
Ministry of Defence Press Officer, Interview, 29 Apr 2008.
Murphy, Verity, BBC *Newsnight* Producer, Interview, 30 Jun 2009.
Reynolds, Nick, Senior Advisor, Editorial Policy, Interview, 14 May 2008.
Robinson, Kate, Assignments Editor of Home Newsgathering, Interview, 19 June 2009.
Sambrook, Richard, BBC Director of Global News (2004–2010), Interview, 11 July 2008.
Sandell, Mark, Editor, BBC *World Have Your Say*, 13 Oct 2008.
———, Editor, BBC *World Have Your Say*, Interview, 10 Dec 2008.
Scullion, Aaron, Senior Product Manager, Future Media and Technology, Interview, 7 May 2008.
———, Senior Product Manager, Future Media and Technology, Interview, 12 Feb 2009.
———, Executive Product Manager, Future Media and Technology, Interview, 26 Oct 2010.
Smyth, Major Paul, Interview, 5 June 2009.
Stone, Jem, Executive Producer, Social Media at BBC Audio & Music, Interview, 9 July 2008.
Tilley, Chloe, Deputy Editor BBC *World Have Your Say*, Interview, 10 Dec 2008.
Twigg, Krassimira, BBC Broadcast Journalist (News Online), Interview, 31 Mar 2009.
Vallance, Chris, BBC Senior Broadcast Journalist, Interview, 28 Jan 2008.
———, BBC Senior Broadcast Journalist, Interview, 8 Mar 2011.
Wardle, Claire, Freelance Consultant for the BBC College of Journalism, Interview, 5 Jan 2010.
Watson, Rob, BBC Defence and Security Correspondent (World Service), Interview, 3 Mar 2009
Wilson, Giles, Editor BBC News blogs, Interview, 3 Nov 2010.
Wyatt, Caroline, BBC Defence Correspondent, Interview, 14 Nov 2008.

Correspondence with Author

Alvarez, Maj Steve, Email Correspondence, 16 July 2010.
Anderson, Fiona, Editor, Coaching, BBC College of Journalism, Email Correspondence, 12 Apr 2011.
Atkins, Ros, Email Correspondence, 15 Mar 2011.
Barron, Peter, Former *Newsnight* Editor (2004–2008), Email Correspondence, 15 Mar 2011.
Blenford, Adam, BBC Senior Broadcast Journalist, Interview, Email Correspondence, 2 Dec 2010.

Bonanno, 1 Lt Amy, US Army PAO, Email Correspondence, 5 Nov 2008.
Bowen, Jeremy, Email Correspondence, 11 Apr 2011.
Corera, Gordon, BBC Security Correspondent, Email Correspondence, 11 Apr 2011.
Costeloe, Silvia, BBC Broadcast Journalist (User Generated Content hub), Email Correspondence, 6 Dec 2010.
Eltringham, Matthew, BBC Head of Interactivity, Email Correspondence, 8 Jan 2009.
Ford, Alex, ('RAF Airman'), Personal Correspondence, 19 Aug 2010.
Gassett, Angela, Weber Shandwick/US Army Accessions Command, Email Correspondence, 14 July 2010.
Hamman, Robin, Former BBC Senior Broadcast Journalist, Email Correspondence, 15 Mar 2011.
Hughes, Stuart, BBC World Affairs Producer, Email Correspondence, 1 July 2010.
———, BBC World Affairs Producer, Email Correspondence, 29 Jan 2011.
Knowles, Jamillah, BBC Broadcast Journalist, Email Correspondence, 12 Dec 2010.
Leithead, Alastair, BBC Asia Correspondent, Email Correspondence 17 Apr 2011.
Mason, Paul, Economics Editor, BBC *Newsnight*, Email Correspondence, 6 Apr 2011.
McDermott, Sarah, Web Team Producer, Email Correspondence, 16 Mar 2011.
Meo, Nick, Sunday Telegraph Foreign Correspondent, Email Correspondence, 6 Nov 2008.
———, Sunday Telegraph Foreign Correspondent, Email Correspondence, 1 Dec 2008.
Mohan, Mukund, Technology Entrepreneur, Email Correspondence, 17 June 2010.
Newman, Nic, Former Controller, Future Media, Journalism (2007–2010), Email Correspondence, 13 Apr 2011.
North, Richard, Email Correspondence, 4 Aug 2009.
Rippon, Peter, *Newsnight* Editor, Email Correspondence, 18 Apr 2011.
Semple, Euan, Former Manager of BBC DigiLab, Email Correspondence, 2 Mar 2011.
Smyth, Major Paul, Email Correspondence, 17 April 2011.
Wardle, Claire, Freelance Consultant for the BBC College of Journalism, Personal Correspondence, 8 Dec 2010.
———, Freelance Consultant for the BBC College of Journalism, Email Correspondence, 8 Apr 2011.
Wood, Paul, BBC Middle East Correspondent, Email correspondence, 16 Mar 2009.

BBC Meetings and Unpublished Documents

Aardt, Tom van, BBC Communities Editor (2008–2009), Audience Interaction Session, BEEB Camp, 28 Nov 2008.
Anderson, Kevin, *BBC Blogs: News as Conversation*, 2005.
Atkins, Ros, BBC Global News Masterclass, 17 Mar 2008.
Barron, Peter, *New Media, New Ways with Audiences, College of Journalism*, 30 May 2008.
BBC Executive Producer, Internal BBC Event, 2008.
BBC Journalist (a), Audience Interaction Session, BEEB Camp, 28 Nov 2008.
BBC Journalist (b), Audience Interaction Session, BEEB Camp, 28 Nov 2008.
BBC News Interactive, Internal blog, 2006–2010.
BBC World Affairs Producers and Researchers, Focus Group, 12 Nov 2008.
BBC World Service Journalists, Focus Group, 23 May 2008.
Blog Guidelines, No Date.
'Blogging and the BBC', *BBC Scotland Interactive*, May 2005.
Clifton, Pete, 'Pete's Weekly Update', *BBC News Online Intranet*, 5 May 2006.
———, 'News Interactive and the Re-Organisation', 2007.
Eltringham, Matthew, Assistant Editor of Interactivity, Social Media Global News Event, Bush House, 16 Sep 2008.
Harris, D., 'BBC Blogs: Qualitative Research Debrief', *BBC MC&A Audience Research*, Sep 2006.

Herrmann, Steve, 'Updates: Mumbai, planning, global news. . .', *BBC News Online Intranet*, 1 Dec 2008.
Hillier, S., 'Are you compliant or are you just ticking a box', *Ariel*, 20 Jan 2009.
Hooberman, Lucy, BBC Innovation Executive, Internal Blogging Wiki, 20 Oct 2005. Internal Blogging Wiki, 20 October 2005.
Horrocks, Peter, 'The newsroom—latest news Sept 8th', *BBC News Online Intranet*, 8 Sep 2008.
Horrocks, Peter, 'The Newsroom—latest news', *BBC News Online Intranet*, 8 Dec 2008.
Marsh, Kevin, Executive Editor of BBC College of Journalism (2006–2011), News Rewired Conference, London, 14 Jan 2010.
McGovern, Anna, Producer, World Service Future Media, BBC Global News Masterclass, 17 Mar 2008.
Peston, Robert, BBC Future of Journalism Conference, 26 Nov 2008.
———, BBC Global News Masterclass, 12 July 2010.
Sambrook, Richard, Internal BBC Blog, 13 Jan 2005.
Sandell, Mark, Editor BBC World Have Your Say, *New Media, New Ways with Audiences, College of Journalism*, 30 May 2008.
Sands, Vivienne, Head of Emerging Media, BBC Monitoring, Internal BBC event, 1 Sep 2008.
Semple, Euan, Internal BBC Blog, 12 June 2002.
Smith, Russell (ed.), 'Livepage Guidelines, Full', BBC Internal Document, No Date.
Smith, Russell, 'Front page session yesterday', *BBC News Online Intranet*, 1 July 2008.
Stone, Jem, *Pan-BBC Blog Trial*, 14 Nov 2005.
Wilson, Giles, BBC News Blogs Editor, Global News Masterclass, 17 Oct 2007.
———, BBC News Blogs Editor, BBC Future of Journalism Conference, 26 Nov 2008.

Published

Speeches, Government, Military and Official Documents

Deputy Secretary of Defense, 'Responsible and Effective Use of Internet Capabilities', *DTM-09–026*, 25 Feb 2010.
Goldstone, R., et al., 'Human Rights in Palestine and the Other Occupied Territories', UN Human Rights Council, 25 Sep 2009.
HQ, Multi-National Corps—Iraq, *MNC-I Policy #9: Unit and Soldier Owned and Maintained Websites*, 6 Apr 2005.
Indian Government Dossier, 'Mumbai Terrorist Attacks, Nov 26–29, 2008', January 2009. Available at *The Hindu*, 'Mumbai Terror Attacks—Dossier of Evidence', http://www.hindu.com/nic/dossier.htm, (Accessed 10 Dec 2009).
MoD, *Contact with the Media and Communicating in Public*, *DIN03–006*, Aug 2007.
MoD, Press Release, 'British Forces Blogging From the Frontline', 1 July 2010.
Ofcom, *Ofcom Communications Market Report*, 2010.
Thatcher, M., Speech to the American Bar Association, 15 July 1985, http://www.margaretthatcher.org/speeches/displaydocument.asp?docid = 106096, (Accessed 15 May 2008).
US Army, 'Operations Security', *AR530–1*, 2007
US Corps, 'IMMEDIATE BAN OF INTERNET SOCIAL NETWORKING SITES (SNS) ON MARINE CORPS ENTERPRISE NETWORK (MCEN) NIPRNET', 3 August 2009.

BBC Reports, Documents, Public Speeches and Cited Broadcast Material

Baker, Jonathan, Deputy Head of Newsgathering (2006–10), *War Reporting—Where does a journalist's duty lie?*, St Bride's Church, London, 9 April 2008.

Budd, A. et al, *Report on the Independent Panel for the BBC Trust on the Impartiality of BBC Business Coverage*, April 2007.

BBC Editorial Guidelines, 2005, http://downloads.bbc.co.uk/guidelines/editorialguidelines/Legacy_Guidelines/2005-editorial-guidelines-full.pdf.

BBC Editorial Guidelines, http://www.bbc.co.uk/guidelines/editorialguidelines.

BBC Editorial Guidelines, BBC Guidelines on Employees Weblogs and Websites.

BBC Management, 'Review of bbc.co.uk: BBC Management's submission to the BBC Trust's review', Dec 2007.

BBC Online Services Guidelines, Formerly: http://www.bbc.co.uk/guidelines/editorialguidelines/onguide/, (Accessed 9 May 2008). Became part of BBC Editorial Guidelines.

BBC *Newsnight*, 5 Jan 2009.

BBC News: Official tweeters' guidance, June 2011.

BBC News: Social media guidance, July 2011.

BBC *PM* Programme, 5 Jan 2009.

BBC *PM* Programme, 9 Jan 2009.

BBC Press Release, 'BBC News appoints Alex Gubbay as first Social Media Editor', 16 Nov 2009, http://www.bbc.co.uk/pressoffice/pressreleases/stories/2009/11_november/16/gubbay.shtml, (19 Nov 2009).

BBC Producer Guidelines, 2000.

BBC *Ten O'Clock News*, 6 Jan 2009.

BBC Trust, Annual Report and Accounts, 2005/6.

BBC *World Have Your Say*, 9 Jan 2009.

BBC *World News*, 27 Nov 2008.

Bridcut, J., 'From Seesaw to Wagon Wheel: Safeguarding impartiality in the 21st century', *BBC Trust Report*, 2007.

Mair, E., BBC Presenter, BBC Radio 4 *iPM* programme, 24 Nov 2007.

Mortimer, E., 'A BBC Trust report on the impartiality and accuracy of the BBC's coverage of the events known as the "Arab Spring"', *BBC Trust*, June 2012.

Neil, R., et al., The Neil Report: The BBC's journalism after Hutton, June, 2004.

Paxman, J., BBC *Newsnight*, 7 May 2008.

Prodger, M., BBC *Newsnight*, 9 Jan 2009.

Radio 4 Feedback, 'The role of the BBC's news blogs', 27 Oct 2008, http://www.bbc.co.uk/blogs/theeditors/2008/10/the_role_of_the_bbcs_news_blog.html, (Accessed 10 Nov 2008).

Thomas, Q. et al., Report of the Independent Panel for the BBC Governors on Impartiality of BBC Coverage of the Israeli-Palestinian Conflict, April 2006.

Rt. Hon. The Lord Hutton, Report of the Hutton Inquiry, Jan 2004, http://www.the-hutton-inquiry.org.uk/, (Accessed 20 May 2008)

Sambrook, Richard, BBC Director of Global News (2004–2010), Reuters 'News of the World' Panel, 16 June 2009.

Webb, J., BBC *Ten O'Clock News*, 5 Jan 2009.

SECONDARY SOURCES

Books

Adie, K. (2002), *The Kindness of Strangers*, London: Headline.

Allan, S. (2006), *Online News*, Maidenhead and New York: Open University Press.

Allan, S. and Zelizer, B. (eds) (2004), *Reporting War: Journalism in wartime*, London: Routledge.

Altheide, D. (1996), *Qualitative Media Analysis*, Thousand Oaks, CA: Sage.

Andén-Papadopoulos, K. and Pantti, M (eds) (2011), *Amateur Images and Global News*, Chicago: University of Chicago Press.

Beckett, C. (2008), *SuperMedia: Saving journalism so it can save the world*, Oxford: Blackwell.

Belsey, A. and Chadwick, R. (eds) (1992), *Ethical Issues in Journalism and the Media*, London: Routledge.

Benkler, Y. (2006), *The Wealth of Networks: How social production transforms markets and freedom*, New Haven and London: Yale University Press.

Born, G. (2004), *Uncertain Vision*, London: Secker and Warburg.

Bourdieu, P. (1998) *On Television*, English translation by P. Parkhurst Ferguson, New York: The New Press.

Briggs, A. (1961), *The History of Broadcasting in the United Kingdom, Vol. I: The birth of broadcasting*, Oxford: Oxford University Press.

———. (1970), *The History of Broadcasting in the United Kingdom, Vol. III: The war of words*, Oxford: Oxford University Press.

Burden, M. (2006), *The Blog of War: Front-line dispatches from soldiers in Iraq and Afghanistan*, New York: Simon & Schuster.

Buzzell, C. (2005), *My War: Killing time in Iraq*, New York: Penguin.

Carruthers, S. (1999), *The Media at War*, London: Palgrave MacMillan.

Castells, M. (2000), *The Information Age: Economy Society and Culture, Vol 1: The rise of the network society*, 2nd Ed., Oxford: Blackwell.

———. (2009), *Communication Power*, Oxford, New York: Oxford University Press.

Clutterbuck, R. (1981), *The Media and Political Violence*, London: Macmillan Press.

Davies, N. (2008), *Flat Earth News*, London: Chatto & Windus.

Ericson, R.V., Baranek, P.M. and Chan, J.B.L. (1989), *Negotiating Control: A Study of News Sources*, Toronto: University of Toronto Press.

Fenton, N. (ed) (2010), *New Media, Old News: Journalism and democracy in the digital age*, London: Sage.

Fishman, M. (1980), *Manufacturing the News*, Austin: University of Texas Press.

Ganor, B. et al (eds) (2007), *Hypermedia Seduction for Terrorist Recruiting*, IOS Press.

Gans, H. (2004), *Deciding What's News*, 2nd Ed., Evanston, IL: Northwestern University Press.

Gallagher, M. (2010), *Kaboom: Embracing the suck in a savage little war*, Cambridge MA: Da Capo Press.

Giddens, A. (2002), *Runaway World*, 2nd Ed., London: Profile.

Gillmor, D. (2006), *We the Media: Grassroots journalism by the people, for the people*, 2nd Ed., Sebastopol, CA: O'Reilly Media Inc.

Gitlin, T. (1980), *The Whole World is Watching: Mass media in the making and unmaking of the New Left*, London: University of California Press.

Goldenberg, E. (1975), *Making the Papers: The access of resource-poor groups to the metropolitan press*, Lexington, MA: D.C. Heath & Co.

Hall, S. et al., (1978), *Policing the Crisis: Mugging, the state, and law and order*, London: Macmillan.

Hallin, D. (1989), *The "Uncensored War": The media and Vietnam*, London: University of California Press.

Harcup, T. (2005), *Journalism: Principles and practice*, London: Sage.

Hargreaves, I. (2003), *Journalism: Truth or dare*, Oxford: Oxford University Press.

Harrison, J. (2006), *News*, London: Routledge.

Herman, E.S. and Chomsky, N. (1988), *Manufacturing Consent: The political economy of the mass media*, New York: Pantheon.

Hoskins, A. and O'Loughlin, B. (2010), *War and Media: The emergence of diffused war*, Cambridge: Polity Press.

Innes, M. (ed.) (2007), *Denial of Sanctuary: understanding terrorist safe havens*, Westport, CT: Greenwood Publishing Group.

Kampfner, J. (2004), *Blair's Wars*, 2nd Ed., London: Free Press.

Keeble, R. (2001), *Ethics for Journalists*, London: Routledge.

Kellner, D. (2005), *Media Spectacle and the Crisis of Democracy: Terrorism, war, and election battles*, Boulder: CO, Paradigm Publishers.

Knightley, P. (2003), *The First Casualty: The War Correspondent as Hero, Propagandist and Myth-Maker*, London: Andre Deutsche Ltd.

Lévy, P. (1999), *Collective Intelligence: Mankind's Emerging World in Cyberspace*, tr. Robert Bononno, Cambridge, MA: Perseus Books.

Lindley R. (2002), *Panorama: Fifty years of pride and paranoia*, London: Politico's Publishing.

Manning, P. (2001), *News and News Sources: A critical introduction*, London: Sage.

Matheson D. and Allan, S. (2009), *Digital War Reporting*, Cambridge: Polity Press.

Moeller, S. (1999), *Compassion Fatigue: How the media sell disease, famine, war and death*, London and New York: Routledge.

Monck, A. with Hanley, M. (2008), *Can You Trust the Media?*, Cambridge: Icon Books.

Morozov, E. (2011), *The Net Delusion: How not to liberate the world*, London: Allen Lane.

Pavlik, J. (2001), *Journalism and New Media*, New York: Columbia University Press.

Pax, S. (2003), *Salam Pax: The Baghdad Blog*, London: Atlantic Books.

Philo, G. and Berry, M. (2004), *Bad News from Israel*, London: Pluto Press.

Rettberg, J.W. (2008), *Blogging*, Cambridge: Polity Press.

Rheingold, H. (1993), *The Virtual Community: Homesteading on the electronic frontier*, Reading, MA: Addison-Wesley.

Rosenberg, S. (2009), *Say Everything: How blogging began, what it's becoming and why it matters*, New York: Crown.

Sanders, K. (2003), *Ethics and Journalism*, London: Sage.

Schlesinger, P. and Tumber, H. (1994), *Reporting Crime: The media politics of criminal justice*, Oxford: Oxford University Press.

Schudson, M. (2003), *The Sociology of News*, New York: W.W. Norton & Co.

Shirky, C. (2009), *Here Comes Everybody: How change happens when people come together*, 2nd Ed., New York: Penguin.

Seaton, J. (2003), *Power without Responsibility: the press, broadcasting and new media in Britain*, 6th Ed., London: Routledge.

Seib, P. (2004), *Beyond the Front Lines: How the news media cover a world shaped by war*, New York: Palgrave MacMillan.

Sigal, L.V. (1973), *Reporters and Officials: The organisation and politics of newsmaking*, Lexington, MA: D.C. Heath & Co.

Simpson, J. (2000), *A Mad World, My Masters*, Basingstoke and Oxford: Macmillan.

Tankel, S. (2011), *Storming the World Stage: The story of Lashkar-e-Taiba*, London: Hurst & Co and New York: Columbia University Press.

Tremayne, M. (ed) (2007), *Blogging, Citizenship and the Future of Media*, New York: Routledge.

Tuchman, G. (1978), *Making News: A study in the construction of reality*, New York: The Free Press.

Tumber, H. (ed) (1999), *News: A reader*, Oxford: Oxford University Press.

Tumber, H. and Webster, F. (2006), *Journalists Under Fire: Information war and journalistic practice*, London: Sage.

Zelizer, B. and Allan, S. (eds) (2002), *Journalism After September 11*, London: Routledge.

Articles, Papers and Theses

Akhvlediani, M. (2009), 'The Fatal Flaw: The media and the Russian invasion of Georgia', *Small Wars & Insurgencies*, 20 (2), pp. 363–390.

Allan, S. (2002), 'Reweaving the Internet: Online news of September 11' in B. Zel-izer & S. Allan, (eds.), *Journalism After September 11*, London: Routledge, pp. 119–140.
———. (2007), 'Citizen Journalism and the Rise of Mass Self-Communication', *Global Media Journal*, Australian Edition, 1 (1), pp. 1–20.
———. (2004), 'The Culture of Distance: Online Reporting of the Iraq War' in S. Allan and B. Zelizer (eds) *Reporting War: Journalism in wartime*, London: Routledge, pp. 347–365.
Allan, S. and Zelizer, B. (2004), 'Rules of Engagement: Journalism and war' in S. Allan and B. Zelizer (eds) *Reporting War: Journalism in wartime*, London: Routledge, pp. 3–21.
Andén-Papadopoulos, K. and Pantti, M. (2011), 'Transparency and Trustworthi-ness: Strategies for incorporating amateur photography into news discourse' in Andén-Papadopoulos and M. Pantti (eds), *Amateur Images and Global News*, Chicago: University of Chicago Press, pp. 97–112.
Bardoel, J. and Deuze, M. (2001), 'Network Journalism: Converging competences of Media professionals and professionalism', *Australian Journalism Review*, 23 (2), pp. 91–103.
Benkler, Y. (2011), 'A Free Irresponsible Press', *Harvard Civil Rights-Civil Liber-ties Law Review*, Available at http://benkler.org/Benkler%20Wikileaks%20CRCL%20Working%20Paper%20Feb_8.pdf, (Accessed 31 Mar 2011).
Bennett, D. (2011), 'A Twitter revolution in breaking news' in J. Mair and R. Keeble (eds), *Face the Future: Tools for the modern media age*, Bury St Edmunds: Abramis, pp. 63–73.
Bennett, W.L. (1990), 'Toward a Theory of Press-State Relations in the United States', *Journal of Communication*, 40 (2), pp. 103–127.
Betz, D. (2008), 'The Virtual Dimension of Contemporary Insurgency and Counter-insurgency', *Small Wars & Insurgencies*, 19 (4), pp. 510–540.
Bowman S. and Willis C. (2005), 'The Future is Here, But Do Media Companies See It?', *Nieman Reports*, Winter, http://www.nieman.harvard.edu/reports/05–4NRwinter/05–4NFwinter.pdf, (Accessed 28 July 2008).
Bruns, A. (2009), 'News Blogs and Citizen Journalism: New Directions for e-Journalism' in Prasad, K. (ed.), *e-Journalism : New Media and News Media*, New Delhi: BR Publishing, pp. 101–126.
Caldwell IV, Lt. Gen. W., Murphy, D. and Menning, A. (2009), 'Learning to Lever-age New Media', *Australian Army Journal*, 6 (3), pp. 133–146.
Cammaerts, B. and Carpentier, N. (2009), 'Blogging the 2003 Iraq War: Challenging the ideological model of war and mainstream journalism?', *Observatorio*, 3 (2).
Deuze, M. (2005), 'What Is Journalism?: Professional identity and ideology of jour-nalists reconsidered', *Journalism*, 6 (4), pp. 442–464.
Domingo, D. and Heinonen, A. (2008), 'Weblogs and Journalism: A typology to explore blurring boundaries', *Nordicom Review*, 29 (1), pp. 3–15.
Etling, B. et al., (2009), 'Mapping the Arabic Blogosphere: Politics, Culture and Dissent', Berkman Center for Internet & Society, June, http://cyber.law.harvard.edu/sites/cyber.law.harvard.edu/files/Mapping_the_Arabic_Blogosphere_0.pdf, (Accessed 24 Aug 2009).
Fadda-Conrey, C. (2010), 'Writing Memories of the Present Alternative Narra-tives about the 2006 Israeli War on Lebanon', *College Literature*, 37.1 (Winter, pp. 159–173.
Fenton, N. (2010), 'NGOs, New Media and the Mainstream News' in N. Fenton (ed) *New media, Old News: Journalism and democracy in the digital age*, London: Sage, pp. 153–168.
Gieber, W. and Johnson, W. (1961), 'The City Hall beat: A study of reporter and source roles', *Journalism Quarterly*, 38 (3), pp. 289–297.

Gilbert, P. (1992), 'The Oxygen of Publicity: Terrorism and Reporting Restrictions' in A. Belsey and R. Chadwick (eds), *Ethical Issues in Journalism and the Media*, London: Routledge, pp. 137–153.

Golding, P. and Elliott, P. (1999), 'Making the News (Excerpt)' in H. Tumber (ed), *News A Reader*, Oxford: Oxford University Press, pp. 112–120.

Gowing, N. (2009), '"Skyful of Lies" and Black Swans: The new tyranny of shifting information power in crises', *Reuters Institute for the Study of Journalism*.

Granovetter, M. (1973), 'The Strength of Weak Ties', *American Journal of Sociology*, 78 (6), pp. 1360–1380.

Hammond, P. (2004), 'Humanizing War: The Balkans and beyond', in S. Allan and B. Zelizer. (eds), *Reporting War: Journalism in wartime*, London: Routledge, pp. 174–189.

Hänska-Ahy, M.T. and Shapour, R. (2012), 'Who's Reporting The Protests', *Journalism Studies* 13, http://dx.doi.org/10.1080/1461670X.2012.657908.

Harb, Z. (2009), 'The July 2006 war and the Lebanese blogosphere: towards an alternative media tool in covering wars', *Journal of Media Practice* 10 (2&3), pp. 255–258.

Harrison, J. (2010), 'User-Generated Content and Gatekeeping at the BBC Hub', *Journalism Studies*, 11 (4), pp. 243–256.

Hartley, J. (2000), 'Communicative Democracy in a Redactional Society: The future of journalism studies' *Journalism*, 1 (1), pp. 39–48.

Haugbolle, S. (2007), 'From A-list to Webtifada, Developments in the Lebanese Blogosphere 2005–2006', *Arab Media and Society*, 1 (Spring), http://www.arab-mediasociety.com/?article=40, (Accessed 10 Oct 2008).

Horrocks, P. (2009), 'The End of Fortress Journalism', in C. Miller (ed), *The Future of Journalism*, BBC College of Journalism.

Hermida, A. (2008), 'The BBC goes blogging: Is 'Auntie' finally listening?', http://online.journalism.utexas.edu/2008/papers/Hermida.pdf, (Accessed 1 Aug 2008).

———. (2009), 'The blogging BBC: Journalism blogs at "the world's most trusted news organisation"', *Journalism Practice*, 3 (3), pp. 1–17.

———. (2010), 'From TV to Twitter: How ambient news became ambient journalism', *Media and Culture Journal*, 13 (2), http://journal.media-culture.org.au/index.php/mcjournal/article/viewArticle/220, (10 July 2010).

Herring, S., et al., (2007), 'Longitudinal Content Analysis of Blogs: 2003–4' in M. Tremayne (ed), *Blogging, Citizenship and the Future of Media*, New York: Routledge, pp. 3–20.

Jenkins, H. (2004), 'The Cultural Logic of Media Convergence', *International Journal of Cultural Studies*, 7 (1), pp. 33–43.

Jönsson, A.M. and Örnebring, H. (2011), 'User-Generated Content and the News: Empowerment of citizens or interactive illusion?', *Journalism Practice*, 5 (2), pp. 127–144.

Kalb, M. and Saivetz, C. (2007), 'The Israeli–Hezbollah War of 2006: The media as a weapon in asymmetrical conflict', *The Harvard International Journal of Press/Politics*, 12 (3), pp. 43–66.

Kelly, J. and Etling, B. (2008), 'Mapping Iran Online Public: Politics and Culture in the Persian Blogosphere', The Berkman Center for Internet and Society, http://tinyurl.com/4ht9y4, (Accessed 31 July 2008).

Kinniburgh, J. and Denning, D. (2006), 'Blogs and Military Information Strategy', *Joint Special Operations University*, Report 06–5, pp. 5–13.

Korns, S. and Kastenberg, J. (2008–9), 'Georgia's Cyber Left Hook', *Parameters*, XXXVIII, (4, Winter), pp. 60–76.

Lasica, J.D. (1999), 'Conveying the War in Human Terms', *American Journalism Review*, June, http://www.ajr.org/Article.asp?id=426 (3 July 2010).

———. (2003), 'Blogs and Journalism Need Each Other', *Nieman Reports*, 57 (3), pp. 70–74.

Lee-Wright, P. (2010), 'Culture Shock: New media and organisational change in the BBC' in N. Fenton (ed), *New Media, Old News: Journalism and democracy in the digital age*, London: Sage, pp. 71–86.

Leskovec, J., Backstrom, L. and Kleinberg, J. (2009), 'Meme-tracking and the Dynamics of the News Cycle' *ACM SIGKDD International Conference on Knowledge Discovery and Data Mining (KDD)*, http://cs.stanford.edu/people/jure/pubs/quotes-kdd09.pdf.

Lowrey, W. (2006), 'Mapping the Journalism-Blogging Relationship', *Journalism*, 7 (4), pp. 477–500.

Lowrey, W. and Burleson Mackay, J. (2008), 'Journalism and Blogging': A test of a model of occupational competition', *Journalism Practice*, 2 (1), pp. 64–81.

MacKinnon, R. (2007), 'Blogs and China Correspondence: How foreign correspondents covering China use blogs', Paper for the World Journalism Education Congress.

Matheson, D. (2004), 'Weblogs and the Epistemology of the News: Some trends in online journalism', *New Media & Society*, 6 (4), pp. 443–468.

McChesney, R.W. (2003), 'The Problem of Journalism: A political economic contribution to an explanation of the crisis in contemporary US journalism', *Journalism Studies*, 4 (3), pp. 299–329.

McNair, B. (2005), 'What is Journalism?' in H. De Burgh (ed), *Making Journalists*, London: Routledge, pp. 25–43.

Merelo, J. and Prieto, B. *Blogosphere Community Formation, Structure and Visualisation*, http://webdiis.unizar.es/~ftricas/Articulos/Blogosphere%20community%20formation.pdf, (Accessed 1 Aug 2008).

Messner, M. and Watson Distaso, M., (2008), 'The Source Cycle: How traditional media and weblogs use each other as sources', *Journalism Studies*, 9 (3), pp. 447–463.

Molotch, H. and Lester, M. (1974), 'News as Purposive Behaviour: On the strategic use of routine events, accidents, and scandals', *American Sociological Review*, 39 (1), pp. 101–112.

Neuberger, C. and Nuernbergk, C. (2010), 'Competition, Complementarity or Integration?', *Journalism Practice*, 4 (3), pp. 319–332.

Newman, N. (2009), 'The Rise of Social Media and its Impact on Mainstream Journalism', *Reuters Institute for the Study of Journalism*, Oxford.

Papacharissi, Z. (2007), 'Audiences as Media Producers: Content Analysis of 260 Blogs' in M. Tremayne (ed), *Blogging, Citizenship and the Future of Media*, New York: Routledge, pp. 21–38.

Phillips, A. (2010) 'Old Sources: New bottles' in N. Fenton (ed) *New Media, Old News: Journalism and democracy in the digital age*, London: Sage, pp. 87–101.

Rabasa, A. et al. (2009), 'The Lessons of Mumbai', *RAND Corporation*, Jan.

Robbins, Maj. E.L. (2007), 'Muddy Boots IO: The Rise of Soldier Blogs', *Military Review*, (Sep-Oct).

Robinson, S. (2006a), 'Gateway or Gatekeeping: The institutionalisation of online news in creating an altered technological authority', *International Symposium on Online Journalism*.

———. (2006b), 'The Mission of the J-Blog: Recapturing journalistic authority online', *Journalism*, 7 (1), pp. 65–83.

Sambrook, R. (2005), 'Citizen Journalism and the BBC', *Nieman Reports*, Winter, http://www.nieman.harvard.edu/assets/pdf/Nieman%20Reports/backissues/05winter.pdf, (Accessed 28 July 2008).

———. (2010), 'Are Foreign Correspondents Redundant?', *Reuters Institute for Journalism*, Oxford.

Scammell, M. (2000), 'The Internet and Civic Engagement: The age of the citizen-consumer', *Political Communication*, 17 (4), pp. 351–355.

Schlesinger, P. (1978). 'Putting reality together: BBC News', in H. Tumber (ed) (1999), *News: A reader*, Oxford: Oxford University Press (1999), pp. 121–133.

Singer, J.B. (2005), 'The Political J-Blogger: "Normalising" a new media form to fit old norms and practices', *Journalism*, 6 (2), pp. 173–198.

Steven, D. and Weston, M. (2003), 'Whose Agenda? The BBC's Reporter's Log on Iraq', 25 Sep, http://ics.leeds.ac.uk/papers/pmt/exhibits/1759/Whose_agenda.pdf, (Accessed 12 Jan 2010).

Shyam Sundar, S. (1998), 'Effect of Source Attribution on Perception of Online News Stories', *Journalism and Mass Communication Quarterly*, 75 (1), pp. 55–68.

Thurman, N. (2008), 'Forums for Citizen Journalists? Adoption of user generated content initiatives by online news media', *New Media & Society*, 10 (1), pp. 139–157.

Tuchman, G. (1972) 'Objectivity as Strategic Ritual: An examination of newsmen's notions of objectivty', *American Journal of Sociology*, 77 (4), pp. 660–679.

Tumber, H. (2005), 'Journalism and the War in Iraq' in S. Allan (ed), *Critical Issues in Journalism*, Maidenhead and New York: Open University Press, pp. 370–380.

Wall, M. (2005), "Blogs of War': Weblogs as news', *Journalism*, 6 (2), pp. 153–172.

———. (2006), 'Blogging Gulf War II', *Journalism Studies*, 7 (1), pp. 111–126.

Ward, W. (2007), 'Uneasy Bedfellows: Bloggers and mainstream media report the conflict in Lebanon', *Arab Media and Society*, 1 (Spring), http://www.arabmediasociety.com/articles/downloads/20070312144654_AMS1_Will_Ward.pdf (1 Aug 2008).

Wardle, C. and Williams, A. et al. (2008), 'UGC@theBBC: Understanding its impact upon contributors, non-contributors and BBC News', http://www.bbc.co.uk/blogs/knowledgeexchange/cardiffone.pdf, (Accessed 3 Nov 2009).

Weimann, G. (2007), 'Using the Internet for Terrorist Recruitment and Mobilisation' in B. Ganor et al. (eds), *Hypermedia Seduction for Terrorist Recruiting*, Amsterdam: IOS Press, pp. 47–58.

Wellman, B. (2001), 'Little Boxes, Glocalisation and Networked Individualism', *Revised Papers from the Second Kyoto Workshop on Digital Cities II, Computational and Sociological Approaches*, http://homes.chass.utoronto.ca/~wellman/publications/littleboxes/littlebox.PDF, (17 Mar 2011).

Zuckerman, E. (2008), 'Meet the Bridgebloggers', *Public Choice*, 134 (1), pp. 47–65.

Index

For Product Safety Concerns and Information please contact our EU
representative GPSR@taylorandfrancis.com
Taylor & Francis Verlag GmbH, Kaufingerstraße 24, 80331 München, Germany